China Today

Joan Lebold Cohen and Jerome Alan Cohen

With Photographs by Joan Lebold Cohen

China

And Her

Harry N. Abrams, Inc

Third Edition

Today

Ancient Treasures

Publishers, New York

To our parents and our children

First Edition 1975
Second Edition 1980
Third Edition 1986

NOTE: When the first and second editions of *China Today* were
prepared, the Wade-Giles was the system most widely used for
the transliteration of Chinese words. Subsequently, the Chinese
mandated the use of the pinyin system, and in the third edition,
newly added names are so transcribed. The other names have
not been altered.

Library of Congress Cataloging in Publication Data
Cohen, Joan Lebold.
    China today and her ancient treasures.

    Bibliography: p. 422
    Includes index.
    1. China—Description and travel—1949—
2. China—Civilization.   3. China—Antiquities.
I. Cohen, Jerome Alan.   II. Title.
DS 711.C59   1985   951.05   85–4084
ISBN 0–8109–0798–4

Printed and bound in Japan

CONTENTS

Introduction • 7

The Prehistoric Period • 41

Ancient China • 53

The Founding of the Empire • 73

The Han Dynasty • 81

The Northern Wei, Sui, and T'ang Dynasties • 109

The Sung and Yüan Dynasties • 145

The Ming Dynasty • 167

The Ch'ing Dynasty • 213

The Republic of China • 227

Contemporary China • 245

The Arts in China Today • 381

Bibliography • 422

Index • 427

Chronology • 431

Map of China • 432

ACKNOWLEDGMENTS

A book of this scope, covering several thousand years of Chinese history, plainly rests upon the support of many scholars. We have benefited not only from the works cited in the bibliography but also from the personal advice of a number of colleagues and friends, including Anne Clapp, Nelson Wu, Max Loehr, Mino Yutaka, Ezra Vogel, Dwight Perkins, Donald Klein, Merle Goldman, Joseph Cheng, Nathan Sivin, Susan Bush, David Waterhouse, Michael Dalby, Mayching Kao, Jimmy Wang, and Christine Kanda. A number of scholars at Harvard University's Fogg Museum have been helpful. We especially want to thank Bertha Ezell for her skillful and patient typing of the manuscript, and we pay tribute to Margaret L. Kaplan, an extraordinary editor, Nai Y. Chang, a gifted designer, and Paul Anbinder, a guiding spirit.

INTRODUCTION

◄2. Shopping with Grandpa in the People's Market, Peking. The government provides both day and night nurseries to ensure women full participation in the work force, but many children are cared for by their retired grandparents. The little girl here, munching on a deep-fried bun similar to a cruller, rides in a Chinese-style perambulator. The shopping bundles will be put into her carriage.

SINCE THE DAYS OF MARCO POLO, China has evoked ever-changing images in the West. At present our perceptions of China are being transformed by a new Chinese imagery. The myths and symbols of the Chinese Communist revolution are being integrated into our view of China's history, and there has been a new receptivity toward China on the part of Westerners since the turmoil of the Great Proletarian Cultural Revolution of 1966–76 came to an end and China again began to present a hospitable face to the world.

Browsing in the China section of a well-stocked library, amid the thousands upon thousands of books that have been published in the last hundred years, can be as enlightening about our shifting vision of China as it is about Chinese history itself. Period pieces from the nineteenth century conjure up the "mysterious Orient": *In Forbidden China; The Mystic Flowering;* and *Foreign Devils in a Flowery Kingdom,* for example. The chaotic conditions of early twentieth-century China are suggested by *China in Crisis* and *What's Wrong with China?* From the same period, *Kind-Hearted Tiger* illustrates the sentimental view of a China innately good although politically impotent. Somewhat later, Westernized Chinese writers show nationalistic fervor in titles such as *China, My China* and *My Country, My People.* After World War II, jubilant Communist titles such as *The East Is Red* elicit Cold War responses, including *Secret Diary from Red China.*

Today, which is the "true" view of China? Since the historic Ping-Pong matches of April 1971 initiated a Sino-American reconciliation, Americans have been struggling to develop a new image of a China that has become increasingly accessible. Of the few thousand carefully selected Americans who were granted entry to China from 1971

9

to 1973, many suffered from a severe case of an illness that can best be described as "Marco Poloitis." They intensely admired what appeared to be an austere giant managing, against all odds, to cope with enormous problems. Theirs was a romantic image full of "miracles" of modernization wrought by a government that seemed to enjoy the active support of most of its poor but able, energetic, collective-minded, and patriotic—indeed militant—people. According to this view, the "real China"—that is, not the authorities on Taiwan recognized by the United States until 1979 as the official government of China—had banished such scourges as hunger, homelessness, unemployment, inflation, and crime. This new vision gave rise to renewed hope for a vast China market, a hope that has recurringly excited American businessmen ever since the first Yankee Clipper ship arrived in Canton in 1784.

"China watchers" who sought to moderate this vision, whether they were journalists, academics, government officials, or businessmen, were sometimes derided for not freeing themselves from the shackles of hostile American propaganda that for a quarter century had sought to depict the People's Republic of China (PRC) as a tyranny totally devoid of redeeming virtues. In 1973, most Americans were not interested in such current books as Jean Pasqualini's *Prisoner of Mao,* even though that vivid first-hand account of seven years in the PRC's equivalent of the Gulag Archipelago deservedly became a best-seller among less naive Frenchmen. Unpleasant reminders of the darker side of Chinese life were simply out of step with the trend. Americans had "progressed" from unfairly damning contemporary China's rulers to uncritically praising them.

Yet the bloom began to fade from the rose by the mid-1970s. Again, political and economic developments played a role in shaping our vision. Efforts to "normalize" diplomatic relationships between Washington and Peking were proving unsuccessful. Peking was insisting upon recognition as the only legitimate government of China. Washington was insisting upon continuing protection for the people on Taiwan against completion of the Chinese civil war that had been interrupted in mid-1950, when President Harry Truman positioned the Seventh Fleet in the Formosa Strait immediately following the outbreak of conflict in Korea. Moreover, Sino-American trade, which had begun to skyrocket after "Ping-Pong diplomacy" had opened the door a crack, began to plummet, creating another in the series of disillusionments that have inevitably followed exaggerated expectations of China. Our Chinese cousins, it was discovered, do not share our belief in man's natural right to own his own automobile.

The new climate generated by the slowdown in bilateral relationships facilitated the publication and appreciation of books that presented a real China strikingly different from that introduced in the early 1970s. Simon Leys's *Chinese Shadows* and Chen Jo-hsi's *The Execution of Mayor Yin and Other Stories* . . . depicted the hideous costs in human tragedy exacted by a totalitarian system that had run amok

3. Line of nursery-school children at the Peking University Nursery School, Peking, where University employees can leave their children in good hands during work hours. Each toddler keeps in line behind the teacher by holding onto a handkerchief tied to the child ahead.

◀4. Sweeping a courtyard in the
Imperial Palace, Peking.

5–7. Three young women of
China. Left: People's
Liberation Army (PLA)
soldier. Center: Tibetan
woman in native costume.
Right: China Travel Service
guide.

during the decade of the Cultural Revolution, inflicting suffering on an estimated one hundred million people. Political developments in China added credibility to this more sober view. Major rioting occurred in Peking's T'ien-an-men Square in April 1976, when police prevented a large crowd from publicly mourning Premier Chou En-lai. The death of Communist Party Chairman Mao Tse-tung in September of that year intensified the power struggle among top PRC leaders that culminated, a month later, in the dramatic arrest of the Chairman's widow, Chiang Ch'ing, and three high-ranking associates. The "Gang of Four," as they were immediately dubbed by their victorious rivals, was then vilified in a massive, ongoing campaign that made them responsible for all the evils and failures of the political-economic system. This campaign produced an outpouring of horror stories about a despotism so arbitrary and widespread as to compare with the worst excesses of Stalinism. And PRC leaders began to concede in public that hunger, housing, unemployment, inflation, and crime were still serious problems.

By late 1978 these revelations seemed to have swung the pendulum of American public opinion from high enthusiasm to a disillusionment that overlooked the many impressive achievements of a regime that had done much to organize, feed, clothe, house, and bring social benefits to the world's largest population, by then roughly a billion people. Yet the sudden announcement that Washington and Peking would establish formal diplomatic relations early in 1979 rekindled American interest in China, albeit this time in more appropriately muted fashion. The visit to Washington and other cities by diminutive and colorful Vice Premier Teng Hsiao-p'ing, who had been ousted from office during the Cultural Revolution and, again, in 1976 by the "Gang of Four," increased the enthusiasm.

The "normalization" of diplomatic relations, which was made possible by a compromise that assured the continuing security of Taiwan, spawned a network of political, economic, scientific, educational, and cultural agreements and exchanges that is giving Americans and Chinese their best

8. Comrades bathing in the river along the northern border of Peking's old Ming city near an old northwest gate (Te-sheng-men).

9. Blackboard painting.
The idyllic farm scene drawn in colored chalks includes trees and flowers, a tractor, green fields studded with slogans, school buildings, and a long white cloud. Above, in red characters outlined with yellow, it says: "We enthusiastically welcome the visit and guidance of American friends."

opportunity to get to know each other since the founding of the People's Republic in 1949. This has presented Mao's successors, Teng Hsiao-p'ing and his government, with a genuine problem. On the one hand, they need American political support against the Soviet "Polar Bear" to the north and its Vietnamese and other allies; also, they want to attract our capital goods, bank loans, investment, and technology; they want not only to learn our management skills and marketing techniques but also to understand our educational institutions and even our legal system; and they know that their people crave intellectual, literary, and artistic contacts with a world from which they have been too long cut off. On the other hand, they know that such contacts present fearsome risks to their government by substantially increasing the Chinese people's access to information, ideas, and lifestyles that may further erode their confidence in their government. Even before the recent acceleration of contacts with the United

15

10. Little girl climbing on
pebbles on Sha-mien
Island, Canton
(Kwangchow)

11. Young girl with rouged cheeks eating bread. The government now boosts bread as better, faster, and more nutritious than rice.

12. Old woman carrying bundles on a yoke at Shunchün, Kwangtung province, at the border to Hong Kong. She wears what used to be the "uniform" for mature women in traditional China.

13. Playing pat-a-cake on a bronze lion in the Imperial Palace, Peking.

14. Gardener watering potted plants in the garden of the Kwangtung Province State Guest House, Canton (Kwangchow).

States and other industrialized democracies, many Chinese were questioning why some countries have enjoyed both political freedom and economic development, why others have at least enjoyed economic development, and why the PRC seemed to enjoy too little of either. The modest liberalization that, since the late 1970s, Teng and other leaders have attempted has not only increased China's exposure to potentially subversive foreign influences but has also allowed its people increased opportunity to voice their reactions to those influences in conversations, debates, letters to the editor, essays in newspapers and magazines, and, for a brief period, in wall posters, protest marches, and sit-ins.

We should not forget that mood swings in perceiving a foreign society are not exclusive to Americans. After more than two decades of officially fostered anti-Americanism, the 1970s brought a shift in Chinese official and popular attitudes. Signs that exhorted the masses to "defeat the American imperialists and their running dogs" were gradually balanced by others that pointedly read: "We want to be friends with all the people of the world, including the American people." Moreover, although the United States remained "the other superpower," the Chinese press began to paint the United States less unfavorably than it did the USSR. By the end of the 1970s the Chinese people, many of whom had never abandoned their pre-1949 admiration and friendship for America, eagerly awaited "normalization" of relations between the two countries. Its announcement set off a wave of officially fostered euphoria, which rose to fever pitch as a result of PRC media coverage of Teng's visit to the United States. After all, who could blame the Chinese for marveling at the American standard of living when Peking television broadcast an interview with a "typical American worker" who turned out to be a corporate executive with his own home, two cars, and an income of almost $35,000 per year?

During the weeks that followed Teng's trip, the visitor to China was often amazed at, and discomfited by, the naive enthusiasm for America that even many officials shared. Virtually everyone seemed to think that the streets of New York were paved with gold and to want to go there. Many Chinese gave the impression that nothing in their country worked, and unfairly ignored the economic and social advances of the past generation. The society that had advertised the virtues of "self-criticism" seemed to be engaging in an orgy of it. Some wall poster writers called not only for an end to the Communist Party's monopoly of power but also for implementation of the principles of the American Declaration of Independence. When asked what he thought of the posters, a young worker said: "Many of us agree with them but we don't dare put up our own. Those guys are crazy. Some of them even attach their names and addresses so that people who agree with them can get together. If the Party line changes, they'll really get it." Why then was the worker willing to talk to a foreigner in public in a "little eating place"? "I never would have before," he said, "but in the present situation I decided to take a chance. I'm scared, however. Fortunately, I don't live in this neighborhood, and I came here by bicycle. As soon as we finish talking, I'm going to ride away from here as fast as I can."

As the worker anticipated, the Party did not allow the situation to last. By spring it moved to curb the political liberalization that had included the first contacts with foreigners since 1949 and to modify the favorable view of the outside world, especially the United States. A number of the most courageous poster writers were arrested and others intimidated. Contact in "little eating places," where conversations with ordinary people are sometimes easy, became more strained. Dancing with foreigners, which during the winter had been possible for certain elite Chinese in a few cities, began to diminish. Articles began to appear in the press, such as an interview with the chef at the Peking Hotel, who confided that he had been cooking for foreigners for forty years and that they were all worthless.

Since the spring of 1979, the Party line has changed repeatedly, sometimes moving toward a more open, relaxed society and at other times, as during the 1983–84 campaign against "spiritual pollution," increasing the pressure of conformity and intellectual repression. Party leaders have evidently had difficulty in steering a middle course that is neither too reactionary nor too liberal, and in attaining a "balanced" assessment of other countries. This has complicated their task of creating a new and more favorable vision of post-Mao China in those countries.

"Vision" is an appropriate term, for the predominant impressions with which most visitors return home are visually derived. Although the PRC now publishes more books and periodicals than were available during the intellectual drought of 1966–76, relatively few are translated. Similarly, Chinese newspapers today print more informative stories than during the previous era, and foreigners are no longer prohibited from buying most local papers, but the press continues to

15. Three schoolgirls wearing red scarves that signify membership in the Young Pioneers, a national youth organization. Two wear skirts, and all act coquettish—a far cry from the militantly earnest atmosphere of 1966–76.

serve largely didactic and propagandistic functions and cannot be compared to that of free societies.

Oral communication is a fragile vehicle in any society; in China it remains a limited and sometimes unreliable source of information. While opportunities for visitors to talk with ordinary Chinese seem to be improving, the Party line has wavered so often that workers, peasants, and soldiers, not to mention intellectuals, have little reason to feel secure about such exchanges. Most visitors can neither read nor speak Chinese, so they must rely on interpreters who, however skillful, inhibit candid communications. The people whom the visitor usually comes to know are the cadres—officials who serve as escorts, guides, and interpreters, and who run the farms, factories, schools, hospitals, and other units on his itinerary. The cadres who are exposed to foreigners are generally those in whose discretion the regime has confidence. Nevertheless, in keeping with the current slogan of "seeking truth from facts," some of them are now willing to engage in fairly frank discussions. Others, however, continue to say little or to dispense a bland version of reality that sometimes contradicts franker statements published by the media.

Since reading and talking offer limited possibilities for insight, seeing becomes correspondingly more important to the traveler. Fortunately, large portions of the country that were previously out of bounds to foreigners have gradually begun to open up. Trips to the mountain fastnesses of Yunnan province and the fabled Yangtze River gorges in Szechwan are now becoming routine, and even Tibet and Sinkiang are

16. Chinese travelers smile and wave at foreigners, and also photograph them from train windows in Nanking station. This illustrates both the new enthusiasm for foreign visitors and the photomania sweeping China.

more accessible. To be sure, for political reasons provincial cities still occasionally close mysteriously, and certain sites remain off limits within the areas to which one is admitted. Yet, as Peking itself demonstrates, many museums, libraries, parks, and other places of interest that were formerly "closed for repairs" (which included ideological repairs) are now open to the public. If in the early 1970s, as many observers now appreciate, the People's Republic was still in some respects a "Potemkin village," a false facade designed to delude the visitor, it is less of one today. We should not overestimate, however, our ability to make meaningful contact with the 80 percent of the population that lives in the countryside or to understand their conditions, for the peasants of China remain remote even from their compatriots in the cities.

As part of its effort to acquire the foreign exchange required to purchase badly needed capital goods and technology from abroad, China has recently developed a flourishing tourist industry. As accommodations, transportation, and other facilities gradually improve, larger numbers of foreigners can expect to visit China, at least so long as the leadership believes that the negative effects of such contacts are tolerable. As of now, however, although visas are quite available, visiting China remains an unusual experience. Thus, a few observations about the cultural adjustments that a Western visitor must be prepared to make may prove helpful.

Those who visit China for the first time tend to be under certain psychological pressures. Most have waited years for

17. Pomegranates in the Imperial Palace, Peking.

18. Stone bridge at Botanical Gardens, Canton (Kwangchow). In the past, round-backed bridges graced the great water gardens and quaintly spanned the canals.

19. Blue-jacketed worker in a green
hat stares while shopping at the
People's Market, Peking.

the opportunity. Many have come at considerable financial sacrifice. Some feel the strain of being cut off from the world in a strange land whose language they do not understand and whose political system they have been taught to fear. Whether excited or apprehensive, virtually all are determined to get as much out of the brief trip as possible. If, as is usual, they are members of a heterogeneous group, the attempt to reconcile divergent interests within the group prior to proposing an itinerary to the hosts often drains individual energies and good humor. Moreover, some people arrive in China tired from a long journey or so eager not to miss anything that they spurn such time-honored Chinese practices as napping after lunch and going to bed early, so that they court exhaustion and often fall ill. The fierce extremes of summer or winter and an occasional all-night train ride or long transportation delay may also contribute to the discomfort of visitors. Whatever the reasons, foreigners frequently seem to be more than usually tense, irritable, and high-strung while in China. In these circumstances they sometimes are inordinately sensitive to experiences that more detached observers would dismiss as unworthy of notice. Occasionally their reactions to these experiences are unfortunate and complicate cultural contacts.

In the United States conspicuous foreign visitors are often stared at, especially once they leave our big cities, and Americans abroad are accustomed to being scrutinized by the local population. In China staring at visitors is something else again (plate 19). Relatively few foreigners are seen there, and staring at them seems to be a national pastime. The Chinese do not hide their immense curiosity about non-Chinese. They stare with forthright intensity and at as close a range as possible, up to three inches—even in the urban centers that are standard sight-seeing stops. One often sees groups of Chinese assembled outside the leading hotels waiting to catch a glimpse of the exotic foreigners, and at the excellent zoos of Peking, Shanghai, and Canton the people stare at foreigners while the foreigners stare at the animals.

There is no point trying to look baggy-panted in an effort to melt into the crowd. Foreigners, and especially women, will be stared at no matter what they wear. However, it is well to know that the Chinese are offended by décolleté necklines on women and that sleeveless shirts have only recently become accepted as appropriate attire.

Foreign visitors, of course, watch the local fashions, which are another indicator of the relaxed climate in the post "Gang

24

20. Straw-hatted photographer at the Sun Yat-sen Mausoleum in Nanking. Professional photographers are often stationed at major monuments to make photos that become both a patriotic and a sentimental remembrance.

of Four" era. By 1978 there were at least twelve approved hairstyles, many more than had been allowed from 1966–76. Today, Chinese women can have curls, and some have permanent waves. In winter, brightly colored diaphanous neck scarves indicate young women's interest in relieving their drab and formless outfits. In summer, some women wear colorful skirts and blouses instead of the ubiquitous baggy pants. The windows of photographic studios display inviting photos of women made up like 1940s American glamour girls. Graceful femininity, form-fitting clothes, and decorative jewelry are also to be seen on stage in the theater—a model for the Chinese masses. Although the changes in how Chinese women look must be measured on a Chinese scale—not in relation to Japanese and Western fashion—the trend is definitely toward the more decorative and feminine.

Many Chinese practices are only comprehensible in Chinese terms. For example, some visitors find it difficult to get used to the consistent differentiation among guests according to status. The Chinese insist that the leading members of every foreign delegation be ranked in hierarchical order, diplomatic style. The hosts then respect this order every day in every way. If cars are used rather than buses, they are allocated so that the head of a delegation usually rides in the biggest, the deputy head in a somewhat less prestigious vehicle, and the number three person in a more modest one. Similar protocol is followed in arranging places at banquets, allocating hotel rooms, making introductions, and reporting in the press. The Chinese defend this policy on grounds of

21. Bicycle traffic on a main boulevard, Peking. Bicycles are the principal means of
transportation for the masses of China. Cycling is considered practical, economical,
and health-building.

politeness and explain that it avoids confusion and facilitates efficient arrangements. Surely this is true, but the extremes to which they carry the practice disconcert many visitors unused to diplomatic protocol.

Another startling factor is the way the Chinese handle the automobile. Wildly honking cars bearing foreign guests unceremoniously shunt aside cyclists and pedestrians. Cars are in very short supply in China, and few are privately owned. Although buses and trucks assume a good deal of the burden of local transportation, great numbers of people rely on their bicycles or walk (plate 21). Perhaps because of the scarcity of motor vehicles, Chinese cyclists and pedestrians appear to be among the most undisciplined in the world, a surprising fact in a country that is governed so rigorously. Thus, a certain amount of horn blowing is required by those who seek to navigate the sometimes chaotic urban streets. But in China it seems that the gas pedal and the horn are linked, so that one cannot move an inch without mindless honking, preferably while driving at a relatively high speed that sends pedestrians scurrying for safety. It is interesting to note that a similar phenomenon occurred in Tokyo in the years just after World War II, before the automobile became commonplace. Whatever the explanation, so irksome is the experience that an occasional visitor will refuse to continue riding in cars, to the puzzlement and discomfort of his escorts, who find crowded buses and hot hikes far more annoying than the excesses of the

characteristic Chinese chauffeur. Heightened consciousness of noise pollution in recent years has led to an effort to curb horn blowing that can be expected to be increasingly effective.

Other examples of privileged treatment for foreigners abound: clearing people away from a museum exhibition they were enjoying so that foreigners can quickly gain an unobstructed view; providing special restaurants or private dining rooms in which foreigners eat far better than the masses; ushering foreigners into special lounges during intermissions at the theater; and so forth. These arrangements may be frustrating for visitors who would like to narrow the inevitable gap between themselves and the Chinese people, and they undoubtedly create popular resentment against both foreigners and the officials who share these privileges. It should be borne in mind, however, that they are intended as gestures of consideration and that such privileged treatment, which in prerevolutionary days was a hated symbol of foreign domination, is now granted through China's free choice, a decision proudly made by the host as a courtesy to guests. Whether the ordinary people of China would make the same choice is another question.

The visitor to China is offered many conveniences. Activities are thoughtfully and efficiently arranged, enabling him to make maximum use of his time. The guests are consulted by the host organization, which does its best to meet the varied interests of the members of each group. And the Chinese patiently tolerate the foibles of foreign group dynamics as the guests struggle among themselves to order their priorities.

Yet, when all is said and done, the Chinese expect us to concentrate upon the China they perceive and want others to understand. Ordinarily this poses little problem, for most visitors enjoy the variety of the usual tour to selected factories, schools, communes, medical facilities, and cultural monuments. But the foreigner who comes as a specialist, with the hope of concentrating on what China has done in his particular area of expertise, may become frustrated. If, as would be natural in most countries, he seeks to meet Chinese who pursue the same line of work, he may be disappointed. Fortunately, artists, art historians, writers, law professors, judges, and sociologists, who were among those unavailable to visitors from the beginning of the Cultural Revolution until 1978–79, have surfaced to an increasing extent. Scientists, engineers, doctors, journalists, local officials, and others were already accessible. Yet, even if one is fortunate enough to meet his professional opposite number, it is often in circum-

22. Far left: Chinese dance "The Hustle" at the International Club, Peking, in March 1979. No single change was more surprising or more significant a measure of the new atmosphere in China since the "Gang of Four" was smashed than the revival of social dancing. But mixed dancing between Chinese and foreigners is still a sensitive subject.

23. Left: Youths celebrate at a boisterous eating and drinking party in a restaurant.

24. Vegetables in a showplace market in Peking. This ideal market was shown to foreign visitors in the early 1970s as typical, but in fact only foreigners were allowed to buy here. The Chinese consumer cannot choose from such a variety.

stances that do not lend themselves to sustained substantive conversations. Most meetings take place in groups and under the watchful eyes of one's escorts and hosts, and in those circumstances candor is sometimes in short supply, even today. Moreover, because of the desire to show visiting experts the overall transformation of new China within which developments in individual fields must be understood, the demands of the schedule usually ration opportunities for exchanging experiences with experts.

Most guests simply accept the fact that, at least on their first trip to China, there will be limits upon the pursuit of specialized interests unless special arrangements are made in advance. Once in a while, however, a human explosion occurs and disturbs the good feeling which generally prevails. Such unattractive incidents strain Sino-American relations,

25. A little boy with a popsicle waits
in a Chinese-style perambulator
at a market in Loyang, Honan
province.

and the lesson to be learned is that if you are not prepared to
do it the Chinese way, don't go to China.

Gifts are a problem that occasionally arouses sensitivities.
Visitors usually want to express their appreciation to the cadres who accompany them during their stay, and they often
want to take something to the organization that has invited
them and to the institutions that receive them. Gifts such as
clothing, household objects, or personal trinkets used to be
out of the question for cadres. In today's more relaxed atmosphere, however, they are accepting items ranging from
fountain pens to pocket calculators. The People's Republic
has done much to eliminate the endemic corruption of previous Chinese governments, and it is especially concerned
about officials succumbing to what the Party calls "the silver-
coated bullets of the bourgeoisie." The relaxation of recent

31

26. Hall of Supreme Harmony (T'ai-ho-tien), Imperial Palace, Peking. Ming dynasty (1368–1644), with renovations of the Ch'ing dynasty, the Republic, and the People's Republic. Height of hall 87 feet, length 210 feet, width 115 feet.

years and the increasing contacts with foreigners have presented new opportunities for corruption, especially in economic transactions. Stories now circulate about Chinese officials who exact gifts of items such as wristwatches, tape recorders, and even Mercedes Benz autos from foreign traders, especially overseas Chinese. Such stories, together with revelations of continuing corruption in domestic affairs, have stimulated the government to adopt new, strict anticorruption measures. Tourists usually need not be concerned on this score, but it is a problem that warrants the serious consideration of foreign businessmen.

Books are currently an appropriate present, and not only from academic or professional guests. Whereas previously such gifts were often carefully screened, and sometimes rejected because of fear of contamination by potentially "coun-

terrevolutionary ideas," the situation has markedly changed. The traditional Chinese lust for learning has been allowed to reassert itself to a considerable extent, and old classics and new works are being published. Bookstores are mobbed with eager readers. Outside, one frequently sees circles of squatting citizens exchanging scarce items. There is a hunger for all information, just as there is an endless appetite for entertainment and the arts, and for special consumer goods that have long been hard to obtain. As many overseas Chinese have discovered, their relatives in the motherland do not want them to send a black-and-white television set but a color model!

One excellent solution is to take along a Polaroid camera, so that one can give instant mementos to people who are particularly kind. Escorts also appreciate photographs mailed to them after the visitor returns home.

27. Plowing a flooded rice paddy in a commune near Shanghai. The young man rides a plow while holding the tail of a water buffalo.

28. Rice paddies of Kwangtung province. Some paddies are flooded in preparation for planting, others are green with young plants.

No impressionistic account of adjusting to Chinese society could be complete without some reference to what may well be the world's best cuisine. If hotels are generally still spartan, the same cannot be said of the food. Several aspects are noteworthy. At one end of the social spectrum are the workers' restaurants. The differences between the food served there and that to which visitors are usually exposed are noticeable. Rice, for example, tends to be somewhat harder, smaller grained, and grayer than that served visitors, but still quite edible even for Westerners. The meat is rather fatty, for this is traditional Chinese preference, but the workers' meals as a whole are tasty. At the other end of the spectrum, the interesting culinary feature of state banquets in the Great Hall of the People is the predominance of soft, easily digestible dishes and soups, a menu suited to the needs of China's aging leadership.

Although the quality of the cuisine varies with the hotel, restaurant, area, price, status of the guests, knowledge of those who order, and other factors, it is, by and large, quite high. Apart from the occasional ceremonial banquet, group tours tend to get fed less well than persons who order from the menu. For foreigners in recent years the cost of dining out has escalated substantially. Unless they manage to talk themselves into seats in the regular Chinese sections of restaurants, still a feat, they should take the precaution of inquiring about prices in advance. Some of the most famous restaurants in Peking and a few other major cities now charge prices that exceed those of their counterparts in New York and surely Hong Kong and are not necessarily better. If one is an official guest, one need not worry about such mundane matters as the cost of meals, but being a guest of the state is often more confining than seeing China in a less exalted capacity.

One area in which the government allows visitors great freedom is in taking photographs, and the requirement that all film be developed prior to departure from China has long been abolished. However, because some foreigners have published some archaeological material before the Chinese, photography is often barred at museums and historical and archaeological sites, even if no color slides are yet on sale there. Virtually everything else in sight is fair game for the lens, although a surprising number of people are reluctant to be photographed—almost as though they are afraid that the camera's "evil eye" will possess their souls. Only a Polaroid seems to break down their defenses.

The Chinese guides do not insist that their guests photograph tractors instead of water buffalo (plate 27), workers

35

29. Playing basketball in the Imperial Palace, Peking. In the setting is the Gate of Military Prowess (Wu-ying-men), southwestern section of the Imperial Palace. Ming dynasty (1368–1644), with renovations of the Ch'ing dynasty and the People's Republic.

instead of peasants, or handsomely dressed children instead of traditional-looking older people in an attempt to make their country seem more "modern" than it actually is.

The camera thus could capture much, if not all, of the reality of China: naturally lush southern rice fields and arid central plains that have become fertile through heroic feats of irrigation; huge factories and the ubiquitous small workshops; various means for transporting agricultural commodities and manufactured products—man, beast, bicycle, boat, wheelbarrow, and truck; central markets and neighborhood stalls; run-down city courtyards and recently built workers' apartments; peasant houses and dim cave dwellings; nursery schools and universities; neighborhood clinics and city hospitals; churches restored to their original use and Confucian temples turned into revolutionary museums; families picnicking at the Great Wall, the emperor's Summer Palace, or the many parks; children swimming in the moat of the Imperial Palace, playing basketball within the former Forbidden City (plate 29), or singing as they hike to the fields to help with the harvest; revolutionary movies, ballets, concerts, operas, and parades; national and international athletic events; chic but ineffectual traffic policemen and baggy but lionized soldiers; images of Chairman Mao and other heroes immortalized in paintings and photographs, and inescapable selections from the writings of the leaders carried by billboards, banners, broadcasts, and books.

30. Reading Wall posters, early in 1979. During this period, shortly after the United States and China normalized relations, there was a great burst of free expression. Courageous Chinese put up wall posters demanding human rights, legal guarantees against arbitrary government actions, and official rehabilitation of people who had been unfairly treated.

31. Women of Foshan, Kwangtung Province, show great pride in their recently renewed old city. The women's traditional black "pajamas" make a dramatic contrast with the freshly whitewashed walls.

32. Couples "love talk" under the blossoms in the Imperial Palace garden, Peking. Although the 1950 marriage law allowed men to marry at twenty and women at eighteen, for many years government policy has dictated that couples should not marry until their mid to late twenties, a policy that has been carried out more consistently in the cities than in the countryside.

33. Pearl River, Canton (Kwangchow).

34. Orchid Garden, Canton (Kwangchow).

This kaleidoscope of contemporary China fails to suggest the continuing prominence that the architectural monuments and art objects of traditional China enjoy today, not only for foreign tourists but also for the Chinese themselves. In line with the classic Party slogan "Make the past serve the present" the masses can now enjoy some of the previously inaccessible preserves of the emperors. Indeed, one of the happier reminders of the vast changes that have been wrought in China in this century is the sight of peasants sipping tea in one of the gardens of the Forbidden City or workers napping on the railings of the Summer Palace. But China's artistic heritage serves the present in broader ways than by demonstrating the egalitarianism of contemporary society. It is an important factor in fueling the sense of national pride, which in turn sustains the spirit of nationalism that has spurred China's progress and made almost four decades of sacrifice endurable for the masses. It is also, at least in the hands of skilled archaeologists, historians, museum curators, and propagandists, an important vehicle for educating the masses about both the evils and the

35. Tomb figure of an equestrian musician. T'ang dynasty (618–907). Pottery with yellowish glaze, painted with red and black cold pigments.

36. Stele with Buddhas from Ch'ang-an, Shensi province. 501 (Northern Wei dynasty). Sandstone, 23 5/8 × 22 inches. Shown at the Historical Museum, Sian, Shensi province.

accomplishments of the old society, the enormous social and economic price paid for aesthetic attainments, and the unfolding of the class struggle throughout China's history. And it is a peerless instrument for winning the admiration and respect of the outside world, as demonstrated by the response to the great traveling exhibitions of Chinese art.

For these reasons, revolutionary China has allocated substantial resources to preserving, restoring, rediscovering, and displaying the artistic achievements of the past. The excesses of the Cultural Revolution resulted in damage to some cultural artifacts and historic buildings, but vigorous measures by Chou En-lai and various other leaders limited the destruction, and in recent years a considerable effort has been made to repair the damage. The People's Republic has also gone to great lengths to exhibit the many priceless treasures that were unearthed during the Cultural Revolution, in order to cast a more positive light on contemporary China both at home and abroad.

As a result, foreign visitors can rejoice in some of the glories

37. Hexagonal window with a rare azalea plant in the covered gallery of a Shanghai nursery. People's Republic.

of ancient Chinese civilization in addition to witnessing the social and economic progress of the present government. Indeed, itineraries have come to reflect an easy counterpoint between tradition and transformation. In Peking one may see the Children's Hospital in the morning and the Temple of Heaven in the afternoon. In Shanghai a long trek through the massive Industrial Palace may precede a leisurely appreciation of the sixteenth-century garden of the Yü Yüan. And in Loyang a tour of the magnificent Buddhist sculptures in the Lung-men caves is balanced by an inspection of the country's largest tractor factory.

The aim of this book is to achieve a similar balance between past and present. The photographs and commentary reflect impressions gained during numerous visits to China and attempt to show the magnificent artistic heritage of the Chinese people in the context of their society today.

THE PREHISTORIC
PERIOD

38. Model for Pan-p'o, a Neolithic village of about 4000 B.C. Shown at the Pan-p'o Museum. This modern reconstruction is based on foundations excavated near Sian, Shensi province. About one-fifth of the total area of the village has been excavated. The circular and quadrangular housing and pits were surrounded by a ditch.

◀39. Landscape east of Sian, Shensi province. The loess beds of north-central China near the Yellow River have been cultivated since prehistoric times, but now the mountainsides have been terraced to expand agricultural production.

THE PREHISTORY OF CHINA is a fascinating puzzle of archaeological and geographical facts, engaging myths, and vast numbers of unanswered questions. According to the Confucian Classics, Chinese civilization stretches back to the third millennium B.C. They tell of sage kings who showed the great Yellow River the way to the sea and taught their people how to drain the marshes and burn the forests for planting, how to carry on agriculture and spinning, and how to cast bronze. They tell of three successive glorious dynasties—the Hsia, Shang, and Chou—founded by kings who through their virtue and humility were granted the "mandate of heaven" to rule as temporal monarchs. Each of the three dynasties eventually came under the rule of tyrannical kings lacking in virtue and humility, who thereby lost the "mandate of heaven" and caused their dynasties to fall.

The Chinese, who have always been proud of and consumingly interested in their long history, accepted these mythic stories as fact until the early twentieth century, when a new breed of Chinese scholar began to question the antiquity of Chinese civilization. These skeptics viewed the "history" in the Classics as mythology. They proved that the larger part of the Classics was written no earlier than the sixth century B.C. and pointed out that there was no archaeological evidence of Chinese civilization before the Chou dynasty (?1027–256 B.C.). Li Chi, a distinguished archaeologist born in 1896, poignantly recalls his encounter with this new intellectual atmosphere. As a schoolboy before the revolution of 1911 (which marked the end of the Ch'ing dynasty and the beginning of the Republican era), Li Chi had learned that there were five thousand years of history; now this impressive time span was

43

being considerably shortened for lack of evidence. In subsequent years, Li Chi and others devoted themselves to reconstructing China's ancient history with evidence solid enough to meet the skeptics' standards.

At the beginning of the twentieth century, archaeology had not yet been scientifically applied to the study of China's past. There are a number of reasons why this was so. Modern archaeology is itself a relatively new discipline among the time-honored classical academic pursuits. Furthermore, the heart of archaeological work is digging in the earth to find buried relics of the past. The traditional Chinese considered disturbing the earth inauspicious; to dig wantonly would upset the precarious balance of forces between heaven and earth. And it was entirely taboo to dig up grave sites and disturb the spirits of the ancestors.

Bronze vessels presumed to be from the period of the Shang dynasty (?1523–?1027 B.C.) and coveted by connoisseurs and antiquarians had been looted surreptitiously from tombs by generations of grave robbers. But these bronzes appeared mysteriously on the market, without records of provenance or archaeological context that might prove their antiquity. Thus the existence of both the Shang dynasty and, by extension, the earlier Hsia, which had been written about in the Classics, was questioned. Beyond that no prehistoric Chinese materials had been excavated. Some scholars assumed that human habitation in China was relatively new compared to the Near East and Europe.

Several dramatic archaeological discoveries in the 1920s and 1930s renewed China's confidence in the antiquity of its civilization. While making a survey in north-central China in 1921, J. G. Andersson, a Swedish geologist who became a great archaeologist, uncovered Yang-shao, a Neolithic site (third millennium B.C.) which gave its name to one of the principal cultures of the "cradle of China." Andersson also made repeated visits to the Chou-k'ou-tien cave site, roughly thirty miles southwest of Peking. This site was extensively excavated from 1927 to 1929. Vast numbers of late Stone Age fossils were found there, but of greatest importance were the skull, teeth, and bones of Peking man, who flourished 500,000 years ago. When these remains were eventually analyzed, they served as conclusive proof of the antiquity of Chinese habitation.

In the late 1920s the ancient city of Anyang, the last Shang capital (flourished ?1300–?1027 B.C.), became the third important discovery and the subject thereafter of large-scale excavations. However, although Neolithic remains near Anyang showed that the area had been settled for an undetermined period prior to its occupation by the Shang, the Hsia dynasty mentioned in the Classics is just being positively identified and therefore is reaccredited from mythology to history, according to archaeologists.

The excavation of Anyang was the first Chinese-government-sponsored archaeological dig. Conservative officials had effectively opposed previous plans in the 1920s, but a group of Chinese archaeologists gained the support and protection of Chiang Kai-shek and uncovered a sophisticated, ordered urban center of impressive proportions.

This period was the heyday of foreign collectors of Chinese antiquities. Ancient bronzes, jades, and ceramics could easily be bought in the curio shops of Peking, Shanghai, and Canton. Although Chinese law proclaimed all objects found in the earth to be the property of the Chinese government, the law was ignored and some officials even received a share of the profits from illicit sales. It was then that the great collections of Chinese art in Japan, Europe, and America were formed.

Today, while the treasures of India and other Asian countries continue to be pillaged for the benefit of the international collector, China and Japan have effectively stopped the cultural drain. The techniques of control are different in those two countries: Japan has designated and listed national treasures and important cultural properties which may not be exported. The Chinese government has simply taken over all museums, temples, collections, and art stores, and sells only what it considers unimportant to the national heritage.

Chinese archaeology changed greatly after 1949. Although it is hardly a first priority in a nation concerned primarily with advancing its industrialization and agriculture, emphasis has been placed upon increasing the knowledge of ancient China through a number of excavations that recognize the role of archaeology in glorifying the great tradition of Chinese civilization both at home and abroad.

Most Chinese archaeological sites have been found accidentally, including the Neolithic village of Pan-p'o, which was uncovered when foundations for a factory were being excavated. Rarely has the archaeologist in China gone to the plains with the Classics in hand to locate a lost city, as has happened in the Mediterranean areas with the Bible or Homer as guide. Some Chinese excavations have, however, been plotted out in advance, like that of the tomb mound of Ming dynasty Emperor Wan-li (r. 1573–1620).

Communist Chinese literature explains that when archaeological sites are discovered by chance, they are reported to the regional archaeological committee, which in turn informs the national organization for archaeology. Excavations are organized by archaeological teams who may call on the army and on local peasants and workers for help. A dig is often carried out with extraordinary speed, judging by Western standards. A few months have sufficed to complete some major excavations that in the West would take years. While it is true that loss and breakage may occur when digging by untrained manpower proceeds with such speed, the Chinese have certainly exhibited and published information about many remarkable treasures found since 1949.

The village of Pan-p'o (c. 4000 B.C.), four miles northeast of Sian, was excavated during the period 1953–57, a time span which does not reflect the inordinate speed of other digs. One-fifth of the total village was excavated and roofed over for preservation; adjoining the site, a museum was built to display a number of objects accompanied by extensive explanatory labels.

The people of Pan-p'o were part of the Yang-shao Neolithic culture, which had settlements on the terraces of fine-grained, wind-blown soil called loess, in north-central China near the Yellow River and in northwest China. They are identified by a fine ceramic ware ranging in color between buff and red and decorated with black and red geometric patterns. This same Yang-shao culture also produced a coarse sandy ware often decorated with impressions made by pressing cord or woven-grass matting against the wet clay. Remains of another Neolithic culture, called Lung-shan, which produced a black ware, have also been uncovered in north-central China and in the eastern provinces. Relative dating of these two cultures is under debate, although it is known that Yang-shao was the earlier—lasting from about 4000 to 2000 B.C.—and that Lung-shan thrived from about 2000 B.C. until the beginning of the Shang dynasty, with pockets remaining during the Shang and continuing into the Chou period. But recent finds have brought to light fresh material which may serve to reorganize all scholarship on prehistoric China.

There is a wealth of information on the village of Pan-p'o, which is typical of many hundreds of other Neolithic settlements. It is situated near a tributary of the Wei River, itself a

40. Bowl in the style of Miao-ti-kou, Honan province. Yang-shao culture, c. 3500 B.C. Buff earthenware decorated with reddish slip and black pigment. Shown at the Imperial Palace, Peking.

41. Earthenware vessels. Lung-shan culture, c. 2000 B.C. Shown at the museum in Wang-ch'eng Park, Loyang, Honan province. Such tripod shapes are extremely practical for cooking over a small fire.

tributary of the great Yellow River. The community was basically sedentary, with agriculture providing the primary food source. Hunting, fishing, and gathering supplemented the diet. Because of the number of prehistoric communities clustered near the southern reaches of the Yellow River, the area has been called the "cradle of China." But there are great differences between the "cradle of China" and the "cradle of civilization" communities which grew up along the banks of the Tigris and Euphrates rivers and the Nile. The Chinese settlements were located some distance from the river, presumably to avoid the great seasonal floods. Mesopotamian and ancient Egyptian agricultural communities contemporaneous with Neolithic China utilized the annual inundation for fertilization of the soil and the trapped waters for irrigation. The ancient Chinese did not use irrigation but depended on the small annual rainfall to grow millet and sorghum.

The settlement of Pan-p'o itself was quite large, covering roughly 70,000 square meters. The foundations of forty-six houses, over two hundred storage pits, and remains of thousands of tools and pieces of ceramic have been unearthed. It has been estimated that as many as two hundred families could have lived in this village at any one time. A ditch surrounded the housing area, which covered roughly 30,000 square meters. Chinese archaeologists called this a "defense" ditch, but it was more likely used for drainage and to keep dogs and pigs from wandering away into the fields. All indications point to a peaceful existence.

Two kinds of houses were built at Pan-p'o; most were round, but some were quadrangular. Similar building techniques were used for both styles. The floors of the buildings were sometimes sunken and sometimes at ground level. The floors and wattle-and-daub walls were plastered with clay. Grasses collected from the plain were soaked in mud to provide a cohesive thatch roofing material, and the roof was supported by wooden pillars made of hewn logs driven into clay-lined holes in the earth. The entrances of all the houses faced south, to avoid the bitter north wind of winter. Interior areas for eating and sleeping appear to have been defined by pounded-earth platforms. Woven-grass matting and animal skins were probably used as bedding and decoration. A central fire pit served for cooking and heating. Warm clothing was sewn by the women, who used bone needles.

The larger quadrangular houses had roughly twenty square meters of space, which was enough for a family of four, ac-

42. Speculative reconstruction of a circular house at Pan-p'o, made of wattle and daub with a thatched roof. The Pan-p'o excavations have been roofed over for protection.

43, 44. Stone-and-wood ax and dibble from Pan-p'o. Shown at the Pan-p'o Museum.

cording to Dr. Judith Treistman (*The Prehistory of China*, p. 44).

The skillful craftsmanship of the Pan-p'o inhabitants is shown by their agricultural tools, such as axes, adzes, and dibbles (used to make holes in which to plant seeds), and gear for hunting and fishing, such as arrowheads, fish hooks, and net sinkers. The tools are designed with elegant simplicity and have a direct appeal, a rustic aesthetic which delights eyes weary of overdesigned machine-age tools.

It is the pottery, however, that best exhibits the exuberance and skill of the Yang-shao people. It is of high quality, varied in shape and design, and appears to share some characteristics with ceramics contemporaneously made in the Near East and notably in Central Asia. No one has yet established a defi-

49

45. Buff earthenware bowl from Pan-p'o, decorated with black paint. Shown at the Pan-p'o Museum. The potter who decorated this bowl captured the essential quality of the fish with great skill and economy of means.

nite link between these cultures at that time, although later intercourse between China and these areas is well documented. Most scholars maintain that Chinese civilization grew up independently, but some suggest borrowings from other cultures. It may yet be proved that these views are not irreconcilable. If, indeed, the prehistoric Chinese society grew up independently, it may still have been enriched by contacts with Near Eastern or Central Asian prehistoric cultures.

The vast majority of Yang-shao pots are decorated with rhythmic abstract designs of straight lines, diagonals, crosshatching, zigzags, circles, loops, open-ended ovoids, waves, and swirls. These designs are usually executed in black paint, enhancing the form of the pots and harmoniously uniting the flat patterns with the swelling volumes. They make a fit beginning for a culture that was to produce the greatest ceramics tradition in the world.

An outstanding piece of ceramic ware found at Pan-p'o differs from the later Yang-shao ware decorated with abstract designs. Its design borrows from the natural world, with marvelous fish swimming around the outside. One fish on the exterior wall is open-mouthed, with black teeth and a nose that resembles a pig's snout. Its body is defined by long curving lines containing two black triangles, one to accent the body, the other the tail. Three triangular fins finish the form, and the gill is indicated by an unpainted crescent within the black body triangle.

46. Buff earthenware water vessel
with cord-marked design, from Pan-p'o.
Shown at the Pan-p'o Museum. In the
speculative reconstruction of the circular
house (plate 42), this vessel is shown
suspended by cords passed through the
handles. It may have been used in this way,
or it may have been sunk into soft earth—
perhaps both storage methods were used.

This pot reflects an intimacy with aquatic life acquired through sustained observation. It is a joyful recording of the natural world by people who were able to communicate its wonders through schematic visual forms.

Another kind of vessel found at Pan-p'o is a coarse, cord-marked, small-necked amphora with a pointed base, an eloquent example of rustic simplicity. Its pointed bottom suggests that the vessel may have been placed in the ground to keep its contents cool, but in the Pan-p'o reconstruction of a circular house, the amphora is hung on a wall by cording threaded through the earlike holes at the middle of the vessel. To make the decoration, a cord was rolled over the wet surface. Other examples of this kind of ware were decorated by pressing matting onto the surface or simply by "combing" (incising) the surface with a shell or stick. The pieces were fired in the community kiln located to the east of the dwelling area.

The function of pottery extended beyond the everyday cooking, serving, and storage of foods and liquids. Pots were also buried with the dead. In the graveyard, which lies beyond the enclosing ditch north of the housing cluster, most adults were buried with at least a pot or two at their feet. This rite suggests the beginnings of the ritual offerings for the after-life, a custom which was to become ever more important in the later historic periods of Chinese civilization. Children were buried in pots near the houses, presumably to stay near their parents.

Chinese Communist historians have striven to fit the archaeological material into a Marxian periodization of Chinese history. They claim that for tens of thousands of years prior to the Shang dynasty a form of social organization prevailed in China that was a type of "primitive, utopian Communism," so named because people lived in clan communes. The members of each commune, it is said, were all related and elected their own leader. They held land, domestic animals, and tools in common, tilled the soil collectively, and shared the fruits of their labor equally. According to this view, because there was no such thing as private ownership of land or other means of production, society was not divided into classes and there was no economic exploitation of one group by another. Some Communist historians maintain that this primitive society was matriarchal, with women developing and practicing the techniques of agriculture while men hunted and fished. This may be true. At least this interpretation accords well with the present attitude, which seeks to glorify the role of the Chinese woman. Articles in Party organs constantly report female feats of strength, courage, and initiative in jobs formerly thought to be men's work, such as the drilling of wells and the building of bridges and dams. The Pan-p'o finds are seen as confirmation of women's basic right to work shoulder to shoulder with their husbands, brothers, and comrades.

ANCIENT CHINA

47. Ax head. Late Shang dynasty
(?1300–?1027 B.C.). Bronze,
12 3/4 × 13 1/2 inches. Shown at the
Imperial Palace, Peking. Found
in the tomb of an important
personage in Shang society, this
ritual ax may have been used to
decapitate victims chosen to
accompany the deceased. The
face has the round eyes and toothy
grin of a skull, yet the nose,
eyebrows, ears, and side hair, all
features of the living, are
included in stiffly curled forms.
The strange combination of
elements in this monster face
is characteristic of Shang
design.

48. Bronze vessel ("*Tsengcheng Yu-fu*") from
Ching-shan, Hupei province. Western Chou
dynasty (?1027–770 B.C.). Height 33 7/8
inches. Shown at the Imperial Palace,
Peking. This *Fang-hu*, a squarish wine
container, was one of many bronze vessels
used for ritual purposes. Found during the
excavation of the tomb of a Chou nobleman
in 1966, the buried bronze had interacted
with its environment to produce the
handsome patina. The scroll design of the
earlier *ting* (plate 50), with its compactly
designed bands, contrasts with the relaxed
overall linear scrolls of the *Fang-hu*. The
ribbon-like scroll design has lost some of
its intensity, yet the surface design as a
whole has a marvelously lively quality.

THE ARCHAEOLOGICAL AND HISTORICAL EXPLANATIONS of ancient China that one receives in China today reflect a point of
view quite different from tha of either traditional Chinese or
Western-influenced scholarship. Communist historians view
ancient China proudly, while at the same time discrediting
it as a viable model of society. Its achievements have been put
under glass as a sanitized display stripped of ideological authority yet maintained in order to satisfy curiosity and foster
national pride.

According to the Marxist interpretation of history, which
is derived from Western experience, societies evolve in stages
from primitive communism through slavery, feudalism, and
capitalism to socialism, and eventually reach the paradise of
Communism. Chinese Communist scholars have had many
problems fitting their country's millennial heritage into the
Marxist mold. They have found it particularly difficult to
arrive at a consensus about the periodization of ancient history.

At present historians seem ready to reopen the debate as to
exactly when primitive communism ended and when the
"Slave Society" began. The late Kuo Mo-jo, president of the
Academy of Sciences for many years, revised his own views
considerably from the first study he published in 1930. His
final view was that the "Slave Society" commenced with the
Shang dynasty (?1523–?1027 B.C.). Other officials argue that
the "Slave Society" began as early as the twentieth century
B.C. with the Hsia dynasty. Only in the 1980s are the literary
references to the Hsia dynasty being corroborated by archaeological data that tend to confirm the latter theory,
which was widely circulated by the Chinese government
even before the scientific evidence appeared. Marxists say
that the "Slave Society" was a new stage in the "inevitable"
unfolding of history. It is said to have developed because
gradual improvements in agricultural production techniques
had brought about an increasing division of labor, the
accumulation of large production surpluses, and the crea-

tion of a wealthy aristocratic class capable of owning and exploiting slaves. As a result of these changes, a monarchical form of government emerged, in which the king, the biggest slave owner and chief of the nobility, owned all the land but permitted its use by nobles, ministers, and other high officials.

According to Kuo and his followers, "Slave Society" lasted through the early part of the Chou dynasty, usually called the Western Chou (?1027–770 B.C.). Roughly midway during the latter part of the dynasty, called the Eastern Chou (770–256 B.C.), they claim, "Slave Society" gave way to "Feudal Society" because the slave economy had developed into a more complex landlord economy, in which exploitation of serf labor became the dominant form of agriculture and private ownership of land came to be recognized. The Communists use the term "feudal" in a much broader, less technical way than do non-Marxist scholars, bringing within its ambit various types of landlord economy rather than solely that type in which land is held by enfeoffment, as it was in medieval Europe. Thus, in their view, "Feudal Society" lasted for over two millenniums until the Opium War of 1839–42 initiated the process of turning China into what they call "a semi-colonial, semi-feudal" country.

The great philosopher-statesman Confucius (551–479 B.C.) and his disciples, who for over two thousand years exercised the most profound influence over Chinese society, lived during a chaotic transitional era. Confucius maintained that the early Shang period and, even more, the early Chou had been "golden ages" when the world had been ruled by virtue and all had been peace and order. He urged the aristocratic rulers of the Chinese states that were contending for power under the nominal reign of the Chou monarchy to emulate those supposedly model governments of ancient China. During subsequent millenniums, right-thinking Chinese rulers and their bureaucracies adopted the Confucian view of ancient China.

Communist historians, by branding the Shang dynasty and the early Chou as the era of "Slave Society" and by revealing and condemning what they believe to be its true nature, have sought to discredit the "golden age" in the minds of the Chinese people. During the early 1970s they attacked Confucius, calling him a descendant of the declining slave-owning aristocracy who preached an ideology that idealized the traditional virtues in order to uphold the old system and frustrate the slaves' efforts to end their oppression. Indeed, Communist

Party propaganda organs mounted a nationwide campaign against the Sage in 1973–74 that was understood by the Chinese to be an attack on Chou En-lai by Chiang Ch'ing in her struggle for power. Since the fall of the "Gang of Four" in 1976, Confucius has gradually begun to recover some of his prestige.

Although art objects of the "Slave Society" are commended for their beauty, Communist authorities emphasize that Chinese craftsmen were exploited by the ruling class. As Chairman Mao has said of traditional China: "The peasants and the handicraft workers were the basic classes which created the wealth and culture of this society." According to the Chairman, the resources expended to make the objects should have been spent for the welfare of the people, not for the delight of a few.

During the Shang and the early Chou, human sacrifices were made to appease troublesome cosmic spirits or to provide company for the dead in the afterlife. As one learns the details of these sacrifices, the term "Slave Society" takes on a more profound meaning even for those who do not necessarily subscribe to the Marxian analysis of history. Ritual bronze daggers and axes reveal that the victim was often killed with weapons decorated with spiral-relief designs similar to those found on bronze vessels (plate 47). Sometimes they show the hollow-eyed, toothy grin of a skull. Probably some of the people who were killed to accompany the dead were decapitated with these axes. Some excavations reveal that their severed heads were stored in one part of the tomb, their bodies in another. In other burial situations metal clamps held down other victims, who were incarcerated live in the tombs. The Chinese display the clamps along with photographs from the site showing the exact positions of the skeletons around the central chamber. In yet a third burial type victims were drugged or poisoned and then sealed into the tomb.

The "Slave Society" provides Communist historians with archaeological evidence that communicates a poignant object lesson to the masses, a lesson driven home through explanations, photographs in the exhibitions, and publications, lest the new Maoist man become too enamored of the glories of China's past. But while vocal in denouncing the horrors of the ancient elite and their exploitation of the skilled craftsmen and the masses at large, the People's Republic nevertheless preserves and celebrates the remarkable antiquity, continuity, and genius of Chinese civilization.

49. Bronze vessel found near Loyang, Honan province. Eastern Chou dynasty (770–256 B.C.). Height 17 inches, diameter 28 3/4 inches. Shown at the museum in Wang-ch'eng Park, Loyang. This large *kuei* was also used to hold ritual offerings. Monster faces are absent, but the handles are in the shape of demons, recognizable in this case as a cross between a serpent and a tiger.

Shang culture reveals the early stage at which both the arts and sociopolitical institutions developed in China. Writing was an outstanding achievement of this period. The ancient characters have been preserved for us mainly on oracle bones, which were used for divination, and on some early bronzes bearing limited-character inscriptions. When the Communist historian assesses the value of these oracle bones, he disparages their use as superstition but extols the antiquity of the Chinese language. The written language has developed continuously for at least thirty-five hundred years and has served as a singular unifying factor within the immense diversity that is China.

From the Western viewpoint, it may seem strange that Communist historians even today feel the need to discredit the superstitions surrounding oracle bones. One must remember, however, that less than a century ago these bones were still being used in China because of their supposed magical powers and that related superstitions have continued to prevail among the peasants in the Communist era. In the practice of nineteenth-century Chinese medicine, "dragon bones," as they were called, were ground up and used in compounds dis-

50. Bronze vessel (*"Wai-shu"*) from Ch'i-shan, Shensi province. Western Chou dynasty (?1027–770 B.C.). Height 35 inches. Shown at the Historical Museum, Sian. This large vessel (*ting*) was used to hold sacrificial food for ancestors and for the "Great Spirit Who Resides in Heaven." The body and legs of the vessel bear banded relief decorations combining a swirling scroll design with monster faces. The eyes of the profile monsters are small nobs, and their bodies curl ambiguously into birdlike or aquatic forms intertwined with the abstract scrolls.

pensed as cures for a variety of ills, and the owners of medicine shops would buy them from peasants who found them in their fields. These traditional Chinese practices may be more properly viewed within the perspective of the vast popularity that astrology, palmistry, and the occult enjoy in the West of today.

In the last years of the nineteenth century, a Chinese scholar recognized that many oracle bones were inscribed with ancient forms of Chinese characters and began to collect them for study. These bones, some of which are 3,500 years old, from the shoulders of cattle (sometimes also from the shells of tortoises), were inscribed with questions addressed to the spirits of heaven and earth, such as the following: "Is it the proper time to sacrifice to deities? Is the weather right for plowing or planting? Will the next ten-day period be auspicious for hunting, for making war, for a journey?" When a hot stick was applied to a bone by a shaman, the heat caused the bone to crack; then the shaman "read" the crackles, telling the questioner how the spirits had responded. Sometimes the names of the questioners were recorded on the bones along with the oracular response and the subsequent outcome. Thus, these bones reveal to us not only the earliest known forms of the written language and a magical rite performed in the attempt to understand unseen forces but also the foremost concerns of ancient society.

Most Chinese believed that there was a universal harmony between man and nature, as exemplified by the endless cycle of the seasons. To assure the success of all things, they sought to keep this harmony in balance. Thus, by questioning the divine spirits as to the advisability of action, they hoped to avoid creating a disharmony which might trigger a natural or man-made disaster.

Bronze vessels are the quintessential image of ancient Chinese cultural achievement, communicating the aesthetic and technical sophistication of the Shang and Chou craftsmen (plates 48–50). Marvelous decoration enhances the power of the vessel forms, creating a perfect artistic unity. Whether the decoration represented magical figures to the supplicants who offered sacrifices in these vessels is still a matter of debate. Certainly the knob-eyed beings and fanciful hybrid birds and beasts within the sinuous relief swirls possess a powerful artistic magic for us today. And we must acknowledge the technological ingenuity of the ancient Chinese, who cast the vessels

51, 52. Stone chimes, above, and bronze
bells, opposite page. Eastern Chou
dynasty (770–256 B.C.). Shown at the
Imperial Palace, Peking. Both were
hung and played by striking.

in intricately carved piece molds (composed of a number of sections).

The zenith of their achievement came during the late Shang (from about 1300 B.C.) and Western Chou (to 770 B.C.) periods. Thus, these bronze vessels serve as a bridge to the past, telling us about the highly developed rituals of an ancient society. They were made for the presentation of food and drink to the primordial ancestor (the "Great Spirit Who Resides in Heaven"), all the ancestors of the ruling dynasty, and the ancestors of aristocratic families who participated in sacrifices. The spirits of wind, water, mountains, and various crops may also have been cajoled and honored by offerings, as they were in later times.

Details of the ceremony for the dead may be found in a legend usually ascribed to the third century B.C., the story of a late Chou king whose favorite concubine died. She had accompanied the king on a hunting trip and had caught cold in the damp marsh. A description of this lady's funeral appears in *The Freer Chinese Bronzes* (John A. Pope *et al*, p. 8). However, the translators warn that the date of the legend is unsure and may be as late as the first century A.D. If the story was written

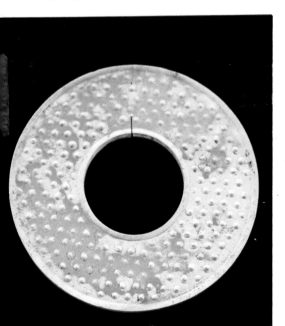

53. Jade disk (*pi*). Eastern Chou dynasty (770–256 B.C.). Shown at the Imperial Palace, Peking. Officials probably wore jade disks as badges of rank. Numbers of these disks have been found in some coffins; they were placed beside the head, arms, and feet of noblemen.

in the first century, the funerary practices it describes may vary somewhat from those of the Chou, yet they are surely worth recalling here:

The sacrificial officer was in charge of the sacrificial tables on which he spread offerings such as meat soup, raw meat, dry meat, minced meat, dates, millet gruel, cold porridge, dry fish, scallions, and a hundred other things. There were twelve *tsu* of raw meat and raw fish and ninety *tou* of cooked meat and forty *ting, tun, hu,* and *tsun* of hot food and wine [*tsu* means platter; *tou, ting, tun, hu,* and *tsun* are different kinds of bronze vessels]. . . .

The sacrificial officer began offering the sacrifices by presenting the soup and wine to the chief mourner . . . who received them with a bow and presented them to the spirit of the dead. The ladies also presented their offerings to the chief lady mourner . . . who performed the ceremonies [as the male mourner had]. The sacrificial officer then gave some of the wine to the court musicians.

Music was a vital part of ancient offering rites. Drums, bells, chimes, pipes, and stringed instruments were all used in early

61

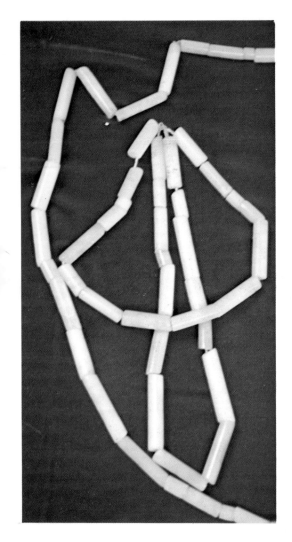

54. Jade beads. Shang dynasty (?1523–1027 B.C.). Shown at the Imperial Palace, Peking. These beads from Hunan province were found inside a bronze vessel along with other jade objects. The smallest has a diameter of about 1/2 inch.

Chinese music. Ancient literature tells of elaborate ceremonies in which music and delicious, pungent foods in bronze vessels were offered not only to the spirits of heaven and of the ancestors but also to celebrate seasons, rains, and military victories. Liturgical chanting and dancing were part of the musical offering. Clothed in appropriate colors, the dancers and musicians sought to convey the mood of the season. Sometimes the dance-mime, using stylized rhythms and gestures, evoked warlike imagery, or the coming of the rains, or honor to the dead.

Because of the fragmentary nature of the archaeological and textual evidence, experts have found it impossible to reconstruct completely the nature of ancient music and dance. Yet some musical instruments have been recovered from tombs, where they were probably put to serenade the deceased with everlasting harmonies.

Two of the most durable types of instrument were stone chimes and bronze bells (plates 51, 52). Both were hung in series from a rectangular wooden frame by silk cords or leather thongs and were played with a striking stick. Although their visual qualities afford aesthetic satisfaction, not to hear them played is like being deaf at the seashore.

The ancient texts tell us that on the battlefield the sound of the stone chimes was a call to arms that would make a man willing to give up his life. If he heard the chimes at home, he would think of heroes who had died in the service of the king. Stone chimes also accompanied dances to invoke rain. Both music and dance imitated the sounds and patterns of wind, rain, and thunder.

Sets of bronze bells, like the stone chimes, varied in size and produced a variety of notes probably often organized in a pentatonic scale. Because no scores have survived (if, indeed, they existed), it is hard to know whether the traditional Chinese music heard today bears much relationship to ancient music.

Bronze bells were cast by the same piece-mold technique used to make bronze vessels. One characteristic pattern of the later Chou period is that of high-relief, decorative bosses which cover the surface area and stand out from it like the quills of an angered porcupine. This design, compared with the lower, integrated relief patterns of the earlier vessels, is almost aggressively virile. Within this design the craftsmen seem to have expressed the martial function of music, which, also using bugles and drums, sent out a call to arms and to stir the hearts of soldiers in battle.

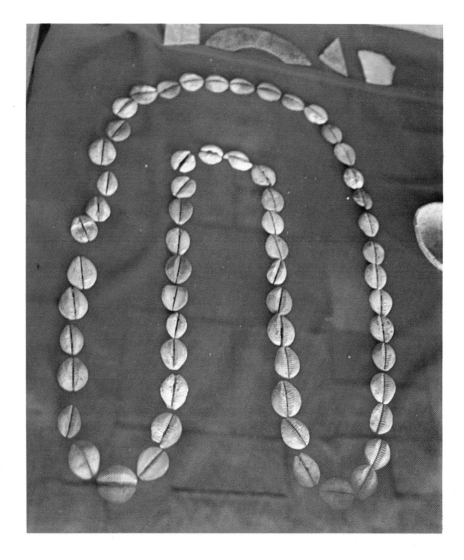

55. String of cowrie shells. Shang–Chou dynasties. Shown at the museum in Wang-ch'eng Park, Loyang, Honan province. The Chinese, like many other ancient and primitive civilizations, treasured cowrie shells for their beauty and provocatively female shapes.

Music in ancient China was bound into prescribed ritual, and contemporary Chinese commentators are quick to point out that art and music in ancient China fed the superstitions which the elite manipulated to enslave the people. They maintain that the new forms of art, music, and literature "serve the people." Although the magical powers of ritual music have been repudiated, music nevertheless constitutes part of the catalogue of ancient achievements presented to bolster national pride, so that the political orientation of Chinese Communist music seems more understandable.

Carved jade has been a favorite medium for ritual and decorative objects since ancient times. Ancient jade is, in fact, nephrite, which may have been mined in China. It comes in a variety of subdued colors ranging from creamy whites and pale greens to red-browns. It was treasured for its uncompromising hardness, for its translucent beauty that hides no flaws, and for the pure tone it produces when struck. These qualities are all

63

associated with virtue. The hardness of jade makes it extremely difficult to carve, even for the modern craftsman who uses
power-driven abrasives. Thus, the patience and skill of the ancient craftsmen are especially remarkable.

Jade objects that were buried with the dead, like other funerary accouterments, tell much about the treasured things
of ancient life. Mysterious long, rectangular objects enclosing
a cylindrical void are thought to be objects of earth worship;
other pieces, circular disks with three notches on the outer
rim, may have been astronomical instruments. Necklaces of
jade beads (plate 54) and small carved plaques of jade sewn
on garments enhanced the beauty and dignity of ritual costumes. A circle of jade was worn as a badge of rank in the service of the king. Jade knives and scepters were fashioned for
ceremonial use. In Eastern Chou, jade pieces were placed in
the openings of the bodies of the dead, and jade disks were
sometimes placed at the head, feet, legs, and arms of the
corpse (plate 53). And later, in the Han period (206 B.C.–
A.D. 220), pieces of jade were sewn together to make complete
funerary garments (plates 69, 82, 83).

Current Chinese burial practices outside the People's Republic continue the tradition of providing for the needs of the
deceased in the afterlife. During 1,500 years of assimilation in

56. Bronze coins. Late Eastern Chou dynasty (403–256 B.C.). Shown at the museum in Wang-ch'eng Park, Loyang, Honan province. These spade-shaped coins, minted by the State of Wei, replaced real spades as a medium of exchange.

China, the Buddhist establishment took over the ancient Chinese practice of outfitting and honoring the dead. It is still possible to visit Buddhist temples in Macao, Hong Kong, Singapore, and Taiwan where elaborate funerary sets are offered. Small-scale houses, cars, food, clothing, and money are fashioned out of paper. These things are burned with the expectation that the rising smoke will deliver the objects to the dead. In watching the preparation and performance of these rituals, one cannot help being impressed by the outstanding quality of the paper fabrications—products of a long tradition of fine craftsmanship—and the thoroughness with which the dead person's possessions are re-created.

The funerary practice of offering money to the dead is not a new phenomenon. Money is commonly found in the tombs of the ancients. Strings of cowrie shells, worn as decorations and kept as magical charms, were also the earliest medium of exchange (plate 55). This kind of shell may have come to China from as far away as the south Indian waters, but cowries, with their provocative female shapes, were used as money in many ancient cultures of the world.

The Chou people, when they came from western China and conquered the Shang about 1027 B.C., not only carried on the sedentary agricultural practices developed in Neolithic times but also absorbed and assimilated Shang culture. Some of the distinguishing Shang characteristics assumed by the Chou, in addition to the mastery of bronze casting for sacrificial vessels and weapons, were a highly developed writing system; a complicated and efficient political and military organization, including the use of chariots; a theocratic state dominated by ancestor worship; underground burials in chambers; an advanced ceramics industry; the development of a sophisticated architecture and decorative arts; the cultivation of silkworms and the technology of silk weaving.

In Chou times the prosperity of China increased along with a developing mercantile economy. Bolts of silk, ingots of precious metals, and cast-bronze objects such as knives and spades were used as mediums of exchange. In the last stages of the Chou, called the period of the "Warring States" (403–221 B.C.), these were supplemented by copper currency. The earliest metal money was cast into miniature replicas of knives and spades (plate 56). Then circular copper coins with square openings at the center came into use. The open centers allowed the coins to be strung together with a cord to make a

65

57. Pavilions, walkways, and moon gates at Hua-ch'ing-kung, Shensi province. This twentieth-century resort, built in the traditional Chinese palace style, freely borrows picturesque elements from the imperial architecture of past millenniums.

"string of cash" (plate 143). This distinctive type of coin, containing the symbolic shapes of heaven (round) and earth (square), along with metal ingots and silk bolts, continued to be an accepted medium of exchange in China into the twentieth century.

Traditional Chinese scholars held that the virtue of the kings was inextricably related to the rise and fall of each ruling house. The character of the monarch ultimately determined the gain, and then the loss, of the "mandate of heaven." In theory, one who was not the hereditary heir could be awarded the ruling mandate because of his flawless virtue. Each new dynasty was supposedly founded by a humble, pious, duty-bound, humanitarian paragon whose conduct served as an example to his people. The Classics tell of the inevitable decline in virtue of the succeeding monarchs, until debauchery and tyranny resulted in the loss of the "mandate of heaven" to a new dynasty. Monarchs who lost the mandate were said to be proud, impious, and unwilling to fulfill their duties. They gave no thought to the welfare of their people and made unreasonable demands upon them, imposing back-breaking taxes and forced labor in order to build unnecessary palaces, wear extravagant clothes, and engage in excesses of wine and women. The death knell of a dynasty was signaled by earthquakes, floods, droughts, eclipses of the sun, rebellions, and invasions.

The histories of Shang and Chou set forth in the Confucian Classics established the pattern of traditional Chinese historical interpretation. Long after the Chou conquest of the Shang, when the story was already several hundred years old, it was written that the last Shang tyrant had been replaced by a glowingly virtuous Chou king. To strengthen the case for Chou legitimacy, the histories relate that the first king was descended from a mythical sage-king. It was said that the favorite concubine of this mythical progenitor went into the fields one day and saw the footprint of a giant. Delighted with what she saw, she put her own foot inside it. As she did so, she became pregnant, and later gave birth to the first of the Chou.

In the last quarter of the eleventh century B.C. the first Chou king established his capital on the Wei River near Sian in Shensi province. An early Chou pleasure palace was built at the foot of Black Horse Hill, thirty-five miles east of Sian. This spot, now called Hua-ch'ing-kung (plates 57, 58), was selected not only for its stately beauty but also for its natural hot springs, and many Chinese rulers have floated in its regenera-

67

58. Hua-ch'ing-kung, the hot springs resort near Sian, Shensi province, built in the twentieth century. Black Horse Hill rises in the distance.

59. Dragon head, detail of marble boat
at Hua-ch'ing-kung, Shensi
province (see plate 58).
Traditional Chinese stories tell
of dragons who reside in clouds,
waterfalls, rivers, and the ocean.
It was thought that dragons
controlled the rains and floods.
Elaborate rituals were performed
to cajole dragons into bringing
rain at times of drought or to
stop the water in times of flood.

tive waters. It whispers tales of kings, concubines, courtesans, and generals from the Chou dynasty to modern times.

The Chinese tell a colorful story of the intemperate Chou monarch whose folly led to the loss of the western part of his kingdom some twenty-eight hundred years ago. Although his favorite concubine was a rare beauty, the king was not completely pleased with her because she rarely laughed. To no avail he imported magicians and acrobats and tried everything to make her gay. One day he hit upon the idea of lighting the signal fire on top of Black Horse Hill, which was an emergency call for help from his vassals. The vassals rushed to the palace to aid the king, only to discover that a joke had been played on them. The concubine, amused to see the king's men embarrassed, laughed out loud. So pleased was the king to see his usually sullen favorite amused that he replayed the joke several times. Inevitably, there came a time of real danger, when the king lighted his signal fire and his angry vassals did not come. The Chou capital was invaded and sacked, and the king was forced to flee to the east, where he established a new capital at Loyang for his sadly truncated kingdom.

When the capital was reestablished in the area of Sian during the Sui (581–618) and T'ang (618–907) dynasties, monarchs once again built palaces and gardens at the foot of Black Horse Hill so that they could enjoy the soothing waters of the

60. Tiled roof of a gazebo at Hua-
ch'ing-kung, Shensi province.
The parades of guardians on the
spines of the roof were positioned
to ward off evil spirits. The tiny
pavilion provides a perfect spot
for moon viewing, solitary
contemplation, or intimate
conversation.

hot springs. Although nothing of the Sui or T'ang palaces remains, a white marble tub shaped like a tiered lotus flower and inlaid with colorful designs is claimed to be the pool in which Yang Kuei-fei, the famous T'ang imperial consort, bathed. After the T'ang period some Taoist temples were built on the site, and the pools were periodically renovated. In the Republican period (1912–49), a full-scale resort was built.

In December, 1936, a major event in modern Chinese history occurred at the hot springs. Generalissimo Chiang Kai-shek, faced with both Communist revolution and Japanese invasion, went to Sian to confer with his ally the warlord Chang Hsüeh-liang. Chiang Kai-shek wanted the so-called "Young Marshal" to carry out a policy of "pacification first, then resistance," which meant that an all-out effort to destroy the Chinese Communist armies was to precede any struggle against the Japanese invaders. However, the Communists had convinced the Young Marshal that all Chinese brothers should unite against the Japanese. They also suggested that the Generalissimo's motive in ordering the Young Marshal's forces to fight the Communists instead of the Japanese was to destroy both rival Chinese armies, thus wiping out all internal opposition to his control of China.

During his stay at the hot springs, Chiang Kai-shek rejected the Young Marshal's proposals for a united front against the Japanese. When the forces of the Young Marshal sought to shoot their way into Chiang's room to take him prisoner,

61. Detail of roof bracketing at Hua-ch'ing-kung, Shensi province. This modern roof line includes elaborate brackets and rooftop course designs. On ancient Chinese buildings such decorative elements were functional. Originally the brackets helped to bear the weight of the roof and the courses worked as weights to hold down the thatch.

Chiang tried to escape in the predawn gloom by climbing out of the window of his ground-floor room and scrambling up Black Horse Hill. After showing visitors his room and the place where he was caught, Chinese guides tell with some relish that Chiang had been in such a hurry that he lost his false teeth and was captured in his nightshirt.

After almost two weeks of bargaining with Communist leaders, including Chou En-lai, the Generalissimo agreed orally to some of the demands, and the scene was set for the ensuing united-front resistance against the Japanese.

Today, the architecture at the hot-springs resort is an elaborate twentieth-century version of the palaces of the past (plates 57–62). The most basic building forms can be traced back to Shang prototypes, such as rectangular halls with wooden columns. The walls are simply protective and decorative screens; they do not bear the weight of the roof. The painted brackets under the roof lines were real supporting members in former times; now they are merely decorative adjuncts (plate 61). The curving "dragon-back" roofs are a parvenu feature, having been used in Chinese architecture for little more than a thousand years. Tile roofs had replaced thatched ones on royal buildings as early as the Chou dynasty, but the tile roof lines continued to recall the original thatch shapes. Today the functions of gable ends as well as those of brackets have been forgotten, and the form is simply decorative—or, as eighteenth-century Europeans called it, "picturesque." It is likely that

62. Lotus pond at Hua-ch'ing-kung, Shensi province. A citizen tries to catch frogs.

the original thatched roofs were topped with wooden logs and that gable ends were bound in spots in order to form a wind baffle weighing down the grass-and-mud mixture. In the tile version the wind baffle is simply copied, even though it has become technologically obsolete, and the old form is incorporated as a decorative element. Thus the rooftop courses, elaborated with bands and crowned with sinuous flowers, are transformed versions of the ancient log wind baffle. The roof guardians may have grown out of the knoblike weights that held down the ridges of the gable ends.

Circular pavilions with humorously curved roofs function as gazebos from which to view the moon and stars (plate 60). Moon gates, curving walls, and latticed screening are all elements of traditional Chinese architecture (plate 57). They have been brought together here in a nostalgic recollection of imperial grandeur that emphasizes the conservative nature of traditional Chinese society, exemplified in the enduring architectural forms.

Water has always been an integral part of palace-garden design. At the hot springs, three formal rectangular halls overlook a small free-form lake (plate 58). Set against the modest mountain with its wrinkled yellow-earth gorge, the lake reflects graceful willow trees, a stone bridge with a pavilion for viewing, an abundant growth of elephant-ear lotus leaves, and a "marble boat." The "marble boat" is, in fact, a pavilion built out into the lake. Two horned dragons pose open-mouthed at the front of the "boat," as if they had just emerged from the watery depths to carry the vessel across the water, aided by a marble paddle wheel (plate 59). This fantasy is a reproduction of the famous nineteenth-century one at the Summer Palace near Peking. In both, the pleasures of the water can be enjoyed without suffering the inconvenience of a real boat.

THE FOUNDING OF
THE EMPIRE

PRECEDING PAGE:

63. A section of the Great Wall, Hopei province. Built in the third century B.C. and rebuilt in succeeding periods. The portion shown here is a modern reconstruction. The Great Wall extends from the Gulf of Pohai to the Central Asian Desert in Kansu province.

64. Sightseers relax on the Great Wall. Most people climb the wall at an easy pace, for the steep grades are tiring. Visiting with friends and eating picnics are all part of the outing.

No MONUMENT is a more potent symbol of the power, glory, struggle, breadth, and antiquity of the Chinese empire than the Great Wall. Several centuries before Christ construction began on this massive rampart, which threads its way from the Gulf of Pohai on the east coast, around mountains, through forests and steppe lands, and deep into the deserts of northwestern Kansu.

The Wall, which separated agricultural, sedentary China from the nomadic, pastoral northern peoples, was built because north China has no natural barrier to stop invaders. To the east and southeast there is the ocean. The dense jungle on the southern borders joins the almost impassable mountains of the southwest. In the far west, the great Central Asian desert forms a natural barrier. North China provides the only easy avenues for entry. Yet the Great Wall, like other permanent lines of defense such as the extensive Roman walls or the Maginot Line, has never been entirely effective in keeping out invaders. The nomadic peoples who roamed the steppe lands continued to sweep down upon China in wave after wave. Even today the old fear of invasion from the north persists—the Soviet Union is now the country the Chinese fear most.

Nevertheless, the Wall has continued to serve as a tangible reminder of the enduring and cohesive nature of Chinese civilization. It is truly overwhelming, a serpentine miracle of engineering that extends for roughly 2,500 miles. Rebuilt and expanded by many rulers of China at different times, it averages 24 feet in height, 21 feet in thickness at the base, and 18 feet in width at the top. It is made of earth and gravel, and was faced with stone until the fourteenth century, when the Ming covered it with brick.

Although the Wall is an amazing construction, it is not forbidding. It seems to blend into the mountains, making it perfect for hiking and picnics, and it has become a favorite spot for Chinese families and friends to spend their days of leisure (plate 64).

65. Distant view of the Great Wall, Hopei province. A miracle of engineering, the wall threads over mountains and through forests, valleys, and deserts. Only a few sections have been repaired; most of it is in ruins. The Ming were the last to rebuild it as a defensive fortification.

One can stroll on it for over a mile near Peking, following the sinuous, precipitous path of its restored sections and luxuriating in vistas of its unbroken thread vanishing into endless mountains. One can climb the lookout towers and stand there as defenders stood for two millenniums under the burning summer sun, where the winds from the desert inflame the crusty earth with gusts of hot air that soar to 130 degrees.

The Wall's powerful configuration does not divulge the suffering, isolation, and death of those who built it, nor does it whisper grandiloquent stories of battles fought on it. It is difficult to imagine the generations of Chinese soldiers who huddled around winter fires or scanned the horizon for marauding hordes. In many places it is so precipitous that one wonders how it could have fulfilled its secondary function of serving as a northern highway for communication and supplies. It seems impossible that couriers, army cavalry riding five abreast, and horse-drawn chariots could, as was reported, have raced from post to post along its top.

The idea of building the Great Wall was conceived and realized by Ch'in Shih Huang-ti, unifier of China and self-proclaimed "First Emperor" of the Ch'in dynasty, which was established in 221 B.C. In ancient China, as in medieval Europe, cities had been made secure from their enemies by building walls around them. Some states, in the fifth and fourth centuries B.C., had extended this military concept by building walls at the edges of their domains to prevent invasion by aggressive neighbors. After the king of Ch'in conquered the other states contending for power in the later stages of the Chou dynasty and formed the empire, he decided to link the walls of the various states and expanded these ramparts into the longest fortification the world has known. Unlike the kings of Chou, who had presided over a system of princely vassal states, the First Emperor developed a centralized, bureaucratic military government that gave him far greater control over the entire populace. He mustered a forced-labor crew of 300,000 men, who worked on the Wall over a ten-year period. In addition, he tried to solve the problem of internal communication with the expanding empire by building roads and canals and standardized not only weights and measures (plate 66) but also the axle lengths of wagons. This last achievement made wagon travel easier by enabling vehicles to travel in the same ruts on the pounded-earth roads.

According to Confucian historians, since the First Emperor was a tyrant—unforgivable in the Confucian judgment—his

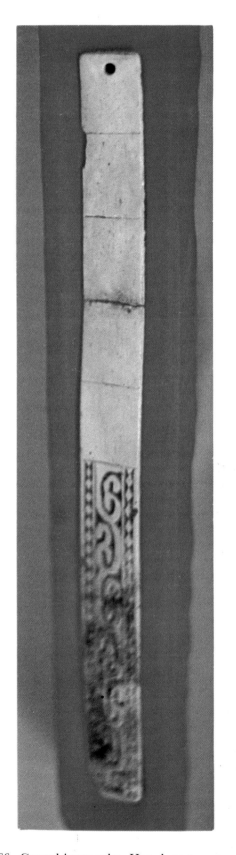

66. Carved ivory ruler. Han dynasty (206 B.C.–A.D. 220). Shown at the museum in Wang-ch'eng Park, Loyang, Honan province. The emperor fixed the measurements at the outset of dynastic rule.

achievements could never outweigh his oppressive methods. Generations of Chinese mourned those who perished while building the Wall and other state projects that consumed the energy and wealth of the country and added to the misery of the peasants. Yet in the early 1970s Communist writers praised the First Emperor for his work in unifying China and establishing a centralized imperial government that assured the development of what they call "Feudal Society" (fifth century B.C. to nineteenth century A.D.). In his day, they maintained, the First Emperor was "progressive" and served as a landmark on the path of historical inevitability, completing the transition from the earlier "Slave Society."

The First Emperor alienated the educated class by burning most books except such "useful" texts as those on agriculture, medicine, and divination. Many of the semisacred books of history, songs and prayers, manuals on rites, and philosophical works were cast into great bonfires in an attempt to wipe out memories and records of the past and to stifle contending philosophies which might imply criticism of his methods of government and his legitimacy. He even went to the extreme of doing away with more than 460 scholars as well as their books. These actions of Ch'in Shih Huang-ti were not the last of their kind in Chinese history, and they suggest an interesting analogy to China during the Cultural Revolution, when few books were permitted, intellectuals were suppressed, and dissent was not tolerated. In defending the First Emperor, the Communist writers of the period pointed out that he did not seek to do away with all books but only those in certain fields, and that he did so in an effort to unify thinking. Similarly, they maintained, he buried scholars alive "not to kill all scholars, but to punish the opposition faction, which stood for restoring the old rules."

This glorification of Emperor Ch'in and attack on Confucius was a typically Chinese way of employing historical figures as a metaphor in a contemporary power struggle. Indeed, they were pawns in Chiang Ch'ing's attempt to praise Mao and discredit Chou En-lai. She proclaimed Emperor Ch'in a true progressive, and the implication was that he was like Mao (and Chiang Ch'ing). Confucius, by contrast, was supposedly a backward-looking reactionary who tried to stop the course of the historical dialectic, and the insinuation was that Premier Chou was like that.

Emperor Ch'in's high place in the Marxist-Maoist pantheon was even more firmly fixed in 1974 through the archae-

67, 68. Terra-cotta horse and warriors. Ch'in
dynasty (221–206 B.C.). Height of
horse, c. 48 inches; of warriors, c. 69
to 73 inches. One group of an army of
6,000 warriors, horses, and chariots
buried in an underground vault east
of the mausoleum of the "First
Emperor," Ch'in Shih Huang-ti.
Excavated about 18 miles east of Sian,
Shensi Province. Shown at the Hall of
the Preservation of Harmony, Imperial
Palace, Peking.

ological discovery of a life-size army of terra-cotta figures (plates 67, 68). They were found in large underground vaults flanking the yet unexcavated mausoleum of Emperor Ch'in. Scholars estimate that there are 8,000 warriors, horses, and chariots buried on the site. Their function probably was to march to eternal victories with the Emperor, or at least to protect his tomb.

The figures have a remarkable presence—the suggestion of an authentic army. It is a bold exercise in scale, the invention of the mind that conceived the Great Wall. For all his inhumane practices, Emperor Ch'in did substitute clay figures instead of sacrificing the living, as had frequently been done in the graves of the Shang and Chou kings. One might theorize that it was precisely this humanistic concern that permitted the artist-craftsmen of Ch'in to create images of warriors with individualized features and costume details. The figures breathe realism, even though they are all ideal warriors—brave, erect, without blemish. Some also carry real weapons of war—halberds, swords, and crossbows.

According to *New Archaeological Finds in China (II)*, Emperor Ch'in began tomb construction the year he inherited the throne, 246 B.C., when he was only thirteen. Building of the tomb complex proceeded throughout his life and for two years after his death in 210 B.C. Histories record that within the walls of Emperor Ch'in's tomb were palaces, rare and exotic objects, official thrones for military and civil servants, and on walls and floors a contour map of China that had simulated rivers made of mercury; on the ceiling the heavens were studded with pearls.

THE HAN DYNASTY

70. Painted tile in a tomb in Wang-ch'eng Park, Loyang, Honan province. 48–7 B.C. (Western Han dynasty). Ink and colors on a clay surface. The tile shows a detail of Hsiang Yü's banquet for Liu Pang. At the left two men watch the banquet, while a third appears from the side to perform a sword dance. Mountains are outlined in the background.

PRECEDING PAGE:

69. Funerary suit of Liu Sheng, from his tomb in Man-ch'eng, Hopei province. Second century B.C. (Western Han dynasty). Jade with gold thread, length 74 inches. Shown at the Imperial Palace, Peking. When Liu Sheng died, in 113 B.C., his body was encased in this suit. The 2,498 pieces of jade were sewed together with about 1,110 grams of gold thread. The silk binding is a reconstruction.

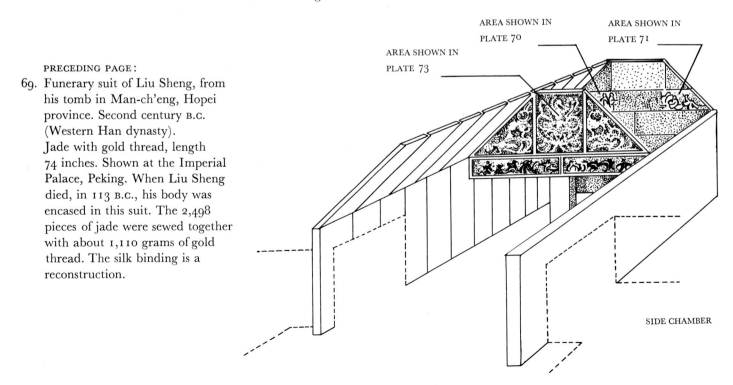

AREA SHOWN IN PLATE 70

AREA SHOWN IN PLATE 71

AREA SHOWN IN PLATE 73

SIDE CHAMBER

71. Painted tile in a tomb in Wang-ch'eng Park, Loyang, Honan province. 48–7 B.C. (Western Han dynasty). Ink and colors on a clay surface. The tile shows another detail of Hsiang Yü's banquet (see plate 70). A man cooks meat over a small brazier while a companion and a horse watch.

A REBELLION ended the rule of the Ch'in dynasty just a few years after Ch'in Shih Huang-ti died (210 B.C.). The insurgent armies were composed of an alliance of oppressed peasants and dispossessed hereditary nobles. The peasants were exhausted and impoverished from the unreasonable tax and labor demands of the Ch'in, and the aristocratic families wanted to restore their power and regain their fiefdoms. In 206 B.C., the second Ch'in emperor was captured and the Ch'in capital at Ch'ang-an was burned and looted. (Ch'ang-an means "eternal peace," and that city is now called Sian). Although this marked the end of the dynasty, it was only the beginning of a struggle for succession which reached its climax in 202 B.C., when Liu Pang, who became Emperor Kao Tsu, founded a new dynasty—the Han.

The story of the struggle for power between the wily peasant, Liu Pang, and the suave aristocrat, Hsiang Yü, the acknowledged leader of the rebellion, lends romance and excitement to histories of the Han. A painted tile depicting this story is shown visitors to a Han tomb in Loyang built sometime between 48 and 7 B.C. (plates 70, 71). Dr. A. Bulling has interpreted this tile and another from the same tomb as scenes from two different plays which were probably performed during the mourning period for the deceased. She suggests that the reason neither literary accounts nor scripts from Han theater have survived may be that the theater, an amusement for women and the illiterate, was considered an unworthy subject for scholars, even though it was an accepted theme for tomb decoration ("Historical Plays in the Art of the Han Period," *Archives of Asian Art*, XXI, pp. 21–37).

Whether the painting represents a theatrical performance or is simply a narrative painting depicting historical events is still a matter of scholarly debate. It does, in any case, tell the story of the struggle for the throne as recounted by the two great Han historians, Ssu-ma Ch'ien and Pan Ku.

The rectangular hollow tile, which looks like a ceramic imitation of a hewn wooden beam, is set into the rear wall of the long central chamber of the tomb. Its surface was covered with white paint as a background for water-based mineral pigments. It shows the confrontation of the contenders for the Han throne at a banquet given by Hsiang Yü in the mountains near Ch'ang-an after Liu Pang's armies had conquered the Ch'in capital and taken the Ch'in emperor prisoner.

While awaiting the arrival of Hsiang Yü, Liu Pang had sealed off the palaces, treasuries, and courts and had forbidden looting. According to the Han histories, Liu Pang had also occupied the critical pass to the capital. When Hsiang Yü approached, he learned of the conquest of Ch'ang-an and the occupation of the pass. He was warned that Liu Pang, formerly greedy and lustful, had touched neither money nor women in Ch'ang-an—an indication that he was planning to seize power and declare himself emperor. Worst of all, the peasant general was said to have the aura of a dragon hovering about him, a sure sign of the "mandate of heaven." Convinced of Liu Pang's treachery, Hsiang Yü, who was a fine general and had an army at least twice as large as Liu Pang's, decided to attack him. Liu Pang learned of the plan and sent a message of apology and explanation. He assured Hsiang Yü that he meant no disloyalty and had, indeed, not only crushed Ch'in resistance for his leader but also had saved the loot for him and his troops; his occupation of the pass was designed only to protect it from bandits (plate 72). The next day Liu Pang came in person to offer his regrets and good will, which Hsiang Yü accepted, inviting him to a banquet.

At the banquet a canny follower of Hsiang Yü began to do

72. Mountains in south-central Shensi province, east of Sian (ancient Ch'ang-an). In 206 B.C., Hsiang Yü gave a conciliatory banquet for Liu Pang in the mountain pass east of Ch'ang-an.

a sword dance, during which he intended to kill Liu Pang, but the latter's companion joined the dance and shielded his master's body with his own. When Liu Pang went out to relieve himself, he and several followers secretly fled the encampment. For more than four years afterward Liu Pang fought Hsiang Yü for control of China.

In the scene on one of the painted tiles, the figures of the two protagonists in the center are almost obliterated. However, one can easily make out other figures at the sides, such as a purple-robed man with a curled mustache and pointed beard who is cooking meat over a flaming brazier while a horse and a companion stand by (plate 71). At the other end of the tile, two long-robed figures outlined against a mountainscape observe the scene, their hands tucked into their long, billowing sleeves (plate 70). Next to them, left hand on hip, a buck-toothed, popeyed sword dancer makes an entrance from the side, sword in hand.

85

73. Painted tile on the gabled
partition of the central chamber
in a tomb in Wang-ch'eng Park,
Loyang, Honan province.
48–7 B.C. (Western Han dynasty).
Ink and colors on a clay surface.
The tile shows the story called
"Killing Three Knights with
Two Peaches." The cutout
partition above is painted with
swirling bodies of men and
wild animals.

The tiles of the Loyang tomb are among the earliest Chinese paintings to survive, yet their facile brushwork and clearly organized composition show that this is not a primitive painting experiment but part of a long, highly developed tradition.

The central tomb chamber is divided into sections by a gabled partition: the post, beam, and gable construction is a translation of wooden building and carving techniques into tile, a more enduring material (plate 73). The central lintel beam, like the one on the rear wall, is a hollow tile with a painting of another historical anecdote. The tile story was identified by Kuo Mo-jo, president of the Chinese Academy of Sciences, as being "Killing Three Knights with Two Peaches," a Confucian parable. Above the lintel swirling bodies of men and wild animals in the mountains appear on the cutout, painted partition. The roof gable is decorated with symbols of the firmament—sun, moon, and stars—which played an important role in the Han religion. Parts of another painted tile remain over the entrance to the tomb, with a beguiling angel flying in the firmament. The embellishment of the rest of the tomb, including the side chambers, consists of patterns stamped into tiles or pressed into bricks. The casket and generous provisions were placed on the floor.

As we have seen, some preimperial funerals included human sacrifices and actual objects, but miniature images made of clay, bronze, or wood were gradually substituted for living people, real musical instruments, and a host of other items. This change was not only humanitarian; it was also a more economical use of resources. And because of it, the poverty of literary sources concerning theatrical entertainment prior to the Sung dynasty (A.D. 960–1279) is somewhat compensated for by wall decorations and small sculptural substitute figures placed on the floors of tombs. Many miniature musicians and performers who were meant to serenade and amuse the dead have been recovered and now delight us.

One of the most remarkable of the much-heralded new archaeological finds, made in 1969, during the Cultural Revolution, is a clay model of a musical performance that features dancers and acrobats (plate 74). Standing on a rectangular base, the show takes place between two groups of large-scaled observers. At one end, next to a large drum on a post, three solemn men, basically cylindrical in shape, with flat hats and black robes trimmed with red, stand in a row, hands in sleeves. Their mouths are pursed into circles, as if they were chanting. At the opposite end of the scene, four men sit watch-

ing, also with hands in sleeves. Two wear tan robes, two wear white robes, and all have white hats crowned with circles that look like doughnuts set on end. Perhaps these figures, larger than the performers, were court officials or ceremonial mourners. While it seems likely that this performance served mourning purposes, it probably was the format for official entertainments as well.

The clay model is also a catalogue of musical instruments. Two players blow a kind of mouth organ *(sheng)*, a set of reed pipes attached to a single base; another plays a kind of zither; and three musicians strike percussion instruments. One of these percussion instruments stands on a stemlike base with a circular top; a second, called *pien ch'ing,* consists of two stone triangles that hang from a wooden frame; the third is a great drum, probably made of hide and wood, mounted on a post. The musicians play their instruments intently, while two female sleeve dancers and four male acrobats perform with graceful agility. At the front of the stage, a larger man in long sleeves seems to act as master of ceremonies. In this lively document of the performing arts, the genius of the Chinese craftsman is displayed through his ability to transform the clay into

74. Acrobats, dancers, and musicians, from Tsinan, Shantung province. Western Han dynasty (206 B.C.–A.D. 8). Painted clay; length of scene 26 3/8 inches, width 18 1/4 inches. Shown at the Imperial Palace, Peking. Originally there were twenty-two figures, but one has been lost. This lively group displays an ancient integrated production of performing arts combining music, dance, acrobatics, and singing.

completely believable, exuberant beings. He has infused his material with the torsion and balance of the acrobats and the rhythmic sway of the dancers.

The new Han materials represent some of the most interesting recent archaeological finds in China and enrich our vision of the Han empire. Liu Pang abandoned many of the more unpopular measures of the first Ch'in emperor, reducing taxes, the terms of corvée labor, and punishments, while at the same time retaining many of the Ch'in innovations regarding central control of the government. His peasant background made him sensitive to the needs and desires of the people, and he adopted the Confucian teaching of "government for the good of the people." Despite a legendary distaste for the pretensions of the literati, he established a precedent for imperial consultation with learned ministers. This consultation was gradually institutionalized into an elaborate civil service. His flair for leadership and his colorful peasant ways make for some of the liveliest reading in Chinese history. In a day before the Chinese had chairs, he squatted—a position assumed by peasants, not nobles—and he used the vernacular language in a most unrestrained way. A biographer writes that one day he grabbed the hat from a scholar's head and urinated in it to express his contempt for the studied affectations of scholars.

As Emperor Kao Tsu, Liu Pang established a firm government, expanded the empire to include more states in all directions, and restored relative peace to the countryside. One of his major problems was the troublesome nomadic people who plagued the northern borders near the Great Wall. He tried to buy peace from the Hsiung-nu, known in the West as the Huns, by sending a Chinese princess to marry their leader and by offering them annual tribute. After Kao Tsu's death (195 B.C.) and a succession of short-lived monarchs, Emperor Wu Ti (r. 140–87 B.C.) consolidated the Han empire and resumed military campaigns against the Hsiung-nu.

Wu Ti, which means "Martial Emperor," decided to make an alliance with some old Han enemies, the Yüeh-chih, nomads who shared the Chinese hostility to the Hsiung-nu because they had been defeated by them. The Yüeh-chih nomads having been chased west by the Hsiung-nu, Wu Ti sent a general to find them. The general was captured by the Hsiung-nu and imprisoned for several years. When he finally escaped, he resumed his quest, and, pushing farther and farther west, eventually discovered the hoped-for allies, now settled in present-day Afghanistan. By this time, however, the Yüeh-chih were no longer interested in revenge against the Hsiung-nu.

This was only one of a number of attempts Wu Ti made to find allies. He sent out expeditions which conquered many oasis cities in the Central Asian desert, initiating what came to be known as the Silk Road. This route extended as far as the shores of the Mediterranean, skirting the Tarim River basin in Central Asia and moving across the Near East through Afghanistan. Roman women eagerly adorned themselves in gossamer Chinese silks. Roman glass and gold were sent in exchange to China, but the Romans bought more than they sold, creating a serious drain of gold from the Roman treasury.

The Han search for allies broadened China's knowledge and control of Central Asia. Among the things encountered on such expeditions were the "blood-sweating horses of Ferghana." These marvelous horses—thought to be foaled by heavenly forebears—were reputed to be able to travel a thousand *li* (over 300 miles) in a day. They were said to be 15 feet high, were heartier than Chinese ponies, had what looked like a double spine similar to a tiger's, and were able to tread on stones without breaking their hooves. Their sweat was red foam. Modern scientists explain that "blood sweating" is caused by parasites which create lesions in the skin. Blood from the lesions mixes with sweat, causing the red foam. When Wu Ti, whose armies were ever in need of horses, heard about these magnificent creatures, he sent an envoy with a gift of a thousand catties of gold and a horse cast in gold to ask the king of Ferghana for some of his fine steeds. But the king was not willing to part with his precious animals. Instead, he slew the Chinese envoy and kept the gold. Wu Ti sent a second expedition against Ferghana, this time with a military force of more than a hundred thousand men. After four years of fighting, the king of Ferghana was killed and the Chinese took three thousand of his horses.

One of the recently discovered Han treasures is a bronze horse (plates 75, 76). Three legs are unsupported, while a single leg is set lightly on the back of a flying swallow. Although this galloping horse was buried as part of a large equestrian funerary entourage between the first and third centuries A.D. — several centuries after Wu Ti received his "gift" from the people of Ferghana—the model was surely meant to represent the "blood-sweating" import from across the desert. Its physical beauty and qualities of speed and motion were so magnificently captured by the skill of the bronze caster that it is easy to believe in the myth of the heavenly descent of the "blood-sweating horses." No ordinary horse could leap through space with such effortless grace.

This horse was one of a large number of bronze objects, including thirty-eight other horses, fourteen chariots (plate 78), and more than twenty military attendants, that have been found in Wu-wei, Kansu, the western area of Han China that served as a gateway to the Central Asian Silk Road.

Despite the fact that clay, wood, or metal figures were substituted for real people in the tombs of Han royal and aristocratic families, real horses and chariots were still sometimes offered. This was true in what is perhaps the most spectacular of the recent archaeological finds—the tombs of the Han royal prince Liu Sheng and his wife, Tou Wan, in Man-ch'eng, Ho-pei province. Among the 2,800 objects in the two tombs was a gilt-bronze spotted dragon, inlaid with turquoise, that probably functioned as a chariot fitting for one of the several chariots and dozen horses found with it (plate 77). Bronze vessels for cooking and storing food and drink, hundreds of ceramic and many lacquer vessels, and sets of figurines were carefully arranged in the enormous tombs, which are referred to by the Chinese as "underground palaces." Both tombs were cut into a rock cliff and entered from the east through underground passages. The vastness of Liu Sheng's tomb is best told through its dimensions: 170 feet long, 120 feet wide, and 23 feet high. Tou Wan's tomb is slightly larger. The plans of the two tombs are similar. Each has a central chamber, with side chambers on the north, west, and south. The west chamber, at the rear of each tomb, held the coffin and the most precious furnishings.

Incense was an essential part of traditional ritual offerings and was also used regularly to perfume the air. Beginning with the Han period, many censers were made in the shape of miniature mountains. When conceiving this shape, Chinese craftsmen apparently intended an association between the vaporous qualities of incense and mountain mists. The ingenious design allows the small-scaled jutting peak to be shrouded in ever-changing rising clouds as long as the incense is burning.

Buried with Prince Liu Sheng was one of the most exquisite examples of all incense burners (plate 79), made of bronze and delicately inlaid with gold. Its protruding forms may represent waves or clouds or strangely shaped rocks. People and beasts appear within the surging "waves." Like similarly formed censers, it is called *po-shan-lu*, which means "Mount

75, 76. Flying horse from Wu-wei, Kansu province. Eastern Han dynasty (A.D. 25–220). Bronze; height 13 1/2 inches, length 17 3/4 inches. Shown at the Imperial Palace, Peking. Transoxianian horses (known to the West as Arabian horses) were imported from Ferghana (Afghanistan) during the Han period. One of those magnificent steeds served as a model for this brilliantly fashioned bronze horse. The sculptor suggests the mythically divine attributes of the horse with one hoof resting lightly on a flying swallow as the horse gallops freely through the air.

Po censer." According to the authors of *Arts of China: Neolithic Cultures to T'ang Dynasty* (Akiyama Terukazu *et al.*, p. 69), the name comes from a hill in Shantung province, the birthplace of a famous maker of incense burners. The mountainous Shantung peninsula, which extends into the Yellow Sea, is the site of several sacred mountains where sacrifices were performed and where Taoists, and later Buddhists, established temples. During the reign of Wu Ti, who was a younger brother of Liu Sheng, Shantung was the home of a number of magicians and the source of many Taoist legends. Possibly Liu Sheng's incense burner represents the legendary Taoist "Islands of the Immortals," which Wu Ti and many others strove to find; perhaps it simply represents a mountain on which royalty enjoyed hunting.

One of the most beautiful objects found in Tou Wan's tomb was a gilt-bronze serving girl holding a lamp (plate 80). Her regular features show a balanced perfection; her wide-sleeved robe covers her body with graceful, easy rhythm. Both she and the galloping horse illustrated earlier demonstrate a new phase of the Chinese mastery of bronze casting quite different from that revealed in the ritual vessels of Shang and Chou. As if by the hand of a magician, the material is convincingly transformed into effortlessly naturalistic renditions of breathing beings. The lamp which the girl holds has an adjustable opening to allow either more or less light, and her sleeve acts as a vent to remove smoke and soot.

Another remarkable object from Tou Wan's tomb is a small bronze leopard, one of a group thought to have been used as sleeve or carpet weights (plate 81). The inlay workmanship is superb and so are the realistically feline form and position. Although many things were made specifically for interment, it seems likely that these leopards were buried after a lifetime of use.

Among the many spectacular treasures found in the tombs of Liu Sheng and his wife, the objects which elicit the most enthusiastic popular response are the two jade funerary suits in which the Han royal couple were buried (plates 69, 82, 83). Jade was not only considered to be beautiful and to symbolize virtue but was also thought to prevent decay of the human body. The ancient Chinese must have hoped that by clothing the body completely in jade they could ensure its eternal preservation. The suits, which include masks, gloves, and shoes, were made of wafers of jade, mostly oblong in shape, sewn with gold thread. The polished jade shimmers in the light and

77. Dragon-head chariot fitting from the tomb of Liu Sheng (d. 113 B.C.), in Man-ch'eng, Hopei province. Second century B.C. (Western Han dynasty). Gilt-bronze inlaid with turquoise, length 8 inches. Shown at the Imperial Palace, Peking. Exquisite fittings for twelve chariots were found in this tomb. Liu Sheng was the brother of the Han emperor Wu Ti (r. 141–87 B.C.).

78. Horse-drawn chariot from Wu-wei, Kansu province. Eastern Han dynasty (A.D. 25–220). Bronze, approximate height of horse 18 inches. Shown at the Imperial Palace, Peking. This chariot was one of 220 funerary objects made of lacquer, gold, bronze, iron, jade, bone, and stone found in the tomb that also contained the flying horse.

79. Incense burner from the tomb of Liu
    Sheng, in Man-ch'eng, Hopei province.
    Second century B.C. (Western Han
    dynasty). Parcel-gilt bronze;
    height 10 1/4 inches, diameter 3 3/4 inches.
    Shown at the Imperial Palace, Peking.
    Many hill censers (*po-shan-lu*) have been
    found in the past, but none so beautiful
    in design and conception as this piece.
    Perfectly cast into a mountain form, it is
    brilliantly inlaid with hairlines of gold to
    accent its undulating peaks and the men
    and beasts who inhabit the scene.

looks as though it were a Chinese version of chain-mail armor.

A total of 2,498 pieces of jade and 1,110 grams of gold thread were used to enshroud Liu Sheng, as compared with smaller-sized Tou Wan, who needed only 2,156 pieces of jade and 703 grams of gold thread. It must have taken numbers of master jade workers years to carve the pieces. Among their most amazing technological feats is the drilling of the four small holes in the corners of each piece, roughly one-eighth inch away from the edge, through which the gold thread was sewn to hold the jade pieces together.

Official records of the period note that princes of the blood were entitled to be buried in jade sewn with gold thread; no-

81. Leopard sleeve or carpet weight, from the tomb of Tou Wan, in Man-ch'eng, Hopei province. Second century B.C. (Western Han dynasty). Parcel-gilt bronze inlaid with stones; height 1 3/8 inches, length 2 3/8 inches. Shown at the Imperial Palace, Peking.

80. Lamp from the tomb of Tou Wan, in Man-ch'eng, Hopei province. Second century B.C. (Western Han dynasty). Gilt-bronze; overall height 18 7/8 inches, figure height 17 1/2 inches. Shown at the Imperial Palace, Peking. A serving girl holds the lamp in her right hand, her arm functioning as the flue. The lamp has an adjustable opening to vary the amount of light.

bles of the rank below prince could have jade suits sewn with silver thread; the lowest of the high-ranking nobles could have jade suits sewn with copper thread. Jade wafers had previously been found scattered in some tombs, but these isolated pieces were incomplete and their exact use had not been ascertained. The discovery of the tombs of Liu Sheng and his consort, together with all the other elements of the find, make it comparable in importance to the discovery of Tutankhamen's tomb in Egypt.

Today in China the significance of this find is expressed in terms of class struggle. In the publication *New Archaeological Finds in China* Ku Yen-wen (pp. 18–19) states:

The archaeological work has mercilessly exposed their [the elite's] evils and extravagance as well as their brutal exploitation and oppression of the labouring people. . . . [It] has once again brought to light a great many precious cultural objects . . . which the labouring people created with their own hands and which in turn demonstrate the craftsmanship of their creators. . . . [Archaeological work] is not

82, 83. Both Liu Sheng and his wife, Tou Wan, were buried in gold-sewed jade funerary suits (see plate 69). The privilege of being buried in such an elaborate shroud was accorded only to the royal family. Above, detail showing the top of the head and the pillow. The jade pillow was enhanced with gilt.

only highly conducive to the study of the history of ancient Chinese society but also provides rich, vivid historical data for widespread, popular education in ideology, politics and class struggle.

In addition to their jade suits, Liu Sheng and Tou Wan had brick-shaped jade pillows on which to rest their heads eternally (the Chinese favored hard pillows, often brick-shaped, for two thousand years; plate 83). Two jade dragon heads, embellished with gilt, peer up at each end of Liu Sheng's pillow. Its surface is covered with low-relief carving which features animal combat, the bodies of animals intertwined with undulating serpentine forms.

At the time of burial, the jade-shrouded bodies were encased in wooden coffins. Although no trace of the wood remains, the gilt-bronze coffin handles have survived (plate 85). Each handle is made in two pieces, with a fastening plaque in the shape of a monster face. Double lines above the eyes curl down into the monster's nose, and curling hair or feathers decorate his brow, which is crowned by triangular ears and a small tiara-like medallion in the center. The handle ring hangs from a snout, but the lower jaw is absent. The absent lower jaw is characteristic of the ancient monster faces found on Shang and Chou bronze vessels, and this full-blown Han motif is a descendant of that zoomorphic tradition.

99

84. Detail of a fish carved on the
stone lintel over the entrance
doorway of a tomb in Wang-ch'eng
Park, Loyang, Honan
province. Eastern Han
dynasty (A.D. 25–220).

85. Coffin handles in the shape of
monster faces, from the tomb of
Liu Sheng, in Man-ch'eng, Hopei
province. Second century B.C.
(Western Han dynasty).
Gilt-bronze. Shown at the
Imperial Palace, Peking. After
Liu Sheng's corpse was encased
in the jade suit, it was placed
in a wooden coffin, of which
only the hardware has survived.

It would appear that monster-face handles were frequently used in Han times. In a tomb dating from the Eastern Han dynasty (A.D. 25–220) that was uncovered at Loyang, the capital during that period, the exterior of the stone doors was incised with monster-face handles (plate 86). Since the tomb was meant to be shut for eternity once the deceased was entombed, the handles had no functional purpose, and the designer of the tomb conceived the relief carving simply as a decorative door symbol. The lintel over the doorway was also carved in low relief; it features a realistically rendered fish within an ornamental motif that includes other aquatic forms (plate 84). The crescent-scaled fish, which traditionally symbolizes fertility and prosperity, swims in lightly carved, angled stripes of water.

The interior of this Loyang tomb is quite similar to the earlier painted Han tomb. The long, rectangular central chamber is divided into two rooms by three posts supporting a lintel surmounted by a carved gable. Two smaller chambers with lower ceilings extend on either side of the central one. Symbols of the zodiac adorn the carved gable, and the center post, looking somewhat like a totem pole, has a smiling carnivore with bared teeth. Bricks impressed with a herringbone design have replaced the pressed-tile wall designs found in the earlier Han tomb.

One side chamber is still lined with ceramic vessels which held provisions for the dead; this chamber also contained a miniature clay pigpen containing a single fat sow (plate 87). The pig was one of the first animals to be domesticated, and pork has always been a favorite at Chinese banquets. Even today, Chinese pigs enjoy the finest care in meticulously kept quarters at communes (plate 88).

Some funerary furnishings found in later Han tombs offer a glimpse of household essentials and accouterments. While these things lack the glamour of the furnishings of Liu Sheng's tomb, they fill out parts of the picture of everyday life (plates 89–93). Two hens peep out of a half-rounded chicken coop shaped like a tiny Quonset hut, and a thick-legged rooster poses grandly under his curling cockscomb. Banquet food is set out waiting to be cooked on a rectangular stove; two turtles, some fish, and other culinary delights are seen near a knife and a deep bowl for soup. Even more basic than banquet offerings are the circular and square ceramic wells ready to quench an eternal thirst and a little house that will mill grain endlessly to replenish the storage jars provided.

88. Piglets at a commune near Shanghai. Domesticated in the prehistoric period, pigs continue to be favorite animals today.

◀87. A small chamber to the left of the central chamber in a tomb in Wang-ch'eng Park, Loyang, Honan province. Eastern Han dynasty (A.D. 25–220). Ceramic vessels hold offerings of food and drink. A miniature ceramic pigpen with a single sow stands in the rear on the right side of the chamber.

Some of these ceramic pieces are unglazed, some are partially painted, and others are covered with a pale-green lead glaze. During the time that the objects remained buried, the glaze underwent a chemical change that produced a softly iridescent patina similar to the look of ancient Roman glass that was also buried for centuries.

Not all later Han objects were mundane; a bronze unicorn assures us that whimsical beasts continued to enliven the Han imagination (plate 95). This particular creature is depicted with such earnest realism that it seems as natural as the bronze horses from Kansu. A remarkable wooden unicorn shown in the 1973–74 traveling exhibition, Treasures of Chinese Art, is similar to its bronze brother. Both have their single-horned heads lowered menacingly, as if ready to charge; they are, no doubt, examples of the legendary flesh-eating unicorn.

Another glamorous later Han treasure recently unearthed is a gilt-bronze, turquoise-inlaid case holding an inkstone (plate 94). It is shaped like a four-legged, horned, toadlike beast and was buried in a nobleman's grave sometime between A.D. 117 and 145. Very likely this inkstone, like Princess Tou Wan's leopards, was a favorite object used in his lifetime by the deceased. The elegance of the inkstone case reveals the esteemed place occupied by Chinese calligraphy. Calligraphy was an essential part of the education of the elite, and members of the small class of literate people aspired to form characters with a fluent, rhythmic style. Poor handwriting was taken to be a sign of bad character. One can imagine that this brilliantly crafted inkstone case inspired its owner to paint in a perfect calligraphic style.

A stone was vital to the preparation of Chinese ink because ink came in a dried stick and had to be ground and mixed with water prior to each use. The use of ink can be documented to the third century B.C. Although its origins are obscure,

it may go back as far as the second millennium. It was made from lampblack; the carbon residue was collected, mixed with glue as a binding medium, and then dried in a mold to produce a stick. When the user ground the stick, he had to take care to grind it evenly, for a crookedly ground stick was interpreted to mean a flawed personality.

A most economical development of the funerary vase appeared later, in the fourth century, during the Six Dynasties period; it has almost everything imaginable piled onto its cover (plate 96). Relief plaques of mountain goats and monster-face handles are studded around the middle of the vase; the top is crowned with a house and walled garden, birds, groups of people, and large vessels with offerings for the dead. This combination house-entourage offering may have spared the family of the deceased the high cost of a large set of funerary objects. The green glaze of the vase is called protoceladon and is a forerunner of the fully vitrified celadon, Yüeh ware, which was developed in succeeding centuries.

Today's Chinese still refer to themselves as "the Han people," and most of the substantial Han territorial conquests are now regarded as part of China proper. Starting out from the "cradle of China," the area around the Yellow River, military action and subsequent settlement expanded the Han empire to include the southeastern coastal provinces of Fukien and Kwangtung, the southwestern provinces of Kwangsi, Kweichow, and Szechwan, and the northeastern province of the region formerly called Manchuria. The most distant reaches of the Han empire included what today we know as North Vietnam, North Korea, much of Mongolia, and many of the oasis cities along the Silk Road in Central Asia. Han rule lasted about four hundred years—from 206 B.C. to A.D. 220, except for a brief period of usurpation (A.D. 9–23)—and its influence in East Asia has been compared by some scholars to the influence in Europe of the partly contemporaneous (27 B.C.–A.D. 395) Roman empire. Most of the vast empire the Han established has endured for the two succeeding millenniums. The Han conquests gave the expanding Chinese population new lands to settle, and as they moved below the Yangtze into the warm, humid south, they developed an intensive rice culture. This great expansion made it necessary for communications to be improved, so that the capital could control distant provinces and goods could be moved from one part of China to another. Even today, internal transportation continues to be a

89-93. Clay funerary objects. Eastern Han dynasty (A.D. 25–220). All shown at the museum in Wangch'eng Park, Loyang, Honan province. Han tombs were often filled with these small models of the essential items of daily life. Recent finds include not only barnyard animals but also wells for drawing water and facilities for cooking and pounding grain into flour.

105

94. Inkstone case, from Hsü-chow, Kiangsu
province. Eastern Han dynasty (A.D. 25–220).
Gilt-bronze inlaid with turquoise. Shown at
the Imperial Palace, Peking. This case, made
in the shape of a horned beast, was buried in
the grave of a nobleman who died between
A.D. 117 and 145.

95. Bronze unicorn. Eastern Han dynasty
(A.D. 25–220). Shown at the Imperial
Palace, Peking.

96. Ceramic funerary urn with Yüeh-type ▶
celadon glaze. Fourth century (early
Six Dynasties). Shown at the Imperial
Palace, Peking. A house, people, birds,
and offering vessels crowd the lid.

major problem for the Chinese. To supply the population of the east coast, it appears to be more economical for the People's Republic to import wheat from abroad than to transport it from the remote west.

The great rivers of China became major routes of transport, and they were supplemented by a network of canals built and maintained by the imperial government. A clay boat from the first or second century A.D., unearthed in Canton, was made as part of a funerary set. It is startling to see how similar the design of many Chinese boats in use today is to this ancient prototype (plates 97, 98).

Professor Joseph Needham, in his monumental study *Science and Civilization in China* (vol. 4, pp. 650–51), points to this model boat to prove that the first-century Chinese used the axial rudder, a sophisticated steering device not developed for

97. Boat on the Pearl River, Canton (Kwangchow). On the rivers of China today one still sees many traditionally styled boats. This marine design goes back at least two millenniums.

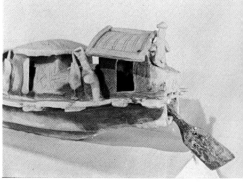

98. Gray pottery boat from Canton (Kwangchow). First century (Eastern Han dynasty). Length, just under 22 inches. Shown at the Historical Museum, Canton (Kwangchow). This boat was found in the tomb of a man who was probably a ship-owning merchant of Han Canton.

another thousand years in the West. He also speculates that the boat was made for a wealthy merchant-venturer and ship-owner of Han Canton.

The boat model provides us with precise detail. A small cabin at the stern serves to shelter the helmsman. Several deckhouses with barrel roofs, probably made of woven matting, serve as cabins or storage space for cargo. The anchor hangs over the projecting bow. Along the sides of the boat there are narrow outboard galleries from which the crew poled. These galleries are broken on both sides near the bow. Needham suggests that this was probably the place for the sail, and that the missing mast would have been placed in the center of the deck in front of the cabins.

Some seagoing vessels sailed beyond the shores of China to Japan and Southeast Asia during the Han period, but the great development of ocean travel came later, in the T'ang period (618–907).

THE NORTHERN WEI, SUI, AND T'ANG DYNASTIES

PRECEDING PAGE:

99. Tomb figure of a warrior, from Li-chüan-hsien, Shensi province. Last half of the seventh century (T'ang dynasty). Pottery painted with color and gold. Shown at the Historical Museum, Sian, Shensi province. The features of this T'ang warrior's face suggest that he was descended at least partially from Central Asian forebears.

00. The Buddha Vairocana. Feng-hsien Temple (Feng-hsien-ssu), Lung-men, Honan province. The inscription on the base is equivalent to a dating of 672–75 (T'ang dynasty). Vairocana is the personification of the original spirit and all-pervasive nature of Buddhist law and the universe. Vairocana sits on a thousand-petaled lotus; each petal represents a universe containing a myriad worlds, each with a Buddha. The cave is about 100 feet square; the height of the figure, including the base, is about 56 feet.

THE DISINTEGRATION of the Han empire—in process for more than a hundred years—was formally acknowledged in A.D. 220 by the fall of the ruling house. For the next four hundred years, north China was overrun by various groups of nomads, and many wealthy and powerful Chinese families moved to the mountains or paddy lands of the south, beyond the reach of the equestrian invaders. Those who stayed in the north to protect their estates had to cooperate with and pay tribute to the barbarians. This was a period of incessant warfare, with a succession of generals proclaiming a series of short-lived dynasties that controlled small segments of what was then China.

The city of Loyang had been the capital of the Eastern Chou (770–256 B.C.), the later Han (A.D. 25–220), and two brief dynasties in the third and fourth centuries. Under the Han, Loyang had been an elegant walled city with lavish palaces, abundant gardens, and an imperial university with an enrollment of more than 30,000 students from all over the empire. When the Han fled from Loyang to escape advancing enemy troops, seven thousand chariots were not enough to move all the books. The vast majority of both official and private books and records perished when the city was sacked and burned by the conquerors of the Han and successive invaders. These fires did more to destroy the written records of ancient China than Ch'in Shih Huang-ti's organized book burning had done in the late third century B.C.

In modern Loyang, virtually nothing remains of the ancient city save the foundations of ramparts and palaces, and Wang-ch'eng (Royal Town) Park, which occupies the site of the Eastern Chou capital. The city walls were torn down in 1939, and the oldest section of the present city goes back no further than the twelfth century. Some narrow lanes lined with handsome old wooden houses roofed with gray tiles evoke the past, but none reveals the imperial grandeur of the old capital city. Some modest tangible proof of once imposing architecture is to be found in rubbings made from decorative

roof tiles (plate 101); these are displayed at the archaeological museum in the Park.

The glory of Loyang did not end with the Han and its immediate successors; the city served again as capital during the last forty-one years of the Northern Wei (386–534) and as a secondary capital during the T'ang (618–907). (The primary capital was Sian, then called Ch'ang-an.) Although no city structures from these eras remain, Lung-men, one of the most impressive Buddhist cave sites in China—indeed, in the Buddhist world—can still be seen about nine miles south of Loyang on the Yi River. The carving of the cave sculptures was begun by the Northern Wei dynasty at the end of the fifth century and continued for another three hundred years.

The Indian religion of Buddhism had been brought to China by foreign missionaries, merchants, and returning Chinese pilgrims over a period of at least five hundred years before the caves at Lung-men were begun. During the troubled times of the later Han dynasty and the succeeding period,

101. Rubbings of decorative roof tiles. Han dynasty (206 B.C.–A.D. 220). Shown at the museum in Wang-ch'eng Park, Loyang, Honan province. Stamped roof tile ends have been found from Chou dynasty buildings, and traditionally styled roofs are still being decorated in a similar manner today. The motifs include mythical beasts, birds, and animals, characters written in the ancient oracle-bone style of writing, and a circle of rope with curls.

the Chinese, faced with constant warfare and no leadership, searched for reassurance and salvation as they saw their world and ideals shattered. These conditions may help to explain why Buddhism was successful in China, despite the fact that its teachings were so different from traditional Chinese ancestor worship and Confucian ideals of filial piety and man's perfectibility.

In the Indian Buddhist view, the life of a being is one small moment in the endless stream of rebirth, and all of life is suffering. In the fifth century B.C., the historical Gautama Buddha had preached that to eliminate suffering one must detach oneself from all cares and desires, including material comforts and beloved family, be celibate, and follow the eightfold path of virtuous living, steering between the excesses of self-mortification and self-indulgence. Through meditation one may become "enlightened," which implies a detachment from all passion and liberation from the cycle of rebirth.

At the beginning of our era Indian Buddhism was five hundred years old and had already developed an alternative course called Mahayana, which means "the greater vehicle." Pious followers were helped to overcome their attachments and passions by devoting themselves in prayer to grace-giving Bodhisattvas and by practicing good works and charity. A compassionate Bodhisattva was an enlightened being who deferred his own entry into Nirvana, or final peace, until all other sentient beings had achieved theirs.

It was Mahayana Buddhism that met with success in China. The main route of transmission was through Central Asia. Upon arrival, it underwent changes which made it understandable and acceptable to the Chinese, and the syncretism of Buddhist and Chinese beliefs is vividly reflected in Chinese Buddhist art forms.

The Northern Wei, who promoted Buddhism as a state religion, were originally the T'o-pa Tartars. They had been invading nomads who pacified north China by A.D. 386, took the Chinese name Wei, and established their first capital, Ta-t'ung, on the northern border near the Great Wall, close to their former pastureland home. They believed that the Northern Wei king was the incarnation of the "Enlightened One." They expressed their piety by carving a huge Buddhist cave complex out of the rocks at Yün-kang, near Ta-t'ung. During more than a century, the T'o-pa Tartars gradually lost their "barbarian" qualities. In the process of assimilating Chinese culture they learned to use Chinese as the official court language, wore Chinese dress, adopted Chinese customs and family names, intermarried with Chinese, and finally moved their capital from the northern edge of the state to Loyang, in the traditional heartland of China.

After the Northern Wei established their new capital at Loyang in 493, they again sought to express their piety at an appropriate nearby site. They chose a defile where the dense, gray, rocky cliffs rise abruptly from the banks of the Yi River. This came to be known as Lung-men, which means "dragon gate," where more than a thousand caves and a hundred thousand Buddhas evidence in tangible form the teachings of the Buddhist religion and the devotion of the Chinese.

The Chinese Communist Constitution of 1954 guaranteed freedom of religion to the people. However, Marxian theory postulates that religion, like other superstitions, will disappear when Socialism removes its causes, and in practice the Communist Party inhibited the free exercise of religion and sought to convert the populace to belief in Mao and the new Chinese state. The government took over the resources of the Buddhist Church and controlled its functions through a carefully monitored Buddhist association. Although Buddhist education was unavailable to the youth of the country, there was a small ongoing Buddhist establishment, which was enough to convince the international community that the Chinese had not abolished Buddhism. In 1963, the Party initiated a policy that regarded Buddhism as a vestigial poison whose roots must be pulled out and destroyed. This policy reached its climax during the violent phase of the Cultural Revolution (1966–69), when the remaining Buddhist establishments that had previously been allowed to perform ceremonies were shut down. In the general relaxation of the post-Cultural Revolution period, the government appears to have returned to its pre-1966 line. Some temples have been reopened and some monks are again permitted to perform services and to meet specially interested foreigners. Moreover, the training of a small number of younger monks has recently been instituted, and popular Buddhist worship has reemerged. Yet in China there is freedom "not to believe," and the assumption is that most younger Chinese will make that choice. As for Buddhist imagery, it is safely categorized within the larger body of historical relics, admired for its craftsmanship but stripped of its religious power.

Chinese guides at Lung-men show that they are sensitive

102. Looking across the Yi River toward the eastern cliffs, Lung-men, Honan province. Lung-men is about nine miles south of Loyang, and means "dragon gate." This was where the Northern Wei began to carve Buddhist caves at the end of the fifth century.

about the pillaging of sculptures for the foreign market before 1949. As visitors tour the caves, they are shown empty places where sculptures that now enhance major foreign museums originally stood. The guides often show great tact, however, in sparing visitors affiliated with a specific institution the embarrassment of seeing where their own museum's piece was hacked out of the stone wall.

Prior to the establishment of the People's Republic, no favorable Chinese interest had been shown in these caves for a thousand years, and the effects of weather, neglect, and wanton destruction by the Chinese themselves during several periods of severe anti-Buddhist persecutions have probably been as damaging as the twentieth-century pillaging for profit. After the T'ang, Chinese cognoscenti did not value Buddhist sculpture as having any religious or aesthetic im-

115

103. The western cliff face at Lung-men, Honan province, showing a honeycomb of cave openings and niches and a pomegranate tree in bloom.

portance. That China's later emperors showed no interest in ancient Buddhist sculpture is demonstrated by its scarcity in the former Peking Palace Collection, now in Taiwan, most of whose treasures, accumulated over a thousand years, were taken from the mainland by the government of Chiang Kai-shek in 1949. Foreign buyers of Lung-men's statuary had no feelings of guilt, because sales were openly transacted and the pieces were sold by Chinese. In addition, collectors felt they could properly care for objects that were being neglected at Lung-men, and that they could transmit the marvels of Chinese Buddhist art to the world beyond China. However, it is quite understandable that the PRC now denounces these removals in the current atmosphere of high national consciousness.

The majority of the Lung-men caves and niches were carved on the western shore of the Yi River; during the T'ang dynasty, comparatively few were carved in the eastern hills (plate 102). As time went on and more niches and caves were fashioned out of the rock, the face of Lung-men came to look like a honeycomb (plate 103). Because Chinese Buddhist art styles evolved over the centuries in which the caves and sculptures were carved, Lung-men serves not only as a type site for

116

104. Seated Buddha in the Pin-yang cave, Lung-men, Honan province. Carved 502–23 (Northern Wei dynasty). This Buddha, located in the center of the rear (west) wall, is the principal image in the cave.

Northern Wei Buddhist art but also as a catalogue of Six Dynasties and T'ang styles.

The process of sinicization of the foreign Buddha image involved transforming the facial features—the Buddha developed Chinese eyes and a small nose—as well as hiding the body behind voluminous layers of drapery. The contours of the body, revealed by diaphanous robes on the foreign image, disappear in the Chinese style in a formal cascade of folds in low-relief linear patterns. In the Pin-yang cave, probably carved for royal patrons between A.D. 500 and 523, there are brilliant examples of the new Chinese synthesis, which occurred toward the end of Northern Wei rule. The main Buddha (plate 104) is seated cross-legged at the central point in the rear of the cave directly opposite the doorway. His slight smile is often compared to smiles seen on archaic Greek statues of the sixth century B.C. Symbolic of his power, his oversize hands stand out from the fluid ripples of the robe, radiating magical reassurance.

There is a group (plate 105) on either side wall of the Pin-yang cave, each consisting of a standing Buddha flanked by smaller attendant Bodhisattvas. Behind the head of each Buddha a circular flaming halo is shallowly carved in low relief, and the whole figure stands within a huge, elaborately carved body halo called a mandorla. The artistic source of halos, in both Buddhist and Christian iconography, is thought to be the Persian gods of light, who were shown encircled by an aura.

The Pin-yang cave was carved over a period of twenty-three years. It has a well-organized plan for all the decorations, including the high- and low-relief sculpture and painting. This is distinctive, because many of the other caves have sections carved by different patrons at different times, resulting in haphazard organization. The dedicatory inscriptions at Lung-men tell us that its patrons included royal, aristocratic, and literati families; monks and nuns (plate 106) who lived at Lung-men and elsewhere; and religious societies that included the common people. Perhaps one of Buddhism's most beneficial effects on Wei and T'ang society was its cohesive force. It offered salvation to all segments of society.

Kenneth Ch'en's *Buddhism in China* (pp. 174–76) summarizes dedications made by the ruling class in honor of the emperor, in memory of ancestors, for the prosperity of the dynasty, for the longevity of the clan, and for the well-being of all the people. The dedicatory purposes of the religious societies reflected the concerns of the masses: to be reborn in a Bud-

107. North wall of a cave carved with Buddhas in niches, Ku-yang (or Lao-chün) cave, Lung-men, Honan province. Cave carved 495–524 (Northern Wei dynasty). The cave is about 42 1/2 feet long, 22 feet wide, and 36 feet high. Below the Buddha niches is a canopy shape including Buddhas, Bodhisattvas, and swagged jewels emanating from monster mouths and floral designs.

106. Worshiping monks. Lung-men, Honan province. T'ang dynasty (618–907). One small niche among the thousands carved with adoring supplicants.

105. Buddha flanked by Bodhisattvas in the Pin-yang cave. Carved 502–23 (Northern Wei dynasty). This is one of two identical sculptured triads, one on the north wall and one on the south wall of the cave.

dhist paradise, to attain enlightenment, to thank the Buddha for boons granted, to obtain benefits such as material wealth, official position, and long life, to express gratitude for recovering good health, and to assure military success in a campaign.

A religious society with only limited financial resources might carve a single niche or part of a wall. Many walls are covered with such unintegrated dedications. A typical example of this kind of wall (plate 107), carved in the Northern Wei style, shows a series of Buddhas cloaked in cascades of drapery, seated on lion thrones in a throne room swagged with curtains, and flanked by disciples and grace-giving Bodhisattvas. Various Buddhas are represented: Prabhūtaratna, the Buddha who presided in a past eon of time and was predecessor to the historical Buddha; Shākyamuni, the historical Buddha born in India in the sixth century B.C.; Maitreya, a Bodhisattva who will become the next Buddha (in other words,

108. Flying musicians at Lung-men, Honan province. T'ang dynasty (618–907). Behind a Buddha's head, a circle of celestial flames was carved in low relief. Heavenly musicians play accompaniment within the halo.

a messiah); Amitābha, the Buddha of Infinite Light, who presides over the Western Paradise. Avalokiteshvara (Kuan-yin), a compassionate Bodhisattva who offers grace to all and assists the worshiper to the Western Paradise of Amitābha, is also shown. There are thousands of representations of paradise enriched with silk swags and jewels, and tens of thousands of smaller Buddhas who float on lotus flowers encircled by radiant mandorlas, attended by a seemingly endless cast of Bodhisattvas. Fastened to what appears to be the proscenium arch of the paradise scene, strings of beaded jewels emerge from the mouths of monsters and from floral designs. Heavenly godlings, called Apsarases (plate 108), are depicted in crisp linear patterns flying about within a flourish of long flowing scarves.

The lotus flower was a favorite Buddhist symbol. In one cave (plate 109) a huge lotus was carved out of the ceiling in the Northern Wei period. Lotus grows wild in Asia; it flourishes in the swamps and marshes without cultivation, attaining its clean and perfect form unscathed by its impure environment. Thus it symbolized the Buddha's beauty and purity.

109. Lotus Flower Cave (Lien-hua-tung), Lung-men, Honan province. The cave is named for the giant lotus flower carved in the ceiling. Most of the carving was done 518–22, with the smaller niches being carved c. 525–75. The cave is about 20 feet wide and 32 feet deep. The height of the standing Buddha is about 20 feet.

He, too, was uncorrupted by the tainted world about him, by the temptations of life.

In A.D. 534, racked by internal struggles, Northern Wei rule collapsed. North China was again divided. Splinters of the ruling house, Eastern and Western Wei, were briefly established, and they in turn were succeeded by two more short-lived dynasties during the second half of the sixth century. During this chaotic time, less carving was done at Lung-men, and the level of activity dropped off almost completely after the second dynastic switch in mid-century. It was only modestly resumed when China was reunited under the Sui dynasty in 581. Although the Sui too was short-lived (581–618), it achieved what its predecessors had been unable to do for more than three hundred years—it created a strong central government with effective military control over much of what had been the heart of Han China. The Sui unification of China set the stage for the long and glorious rule of the T'ang dynasty (618–907), just as the Ch'in unification (221–206 B.C.) had set the stage for Han rule (206 B.C.–A.D. 220).

The establishment of the T'ang ushered China into a golden age of domestic peace and prosperity and one of the periods of greatest imperial expansion in her history. For a brief time in the eighth century, T'ang control of western China extended beyond the Pamir mountains into the Oxus Valley, today part of Afghanistan and the USSR. The T'ang imperial family was of mixed blood resulting from Turkic-Chinese intermarriage. The name of the great Emperor T'ai Tsung (r. 626–49), which means "Grand Ancestor," reflects the unselfconscious cosmopolitan mixture of the imperial blood. This was to be a sign of the broad tolerance enjoyed in T'ang China by all kinds of foreign people, ideas, images, and goods. The capital cities of Ch'ang-an (Sian) and Loyang and the trade city of Canton had areas reserved for foreign traders, officials, and missionaries. Although Buddhism was by far the most widely practiced religion of foreign origin, it had been transformed into a Chinese religion, and many of its ideas were absorbed into the texture of Chinese thought. However, it was but one among a group of religions introduced to China from outside. Others were Zoroastrianism, Manichaeism, Nestorian Christianity, Judaism, and Mohammedanism.

The Buddhist imagery of the T'ang reflects the new cosmopolitan qualities of T'ang thought. It loses much of the specifically Chinese linear stylization that marks the images of the Northern Wei period. Buddhist craftsmen of the T'ang

110. Buddha, east wall of Cave II,
Lung-men, Honan province.
Sui or T'ang dynasty.

111. Buddha in Chai-fu cave
(Ch'ien-ch'i-ssu), Lung-men,
Honan province. First half of the
seventh century (T'ang dynasty).
This awesome Buddha reflects the
early T'ang stylistic shift.

examined freshly imported, full-bodied Indian Buddha images and carved new ones in a new Chinese style (plates 110, 111). The change was partly due to continuing foreign influence, but there was also an indigenous Chinese stylistic development away from the abstract, disembodied Wei ideal and toward an image more closely related to human anatomy. Faces lose the exaggerated elongation characteristic of the Wei style, and the bodies of the deities in the pantheon begin to be defined under their robes. The trend toward a kind of sensual "realism" climaxes during the eighth and ninth centuries, when the facial expressions and revealed torsos of some of the Buddhist images take on a decidedly earthly look, as if they were modeled after T'ang courtiers.

This change is amply reflected at Lung-men. The Cave of Ten Thousand Buddhas, called Wan-fo-tung (plates 112–114), was completed in A.D. 680. Following the general organization of the earlier caves, the central Buddha sits cross-legged on a lotus throne, flanked by disciples and Bodhisattvas. An example of the early T'ang style, this Buddha has an overall rounded feeling quite different from his angular Pinyang counterpart; his face is heavy, his chin sharply defined, and his lips are unsmiling; the torso is clearly suggested under the robe. The cave walls and sculptures were painted at the time they were dedicated, and some were repainted in later pious acts of refurbishing. In the Cave of Ten Thousand Buddhas, the red-painted halos and red-and-white-painted lotus on the ceiling (plate 112) have survived remarkably well.

The name of the cave comes from the thousands of tiny Buddhas that are carved in relief on its side walls. In the Pure Land sect, a major school of Chinese Buddhism in which Amitābha presided over the Western Paradise, rebirth in this heaven was offered as a reward for the practice of "good works" such as repetition of the Buddha's name and repeated creation of the Buddha image. The invention of printing in T'ang China facilitated mass reproduction of Buddha images on paper, but this cave illustrates the pious act in a more durable form.

Close examination of these thousands of Buddhas (plate 113) reveals that the majority of their minuscule heads—no larger than half an inch—have been broken off. It seems unlikely that this vandalism was the work of thieves, for the head fragments would be no more than unrecognizable pebbles. These heads were probably smashed in iconoclastic campaigns against Buddhism. There were three major Buddhist persecutions in

112. The ceiling of the Cave of Ten Thousand Buddhas is engraved and painted with a lotus-flower design.

113, 114. Cave of Ten Thousand Buddhas (Wan-fo-tung or
Yung-lung-tung), Lung-men, Honan province.
Completed in 680 (T'ang dynasty). Carved and
painted stone. The cave is about 19 feet wide and
22 feet deep. The Buddha is flanked by two
disciples and two Bodhisattvas (one of each shown
here) and a host of smaller attendants. The side wall
is carved with thousands of tiny Buddhas (detail at
left). Wan-fo-tung means Cave of Ten Thousand
Buddhas; the other cave name comes from the title
of the period of years beginning in 680 (Yung-lung).

115. The Buddha Vairocana and a disciple (*lohan*), Feng-hsien Temple (Feng-hsien-ssu), Lung-men, Honan province. Statue, 672–75. Vairocana has some of the magical marks that identify Buddhas, such as the cranial protuberance, and the disciple shares other characteristics of the Buddha, such as three folds of flesh at the neck and elongated ear lobes. The size of the colossal statue can be comprehended by comparing it to the height of the man to the right of the disciple.

Chinese history. The most devastating one occurred in 845, only 165 years after the completion of this cave.

The pinnacle of glory reached by Buddhism at the height of its influence—before the crippling persecutions and its displacement as the imperial religion—can be seen in the largest cave at Lung-men, called Feng-hsien Temple (plates 100, 115–118). It is roughly 100 feet square and is called a temple because, unlike the other caves, no natural roof remained when the giant cavity was hollowed out of the hillside. In its day, the temple was covered with a wooden roof. An inscription reveals that the central Buddha was begun in 672 and completed in 675. This colossal figure, measuring 56 feet including its pedestal, has been identified as Vairocana, a newly introduced member of the Chinese Buddhist pantheon who is different from both the historical Buddha and the Savior, Lord of the Western Paradise. Laurence Sickman describes Vairocana in Sickman and Soper, *The Art and Architecture of China* (p. 71), as a personification of "a philosophical concept of the original creative spirit that embraces the Buddhist Law and the cosmos." According to the scriptures, Vairocana Buddha sits on a thousand-petaled lotus; each petal represents a universe containing myriad worlds, each with a Buddha. Vairocana has some of the magical marks which identify Buddhas, such as the cranial protuberance called *ushnīsha*, the reputed location of his special knowledge, and three folds of flesh on his neck. He has a peaceful, introspective expression and in both size and looks fits the awesome cosmic prescription for such a universal spirit. Behind the giant Vairocana Buddha, floating within his flaming nimbus, are many small Buddhas seated on lotus flowers.

The entourage of two flanking disciples and two Bodhisattvas seen in many other Lung-men caves is also carved in gigantic high relief. The principal disciples of the Buddha, Ananda (plate 117) and Kashyapa, appear, although the latter has now been almost completely obliterated. They both had shaved heads and simple monastic robes. The Bodhisattvas wear the crown, jewels, and double-draped skirt (dhoti) of an Indian prince. After all sentient beings become enlightened and reach Buddhahood, the Bodhisattvas, having finished their work, will also become Buddhas and will take off their finery as a symbolic act of renunciation. Their relaxed posture, standing with one hip slightly extended, is an adaptation of the Indian *tribhanga* pose. It contrasts vividly with the stiffly frontal Bodhisattvas in the Northern Wei style. Of the original

116. Two guardian kings in the southern section of Feng-hsien Temple. The one on the left, pagoda in hand, is stamping on a dwarf. The other, by far the fiercer looking of the two, with bulging muscles and eyes, is scantily dressed in jewels, scarves, and a short skirt. Most of the caves have more modestly scaled door guardians of similar appearance.

117. The Buddha Vairocana, a disciple, a Bodhisattva, and fragments of a guardian king in the northwest section of Feng-hsien Temple (Feng-hsien-ssu), Lung-men, Honan province. Originally Vairocana had eight colossal attendant figures, four on each side. Flanking Vairocana were two disciples, beside them two Bodhisattvas, and beside these two pairs of guardian kings.

118. Three seated Buddhas. Lung-men, Honan province. T'ang dynasty (618–907). These figures present a problem in dating and location because they were probably moved from another Lung-men site.

four guardians only one set of two remains intact on the north side (plate 116).

More caves were carved at Lung-men between 640 and 720 than at any other time. Activity later dropped off, especially after the great Buddhist persecution of 845, although some carving continued through the last years of the T'ang dynasty and into the Sung (960–1279). Under the T'ang, the Buddhist establishment grew rich and powerful. The Buddhist Church became a major landholder through imperial and private land grants. It had hundreds of thousands of adherents who took monastic vows; their motivation was not always pious, for doing so made it possible to avoid taxes, corvée labor, and military duties. The fanatical Taoist emperor who engineered the anti-Buddhist repression and confiscation of 845 did so not only for religious reasons. He also feared that his wealth and the strength of his empire would be drained off by the tax-exempt Buddhist properties and the unproductiveness of those who took refuge in monastic life. Records from that period catalogue the destruction of 4,600 monasteries and 40,000

129

shrines, and the return of 260,000 monks and nuns and their 150,000 servants to the tax registers.

By the late T'ang, Chinese Buddhism had lost its inner vitality and never really recovered. Although Confucian scholarship was carried on during the T'ang, some of the ablest leaders of Chinese society studied Buddhist law. In the subsequent Sung dynasty, the elite lost interest in Buddhism, hoping for careers in government. They studied ancient Chinese history and literature, for the civil-service examinations tested a man's mastery of the Confucian Classics. Yet some aspects of Buddhist thought remained within the fabric of Chinese learning, and, although diminished in power, prestige, and wealth, a major Buddhist establishment survived in China into modern times.

Buddhist art left marks on the Chinese landscape, just as many Buddhist ideas became absorbed into Chinese thought. The pagoda—the Chinese equivalent of the Indian stupa, or relic mound—is the most obvious enduring form seen by travelers in China today. In India the stupa was a hemispherical burial mound in which the sacred remains of the Buddha or his disciples were enshrined. In the transmission of Buddhism to China, the repository for such relics took the form of a storied tower. Some scholars trace the origins of the pagoda to the traditional Chinese watch towers built in Han China. Not only were the stupas and pagodas sanctified structures themselves because they housed sacred objects, but their shapes—stupa in Indian Buddhist art and pagoda in Chinese Buddhist art—were also carved or painted on walls in sacred places and were worshiped just as were images of the Buddha.

There are at least thirty-nine small, carved representations of pagodas on the walls of the Lung-men caves (plate 119). The one illustrated here, square-shaped and with five stories, looks as though it has undergone some terrible natural disaster or the ruinous hacksaw of an anti-Buddhist. This style of pagoda was popular in the T'ang period. The Great Gander Pagoda (Ta-yen-t'a; plate 120) in Ch'ang-an looked very much like this Lung-men carved pagoda when it was first built in the seventh century for Hsüan-tsang, the most famous of Chinese pilgrims. He had traveled to India between A.D. 629 and 645 in search of understanding and the true scriptures and had kept a careful account of where he had been and whom he had met. His informative *Record of the Western Regions* is an invaluable document of Indian history, especially because the great body of Indian literature is philosophical in

119. Pagoda carved into the wall of the western cliff face at Lung-men, Honan province. T'ang dynasty (618–907).

OPPOSITE PAGE:

120. Great Gander Pagoda (Ta-yen-t'a), Sian, Shensi province. Originally built in 652, it was rebuilt with two more stories in the eighth century and restored in 1580 and recently. This pagoda was built as a depository for the Buddhist scriptures brought to China from India by the famous monk Hsüan-tsang in the seventh century.

content and does not include the mundane dates and events from which history is reconstructed.

After Hsüan-tsang returned from India to Ch'ang-an via Khotan on the newly opened "southern route" over the Central Asian desert, he was celebrated not only for his adventurous travel, which stirred the Chinese romantic imagination for generations, but also for his great learning. He translated some of the scriptures he brought back from India, and these served as basic documents for some important schools of Buddhism which subsequently flourished in China and Japan. He asked the emperor to build an appropriate repository for this sacred literature. Most Buddhist temple architecture, including pagodas, was built of wood, the form of religious buildings following the models of palace architecture, which were also made of wood. Hsüan-tsang wanted a pagoda made of stone, the more enduring material he had seen used in the great stupas of India. In a very Chinese compromise, the Great

Gander Pagoda was built in five stories of brick. However, soon after the monument for Hsüan-tsang's precious texts was built, it cracked and had to be restored. When it was repaired in the early eighth century, two more stories were added. Although the Great Gander Pagoda was built within the walls of the T'ang city of Ch'ang-an, the setting was then, as it remains now, far from the hustle and crowding of the central city. T'ang aristocrats built pleasure pavilions close by, and twice a year the local populace was allowed to come to picnic, enjoy the country air, and climb the pagoda to look at the spectacular view of the environs and glimpse the mountains of Szechwan at the edge of the north China plateau. The pagoda and adjoining temple burned in the eleventh and twelfth centuries and were restored in the sixteenth century and then again by the People's Republic. The temple complex of rectangular halls, drum towers, and courtyards (plate 121) has been rebuilt in a traditional style.

Funerary ceramics attest to the continuing popularity of the T'ang rectangular pagoda style. Among recent archaeological finds are a ninth-century stoneware ewer (plate 122) decorated with a curving-roofed T'ang pagoda design in relief and covered with a celadon glaze, and a late tenth-century three-colored, seven-story funerary pagoda (plate 123). A companion piece to the latter is a pottery box for preserving Buddhist relics. Its highly unusual shape is a cross between a box with metal edging and a one-story mausoleum. If it is reproducing an architectural form, it is of a vaguely foreign type. A creamy yellow crown of medallions is set around the roof line at the base of the hipped roof, which is flat on top. Under the roof-line decor, the cubic building form is outlined horizontally by green studded beams and by green vertical posts framing the corners (perhaps simply the box's protective edging). White high-relief lions guard the corners, and cream-colored anthropomorphic guardians stand beside the door. Brown, circular medallions with starred centers decorate the walls.

Much foreign artistic influence was absorbed into Chinese forms during the T'ang, reflecting the receptive climate for non-Chinese exotica. The visitor to China today still finds some tangible evidence of this early foreign influence—mosques in various cities, for example, and, of course, early Buddhist temples. In Kwangchow (Canton), a fine pagoda was originally built in 537 as part of a temple complex which came to be known as the Temple of the Six Banyan Trees (plate

122. Ewer from Changsha, Hunan province.
Ninth century (T'ang dynasty). Stoneware
with celadon glaze. Shown at the Imperial
Palace, Peking.

123. Miniature funerary pagoda and Buddhist
relic box, from Mi-hsien, Honan province.
Last quarter of the tenth century (Sung
dynasty). Stoneware with three-color glazes.
Shown at the Imperial Palace, Peking.

125. Bodhi tree (pipal) in the courtyard of the Temple of the Six Banyan Trees (Liu-jung-ssu), Canton (Kwangchow), Kwangtung province. The temple was founded in 479. Buddhist scriptures recount that the Buddha sat beneath this kind of tree at Bodhgaya when he became enlightened. Seedlings from that sacred tree were carried all over the Buddhist world to be planted and worshiped.

◄124. Pagoda (Hua-t'a) adjoining the Temple of the Six Banyan Trees (Liu-jung-ssu), Canton (Kwangchow), Kwangtung province. First built in 537, it was rebuilt in 1098 in Sung pagoda style. Height 180 feet. The polygonal Sung pagoda style is a sophisticated elaboration of the T'ang pagoda.

124). When the pagoda was restored in 1098 after a fire, it was rebuilt in the mode characteristic of Sung dynasty pagodas. A faceted tower rises from an octagonal base, an elaboration on the square T'ang models. The Temple of the Six Banyan Trees includes yet another exotic import, two bodhi (pipal) trees (plate 125); the Buddha purportedly was seated under a bodhi tree at the moment of his Enlightenment. Although the Buddha's sacred tree in Bodhgaya, India, died, seedlings from it were carried to many places, along with Buddhism, its scriptures, and its imagery. Trees from the seedlings still flourish today at Anaradhapura in Ceylon and Borobudur in Java, for example, and it is quite likely that the great bodhi trees in the Canton temple grew from seedlings taken to China by pious Buddhists.

During the T'ang, the largest foreign community in China was in Ch'ang-an, where the imperial court resided. From the seventh to the ninth centuries, this was the seat of power of the largest empire in the world, as well as the world's most populous city, having over two million inhabitants. Ch'ang-an was the richest, most cosmopolitan, most carefully planned metrop-

126. A Radiant King. T'ang dynasty (618–907). Marble. Shown at the Historical Museum, Sian, Shensi province.

127. Lantern with a coiled-dragon base. T'ang dynasty (618–907). Stone. Shown at the Historical Museum, Sian, Shensi province. The watery habitat of the many-headed, coiled dragon is suggested by waves at the base.

olis in the world and expressed the highest achievements of organization, technology, and art of that period.

The visitor to Sian today can see little of T'ang splendor save two pagodas. The T'ang city fell into ruins after the dissolution of the dynasty. What remains of old Sian was built during the Ming (1368–1644) and Ch'ing (1644–1912) dynasties, and its walls (plate 128) enclose a city area one-sixth the size of T'ang Ch'ang-an. Still, even if modestly, the scale of these walls and of their great fortified gateways evokes some sense of the ancient imperial presence. The Ch'ing city is a miniature version of the great T'ang city, arranged in a grid-iron pattern with wide boulevards. For a lover of ruins, old city walls, weathered and unrepaired, possess romance (plate 129). If no palaces remain, there still are little alleys lined with thatch-roofed houses made of whitewashed, pounded earth mixed with clay, the kind of dwelling built by common folk for at least two millenniums. The lanes of Sian are lined with walls which enclose courtyard dwellings (plate 130). A peep through the occasional open gate reveals scenes of housekeeping—water storing, washing, cooking, and kitchen gardening—not so different from those seen in Han funerary sets.

One must go to the museum to find traces of the glory that was T'ang Ch'ang-an. Among many items of high quality are some voluptuous, vigorously carved, white marble Buddhist sculptures (plate 126) from the wealthy Buddhist temples of Ch'ang-an. A marvelously carved lantern (plate 127) held up by a coiled, dragon-like being is probably from a temple and is but a single example from perhaps thousands of elaborate fixtures that once illuminated that city. Ch'ang-an was famous for night-time diversions ranging from Buddhist feasts, dances, and dramatic performances to amusements offered in the gay quarters by beguiling courtesans skilled in musical arts and flattering conversation and by ordinary prostitutes. There were taverns and teahouses offering rare foods and wines not only from China but also from the many foreign countries represented in the local population.

In his brilliant book *The Golden Peaches of Samarkand*, Edward Schafer draws a vivid picture of the foreigners whose ways enriched the texture of Chinese life with what he calls "T'ang exoticism." Li Po, a famous T'ang poet, commemorated one such exotic T'ang creature, a lithe, fair-haired, green-eyed beauty called a "western houri," who seduced the poet and other guests with her intoxicating charms. As translated by Schafer (p. 21), Li Po's poem touches us directly:

128. City wall and gates in Sian, Shensi province, built during the Ming dynasty (1368–1644). Fields of tomato plants can be seen in the foreground.

129. Old pounded-earth wall in Sian, Shensi province. As the modern city of Sian flourishes, old walls fall into ruin or are pulled down.

130. Courtyard housing in Sian, Shensi province. From a small lane, a brick gateway leads to a courtyard shared by a group of traditional-style houses.

The zither plays . . .
The lovely wine, in its pot of jade, is as clear as the sky
. . . our faces begin to redden
That western houri with features like a flower—
She stands by the wine-warmer, and laughs with the breath
   of spring
Laughs with the breath of spring
Dances in a dress of gauze!

Once again, it is the sets of funerary figures that show us a glimpse of local color. Hook-nosed, bearded traders from the Middle East, both Aryan and Semitic, often appear in the timeless entourages (plate 131). These merchants supplied the Chinese nobleman with prized foreign products during his lifetime, and it was presumed that they would continue to do so after his death. Some conquered peoples of Central Asia were brought to Ch'ang-an to serve as slaves for the imperial family and for noblemen, while other foreigners came by choice to trade with or serve the Chinese. Among the funerary figures are a number of fair-skinned youths with black, curly hair, who served as grooms (plate 132). The youth depicted here wears only a single length of cloth, wrapped around his legs and torso below the waist in the form of slightly ballooning shorts. The end of the material crosses over his chest and goes around his neck, although the neck material has been left unpainted. His dark, bushy eyebrows, painted with exuberance, harmonize with his marvelously thick, curling hair, molded in high relief. His dark mane and small red lips are a foil for his fair complexion.

Most of the Central Asian peoples who came to Ch'ang-an —Turks, Uighurs, Tocharians, and Sogdians—traveled to China overland, following the Silk Road. By contrast, their South Asian counterparts—the Chams, Khmers, Javanese, and Sinhalese—came by sea and mainly congregated in Canton. Both international settlements had large groups of Arabs, Persians, and Indians who came to China by both land and sea routes.

The two-humped Bactrian camel (plate 133) made it possible to journey by land around long stretches of desert—the most difficult part of the route. The Chinese obtained these camels through tribute, war booty, and purchase from various Turkic tribes. Bactrian camels were prized as mounts as well as beasts of burden; their fleet gait often sped emergency messages to remote frontier posts. But their most important role in T'ang China was to carry men and goods along the Silk

131, 132. Tomb figures of a merchant from the Middle East, top, and of a foreign youth who served as a groom. Eighth century (T'ang dynasty). Pottery painted with cold pigments. Shown at the museum in Wang-ch'eng Park, Loyang, Honan province.

133. Tomb figures of a Bactrian camel and a groom, from Loyang, Honan province. Eighth century (T'ang dynasty). Pottery with three-color glazes; height of camel 34 inches. Shown at the Imperial Palace, Peking. The Silk Road was difficult, skirting the dry wastes of the Central Asian Desert. The unusual capacities of the Bactrian camel made the trip possible.

Road. Schafer points out (pp. 13–14) that the roads would have been impassable were it not for "the peculiar virtues of the Bactrian camel, which could sniff out subterranean springs for thirsty merchants, and also predict deadly sand storms." He translates an ancient account: "When such a wind is about to arrive, only the old camels have advance knowledge of it, and they immediately stand snarling together, and bury their mouths in the sand." Men in the caravans observed the camels and covered themselves completely for protection against these perilous sand-laden winds and the imminent death they threatened.

Models of these noble desert beasts were often fashioned of clay and included in a funerary entourage. T'ang Bactrian camels and horses like the "blood-sweating horses of Ferghana" were among the most appealing Chinese art objects collected by foreigners in the late nineteenth and the twentieth centuries. Hardly any museum in the West is without a T'ang camel or horse, or at least a good imitation, because eager buyers outnumbered the authentic products and clever forgers could realize high profits.

The brown, green, and creamy yellow glazing seen on the haughty, bellowing Bactrian camel is typical of T'ang funerary ceramics. It is called "three-color ware." T'ang potters

134, 135. Tomb figures of T'ang dynasty court
ladies. Pottery with three-color
glazes; unglazed heads painted with
cold pigments. Shown at the
Historical Museum, Sian, Shensi
province.

did not know the secret of keeping the colors separate, and the glazes dripped beyond the specified areas, despite the use of relief patterns to hold the glazes in place. However, the potters used the dripped blobs of glaze to marvelous advantage, which is part of the charm of T'ang ware. The hollow clay figures were made in a series of molds, with a large opening under the belly of the creature to allow the gases to escape during the firing.

Among the most engaging burial figurines are some lively lady companions, full of self-composed elegance and charm. They wear the modish dresses of the period, when fashions were greatly influenced by various Central Asian styles of dress, coiffure, and makeup. The styles were brought to Ch'ang-an by musicians, entertainers, and courtesans. The voluminous, flowing robes and long sleeves worn in Wei and Han times were replaced by a tight-fitting bodice with equally tight-fitting sleeves, worn over a full skirt (plate 134). The older feminine hair style—parted and combed to the neck—was replaced by a new look featuring a flamboyantly upswept coiffure with one or two knots of hair worn on top of the head. The slim beauties of the seventh century were replaced by robust eighth-century ladies (plate 135) reflecting the economic well-being of the time. Jane Gaston Mahler, in *The Westerners Among the Figurines of the T'ang Dynasty of China* (p. 114), suggests that these ladies must have eaten heartily at banquets of more than fifty courses, which included unusual items such as "longevity gruel . . . dragon brain, unborn phoenix . . . fairy meat . . broiled dragon whiskers, purple dragon dumplings, and elephant tusk dumplings." Evidently these double-chinned ladies enjoyed the banqueting and modified the noble dress to flow loosely over their well-fed bodies. Soft sleeves and a loose torso replaced the tight-fitting bodice so popular in the seventh century. A gossamer scarf fell from the shoulders under the arm and around the undefined waist.

Yang Kuei-fei was the reigning beauty and style setter of the mid-eighth century. She was the favorite of Emperor Ming Huang (r. 712–56). Her flawless complexion, moon face, and ample matronly figure, as well as the love and attention the emperor showered on her, have been celebrated by T'ang poets. There are many tales of how she and Ming Huang enjoyed cavorting in the hot springs at the foot of Black Horse Hill near Ch'ang-an. But the part of her story that has assured Yang Kuei-fei's place in history revolves around the great friendship she and the emperor lavished on An Lu-shan,

136. Tomb figure of a scholar-official, from Li-chüan-hsien, Shensi province. Last half of the seventh century (T'ang dynasty). Pottery painted with color and gold. Shown at the Historical Museum, Sian, Shensi province.

a general of partly Sogdian origin who was a powerful military governor of a northeastern T'ang province in the area of modern Peking. Consort Yang and the general may have had an intimate relationship; if so, it was a shocking indiscretion for an imperial consort. In any event, An Lu-shan became the enemy of Yang Kuei-fei's brother, the chief minister, who dominated court politics in the early 750s. Angered by Minister Yang, An Lu-shan revolted in 756, captured Ch'ang-an, and forced the emperor and his followers to flee. The unhappy imperial soldiers blamed the disaster on Yang Kuei-fei and her brother and demanded their lives. The old emperor sacrificed the great love of his life, the exquisite Yang Kuei-fei, and quit the capital, traveling southwest through the lofty mountains of modern Szechwan. Generations of Chinese have retold the sad story of Yang Kuei-fei and Ming Huang in painting, poetry, prose, and drama.

One can imagine that the imperial horses which accompanied Ming Huang's hapless entourage had decorations of gold and silver on their armor; that An Lu-shan, the rebellious general, wore brilliantly colored red-and-green armor edged in gold (plate 99); and that Yang Kuei-fei's brother, as an important court official, wore a long-sleeved robe enriched with brilliant brocade panels and a black hat (plate 136).

In 1970, archaeologists in China added a fascinating appendix to this story by finding two large ceramic jars that contained more than a thousand objects of extraordinary beauty. The jars were discovered in the suburbs of the present city of Sian, on the site of the mansion of the Prince of Pin, Li Shou-li, a cousin of the Emperor Ming Huang. The Chinese archaeologist Hsia Nai writes in *New Archaeological Finds in China* (p. 4) that this treasure hoard had probably been buried by someone in the princely household of Li Shou-li's son before the nobles fled with the imperial party.

The number of objects in this cache is modest compared to the extensive inventories of the Shōsōin treasure house in Nara, Japan, which contains a wide range of T'ang pieces that had been acquired by Japan's Emperor Shōmu. During the seventh and eighth centuries the Japanese, vastly impressed by the rich and powerful T'ang civilization, engaged in large-scale borrowing of the trappings of the sophisticated mainland culture—its Buddhist religion, its theory of government, its city planning, and its styles of art—including a taste for the foreign goods imported into China. The prince's precious hoard has some items that are similar to those in the Shōsōin

137–39. Treasures found in the hoard of the Prince of Pin, at Ho'chia-ts'un, Sian, Shensi province. First half of the eighth century (T'ang dynasty). Shown at the Imperial Palace, Peking. 137: Silver censer, diameter 1 3/4 inches. 138: Gold dragons, height 1 inch. 139: Silver dish with amethyst crystals.

collection, having been made in the same time period. One such example is a handsome small glass bowl decorated with relief circles (plate 141). Bowls of this kind were made in Sassanian Persia and brought to China over the Silk Road.

Another imported treasure of incredible beauty found in the cache of the Prince of Pin was an onyx rhyton, a gold-tipped drinking vessel carved in the shape of an ibex's head (plate 142). The smooth curve of the magnificent drinking horn is artfully complemented by the graceful reverse curve of the great ibex's twisted horns.

Other banquet accouterments were found in the large pottery jars containing the hoard: over two hundred gold and silver vessels, many of which were silver bowls decorated with gold repoussé designs. Some were round, while others were fashioned into graceful leaf or double-leaf shapes. Decoration includes animal motifs, some native to China—such as the revered tortoise, symbol of longevity—and some Sassanian-inspired animals, such as a fluffy-tailed fox with a long nose like that of an anteater (plate 140).

A tiny spherical incense burner (plate 137), similar to one in the Shōsōin repository at Nara, Japan, is one of the smallest and most engaging objects found in the prince's hoard. It is hung from a chain and cleverly designed so that it can never spill, for within a delicately carved openwork silver case, a tiny bowl to contain burning incense is mounted on concentric rings. No doubt it was worn to ensure a perfumed aura, and it may also have been placed among pillows or bedding to scent the environment.

A set of minuscule dragons made of gold (plate 138) was also among the tiny treasures from the hoard. Although it is not clear exactly how these decorative beasts were used, they are made in the form of the primordial Chinese ancestor, the Dragon King. All through Chinese dynastic art the dragon was an imperial symbol. It was believed that dragons were the presiding spirits of the waters and that they dwelt in rivers, oceans, pools, and clouds. Unlike dragons in the West, which are cast as incarnate evil, Chinese dragons personify creative, life-giving forces as well as the destructive powers of flooding.

The Chinese, perhaps more than other peoples, had a consuming interest in seeking the elixir of immortality. The study and search for the animals, minerals, and herbs which might supply this magical elixir was pioneered by amateurs, many of them initiates into esoteric Taoism, who engaged in alchemy as well as in the preparation of herbal medicines. The Prince

140–42. More treasures from the hoard of the Prince of Pin. 140: Double leaf-shaped dish with repoussé fox designs, silver with gold, diameter 8 7/8 inches. Mid-eighth century (T'ang dynasty). 141: Glass bowl from Sassanian Persia, diameter at mouth 5 5/8 inches. Seventh to eighth century. 142: Onyx and gold rhyton (drinking horn) from Central Asia, length 6 1/8 inches. Mid-eighth century (T'ang dynasty).

143, 144. Silver coins threaded as a string of cash, below, and a silver disk, right, found in the hoard of the Prince of Pin, at Ho-chia-ts'un, Sian, Shensi province. All T'ang dynasty. Shown at the Imperial Palace, Peking.

of Pin, like other nobles and many emperors, engaged the services of a variety of alchemists, magicians, and priests to produce not only the elixir of immortality and substances that might make flight to the heavens possible, but also medicines. Cinnabar, stalactite, amethyst (plate 139), quartz, and litharge were among the medicinal items deposited in the prince's hoard. Chemically treated ground cinnabar, taken by mouth, was thought to be the sure vehicle to immortality.

No true treasure trove would be complete without cash, and, indeed, the Prince of Pin's was well supplied. There were bars of metal, gold and silver Chinese coins (plate 143), inscribed silver disks bearing a date equivalent to 731 (plate 144), gold dust, a Sassanian silver coin (Chosroes II, A.D. 590–627), a Byzantine gold coin (Heraclius, A.D. 610–41), and five Japanese silver coins minted in 708. This international coinage further confirms the cosmopolitan picture of T'ang Ch'ang-an.

The significance of the find is enormous. In Communist terms, Hsia Nai in *New Archaeological Finds in China* (p. 5) says: "This group of precious objects created by the working people finally returned to their hands after 1,200 years." For others, the hoard is a kind of eighth-century time capsule—a magnificent heritage for archaeologist, historian, and art lover alike.

THE SUNG AND YÜAN
DYNASTIES

Sung Dynasty

PRECEDING PAGE:
45. Huang Shan, Yellow Mountains, Anhwei Province, with swirling mist.

46. "The Forest of Steles." Han dynasty (206 B.C.–A.D. 220) through Ch'ing dynasty (1644–1912). Stone. Historical Museum, Sian, Shensi province. The Chinese have inscribed stone tablets for commemorative purposes for several millenniums. Although most of these steles have Confucian inscriptions, some are Buddhist and there is a single Nestorian Christian inscription.

THE T'ANG DYNASTY showed signs of disintegration at least 150 years before its actual collapse in 907. Indeed, the distant reaches of the empire had begun to detach themselves from central control soon after their conquest in the seventh and eighth centuries. Regional generals established themselves as de facto rulers and passed their rule on to their descendants rather than to officials designated by the capital. Increasingly the directives of the T'ang court were ignored, and within a few generations of the great expansion the loyalty of some of the recently acquired territories could not be relied on.

Beset by financial difficulties, the imperial house imposed new taxes in the eighth century, but these were not enough to offset the extravagances of the court. Neither was there enough land available both to make estate grants—the expected imperial reward to loyal officials—and to redistribute land among the burgeoning peasant population. Ordinary peasant farmers, caught in an intolerable economic squeeze, resorted to uprisings and banditry in their quest for survival.

Although the T'ang dynasty collapsed, China endured only fifty years of disunity before the successor dynasty, the Sung (960–1279), reestablished patterns of centralized rule developed under the T'ang. During the T'ang period, the literati officials had won administrative control, taking power from the old nobility through an institutionalized bureaucracy. This shift of power toward the upwardly mobile scholarly class was even more fully developed during the Sung.

Under the Sung, the ruling house no longer embraced Buddhism as a state religion, and bright young men did not spend their energies studying Buddhist law. There was a potent revival and reshaping of Chinese values and a turning inward that closed the Chinese mind to foreign ideas. The Chinese saw no reason to accommodate to outsiders. From China, which means the "Central Realm," they were able to deal with the world at large on their own terms until the Opium War of 1839–42. Their intellectual, technological, and economic

147, 148. Unknown artist. Scenes from *The Ch'ing-ming Festival on the River*. Copy after Chang Tse-tuan (active c. 1120). Probably Ming dynasty (1368–1644). Hand scroll, ink and color on silk. Shown at the Imperial Palace, Palace of Peace and Longevity (Ning-shou-kung), Peking. Above, street hawkers offer food, drink, and fans to the crowd on a Kaifeng street. The buildings in the background are, from left: a tea shop, an antique store with bronze and ceramic vessels and scroll paintings, and the entryway to a temple guarded by stone lions. Right, shops around a residential courtyard and three scholars debating. The bustle of the city shops seems removed from this peaceful courtyard scene. The stylish Ming red-lacquered railings in the courtyard show the Chinese fretwork design so admired by Western adapters.

growth under the Sung served as a model for subsequent dynasties, and their pattern of government was also sustained.

In giving a new look to Confucianism, Sung scholars revived classical thought. The new form, Neo-Confucianism, reemphasized humane values and personal relationships and offered explanations enriched by Buddhist and Taoist ideas concerning the nature of the universe. Neo-Confucianism not only emphasized the need for proper relationships of authority and obedience within the family—between father and son, husband and wife, elder brother and younger—but it also took the family as a model for the relationship of the emperor to his subjects and created a comprehensive public and private code of ethics and philosophy for the Chinese elite.

Neo-Confucianism was only one element in the intellectual flowering of Sung society. Alongside the revival of classical thought there was intensified interest in history and the arts of painting, poetry, and gardening. As part of his learning, any cultivated man was expected to be accomplished in calligraphy, the vehicle for expressing his higher thoughts in words. Moreover, the Chinese traditionally categorized painting as an extension of calligraphy, and the ability to paint was generally expected of a literatus.

Sung art served as an ideal and a frame of reference for future generations of artists. Its influence, which continued throughout the imperial period, closely parallels that of the patterns of government and forms of thought which prevailed into the twentieth century. Because the political, social, and spiritual institutions of China remained relatively static from the tenth

149, 150. Above, scene from *The Ch'ing-ming Festival on the River* (see plates 147, 148). Among the many city entertainments shown on this scroll, a tightrope walker performs before a fascinated crowd. Right, a modern tightrope walker from Kaifeng performs in Loyang. A number of cities in the People's Republic officially support acrobatic troupes which perform in their own cities and nearby regions.

century to the twentieth, John K. Fairbank, Edwin O. Reischauer, and Albert M. Craig call the Sung "early modern China" (*East Asia: Tradition and Transformation*, p. 151). They point to "the uniquely stable and traditionalist society . . . which changed so little, in comparison with Europe," in spite of two foreign conquests—by the Mongols (the Yüan dynasty of 1279–1368) and the Manchus (the Ch'ing dynasty of 1644–1912). During these conquests, neither the ideas nor the images of the conquerors or of other foreigners penetrated the Chinese artistic consciousness in a revolutionary way, as Buddhism and its imagery had done.

The way in which Sung visual art served as the basic reference point for what was to follow can be seen in a painting that probably depicts the annual spring festival called Ch'ing-ming (plates 147–149). It was painted by an anonymous artist of the Ming dynasty (1368–1644), who seems to have used as a model a Sung painting by Chang Tse-tuan, who was active in the Imperial Academy about 1120. Chang Tse-tuan's painting portrayed the Ch'ing-ming festival at Kaifeng, the capital city of the Northern Sung dynasty, and at least thirty-five adaptations of it exist. Our Ming painting, a very long hand scroll, is not a line-for-line copy of the Sung version but, in the manner of post-Sung thematic and inspirational borrowings, is a paraphrase of the older work painted in the current Ming style.

Ch'ing-ming is still celebrated today by Chinese in Hong Kong, Taiwan, and Singapore, though its importance has diminished on the mainland. When the willows first come into

151. North-central China, between Loyang and Sian. Clear air, broad, dry plains, and looming mountains characterize much of the northern Chinese landscape.

leaf, branches are cut to sweep the ancestral graves. It is a joyous time, when people put on their best clothes and enjoy banquets and other entertainments. This event, depicted in the prosperous city of Kaifeng, offers a fascinating view of urban domestic and commercial life along the canals, through the streets, and over the bridges. While coolies carry goods and artisans build houses, some merchants sell silk from shops stocked with great bolts, others deal in antiquities and paintings (plate 147). In the streets, hawkers offer fans and cooked tidbits of food to the monks, officials, and workers who hurry by. In a house built around a courtyard shielded from the teeming humanity outside, scholars carry on an animated discussion (plate 148). The painting clearly documents that wooden houses with tiled roofs continued to be the standard form for elegant living—as they had been for hundreds of years before the Ming.

Landscape painting was one of the loftiest achievements of the Sung. Two types evolved, roughly corresponding to the two major periods and geographic centers of the dynasty: Northern Sung (960–1127) and Southern Sung (1127–1279). They share a basic vocabulary and artistic harmony, yet they reflect both the physical differences in the landscapes of north

152. The Chinese first built a dam to separate the West Lake from the Ch'ien T'ang River in the Han dynasty in an effort to stop flooding and tidal waves. The Sung court took refuge at Hangchow and made it their capital for 150 years after the Jurchen conquered their capital at Kaifeng in 1127. Hangchow's famous water and mountain views have earned it the Chinese encomium "an earthly paradise."

and south China (plates 151, 152) and the psychological differences in the Sung mind during the two periods. The monumental landscapes associated with the Northern Sung school are awesome, as austere and uncompromising as are the northern mountains themselves. They are painted with a self-confidence that comes from technical mastery combined with a sureness of perception, in which truth and beauty are merged into a unified artistic expression.

When the Sung were invaded by the aggressive northern hordes called Jurchen, they were forced to evacuate the capital at Kaifeng and flee to the south. In 1127, remnants of the Sung court set up a "temporary" capital at Hangchow, from which they ruled south China for the next century and a half.

Landscape painting in the south continued to be practiced in the reestablished Imperial Academy. A Southern Sung style evolved in which the painted landscapes, often cloaked in enveloping mists, loom smaller on the silk ground and express a softer, more intimately personal vision than that of the Northern Sung landscape style. Their qualities reflect a new Chinese introspection infused with a kind of lyricism which is absent from the Northern Sung forerunners.

Highly esteemed Sung landscapes served as a model for

subsequent landscape painting. Chinese art historians point to Tai Chin, active during the second quarter of the fifteenth century in the Ming Imperial Academy, as an example of a later painter in whose work this extended influence can be seen. The chauvinistic Ming court, eager to blot out the memory of the foreign Mongols, encouraged Tai Chin to revive the Southern Sung style of painting at the Imperial Academy, and he became the founder of the Che school, whose name derived from the fact that he lived in Chekiang. Although his expression has a decidedly Ming look to it, he strove to re-create the Southern Sung ideals. In his *Mountain Landscape* (plate 153) in Peking's Palace Collection, the foreground has clumps of trees painted with lively vigor, while small rustic pavilions and a few people are painted in an inconspicuous, unaccented way. Just above the tree line, the middle distance is ambiguously disembodied in a subtle band of haze. Towering cliffs accented by inky dots and crowned with clumps of trees dominate the background. Misty profiles of the cliffs beyond linger in the remotest reaches of the painting. The mountain "wrinkles" of the sheerly rising cliffs are mainly defined by "ax-cut" brushstrokes, so called because the ink formation takes on the appearance of an ax mark on wood. All these elements may be traced back to Sung painting, although the Ming master has elaborated on the earlier models. In its more complicated form, the Ming painting does not reveal the striving for subtle harmonies of light and mist, the suggestively incomplete rendering of detail, or the openness of composition manifested in large blank areas so characteristic of Southern Sung painting. Tai Chin's style is relatively dehumidified, quite complete in filling the paper, and assertive in its descriptive precision.

Although Sung painters and poets idealized nature, most of them lived in the cities and only occasionally ventured into the mountains. They were urban dwellers with a romantic vision of unsullied nature somewhat akin to that of Jean-Jacques Rousseau. One of the great masters of Northern Sung painting, Kuo Hsi (c. 1021– c. 1090), wrote *An Essay on Landscape Painting* which has guided generations of Chinese artists. In a translation by Shio Sakanashi (pp. 32–33) we can learn something of Kuo Hsi's thoughts and goals:

Why does a virtuous man take delight in landscapes? It is for these reasons: that in a rustic retreat he may nourish his nature; that amid the carefree play of rocks and streams, he may take delight. . . . The din of the dusty world and the locked-in-ness of human habitation are what human nature

153. Tai Chin (active second quarter of the fifteenth century). *Mountain Landscape*. Ming dynasty (1368–1644). Hanging scroll, ink on paper. Shown at the Imperial Palace, Palace of Peace and Longevity (Ning-shou-kung), Peking. The awesome scale and grandeur of nature, in relation to the tiny people who inhabit it, is a favorite Chinese landscape theme. The individual artistic expression is marked by the artist's conception and technique in presenting his own variation of the usual components, such as mountains, mists, water, rocks, and trees.

habitually abhors; while, on the contrary, haze, mist, and haunting spirits of the mountains are what human nature seeks, and yet can rarely find. When, however, . . . the minds, both of a man's sovereign and of his parents, are full of high expectations of his services, should he stand aloof, neglecting the responsibilities of honor and righteousness? In the face of such duties the benevolent man cannot seclude himself and shun the world. . . . Having no access to the landscapes, the lover of forest and stream, the friend of mist and haze, enjoys them only in his dreams. How delightful then to have a landscape painted by a skilled hand! Without leaving the room, at once, he finds himself among the streams and ravines; the cries of the birds and monkeys are faintly audible to his senses; light on the hills and reflection on the water, glittering, dazzle his eyes. Does not such a scene satisfy his mind and captivate his heart?

Kuo Hsi's statement is also a conceptual manual for gardens. Kuo's ideas particularly apply to the city garden, where a wall affords separation from the urban environment, withdrawal from the world of men's affairs into a special space where time and logic are suspended. The wall defines the garden world in a way that might be compared to the silk or paper backing of a painting. The garden itself is an evocation of mountains and water; it offers a path to the universe, with places to rest, read, drink, view the moon, compose poetry, joke, game, and tryst. Indeed, the content of Chinese gardens tends to be expressed in a series of individual compositions that are concerned with framing a scene, using scale to create illusion, water and shadow reflections, stone patterns suggesting reflections and "borrowing" landscape from neighboring vistas. The visitor experiences these during the passage through the garden, which has a high proportion of architecture in the form of paved courtyards, pavilions, walls, gateways, rockeries, individual rocks, and water, compared to a lower proportion of greenery—trees, shrubs, and potted seasonal flowers.

The PRC has restored a number of gardens in the last thirty-five years, but, judging from the architecture, none of these seem to go back further than the Ming dynasty. No Sung garden survives today in its original form; yet the Wang Shih Yüan, Garden of the Master of Nets, in Soochow was originally laid out in 1140.

It is hard to imagine that any urban dweller would fail to appreciate Kuo Hsi's longing for mist and mountains. However, during the Cultural Revolution his ideals were

154. Gateway called Kuo-chieh-t'a
(Tower Which Bestrides the
Road, also known as the "Cloud
Terrace"), at Chü-yung-kuan
Pass, Hopei province. Inscribed
with date corresponding to 1345
(Yüan dynasty).

quite unacceptable. They were considered to be a hedonistic
appreciation of the countryside that was not only elitist but
an incomplete artistic expression of love of the motherland.
To be acceptable in those years they should have included
direct reference to proletarian class consciousness and identi-
fiable revolutionary content. The concept of "locked-in-ness
of human habitation" was considered reactionary and
revisionist because of its selfishness. It ran counter to the ideal
of the Maoist man who seeks to serve his country wherever
the Party sends him and feels no selfish desire to be elsewhere.

Since the fall of the "Gang of Four" in 1976, the shift in
policy is apparent; Kuo Hsi is again appreciated; landscape
painting and gardens without political content are acceptable.

Yüan Dynasty

During the first half of the thirteenth century the Golden
Horde of the great Genghis Khan swept down from Mongolia
to gain control of north China. By 1279 Kublai Khan, the

155. Detail of the gateway at Chü-yung-kuan Pass (plate 154), showing carving of Buddhas in the passage under the terrace. Travelers to and from the Yüan capital must have been reassured by seeing the carvings of so many Buddhas, and by the inscriptions of Buddhist charms on the gateway, written in the many languages of the people who passed through.

156. Detail of the gateway at Chü-yung-kuan Pass (plate 154), showing stone carving of a celestial guardian. This is one of four guardians, all carved with great animation, who protectively preside over this gateway.

grandson of Genghis, and his fabulous cavalry completed the occupation of south and southwest China, subjecting the country to the most extensive foreign conquest it had known. The Great Khan, as he was known, and his relatives controlled an empire larger than any other the world has experienced. It stretched from China, Korea, and the northern parts of Vietnam and Burma across Eurasia to Persia and the Black Sea and as far as Hungary and Moscow. The success of the well-trained Mongol forces was due not only to their ferocity and brilliant strategy but also to their reputation. Hair-raising tales were told of the horrors that were in store for those who resisted the Mongols, while those who surrendered without a fight were promised leniency and consideration. In addition, the Mongols received ill-considered Chinese cooperation at certain points, especially in defeating the Jurchen barbarians, who had defeated the Sung in 1127 and established themselves in the north as the Chin dynasty (1115–1234). Once the Mongols defeated the Chin, there was no buffer state between the Chinese and the Mongols, and this simplified the completion of the Mongol conquest.

Following the pattern of other barbarian rulers before them, the Mongols took a Chinese dynastic name, Yüan. They used the Chinese bureaucracy to maintain order and collect taxes from the local population, but often placed Mongols or other foreigners in key positions in an effort to control established Chinese patterns of government.

The victorious Yüan leaders extended the despotic power of the central government, which was reinforced by their great military strength, and they supervised the Chinese bureaucrats, who performed for them as though the Yüan emperor were a native Chinese emperor. According to Marco Polo, this system worked extremely well. His tales include accounts of the rich and handsome city of Hangchow, previously the Southern Sung capital, which continued to flourish as a great center of commerce and the arts, and the newly founded Yüan winter capital of Ta-tu (Peking).

The recent uncovering of parts of Ta-tu has somewhat increased the small number of architectural remains from that period. Only a few pieces of molded ornamental yellow and green tile have been exhibited, however, and they tell us little about the sculptural achievements of the Yüan. A most interesting monument seen by visitors en route to the Great Wall is a gate carved at Chü-yung-kuan (plate 154) bearing a date corresponding to 1342–45. It is referred to by Sherman Lee as the "Cloud Terrace" (*Chinese Art Under the Mongols*, p. 6), and is regarded as a key monument for stylistic attribution and dating of Yüan works. Its Chinese name, Kuo-chieh-t'a, translates as "Tower Which Bestrides the Road." The terrace was probably meant to have been topped with a stupa tower. As it is, the marble platform has a commanding view of the countryside and mountains northwest of Peking. The old road to the Yüan capital passed under the carved archway, and, once one had passed the Great Wall, this was the last gateway before the capital.

The walls of the passage are covered with relief carvings of Buddhas (plate 155), celestial guardian kings (plate 156), and inscriptions in six languages. The gesturing Buddha in a flame-edged mandorla decorated with lotus flowers peacefully communicates his intense introspection. His face, body, robe, and snail-curl hair design have an overall schematic harmony and a spirit quite different from that of the angular, disembodied Northern Wei Buddhas or the full-bodied T'ang Buddhas at Lung-men. Hundreds of smaller Buddhas sit within arcades of niches hung with beaded ornaments. One of the guardian kings destroys the enemies of the Buddha with a single pass of the sword. His crown, elegant armor, and flying scarves do not detract from his menacing posture and bulging-eyed ferocity. The inscriptions on the "Cloud Terrace," which are Buddhist prayers or magical charm formulas, spotlight the cosmopolitan mixture of languages within the Mongol empire: Chinese, Tibetan, Mongolian, Uighur Turkish, Tangut, and Sanskrit. Of these scripts, only Sanskrit was not a vernacular tongue; it was the classical language of Buddhism, in which the charms had originally been written.

Many Mongols practiced Tibetan Buddhism, called Lamaism, which emphasizes ritual formulas and secret magical practices. Kublai Khan protected Confucian temples and exempted Confucian scholars from taxation, but he extended the same tolerance to other religious establishments as well. This displeased the educated Chinese, who were also alienated by the Yüan practice of entrusting key administrative positions to foreigners from all over the vast Mongol empire.

After the fall of the Yüan, Ming historians refused to concede that the Mongols had contributed any innovation or achievement. They presented the Mongols as unclean savages interested only in destruction and orgies, and this judgment became the cliché of subsequent Chinese historians. The great painters of the period were not condemned, however, for they

BELOW:
158. Yüeh-ware vase, made in
Chekiang province. Tenth
century (Five Dynasties or Sung
Dynasty). Porcelaneous
stoneware. Shown at the Ceramic
Exhibition, Imperial Palace,
Peking. The potter has achieved
a brilliantly credible integration
of the polygonally ribbed, bulbous
bottom and the long, narrow neck
in this classic vase. The subtle
monochrome glaze adds to the
overall harmony.

ABOVE:
57. Amphora with dragon-head
handles, made at Wa-cha-p'ing
kiln site, Changsha, Hunan
province. Ninth century (T'ang
dynasty). Stoneware with celadon
glaze. Shown at the museum in
Wang-ch'eng Park, Loyang,
Honan province. Chinese
communication with the cultures
of western Asia and the
Mediterranean is clearly
documented by the addition of
many foreign shapes to the
Chinese ceramic repertoire.
Amphoras, along with many other
vessels, were carried over the
Silk Road, and their shapes
were adapted with vigor and
style by T'ang potters.

ABOVE:
159. Bird-headed ewer, made in Sian,
Shensi province. Eighth century
(T'ang dynasty). Porcelaneous
stoneware with Northern Celadon
glaze. Shown at the Ceramic
Exhibition, Imperial Palace,
Peking. When some Sassanian
Persian metal ewers were
unearthed in Russia, it was
suggested that the Chinese vessels
were modeled after these
prototypes. This kind of ewer was
popular in T'ang China and
certainly reflects a foreign
influence.

were native Chinese. The Mongols had no tradition of pictorial art.

Ceramics: T'ang to Ming

160. Jar with spouts and cover, made in Chekiang province. Tenth century (Five Dynasties or Sung dynasty). Porcelaneous stoneware with Yüeh-type celadon glaze. Shown at the Ceramic Exhibition, Imperial Palace, Peking. The lotus petal and four-line wave patterns incised on the surface, and the spouts, which seem to grow out of the vessel's body, have a lively charm. The sculptured, lotiform crown holds a cutout pomegranate.

Ceramics, like landscape painting, achieved supreme perfection in the expression of Sung aesthetics. Just as Sung painting served as a classic prototype for subsequent paintings, so Sung ceramic shapes, glazes, and decoration served as models for potters throughout the imperial period. After the T'ang, no more foreign shapes were added to the vocabulary of ceramic forms, as the round-bodied, small-necked amphora (plate 157) and the bird-headed ewer (plate 159), both of which were inspired by Persian prototypes, had been. Moreover, the T'ang shapes, foreign and Chinese alike, were modified into a more integrated form. The long-necked, blue-green Yüeh-ware vase of the tenth century (plate 158) is a model of the kind of synthesis of forms that occurred in Sung. Between the swollen polygonal bottom and the tall neck which unites the two sections there is the subtlest kind of harmony. The T'ang vessels do not possess such an overall unity; there is a distinct differentiation between the amphora's swollen bottom and its small neck. Yet, compared to the quieter grace of Sung wares, T'ang wares have a lively, robust quality, as though bursting with energy.

Of the many Chinese inventions, perhaps the one that has been most universally appreciated is porcelain. Porcelain can be defined in many ways, but in the Chinese context it means a broad range of high-fired, hard-bodied, nonporous ceramics which ring when struck. When Chinese porcelains began to be exported in large quantities to Europe in the seventeenth century, the principal items were blue-and-white or thin, white, shining, translucent china, painted with overglaze enamel. Thus, Westerners came to think that porcelain was limited to these wares. The body and glaze of porcelain are fused during an intensely hot firing, at about 1,440 degrees Centigrade. In the course of this process, called vitrification, a chemical change transforms the clay body of kaolin and feldspar and the silica glaze into a new, totally nonporous molecular arrangement. Technically, porcelain is a kind of stoneware, which is a broader category of ceramics fired at high temperatures and includes a greater variety of clay body combinations.

The making of porcelain in China dates from at least the Six Dynasties (A.D. 222–589). One probable reason for its development was the desire to utilize fully the space in a Chinese type of kiln. These kilns were built into a hillside and had up to twenty

61. Bowl made at You-chou kiln, Shensi province. Eleventh to twelfth century (Sung dynasty). Northern Celadon porcelain. Shown at the Ceramic Exhibition, Imperial Palace, Peking.

162. Chün-ware dish. Twelfth century (Sung dynasty). Porcelaneous stoneware. Shown at the Ceramic Exhibition, Imperial Palace, Peking.

chambers spaced progressively away from the firebox. The chamber closest to the firebox got the most heat, while the ones farther away were suitable only for wares that could be fired at lower temperatures. In *Chinese Art* (vol. 2, pp. 402–11), William Willetts explains that the economical Chinese potters conducted extended experiments in order to find a clay and glaze which could withstand the intense heat nearest the fire. The result was porcelain, treasured not only in the imperial court but also in Africa, Europe, and America. Ceramics, along with silk, were long among China's most important export items. As indisputable evidence of this, T'ang pots have been found in a number of places in the Near East, and ceramics dating from the Sung on have been found in quantities in the Philippines, Indonesia, and the Indo-Chinese peninsula. This distribution occurred long before the Portuguese arrived in China in the sixteenth century and began to whet European appetites for Chinese porcelains, thereby causing a revolution in Western ceramics industries.

An admiring foreign public calls one of the famous groups of Sung porcelaneous wares "celadon." This label brings to mind pots glazed not only in sea-foam green but also in a

163. Ting-ware pillow in the form of a reclining baby. Eleventh to twelfth century (Sung dynasty). Porcelain. Shown at the Ceramic Exhibition, Imperial Palace, Peking. The Chinese have traditionally favored hard pillows. They were made in a variety of shapes and often decorated.

164. Tz'u-chou pillow. Thirteenth to fourteenth century (Yüan dynasty). Stoneware with three-color glazes. Shown at the museum in Wang-ch'eng Park, Loyang, Honan province.

range of other greens that include tones of gray, olive, brown, and blue. Although there are still many scholarly questions to be answered concerning identifications and classifications within the vast group of green wares, various types of celadons are identified by certain characteristics and by the site of manufacture. For example, the type of celadon called Yüeh ware was manufactured in Chekiang and appeared in a variety of colors, shapes, and designs. A lotus-petal design was incised into the body of a multispouted covered jar (plate 160), which is grandly bathed in a soft gray-green glaze. A long-necked bottle without carved decoration and covered in a soft blue-green glaze is another example (plate 158). Potters in the north made their own versions of Yüeh ware, called Northern Celadon. Gray and olive tones are characteristic of this kind of ware (plate 161), which frequently has intricate patterns carved into the clay body.

Although these celadons were highly prized, they were not among the official wares made for use at the Sung court. One of the imperial wares, called Chün (plate 162), was made at Yü hsien in Honan province during the Sung. Its haunting turquoise glaze is often spotted with splashes of purple. Some modern connoisseurs particularly prize the purple effects, yet the Chinese called the reddish-purple by scornful terms such as "mules' liver" and "horses' lung."

Much about Chinese firing techniques is still mysterious, so that it is difficult to explain exactly how these spots and other subtleties were achieved. We do know that they varied with the metallic contents of glazes (iron, copper, manganese, and cobalt were among the metals used) and the intensity of heat and amounts of oxygen in the kiln. But the precise color and effects were determined by the uneven nature of the wood employed as fuel, the purity of the metals, atmospheric conditions on firing days, and a host of other variables.

A probably apocryphal story about the spots on Chün ware relates that they were first produced when a pig accidentally wandered into the kiln and was burned. This supposedly created a great deal of smoke, which reduced the amount of oxygen in relation to carbon dioxide and produced the purple spots. When the emperor saw this "mistake," he was delighted and ordered more of the same. The hapless potter, having no more pigs and knowing no other way to re-create the effect, sacrificed his daughter in the kiln in an effort to please the emperor.

White Ting ware was also made for official court use. Among the Ting ware shown in the Imperial Palace ceramics

165. Jar. Hsüan-te (1426–1435, Ming dynasty). Blue-and-white porcelain. Shown at the Ceramic Exhibition, Imperial Palace, Peking.

166. Jar with cover, made at Paoting, Hopei province. Fourteenth century (Yüan dynasty). Porcelain with blue and red underglaze. Shown at the Ceramic Exhibition, Imperial Palace, Peking.

exhibition is a porcelain pillow in the shape of a reclining baby (plate 163), formed with such convincing realism that one almost believes a bright-eyed baby could assume such a convoluted posture. Another pillow of great charm (plate 164), in a slightly curving brick shape, shows within its incised lines a child ambiguously either swimming in a green lotus pond or flying above it. Although its greens and mustard yellows are reminiscent of T'ang three-color ware, it was made during the late Sung dynasty (twelfth and thirteenth centuries) and is a type of Tz'u-chou ware.

The story of blue-and-white ware is one part of the history of ceramics which has greatly benefited from the reassessment of Mongol contributions. Perhaps no kind of Chinese ware can compete with blue-and-white for enduring popularity in the West. Since the seventeenth century, it, along with enamel wares, has been imported in vast quantities and copied by almost every European kiln, including Meissen, Delft, and a host of English potteries. Because only a limited amount of Ming (1368–1644) ware had been sent to the West, the blue-and-white designs best known in Europe were creations of

167. Jar. Fourteenth century (Yüan dynasty). Blue-and-white porcelain. Shown at the Ceramic Exhibition, Imperial Palace, Peking.

168. Incense burner in the shape of a bronze vessel. Wan-li (r. 1573–1620, Ming dynasty). Blue-and-white porcelain. Shown at the Ceramic Exhibition, Imperial Palace, Peking.

169. Gourd-shaped vase. Wan-li (r. 1573–1620, Ming dynasty). Porcelain with enamel glazes. Shown at the Ceramic Exhibition, Imperial Palace, Peking.

the Ch'ing dynasty (1644–1912), and these were the models and inspiration for the voguish chinoiserie ceramics of the eighteenth century.

Until recently, few Yüan dynasty blue-and-white pieces had been identified, even though the first manufacture of this ware had been traced to the Yüan. It was assumed that the technology for controlling the colors so that they would not drip or spread beyond their assigned areas had been learned from Persian potters. After all, the cobalt with which to produce the blue had been imported from the Near East during the Yüan and in subsequent periods. For lack of evidence, Yüan blue-and-white was not seriously studied, while Ming examples were celebrated. But more recent scholarship has shown that highly sophisticated blue-and-white pots and bowls were produced under the Yüan. Moreover, some scholars suggest that the technology for separating colors in glazes may well have developed independently in China, concurrent with the Near Eastern achievement.

Two remarkable jars from the Yüan period on display at the Imperial Palace are shown here. Their rich decorations reveal a flamboyant taste quite different from the earlier classical wares. Dragons swim with a kind of electric energy through churning waves, while lobed medallions form a counterpoint design around the collar (plate 167). The underglaze design is painted with the same facility and commitment that Yüan artists displayed when working with brush and ink on paper or silk. The bulbous covered jar (plate 166) has an even more ornate design, utilizing both underglaze blue and red, within an openwork panel carved into a bed of peonies and contained within an undulating medallion. This jar is one of four of its kind known to exist; its twin made financial history in 1971, when it was reputedly sold by a London dealer for half a million dollars.

Ming blue-and-white from the late fourteenth and fifteenth centuries shows a far more restrained use of pattern, at once delicate and forceful (plate 165). It is curvaceous, yet, compared to Yüan designs, austere. It is these early Ming wares, with intertwined chrysanthemums and peonies in a deep blue against a white ground, that the majority of Western collectors have most cherished. Over the almost three-hundred-year Ming rule and in different regions of China, there was great variation in the forms and designs of blue-and-white wares. In addition, the tones range from sky blue to blue-black, depending on the purity of the cobalt used in the glaze. An imposing dark-blue-and-white incense burner (plate 168) from the time of Wan-li (r. 1573–1620) is made in the shape of an ancient bronze sacrificial vessel. Many ceramics were designed not only to follow the Sung repertoire of shapes but also to imitate ancient bronze shapes; these serve as yet another example of the reassertion of the traditional bonds of Chinese culture.

The Ming had fully developed the technique for decorating china with bright, jewel-like colors, as seen in the fine double-gourd-shaped bottle covered with red, yellow, blue, and green overglaze designs (plate 169). The white high-fired porcelain was painted with lead-based glazes and fired a second time at a lower temperature. Overglazing enjoyed great popularity in the late Ming and Ch'ing times. Another innovation can be seen in a nascent form on the lower half of the double-gourd bottle. The birds here are shown in a landscape of curling, stringlike clouds. The rich, glossy quality of the shining white background and the brilliant, opaque colors distinguish this piece from pre-Ming decorated wares.

THE MING DYNASTY

70. "Sacred Way" leading to the tomb of the first Ming emperor, Hung-wu (r. 1368–1398). Nanking. The stone beasts appear to monitor the men and spirits who approach the tomb.

71. Column, one of a pair, in front of T'ien-an-men Gate, Peking. Ming dynasty (1368–1644). Marble. A cloud pierces the shaft of this column carved with an encircling dragon—symbols of heaven. The column represents the bestowal of heavenly power on the dynasty   the "mandate of heaven" to govern the "Central Realm."

TEMÜR, GRANDSON OF KUBLAI KHAN and the last strong Mongol emperor, died in 1307. Although the dynasty lingered until 1368, his successors were unable to exercise effective control over China. Once again, the warning signals of dynastic downfall that had been mentioned in the Confucian Classics occurred in the form of floods and famine accompanied by popular uprisings. A series of contenders emerged from the Chinese rebel forces to claim the "mandate of heaven," and one of them, Chu Yüan-chang, born a commoner like Liu Pang, founder of the Han dynasty, managed to expel the despised barbarians and establish himself as the first Ming emperor. He is generally referred to as Hung-wu ("Vast Military Power"), the name he gave his reigning years (1368–1398). The practice of referring to the emperor by the name he chose for his reign years was perpetuated in the Ming and Ch'ing dynasties.

The Ming followed the general governmental pattern established in T'ang and Sung times, but included the Yüan innovation of personal imperial control over government organs. One inherited imperial institution that reached new heights of influence under the Ming was the Board of Censors, whose function was to serve as the "eyes and ears of the emperor," inspecting the operation of government at all levels and reporting directly to him. Hung-wu, famous for his bad temper and cruelty, set himself up as a virtual despot in Nanking, which he made the capital (plate 170). When he died in 1398, his grandson inherited the throne briefly but was removed after a devastating civil war which an uncle, the fourth son of the late emperor, waged against the heir. The victorious uncle became known as Emperor Yung-lo (r. 1403–1424).

Like his father, Yung-lo continued to expand the empire and to keep the northern barbarians divided and therefore militarily impotent. He moved the capital back to Peking and began to build his own palace—the Forbidden City—which was to house China's rulers until the end of the imperial period in 1912. He selected a site for a tomb northwest of Peking

(plate 172) after the conventional consultation with diviners about an auspicious spot. The emperor wanted to be assured that in death he would not be plagued by hungry ghosts or other malevolent spirits.

Later Ming emperors continued the ancient practice of building tombs for themselves near the capital. Twelve of Yung-lo's successors were buried in the same beautiful valley that he chose, which the Chinese now call the Valley of the Thirteen Tombs. It is roughly an hour's drive by car from Peking, but it must have been almost a day's ride on horseback. During the Ming, the large valley, which stretches three miles north and south and two miles east and west, was sealed off by guards to keep people from cultivating the soil, cutting trees, or taking stones. No one, not even the emperor himself, was allowed to enter the sanctified precincts on horseback.

170

172. Valley of the Imperial Ming
Tombs, northwest of Peking.
Ming dynasty (1368–1644).
Roofs of the tomb complex of
Emperor Yung-lo (r. 1403–
1424), from right to left: gateway,
offering hall, and stele tower. The
tomb itself is buried within the
hemispherical wooded mound at
the extreme left.

Everyone who came to make offerings walked through several
great marble gateways, past an inscribed stele once protected
by a roofed pavilion, and down a long avenue lined on both
sides with impressive but engaging stone animals and human
figures. The avenue (plate 173) is usually called the "Sacred
Way" in English, but a more accurate translation of the
Chinese name *(shen-tao)* is the "Way of the Spirit." Twelve
pairs of animals overlook the initial part of the avenue, which
was recently paved with blacktop. The road turns slightly
after one passes the last of the animals, and twelve human figures line the rest of the avenue. There are four generals (plate
175), four officials, and four retired officials.

In building this avenue, the Ming rulers were perpetuating
the traditional formula for imperial tombs, for Han and T'ang
tombs also had fine stone animals lining their approaches.
Examples of this earlier monumental carving may be seen in
the Historical Museum in Sian, and compared to them the
Ming animals, marvelous though they are, have a certain stiff-
ness and formality. The Ming lion (plate 173) looks decorative, smug, and stony in contrast to the leopard-like Han
feline, whose tense, screeching form looks ready to pounce
(plate 174).

Like Confucian ideals and the institutions of the past, artistic
formulas were accepted as revealed truth and simply adapted and reused. In monumental sculpture and imperial architecture, what was lost in vigor and spirit was made up for
in formality and decorative elaboration.

The tomb of Yung-lo was built at the end of the great avenue. It is a large, impressive area which has been carefully repainted and tended by the current regime. One enters through
a triple-arched gateway into a courtyard, and through a
second great gateway which leads to another, larger courtyard
measuring 500 feet in length. The central pathway leads to a
mammoth building (plate 177) with a carved marble stairway. This structure is the Hall of Eminent Favors (Ling-en-
tien), which is 220 feet long and 105 feet wide. The colossal
hall has a double roof covered with yellow-orange tiles and
supported by tremendous red wooden pillars. It was here that
the descendants of Yung-lo brought sumptuous offerings to a
stele on a central altar. The ceilings (plate 176) are elaborately painted in gold and intense gemlike hues. The central motif
features the imperial golden dragons within square coffers and
on crossbeams.

Beyond the offering hall one passes straight on through an-

173. "Sacred Way" to the Imperial Ming Tombs, northwest of Peking. Fifteenth century (Ming dynasty). This avenue was built by Emperor Yung-lo to run from the valley entrance gateways to the gateway of his mortuary complex. Sculptures line the avenue to oversee the men, beasts, and spirits who approach his tomb.

174. Leopard-like feline (*pi-hsieh*) from a tomb at Hsien-yang, Shensi province. Western Han dynasty (206 B.C.–A.D. 8). Stone. Shown at the Historical Museum, Sian, Shensi province. Processions of animals traditionally guarded the approach to a royal tomb. Mouth open with a great roar, and tongue extended menacingly, this taut beast seems ready to spring. He contrasts vividly with his stationary Ming descendant.

175. General, detail of head and torso. Ming dynasty (1368–1644). Stone. "Sacred Way" to the Imperial Ming Tombs, northwest of Peking. The avenue is lined by statues of twenty-four animals and twelve human figures, among them four generals in elaborate armor.

other great gateway and then a smaller one to a marble altar (plate 178) set with five marble ritual vessels. Just beyond the altar is a massive tower which has a crenellated stone base and is crowned by a double roof. This 70-foot tower contains a 7-foot stone stele inscribed with the emperor's name. From the tower one can enjoy a commanding view of the mountains and of the wooded valley, dotted by distant roofs belonging to funerary buildings of the subsequent Ming emperors. Behind the tower lies a great forested mound in which the tomb itself was built. It has not yet been excavated.

When the Chinese do open the tomb of Emperor Yung-lo, they are apt to find a great number of treasures similar to the ones already excavated from the tomb of Emperor Wan-li (r. 1573–1620). That long-tenured sovereign, who ruled about 150 years after Yung-lo, is not remembered for any of the Confucian virtues. All Chinese historians, including the current Communist ones, tell of Wan-li's awesome extravagances and his irresponsibility about his governmental duties.

In "Opening an Imperial Tomb" (*China Reconstructs*, March, 1959, p. 16), archaeologist Hsia Nai told how the tomb of Wan-li was excavated. He described the objects discovered and set forth the facts in a straightforward way, not mentioning class struggle, exploitation, or other object lessons of Communist history. He noted that the tomb chambers were being repaired and that there would be an underground museum. He also mentioned that the tomb, which took six years to build, cost eight million ounces of silver and that Ming historians recorded the fact that Wan-li ordered an "entertainment" in his funeral chamber upon its completion.

The apolitical tone of Hsia's 1959 article contrasts with that in his article in the 1972 volume *New Archaeological Finds in China*, which combines archaeological revelations with ideological object lessons about the evil exploitation of the laboring classes during the "Feudal Period." Nor are such lessons lacking in the completed underground museum in Wan-li's tomb. Visual and written explanatory materials on the walls present a vivid image of peasant suffering and glorify peasant uprisings during the Ming period. The educational messages detail how many bushels of rice would have been available to feed how many hungry people for how many years if the capital and labor lavished on the tomb building and its treasure had been used for the people instead.

Among the array of jeweled and ceramic vessels, lamps, lacquered coffins, silks, and ornaments, a supreme treasure

176, 177. Offering hall and detail of ceiling, Hall of Eminent Favors (Ling-en-tien), Tomb of Yung-lo (r. 1403–1424). First quarter of the fifteenth century (Ming dynasty), recently renovated. Courtyard length 500 feet, hall length 220 feet, width 105 feet. This immense building is one of the largest wooden halls in Asia. The wooden ceiling, like those in the Imperial Palace, is coffered and brightly painted with colors and gold. Golden dragons writhe within the coffers and on the cross beams.

178. Altar in front of stele tower,
Tomb of Yung-lo (r. 1403–1424).
First quarter of the fifteenth
century (Ming dynasty). Marble.
Offering vessels were usually made
of lacquer, metal, or ceramic, but
here they have been fashioned for
posterity out of marble. The
central vessel simulates a censer
in a *ting* tripod shape. The
sculptor has formalized the
vaporous emissions, like a great
conical hat. A dragon resides in
this cloud.

found in Wan-li's tomb belonged to one of the two empresses
who were buried with him. It was probably a bridal headdress
and is called a phoenix hat (plate 179) because the female imperial symbol dominates the top of the pearl-encrusted, gem-
studded crown. Outlined in gold, the marvelous blue phoenix
looks as if made of enamel, although some authorities say it is
made of kingfishers' feathers. Three small golden dragons ride
on the crest of the hat. The dragons on each side hold strings
of pearls in their mouths. The strings are intermittently punc-
tuated with gold star-studded medallions.

An interesting contrast in style may be seen by comparing
this Ming tomb with the 1957 tomb (plate 180) commemorating the Communist martyrs who were killed by Chiang Kai-
shek's forces in what today is called the Canton Commune
Rising of 1927. The latter contains the remains of 5,000 victims in a huge hemispherical mound, encircled by a marble
wall. It is designated by characters carved into the wall and
is guarded by traditionally conceived lions that sit atop the

wall. Potted plants grouped in front of the inscription serve to honor and decorate the monument. In their search for a Chinese Communist style, the designers consciously departed from the imperial Ming prototype and created a distinctive monumental form. Bronze doors in the marble wall bear an unmistakable international Communist red-star symbol.

Areas near Peking have been the site of human habitation since at least 500,000 B.C., as the discovery of the bones of Peking man proved. The remains of early settlements and references to it in ancient literature have revealed something of Peking's long history. Yung-lo made it the Ming capital in 1421 and built his palace over areas where the ruined Mongol palace and city had been. He laid out a new, enlarged city which excluded some of the northern sections of the older city and extended south beyond the old Yüan walls. The city walls erected by the Ming enclosed Peking until recently, when the Communist authorities pulled them down in the course of modernization. Unfortunately, this has deprived the city of much of its distinctive atmosphere, although the old gates still stand. Peking now sprawls in the same way that Western cities do, to the dismay of its admirers.

The Ming city, virtually unchanged by the Ch'ing, was constructed in the shape of two adjoining rectangles, one north of the other, and planned on axes governed by the four cardinal points—north, south, east, and west. The northern rectangle was built over much of the old Mongol city and includes the Imperial Palace, parks, and drum and bell towers. The southern rectangle was somewhat wider, extending slightly east and west beyond the walls of the northern part, but was shorter in length than the northern section. Buildings for imperial worship, such as the Temple of Agriculture and the Temple of Heaven, were built within the southern part of Ming Peking.

The Temple of Heaven complex (T'ien T'an), built in 1530–40, restored in 1749 and again recently, is several miles long. It is in the southernmost part of the Ming city and lies east of the central north-south avenue that bisects that part of the city. Here, at the time of the winter solstice, the emperor used to address Heaven and offer sacrifices.

Let us approach the main ceremonial axis from the south and proceed north, as the emperor did on ceremonial occasions. A vast walled square area encloses the southern section. We enter through a triple gate, proceeding north to a circular wall and through another triple gate. In the center of the

179. Phoenix hat, from the tomb of Wan-li (r. 1573–1620) and his consorts. Reproduction(?). Last quarter of the sixteenth or first quarter of the seventeenth century (Ming dynasty). Gold, gems, pearls, and blue enamel or kingfisher feathers. Shown at the Imperial Palace, Peking. This was probably worn by one of Wan-li's empresses as a bridal headdress.

180. Tumulus in the Park of the Martyrs of the Canton Commune Uprising, Canton (Kwangchow). Built in 1957. Marble wall and lions. The mound holds the remains of the 5,000 victims killed when the Kuomintang crushed the Communist commune in Canton in 1927.

round courtyard there is a marble platform—the Altar of Heaven (plate 181). Open to the sky, this is the altar from which the emperor's signed declaration was read to the "Great Spirit Who Resides in Heaven." The marble altar is a flat-topped circular platform rising up in three tiers, with stairways located in the four cardinal directions. Its only embellishments are the carved marble balustrades. It is a marvelously simple construction which reflects the crisp formulation of the traditional Chinese symbols of Heaven (round) and Earth (square), using architecture to invoke the ideal harmony of the two. Multiplication of elements grouped in nines recurs frequently; the number nine is the symbol of the sky and the emperor.

Proceeding northward from the altar, we go through two more sets of marble gates, the northern openings of the circular and square walls. Those walls, like the altar itself, have four gates or stairway approaches, one in each cardinal direction. The stone walls are painted red and roofed with deep-azure tiles, the color of the innermost recesses of the vaulted

181. The Altar of Heaven (Yüan-ch'iu-t'an) within the Temple of Heaven complex (T'ien T'an), Peking.
Built in 1530 (Ming dynasty), enlarged in 1749. Marble. During the Ming and Ch'ing dynasties,
each year at the time of the winter solstice, the emperor offered prayers on this altar to the "Great
Spirit Who Resides in Heaven."

182. Walls and gateways between the Altar of Heaven (Yüan-ch'iu-t'an) and the Imperial Heavenly Vault (Huang-ch'iung-yü) in the Temple of Heaven complex (T'ien T'an), Peking. Ming dynasty (1368–1644), rebuilt in 1749. The Altar of Heaven is surrounded by a circular wall and a square wall, each with three gateways in the four cardinal directions. This view looks north from the altar through gateways of both walls.

heavens. As on most traditional roofs, the ends of the circular and semicircular tiles are decorated with relief designs. For this imperial monument, the tile ends are stamped with five-clawed dragons flying in clouds (plate 183), symbols of Heaven. Larger, rounded tile heads of *makaras* (mythical water demons) emerge from the tops of the spines of the tile roofs near where the roofs end at the marble gateposts. The most distinctive features of the post-and-lintel gates (plate 182), besides their obvious translation from wooden construction into stone, are the flat carved-stone clouds which pierce through the tops of the posts. It is an extraordinary image which reminds the visitor that he is not treading on mundane soil, but walking within the Chinese conception of Heaven.

Professor Nelson Wu brilliantly interprets the Temple of Heaven complex in *Chinese and Indian Architecture* (pp. 41–45). He suggests that the round Altar of Heaven set within the square courtyard (Earth) is the earthly base for this monument, and that the other gateways and buildings along the main northern axis were conceived in the Chinese mind as ascending at each stage and stretching up toward the heavens. In other words, the next building, the Imperial Heavenly Vault, a single-storied wooden structure with a dazzling blue-tiled roof, was to be understood as being above the Altar of Heaven. And beyond it, the circular, triple-roofed Hall of Prayer for Good Harvests (commonly referred to as the Temple of Heaven) was mentally conceived to be directly above the Imperial Heavenly Vault, brushing the clouds in the heavens.

As we leave the Altar of Heaven and proceed north, which we now understand to be up, we enter the gate, courtyard, and then round pavilion of the Imperial Heavenly Vault (plate 185). Within this building, stone tablets were placed on the altar, and sacrifices were performed before them. One can still see the carved marble altar (plate 184) with stairs and the wooden case which once held the stele that rests atop the altar. The tile roof is supported by great wooden pillars which were covered with elaborately decorated relief designs in a gesso-like material (plate 186). The surface design of these pillars has flaked away over the years, and since the Imperial Heavenly Vault has not yet been as fully restored as the Hall of Prayer for Good Harvests, one can see just how the decoration was applied in layers.

We continue our northward journey to a half-rounded wall —the gate through the dome of heaven—and proceed on a mile-long marble avenue to the gateway of the Hall of Prayer

183. Detail of roof tiles on wall (plate 182).

for Good Harvests. The enormous circular triple-roofed building (plate 188) rests on a huge circular base within a vast rectangular courtyard. This climactic building lies at the north end of the complex; the encompassing wall of the whole complex is rectangular (Earth) at the south end but rounded (Heaven) at the north end, which further bolsters Professor Wu's vertical theory. The temple has been repainted quite recently with gold and the rainbow colors. The crossbeams and domed vault are embellished with designs which include dragons, phoenixes, clouds, and medallions (plate 187). Great pillars, decorated with gilded flowers and leaf designs, support the dome. The wooden pillars were made from giant trees from Yunnan. All this decoration creates an extraordinarily rich and elaborate vision of the heavens.

The restoration gives the monument quite a different appearance from the way it looked during the violent phase of

184. Altar in the Imperial Heavenly Vault (plate 185). Altar, marble; stele box, carved screen, and pillars, wood. During the Ming and Ch'ing, tablets honoring gods and royal ancestors were worshiped on this altar.

OPPOSITE PAGE:

185. The Imperial Heavenly Vault (Huang-ch'iung-yü) in the Temple of Heaven complex (T'ien T'an), Peking. Built in 1530 (Ming dynasty), restored in 1752. Temple diameter 51 feet, height 63 feet. The imperial entourage traveled north from the Altar of Heaven through two sets of gateways (plate 182) and then through the covered gateways of the encircling wall of the Imperial Heavenly Vault.

the Cultural Revolution (1966–69). The imperial decoration was eclipsed by giant pictures of Chairman Mao hung both outside and inside. By 1972, however, the only ideological reminders within the Temple of Heaven complex were a discreet bulletin board at the western approach that exhibited photos of friendly delegations visiting China, and a large red billboard on the mile-long marble roadway. The billboard, which looks much like those used in the West for outdoor advertising, artfully reproduced Chairman Mao's poem "Snow" in his own calligraphy. The poem classically extols the awesome grandeur of the winter landscape in the highlands of Shensi and Shansi provinces, which has been so admired by Chinese leaders of the past. Mao used the poem to remind his followers that the present generation must produce its own leaders—men of vision.

The Temple of Heaven complex provides an example of how an old monument is put to new use following the Chairman's directive to "let the old serve the new." During the Ming and Ch'ing, only the emperor and his entourage could enter its sacred precincts. After the collapse of the empire in 1912, it was opened to the public, and some festivals were held and offerings made there during the earliest years of the Republic. Now the notions of Heaven's power and of sacrifice to spirits have been derided as superstition, and the complex serves sightseers and strollers, showing the masses the "glorious achievements of the craftsmen of the past." Only a single billboard is needed to remind them that universal power no longer resides in the heavens but within Chairman Mao's Chinese Communist Party. Sacrifices, once made in the form of cooked offerings, must be understood as self-sacrifice to be made in everyday service to the state. Ultimate truth, once thought to be found in the Confucian Classics or imperial edicts, now resides in the "Thought" of Chairman Mao.

Just north of the center of the old city of Peking is perhaps the best-known Ming monument, the Imperial Palace (now called Ku-kung, which means "old palace"), also called the Forbidden City. It was called the Forbidden City (*Tzu-chin-ch'eng*) because, during the centuries of Ming and Ch'ing rule, entrance into its vast confines was strictly forbidden to all except the emperor and his entourage of concubines, eunuchs, officials, guards, palace staff, and craftsmen. It is hard to conjure up a vision of this exclusiveness today, when thousands of visitors from all over China and from abroad stream through the palace daily. In good weather one can see children and

186, 187. Below, pillar in the Imperial Heavenly Vault (plate 185). Wood with layers of gesso. In contrast with the brightly painted pillars of the Hall of Prayer for Good Harvests at right, the aging pillars in this building reveal how the relief decoration was applied to the wood surface.

adults posing for photographs on the great ornamental sculptures, a game of basketball being played in the outer precincts of the palace, and swimmers diving into the moat surrounding its walls.

Let us approach the Forbidden City from T'ien-an-men Square (plate 252). "T'ien-an-men" means "Gate of Heavenly Peace," and the square takes its name from the old imperial gate located at its north end (plate 338). It is in the center of the capital and is considered to be the heart of the People's Republic of China. T'ien-an-men is the ceremonial center where the major demonstrations and parades take place. The area was formerly much smaller, but the Communists cleared away enough buildings to create a 98-acre space. It is estimated that the square can hold a million people. When great parades are held, officials watch from a reviewing platform on T'ien-an-men's gateway. The current government has built two enormous structures on the east and west sides of the square—the Museum of History and the Revolution and the Great Hall of the People. In the middle of the square there is a huge monument to the People's Heroes.

During the Ming and Ch'ing, the emperor passed through T'ien-an-men when he went to make sacrifices at the Temple of Heaven, and imperial edicts were handed down from the top of the gateway. The edicts were placed in the mouth of a golden, phoenix-shaped box and lowered to a kneeling official, who had them copied and distributed throughout the empire.

188. Hall of Prayer for Good Harvests (Ch'i-nien-tien), Temple of Heaven complex (T'ien T'an), Peking. Originally built in 1420 (Ming dynasty), restored in 1751, burned in 1889, rebuilt in the 1890s, restored recently. Terrace height 36 feet, diameter at broadest point 195 feet. Hall overall height 123 feet, diameter 96 feet. This nineteenth-century reconstruction is perhaps the best-known building in the Temple of Heaven complex. Its distinctive profile, with a triple roof, is often used as a logo on Chinese printed materials.

189. Swimming in the moat surrounding the Imperial Palace, Peking. Moat, Ming dynasty (1368–1644). The masses of China come in great numbers to visit monuments of the past, and the new generation as well as the supervising cadres exhibit a certain lack of awe of the once forbidden precincts.

When the present government cleared the space, pairs of huge imperial sculptures which had lined the approach to the T'ien-an-men gate were moved north closer to the gate to permit construction of an east-west avenue. Within this group was a pair of columns, one of which is shown here (plate 171). It is encircled by a relief carving of a dragon in clouds and is pierced by a flat cloud. The column's surface is carved in a low relief that makes it look as though it had been flat and was then rolled into a cylinder. However, its piercing cloud element introduces a surprising third sculptural dimension. This column provides a highly distinctive image, using elements similar to the Temple of Heaven gateway motif (plate 182). It is only one of the imperial symbols at T'ien-an-men which mingle with Communist iconography such as slogans and giant poster photographs of Chairman Mao.

190. Gateway at the north end of the corridor between the Three Rear Palaces (Hou-san-kung) and the Six Western Palaces (Hsi-liu-kung), Imperial Palace, Peking. Ming dynasty (1368–1644), with renovations of the Ch'ing and People's Republic. The walls of the Imperial Palace were painted reddish purple, believed to be the color of the North Star, and therefore auspicious, and the roofs were covered with yellow tiles, the color associated with the emperor.

As we leave T'ien-an-men Square proceeding northward toward the Imperial Palace, we enter the central arch of T'ien-an-men gateway, one of the five openings through the Gate of Heavenly Peace. Previously, only the emperor passed through the central gate. Proceeding along a straight roadway that goes through three more gateways, we pass the area where the imperial guard was once quartered, now a public park. We approach the great Wu-men, Gate of the Midday Sun. The Wu-men bridges the moat (plate 189) to the inner palace city, which covers 250 acres and lies within the greater Imperial City. The palace plan, conceived by Yung-lo in the early fifteenth century, was essentially unchanged by the subsequent Ming and Ch'ing emperors, although they frequently renovated and added buildings. All the Imperial City walls (plate 190) were painted a reddish purple, believed to be the

191. Stair terrace of the Hall of Supreme
Harmony (T'ai-ho-tien), Imperial
Palace, Peking. Ming dynasty
(1368–1644), with renovations of
the Ch'ing and People's Republic.
Marble. The emperor presided over
official ceremonies in three great
Halls of Harmony at the heart of
the Forbidden City. Triple stairways
provide access to the ceremonial
platform, the base for all the three
halls. A panel in the central
stairway, carved with clouds and
dragons, was the space over which
the emperor's chair was carried.

color of the North Star and therefore auspicious. The palace
roofs were golden yellow. In the Chinese reckoning, there
were five "positions": north, south, east, west, and center;
yellow was the color of the center and was selected by the
Ming and Ch'ing to be the color for the Son of Heaven—the
emperor—who ruled the "Central Realm."

Within the first courtyard, a rectangular space so vast that
the scale of a human being is reduced to total insignificance,
there are five marble bridges over the River of Golden Water
leading to another gate. There is a geometric and axial
tyranny throughout the Forbidden City; the courtyard plans
are uncompromisingly rectangular, and the gates correspond
to the cardinal directions—north, south, east, and west. So
strong is the main axis, which runs north-south, that man's
impulse to meander or diverge from this awesomely severe
orientation is totally subjugated.

At the rear of the next courtyard a great triple-tiered platform stretching north in the shape of an "I" is the base for
the Hall of Supreme Harmony (plate 191), the Hall of Perfect

188

Courtyard of the Hall of Military Prowess (Wu-ying-tien), southwestern section of the Imperial Palace, Peking. Ming dynasty (1368–1644), burned and rebuilt in the Ch'ing, renovations in the People's Republic. During the Ming and Ch'ing, this hall housed the imperial printing presses which produced anthologies of imperial poems, encyclopedias, and collections commissioned by the emperor. It is now used to display some of the archaeological treasures found during the Cultural Revolution.

Harmony behind it, and the Hall of the Preservation of Harmony behind that. This courtyard is even larger than the preceding one, further dwarfing the individual and reinforcing his status as a humble subject of the Son of Heaven. The three Halls of Harmony were part of the original Ming plan. The emperor sat in all three halls on various great occasions such as his birthday, the winter solstice, the New Year, the selection of generals, the reading of the names of scholars who had passed the highest civil-service examinations, the inspection of the annual harvest seed for the next year's planting, and the banquets for the representatives of tributary states or for officials within the imperial government. During times of official celebration, the vast courtyards were filled with legions of men carrying pennants and streamers while orchestras played accompaniment on stone chimes and gilt-bronze bells.

There is a great carved marble slab with dragons and phoenixes in clouds in the center of the triple stairway that ascends the platform to the Harmony halls (plate 191). The emperor was carried over this in his sedan chair. All the

189

193. Gate of Heavenly Purity (Ch'ien-ch'ing-men), Imperial Palace, Peking. Ming dynasty (1368–1644).
The stair descends from the north end of the platform that holds the three great halls of state (Halls
of Harmony) to a large courtyard and gateway entrance to the imperial residences located in the
northern section of the Forbidden City.

Balustrade post with dragon-phoenix-cloud motif, Imperial Palace, Peking. Ming dynasty (1368–1644), with renovations of the Ch'ing and People's Republic. Marble.

Bird-and-flower wall medallion, Imperial Palace, Peking. Ming dynasty (1368–1644), with renovations of the Ch'ing and People's Republic. Plaque and wall, glazed ceramic.

north-south-oriented stairs and other east-west stairs within the pattern of imperial movement had similar carved slabs—spaces which only the emperor could enter. These long marble cloud-and-dragon rectangles look like patterned carpets and are a distinctive imperial motif seen also at other places the emperor visited, such as the Temple of Heaven, the Summer Palace, and the Ming tombs.

The palace and other imperial monuments were also decorated with miles of elaborate marble balustrades such as one finds along the tiered platforms supporting the three Halls of Harmony. The tops of the upright cylindrical posts were carved with the same dragon-phoenix-cloud motif (plate 194).

The vast marble courtyards repeat themselves; all are entered through gates and all have wooden, tile-roofed halls arranged geometrically around the courtyard. Currently they share an austerity which must have been somewhat modified during the imperial period by the perpetual mist of incense that rose from huge censers on the stairs and platforms (plate 192). The aromatic clouds curled around the emperor's buildings and softened their appearance. And on special occasions the human pageantry would, of course, fill up the courtyards. Yet it seems clear that an architectural conception employing such colossal, inhuman spaces walled off from the everyday world and a rigid orientation that assumes such an unyielding hierarchy must reflect how the emperor saw himself in relation to his court and to the people of China. Court protocol was as strict as the architectural design. For a petitioner or an ambassadorial tribute bearer there was no possibility of informal access or conversation. If an emperor wished to be informed of the realities of Chinese life, he had to leave the confines of the Forbidden City. Some emperors had no such desire. The Son of Heaven was not an ordinary mortal; as recipient of the "mandate of heaven" he was the ceremonial head and key power in rigidly organized and categorized institutions. Some Western historians attribute the decline of the Ming dynasty and, indeed, the whole dynastic system to the fact that there was no higher law or institutionalized check on the arbitrary imperial power. Traditional Chinese historians used the stock Confucian explanation that the collapse of the Ming occurred because of the personal failings of various emperors. The emperor's virtue and sense of social responsibility were certainly crucial factors in a successful reign, but no matter how conscientious the emperor was, the Confucian ideal ruler could never have been the Marxian one because of

191

196. Guardians on corner roof tiles of the hall next to the West Flowery Gate (Hsi-hua-men), Imperial Palace, Peking. Ming dynasty (1368–1644), with renovations of the Ch'ing and People's Republic.

197. Looking south in the corridor between the Three Rear Palaces (Hou-san-kung) and the Six Eastern Palaces (Tung-liu-kung), Imperial Palace, Peking. Ming dynasty (1368–1644), with renovations of the Ch'ing and People's Republic. The residential palaces were built on a north-south axis and surrounded by walls. Long walkways run between the compounds. Gateways open onto these corridors.

the emperor's class consciousness, class origins, and exploitation of the working people. To Communist historians the collapse of the dynastic system was historically inevitable and was caused by the failures of the system itself, rather than those of the emperor.

The private living quarters of the imperial family, the concubines, and the ever-watchful eunuchs were in the northern section of the walled palace quadrangle (plate 193). Some of the smaller palace courtyards, though hardly cozy, have a more human scale. This is especially true of the concubines' quarters, placed on a north-south axis just west of the main palace. Here the smaller scale allows the charming green-and-yellow ceramic wall plaques of dragons, flora, and fauna and the delightfully tiled roofs to come into focus (plate 195). There is a parade of guardians at each corner of all of the thousands of roofs within the Imperial Palace (plates 196, 198). Their function is to guard the gate or hall from the malevolent spirits who reside in the four diagonal directions—northeast, northwest, southeast, and southwest. Some of the parades include a dragon, nine whimsical feline or birdlike creatures, and an official riding on the back of what appears to be the top half of a giant rooster. Other, more modest groups have only three guardians between the dragon and the mounted official.

There are long narrow walkways between the various sections of the palace (plate 197). These are lined by the ubiquitous reddish-purple walls that enclose each section. Most courtyards are entered from the south through a main gate (plate 200), and many are planted with handsome trees. Directly in front of the gate, the smaller courtyards have wooden screens to protect the occupants from visitors' eyes (plate 199). The rectangular hall at the rear of the courtyard is generally entered from the center. Usually there is a small courtyard and a second hall in back of the first, with a connecting walkway. Since the succession of Ming and Ch'ing emperors who resided in the Forbidden City renovated the apartments that they and their entourages occupied, what we see today is only the shell of the original Ming palace. The apartments that are open for inspection are furnished in the nineteenth-century, late Ch'ing taste. The decoration features an elaborateness reminiscent of its Western equivalent of roughly the same period—Victorian taste (plates 203, 224). In the ceiling of one imperial apartment (plate 201) a marvelously carved golden dragon writhes within a star. Suspended from this golden relief and surrounded by golden fringes is a silver orb that hangs

198. Guardians on corner roof tiles,
Imperial Palace, Peking. Ming
dynasty (1368–1644), with
renovations of the Ch'ing and
People's Republic. Orange-
yellow ceramic.

199. Entrance courtyard with screen
on left, Ch'eng-ch'ien-kung,
northeastern section of the
Imperial Palace, Peking. Ming
dynasty (1368–1644), with
renovations of the Ch'ing and
People's Republic. In this complex,
which is similar to the Palace of
Permanent Peace (plate 200), the
screen-gate is closed (left). The small
courtyard with trees has a relatively
intimate scale and must have been
a pleasant place for the women to
sit and talk and play games.

200. Entrance to the ceramics exhibition
in the Palace of Permanent Peace
(Yung-ho-kung), northeastern
section of the Imperial Palace,
Peking. Ming dynasty (1368–
1644), with renovations of the
Ch'ing and People's Republic. The
sign reads: "Ceramics Hall, latter
section." Currently used as an
exhibition hall, this small complex
used to house women of the court.
The main entrance to the courtyard and hall is from the south. In
times past, when the gateway
was opened for a caller, he would
have been confronted by a closed
screen-gate which hid the courtyard from curious or unworthy
eyes. Here the screen-gate is open.

201. Carved ceiling in an apartment in the Six Western Palaces (Hsi-liu-kung), northeastern section of the Imperial Palace, Peking. Ming dynasty (1368–1644), with renovations of the Ch'ing and People's Republic. Ceiling, carved wood with paint and gilt; hanging, mirrored ball and golden pendants.

like a crown with long pendants. Couchlike thrones, sometimes called *k'ang*, served for sitting or reclining. Calligraphy and paintings decorated the walls.

The women of the court stayed in their quarters. A force of eunuchs served and oversaw their feminine charges. The women whiled away their days dressing up, playing games, gossiping, and intriguing. The concubine whose son became the heir apparent was afforded all the prerogatives of a full-fledged consort. Occasionally, as in the case of the Empress Dowager Tz'u-hsi (1835–1908), such a woman, supported by faithful eunuchs and trusted officials, attained power through a triumph of court intrigue. But, in general, women played an extremely subservient role.

Especially under the Ming, the unchecked power of the imperial eunuchs was a persistent evil that contributed to the dynasty's disastrous end. Upon the fall of the Mongol dynasty, the scholar-official class had rejoiced at ridding China of the despised foreign rulers, but enlightened government was not necessarily fostered by Chinese rulers. As the Ming dynasty went on, the eunuchs managed to dominate the emperors and officialdom. They created so much factionalism and conflict at court that even the most dedicated literati officials became discouraged and humiliated; sometimes they were even in danger of losing their lives. The literati class, which had

195

202. Entrance to the Hall of Military Prowess (Wu-ying-tien), southwestern section of the Imperial Palace, Peking. Ming dynasty (1368–1644), burned and rebuilt in the Ch'ing, with renovations in the People's Republic. Sculpture, gilt bronze; stairway, marble; walls, painted plaster with ceramic decoration; tiled roof. Mythical beasts guard the entrance.

203. Reception hall in an apartment in the Six Eastern Palaces (Tung-liu-kung), northeastern section of the Imperial Palace, Peking. Ming dynasty (1368–1644), with renovations of the Ch'ing and People's Republic. A few apartments in this section of the palace have recently been refurnished with Manchu accoutrements.

emerged victorious in its power struggle with the old noble class in the Sung, was quite helpless to counter the eunuch influence. Eunuchs were companions and friends to young emperors in their formative years, were masters of plots and gossip, and were unencumbered by family obligations. They sublimated their sexual incapacity in a lust for power and extravagance.

In this period the scholars, who were regarded as paragons of Confucian virtue, often chose not to serve in government or else retired early in order to escape the unprincipled schemes at court. While the power elite paid lip service to Confucian morality, it was in fact utterly corrupt.

Literati protest against imperial service was not a phenomenon that began with the Ming. As early as the fifth century, a poet-official named T'ao Ch'ien (also known as T'ao Yüan-ming; d. 427) resigned his official position in protest and retired to private life, commemorating his feelings in a poem, "Going Home."

In a period when official service was especially perilous, such as the Ming, this theme of the courageous official who retires from public life to cultivate his spirit and pursue the fine arts of painting, poetry, and friendship enjoyed great popularity among the literati. Wang Chung-yü, an early Ming artist who was active in the late fourteenth century, painted his version of the poet T'ao Yüan-ming with scroll in hand (plate 204). In his retelling of the story, Wang used as his model an earlier painting on this theme. The figure of the protesting poet, although somewhat haughty, is painted in a sweep of lines more decorative than defiant. His hat, fur cape, and flowing robes fit into a gentle crescent curve. The figure floats in an undefined background, and its elegant lines produce a graceful rhythm rather than emphasize the literary message. Since the message was already well known to the literati audience through paintings on the same subject from the T'ang and Sung periods, the Ming painter could devote himself, if he preferred, to the enjoyment of the abstract, decorative qualities of line.

This painting of T'ao Yüan-ming shows why Ming painting is often difficult for the uninitiated Westerner to appreciate fully. It is based on references to classical literature and art that the artist assumes his audience knows. The situation is somewhat analogous to that of a Chinese who has learned English but knows nothing of Western civilization, ancient or modern, and tries to read James Joyce's *Ulysses*. While some words may have a familiar ring, without a thorough grounding in classical and contemporary culture it is quite impossible to understand the meaning. In a similar way, we are ill equipped to approach the subtle antiquarian references and currents so familiar to Wang Chung-yü's audience.

The most revered Yüan painters were all native Chinese. Since most of them had no official connection with the Mongols, their reputations were untouched by the Ming condemnation of the Mongol era, and their work continued to be admired. Ni Tsan (1301–1374) was one of the most influential Yüan artists, among both his contemporaries and succeeding generations. Indeed, were it not for the inscription and signature of the artist, a painting by Wang Fu (1362–1416) in Peking's Palace Collection (plate 205) could well be mistaken for a painting by the Yüan master himself or one of his circle. Wang Fu paraphrased one of Ni Tsan's favorite themes of bamboos, trees, and rocks, painting it in the Yüan master's crisp, dry style. The painting is of superb quality. Because of the graceful arrangement of the composition and the beautifully rendered brushstrokes that define the branches, leaves, and rocks, any connoisseur would cherish it. From the standpoint of originality, however, it is clearly imitative, displaying a cultivation of Ni Tsan's style. Virtually all later Chinese painters, sculptors, architects, and bureaucrats worked within the frame-

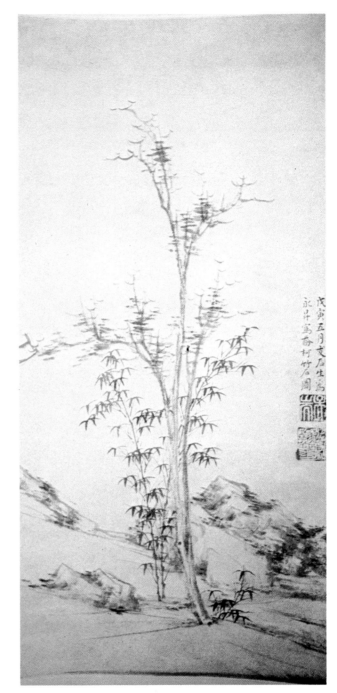

204. Wang Chung-yü (active late fourteenth century). *The Poet T'ao Yüan-ming* (365–427). Inscribed. Ming dynasty. Ink on paper. Shown at the Palace of Peace and Longevity (Ning-shou-kung), Imperial Palace, Peking. The artist does not emphasize the subject's psychological dilemma—he has painted with flowingly rhythmic strokes.

205. Wang Fu (1362–1416). *Tall Tree, Bamboo, and Stone*. Kiangsu province. Inscription says it was painted in 1398, when the artist was thirty-six, for a friend, Yung Sheng. It is signed and dated. Ming dynasty. Ink on paper. Shown at the Palace of Peace and Longevity (Ning-shou-kung), Imperial Palace, Peking. To paint the innermost essence of a subject—the hardness and massing of rock, the delicacy and flexibility of bamboo, and the vibrant growth of a tree—was an important goal for a painter.

work of the past. In effect, the subject of the art was its own classical past, with new and highly creative stylistic variations. The artist worked with age-old patterns, which he freely re-interpreted.

One of the greatest artists of the Ming, who was also a great admirer of Ni Tsan, was Shen Chou (1427–1509). Remaining in his native city of Soochow, Shen Chou avoided an official career and pursued his art just as Ni Tsan had done. He is considered the founder of the Wu school, so named because Soochow was in the ancient State of Wu. But Ni Tsan's was only one of the older styles of painting that Shen Chou practiced. In Peking's Palace Collection there is a splendid painting (plate 206) executed in the "blue-green landscape" style revived from T'ang times. In a detail of that painting we see a man dressed in long robes and holding a walking stick, standing in a small clearing on a wooded hillside contemplating the true nature of the universe.

Another outstanding painting by Shen Chou in this collection is a self-portrait (plate 207) painted in 1506, when the artist was seventy-nine years old. Portraiture was rare in the Wu school, and this half-length portrait may be unique in Shen's oeuvre. It is in the style of ancestor portraits, which were generally painted by professional artists and not by the literati artists of the Wu school. The artist's inscription states that he was trying to reveal character rather than make an exact likeness. Nevertheless, the painting appears to be a remarkably careful study of advanced age—the facial wrinkles, freckle-like discolorations, even the hair, beard, and eyebrows are clearly those of an old man. The face is very much alive: the lips seem almost ready to utter a phrase, and the intense eyes are piercing. This vitality contrasts with the formal, abstract patterns of the scholar's black hat and pale-brown robe.

Another scholar's portrait, at the opposite end of the stylistic gamut from Shen Chou's self-portrait, is Hsü Wei's *Scholar on a Donkey* (plate 208). Hsü Wei (1521–1593) was an individualist, aligned with no particular painting school. In keeping with the spirit of literati "amateur" painting, his scholar is painted with rapid calligraphic strokes that outline only the barest essentials of the robe. His dotted eye and hat and the donkey's ears and legs have each been formed with a single stroke. Here the brush was used in a completely calligraphic way. The Chinese have always categorized painting as an offshoot of calligraphy, and Hsü Wei's painting is an excellent example of the close relationship between them.

206. Shen Chou (1427–1509). *Landscape* (detail), in blue-green T'ang style. Ming dynasty. Ink and colors on silk. Shown at the Palace of Peace and Longevity (Ning-shou-kung), Imperial Palace, Peking. Adapting an ancient style of painting for the background color, Shen Chou created figurations of his own, clear and firm and deceptively simple.

201

208. Hsü Wei (1521–1593). *Scholar on a Donkey* (detail). Chekiang province. Inscribed. Ming dynasty. Ink on paper. Shown at the Palace of Peace and Longevity (Ning-shou-kung), Imperial Palace, Peking. The artist has painted the humorous juxtaposition of a dignified scholar and a long-eared donkey with calligraphic skill and economy of line.

207. Shen Chou (1427–1509). *Portrait of the Artist* (detail of lower half). Inscribed in upper half with date, 1506, and comments by the artist. Ming dynasty. Ink and colors on silk. Shown at the Palace of Peace and Longevity (Ning-shou-kung), Imperial Palace, Peking.

In a final example of Ming painting from Peking's Palace Collection we see a picture executed in a professional style which was in vogue at the court. Yu Ch'iu (active c. 1570–1590) painted a subject borrowed from the past, showing the Sui dynasty (581–618) minister Yang Su surrounded by beauties in a garden courtyard (plate 209). The figures are painted in a finely drawn style which was favored by the aristocratic taste-makers. This kind of painting was cultivated in the Sung court also and continued in the Ming period. Most amateur-literati artists rejected the meticulously detailed and highly finished look of professional artists such as Yu Ch'iu, preferring more intuitive and unschooled styles. While both amateur and professional artists practiced a conscious archaism, the amateur artists valued qualities of "naturalness," which were, however, highly intellectualized and contrived, sharing many of the ideals and characteristics of the highly cultivated rusticity of the Japanese "tea taste." Yu Ch'iu's painting, by contrast, has a refinement and artifice quite different from the other paintings we have seen.

Yu Ch'iu's painting of Yang Su provides a wealth of documentary evidence about Ming costuming and furnishing: the design of the ceramic garden seat in the foreground, on which the visiting official sits; Minister Yang's wooden bench with turned-up feet and a matching side table, both covered with brocaded or woven tops; the side-table display of the vase of flowers and an ancient bronze tripod from the minister's collection; the rolled-brocade edging of the table and bench that matches the pattern worn at neck and sleeve by the ladies in their flowing robes; and the pattern of the woven-mat background for the blank screen. The most exotic detail in this painting to Western eyes is the rocky outcropping on the upper right side. This puzzling vision of grotesquely shaped rocks is also found on later Chinese porcelains.

These rock forms were not just a fantasy in the artist's mind. Hollowed out and molded by wind and water over a span of eons, they were collected from the various areas of China and set into Chinese gardens to suggest rugged mountain peaks (plates 210, 214). According to the theory of garden planning, which evolved in ancient times and was fully developed by the Sung, the two most fundamental elements in Chinese gardens were hills or mountains and water. Some writers on the subject of garden theory equate the universal principles of *yin* and *yang* with these elements: *yin* is passive, dark, and moist—that is, water; *yang* is active, bright, and aggressive—the moun-

209. Yu Ch'iu (active c. 1570–1590).
The Sui Minister Yang Su (detail).
Ming dynasty. Ink on paper.
Shown at the Palace of Peace
and Longevity (Ning-shou-kung),
Imperial Palace, Peking.
A minister surrounded by
beauties in a garden setting was
a favorite subject for court
paintings. This theme was adapted
for porcelain decoration in the
Ch'ing period and exported to the
West, where it provided a vision
of China for Europeans in the
seventeenth and eighteenth
centuries.

tain. A harmonious arrangement of mountains and water
in a garden could evoke the spirit of universal harmony of *yin*
and *yang* for the beholder. Of course, gardens also had trees,
shrubs, flowers, bridges, and architectural elements. Most important, the arrangement of a garden was quite the opposite in
conception of the formal rectilinear courtyard pavilion arrangement of formal palaces and mansions. Chinese gardens,
like Japanese ones, are miniature versions of nature's way.
The formal geometric gardens of eighteenth-century France
are the exact opposites of the Chinese organic adventures,
which offer surprise after surprise along the winding pathways
that lead one past ever-changing vistas. It is not intended that
the viewer be able to comprehend the whole garden from any
given point. He must journey past the miniature evocation of
mountains, streams, and forests, enjoying each sensation as a
traveler would in the countryside. Osvald Sirén in *Gardens
of China* (pp. 3–13) compares the journey through a Chinese
garden to the viewer's journey through a Chinese hand-scroll
painting of the landscape, which, as it unrolls, has a kind of
cinematic effect.

The garden in the Forbidden City has some of the ideal
characteristics of such a garden, but, in keeping with the overall
rigidity and large scale of the Imperial Palace scheme, it was
not planned with the complete freedom of an organic, curvi-
linear, asymmetrical creation, nor does it contain the intimate
surprises found in smaller gardens. The gardens have many
rock arrangements. Some are enclosed by marble railings
and covered with ivy. Other rockeries are mountainous
settings for pavilions; still another is a great rugged wall with
a fountain. Yet these gardens are denied a sense of mystery
because of the inflexible palace environment. Another treatment of the strangely formed stones may be seen in the northeast corner of the Imperial Palace, in the courtyard outside
the private apartments built by the Ch'ing emperor Ch'ien-
lung (r. 1736–95). Mounted with awesome formality, the
stone is displayed as a piece of nature's finest art (plate 210).
Although its mannered form can be fully admired, in this setting it is robbed of its potential to evoke a mountain.

If we turn from the dignified gardens of the Imperial Palace
to a garden in the old Chinese section of Shanghai, we can see
an example of a Ming city garden built in the spirit of fantasy
so sought after by the literati. The Yü Yüan, a mandarin's
garden (plates 211–218), was built in 1537 by an official and
is similar to the kind of garden in Soochow in which Shen

210. Stone outside the Hall of Repose (Yi-ho-hsüan), Imperial Palace, Peking. Ch'ing dynasty (1644–1912), renovated in the People's Republic. Carved by the forces of wind and water over eons of time, this rock, mounted on a base, is shown as a fascinating and artful achievement of nature.

211–15. The Yü Yüan, Shanghai. 1537
(Ming dynasty), restored 1956.
Right, the top of the wall
undulates like the back of a
writhing dragon. Lions stand guard
at the gateway. Opposite page: a
vase-shaped gate; a garden
pavilion made of lacquered wood,
with marble table and seats; a
two-story pavilion atop a rockery,
giving the effect of a mountain
retreat; a courtyard enclosed
by a roofed gallery with a moon
gate at the right. The Yü Yüan
consists of a series of enclosed
courtyards, each offering new
visual delights, with the
combination of linear elements—
undulating, circular, triangular,
and straight—producing
extremely lively settings.

Chou and his circle drank wine, composed poetry, played music, created and viewed paintings, played chess, and admired specially cultivated flowers. The Yü Yüan followed the city garden formula; built in the heart of a city, sandwiched between crowded buildings, it was shielded from the activity outside by a high wall. Perhaps it was stocked with exotic birds, whose songs drowned out the street noises of hawkers calling their wares.

Once inside the gate, the visitor is enveloped in a fanciful, contemplative environment. A walk through the first pavilion, made of wood lacquered a rich red-brown, leads to a decorative gallery. (plate 213). From this spot one can view the first garden (plate 216), which includes a great rock formation, a small lotus pond, and a covered gallery. The spines of the tiled roof of the gallery and the pavilion turn up at the ends in such a gaily absurd way that they make one laugh aloud. Also, one appreciates that the European creators of chinoiserie were honest men—faithful to the spirit of their models.

A white wall surrounds the garden and provides a perfect backdrop for the baroque rock shapes. The line of black roof tiles on the wall undulates like the back of a great dragon (plate 211). The rockery is not only a mountain with a circuitous path to the summit; it also invites the wanderer into its caverns and grottoes. Then the path leads to a vase-shaped gate (plate 212) through a wall which encloses another section of the garden. Again the wall is a background for fantastic rocks; one fairly restrained arrangement clearly shows the close relationship between Japanese and Chinese gardens. With great economy of elements, a few rocks and a tree suggest a totality of nature. Across the courtyard from this understated group there is the mountainous mass of a second great rockery. A two-story pavilion with humorously curled-up roofs is perched on top of this mountain (plate 214). Other small buildings include a theater.

The path continues through ornamental gates revealing more courtyards with pavilions and lakes, all full of surprises and flights of fancy. The silhouettes of the various elements fairly dance with picturesque exuberance where moon gates, dragon-back walls, and triangular roof lines meet (plate 215). Changes of season are reflected by trees and potted shrubs. In courtyards where there is no water, paving stones are laid in wave patterns.

Just as the gardens have been meticulously restored, so have

216. Lotus pond and *Heroes of the Revolution*, Yü Yüan, Shanghai. Garden, 1537 (Ming dynasty); sculpture, People's Republic, late 1960s/early 1970s. This revolutionary group exemplifies the art ideals of the Cultural Revolution. The rising proletarians are cast cement figures and maintain a color harmony with the rockery.

217. The same lotus pond and rockery as seen above. The revolutionary sculpture group was removed and the rockery restored sometime between 1976 and 1979, during the post-Cultural Revolution political relaxation that deemphasized militant themes in art.

218. Broken-axis stone bridge over a lotus pond, next to the Yü Yüan, Shanghai. The bridge is a remarkable example of the designer's search for the picturesque through the elaboration of form.

219. Garden of a nursery, Shanghai. Billboard: "It is the people, only the people, who are the moving force in the creation of world history."

220. Interior of a living hall, Yü Yüan, Shanghai. 1537 (Ming dynasty), restored 1956. Painting in the style of the Peking Academy, ink and color on paper, People's Republic. Although the garden is full of asymmetrical elements, the living halls were designed with the traditional rectangular definitions common to palace and domestic housing.

the pavilions been refurbished and fitted out with appropriate furniture. Carved openwork grilles frame room sections hung with landscape paintings (plate 220). Marble and ceramic garden seats are used outdoors; carved mahogany chairs and tables indoors. One pavilion, in which visitors may be offered tea by the cadre in charge of the Yü Yüan, is furnished with chairs made from the gnarled roots of elm trees, whose fantastic forms parallel the grotesque rocks outside.

During the Cultural Revolution the entrance pavilion had a large golden statue of Chairman Mao and the large rockery had a cement sculpture group of proletarians breaking their chains. These were the artistic expressions of the heightened political atmosphere. The sculptures in the Socialist Realism style on the rockery expressed the anger of the masses as they emancipated themselves. Because they were made of harmonizing rock-colored cement, they did not totally disrupt the overall Ming ambiance, and they provided an imaginative artistic solution to the political necessity of that time. It was

221. Grand Canal at Yangchow. The original Grand Canal was begun in 610 and ran from Hangchow west to Ch'ang-an (Sian). In the early fifteenth century the Yung-lo Emperor expanded the canal north to Peking. It became the principal food supply route from the south to Peking and remains a major artery.

not enough in the Cultural Revolution years for a garden to be just a garden, it had to display revolutionary vigor.

The relaxation of political pressures since Mao's death can be charted in this garden. The rockery was restored to its Ming concept and the entrance hall has no sculpture of a political leader.

Most Chinese gardens have been depoliticized since 1976. Only a few red billboards with political exhortations remain. Evidently the Communist Party propaganda department now believes that the masses will learn elsewhere that "it is the people, only the people, who are the moving force in the creation of world history." The garden stroller is allowed his own thoughts.

THE CH'ING DYNASTY

PRECEDING PAGE:

222. Bridge at the Summer Palace (I Ho Yüan), K'un-ming Lake, northeast of Peking. Ch'ing dynasty (1644–1912) and People's Republic. Marble, wood, and tile. Of all the imperial monuments around Peking, none is used with more frequency and joy by the masses of China than the Summer Palace.

223. Courtyard of the Hall of Repose (Yi-ho-hsüan), northeast corner of the Imperial Palace, Peking. Ch'ing dynasty (1644–1912). Private apartments used by Ch'ien-lung (r. 1736–1795) and the Empress Dowager Tz'u-hsi in the last half of the nineteenth century.

THE CH'ING, OR MANCHU, DYNASTY (1644–1912) is best remembered for its careful preservation of Confucian culture. As foreign conquerors of China, members of the Ch'ing elite were more self-consciously traditional than native Chinese leaders had ever been. When the Ch'ing rebuilt and redecorated the Imperial Palace (plates 223, 224) and the Temple of Heaven, for example, the restoration was carried out as an extension and elaboration of Ming forms. Yet both have a distinctive Ch'ing spirit.

In the sixteenth and seventeenth centuries, as the Ming government became increasingly paralyzed by imperial irresponsibility and the excesses of eunuch power, uprisings were led by bandits who developed into regional leaders. The leader who established the most effective power base and became most significant to subsequent Chinese history was a Manchu named Nurhachi (1559–1626), a descendant of the Chin dynasty rulers who had dominated north China from 1115 to 1234. Aided by the official Ming policy of sinicizing the barbarians, Nurhachi organized the Manchu clan society into an effective administrative entity in a modified Chinese style. His bureaucratic government included many Chinese, who worked side by side with Manchu clansmen. While he was consolidating his Manchurian territories, Nurhachi also adapted the Mongolian alphabet to develop a written Manchu language. This facilitated administration and made it possible for the Chinese Classics to be translated into Manchu. Nurhachi thus created a highly sophisticated Confucian bureaucracy which he eventually used to rule China.

In 1644 Peking was attacked by a rebel force from western China and threatened by Manchu forces from the northeast. The Ming general in charge chose to ally himself with the Manchus, who were led by one of Nurhachi's sons. Then the Manchus and the Ming army combined to crush the rebels from the west, and a grandson of Nurhachi was set upon the Chinese throne. The barbarian invaders from the northeast took the Chinese dynastic name Ch'ing ("Pure") and conducted traditional Chinese-style government with an ease and skill that came from years of practice before their conquest of China.

The situation had some similarities to the Communist "liberation" of China in 1949. By the time Chairman Mao and his forces gained control of the national government, they had already had over two decades of experience in governing large rural areas. This administrative experience offered invaluable preparation for their nationwide tasks, and its mark can still be seen in the political system of the People's Republic. Here the similarities between Communists and Manchus abruptly ends, however, because, once in control of the national government, the Manchus simply strengthened the existing Confucian system, while the Communists abolished the government of Chiang Kai-shek with an awesome finality and created a new system for controlling China.

Throughout the late seventeenth and the eighteenth centuries China enjoyed peace and prosperity. The Ch'ing emperors of that period were conscientious rulers who governed at least as well as the best of their predecessors in previous dynasties. China remained largely aloof from the world behind a cultural and economic wall built on a belief in her own superiority and self-sufficiency. This attitude was well expressed by Emperor Ch'ien-lung in 1793, when he rebuffed Lord Macartney, whom King George III had sent to the Ch'ing court in an effort to persuade the emperor to expand British trade facilities in China. The emperor told Macartney, "Our celestial empire possesses all things in prolific abundance." Despite the fact that Britain presided over a very different type of imperial system from China's, the Son of Heaven in Peking sought to make Macartney's visit conform to the protocol of the hierarchical East Asian system. Thus the British gifts were labeled "tribute," and court officials tried unsuccessfully to make Macartney prostrate himself before the emperor in the tribute bearer's customary kowtow.

Ch'ien-lung's spurning of George III represented a classic example of pride going before a fall. Within half a century the British began to force China to trade on their terms, and the Opium War of 1839–42 inflicted the first of a series of humiliating military defeats on the "Central Realm." By the mid-nineteenth century China was also suffering grave domestic problems. Swift population growth, natural disasters, official corruption and mismanagement, and economic discontent

224. Hall with throne, Imperial
Palace, Peking. Ming dynasty
(1368–1644), with renovations
and furnishings of the Ch'ing
dynasty (1644–1912), restored in
the People's Republic.
Wooden hall with glass windows;
lacquered and gilt-wood furniture
with brocade upholstery;
gilt-bronze urns. This throne
room is modestly scaled compared
to the elaborately carved
high throne in the Hall of
Supreme Harmony.

stimulated severe internal upheavals, which came to a climax
in the T'aiping Rebellion of 1850–64. Western aid eventually
helped the Ch'ing suppress the T'aipings, but not before another round of Sino-Western conflict had culminated in 1860
in a treaty system that granted the major Western nations
broad trading privileges and extraterritorial rights.

The 1860 treaty negotiations had been marred by an ugly
incident that led to the destruction of Emperor Ch'ien-lung's
favorite palace. Despite the fact that a truce had been declared, the Chinese captured the chief British negotiator and
his entourage and killed twenty members of his group before
releasing him. In retaliation against the emperor, Lord Elgin,
leader of the British forces, ordered his men to sack the Summer Palace, Yüan Ming Yüan, which was located about six
miles northwest of the Peking city wall. They destroyed more
than two hundred buildings. (It was this Lord Elgin's father
who removed the marble carvings known by his name from

225. Balustrade at the Summer Palace. Ch'ing dynasty (1644–1912). Marble.

227. Stage and courtyard, Palace of Virtue and Harmony (Te-ho-yüan), Summer Palace. Ch'ing dynasty (1644–1912), with renovations of the People's Republic. Railing grillwork, metal; gallery, stone and wood. Chinese opera was performed on this platform stage for the Empress Dowager Tz'u-hsi.

228. Aquatic garden in K'un-ming Lake. Balustrade and decorative windows in a covered gallery, Eastern Palaces, Summer Palace. Ch'ing dynasty (1644–1912), with renovations of the People's Republic. From inside the gallery viewers can enjoy the scene through a great variety of window shapes.

229. Stork. Ch'ing dynasty
(1644–1912). Gold, gems, and
pearls. Shown at the Hall of
Happiness and Longevity
(Le-shou-t'ang), Imperial
Palace, Peking. The Empress
Dowager Tz'u-hsi especially
coveted delicate sculptures made
of precious metal and stones.
On her birthday many treasures
like this one were presented
to her.

and K'un-ming Lake is a favorite spot for swimming and boat-ing in the summer and skating in the winter. Huge crowds of vacationing Chinese pour into the previously exclusive imperi-al hideaway. Compared to the rigid geometric plan of the Forbidden City, the overall layout of the Summer Palace is rambling and informal. Solitary gazebos and palace complex-es follow the contours of the shoreline and ascending hills in order to take advantage of lovely vistas. Yet it is interesting to note that individual palace buildings were subjected to the same rigid geometry as that seen in the Forbidden City. Even the yellow-orange tiles in the Forbidden City are found again in the pavilion roofs of the Summer Palace (plate 226). Besides elaborate living quarters, there are facilities for various diver-sions. Decorated walkways, viewing pavilions, gardens, ele-gant courtyards, and a stage for theatrical performances (plate 227) indicate some of the imperial recreations. The Empress Dowager watched presentations of Chinese opera from a pa-vilion across the courtyard from the stage, and it is said that she herself occasionally appeared in these theatricals masked as the Buddhist Goddess of Mercy, Kuan-yin.

Another favorite activity of the Empress Dowager was col-lecting jewels. At the Summer Palace there is a sumptuous dis-play of birthday presents received by her, including rows of pot landscapes made of jade, garnet, amethyst, lapis, tur-quoise, and other semiprecious stones. Among the many items at an exhibition of imperial treasure at the Imperial Palace in Peking there is a small golden stork, cloaked in pearls, that carries a jeweled branch in its beak (plate 229).

Evidently the Empress Dowager enjoyed power as much as she did jewelry. Originally the consort of Emperor Hsien-feng, after his death in 1861 she and his brother, Prince Kung, seized power under the nominal reign of her son, the new boy-emperor. Histories tell how she dominated her son, and gossip has it that she encouraged the excesses which caused his pre-mature death in 1875 at the age of nineteen. She then success-fully connived to have her four-year-old nephew appointed Emperor Kuang-hsü. This was unprecedented, since he was of the same generation as his predecessor and therefore could not properly fulfill the ritual obligations of filial piety that each emperor owed the previous one. The Empress Dowager's bold maneuvering enabled her to continue to dominate the court for another fourteen years until Kuang-hsü's maturity brought about her retirement in 1889.

Japan's stunning defeat of her traditional big brother, China, in 1894–95 seemed to signal the impending division of China by the imperialist powers. "Self-strengthening" had proved to be too little and too late. Thus a more radical group of Chinese reformers sought to persuade Kuang-hsü to adopt a program of profound change, comparable to that implemented by Meiji Japan a generation earlier. But most of the reforms of the "Hundred Days" of 1898 were short-lived, for they provoked an ultraconservative reaction in the form of a coup d'etat by the Empress Dowager against her nephew. Thereafter she kept Kuang-hsü a palace prisoner for the last ten years of his life, and it is said that she even forced his favorite concubine to drown herself in a well in the Forbidden City. Mysteriously, he predeceased the Empress Dowager by one day, in 1908. Although contemporary guides show some embarrassment when the subject of concubinage is brought up, the cruel death of Emperor Kuang-hsü's beloved is mentioned crisply as another example of the evils rampant in pre-Communist China.

Only after the failure of the so-called Boxer Rebellion of 1900—actually a war against the foreign powers, in which imperial troops joined forces with a xenophobic mass movement—did the Empress Dowager grudgingly support many of the reforms she had previously frustrated. But even the broad program of political, administrative, legal, fiscal, educational, military, and other changes that was launched during the next decade and that promised eventually to produce a self-governing constitutional monarchy could not save the tottering Manchus. They, and indeed the millennial imperial system, were engulfed by a rising tide of Chinese nationalism that culminated in the revolution of 1911 and the establishment of the Republic of China.

The Ch'ing were great patrons of the arts, including that of ceramics, which came to be well known in the West. Although Sung wares have been preferred by the cognoscenti of the twentieth century, generations of Westerners prized Ch'ing wares.

During the seventeenth century, the ceramics industry was reorganized and was enthusiastically patronized by the court, affluent Chinese, and the foreign market. Although Ch'ing ceramics may lack true originality, they exhibit inventiveness in the handling of materials and glazing, superb execution, elegance, refinement, and charm. If, on the one hand, Ch'ing potters re-created or elaborated on old designs, on the other

230. Shells. Ch'ien-lung (r. 1736–1795), Ch'ing dynasty. Porcelain, enamel glazes. Shown at the Ceramic Exhibition, Imperial Palace, Peking. The potter observed these shells so carefully and crafted them so skillfully that even fishermen could be fooled.

hand their glazed hues introduced intensity, subtlety, and novelty. No form or color seems to have been too difficult for them to make.

Indeed, the remarkable realism they achieved makes many of their objects masterpieces of trompe l'oeil. Several such examples from the eighteenth century are shown in the Imperial Palace's ceramics exhibition. There are some ceramic shells (plate 230) and a circular ceramic box (plate 231) made to look like lacquered wood. The shells look so real that it is hard to believe they are not organic. The ceramic box fools the eye because it looks so convincingly like the kind of carved lacquer that enjoyed great popularity in Ch'ing times. The box is actually painted with lacquer, while the colors of the shells come from overglaze enamels. Two other examples of ceramics masquerading as natural objects are a decorative duck (plate 232) and a leaf dish (plate 233). The feathers and down of the duck, its shiny beak, and webbed feet are all treated with the utmost realism. The incised and sculptured decoration and slick glazes are extremely skillful. The pose has a distinctly duck-like quality. The delicately formed leaf plate, tied with a single flower and some leaves, evokes a pleasantly romantic image. Both duck and leaf are colored with overglaze enamels.

Critics have attacked this kind of technical tour de force, pointing out that trickery, rather than revelation of the innate potential of the material, was its goal. They call these things "kitsch"—stylish objects without artistic value. Yet these ob-

231. Box with cover. Ch'ien-lung (r. 1736–1795), Ch'ing dynasty. Porcelain with lacquer. Shown at the Ceramic Exhibition, Imperial Palace, Peking. The potter plays a joke on the maker of carved lacquer with a deceptive porcelain imitation.

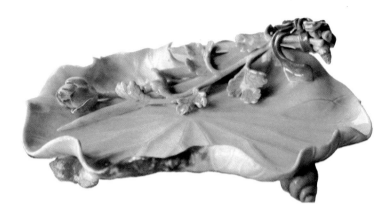

233. Leaf dish. Ch'ien-lung (r. 1736–1795), Ch'ing dynasty. Porcelain with enamel glazes. Shown at the Ceramic Exhibition, Imperial Palace, Peking.

232. Duck. Ch'ien-lung (r. 1736–1795), Ch'ing dynasty. Porcelain with enamel glazes. Shown at the Ceramic Exhibition, Imperial Palace, Peking. No detail of this quacking duck has been overlooked to assure its authenticity in clay.

jects do document China's cultural history and are evidence of a ceramics technology so fully developed that virtually anything could be represented.

The Chinese artist has always had remarkable rapport with the natural world. The Ch'ing potter continued to use animal, vegetable, and mineral objects as his models, regardless of the shift in presentation from abstract decorative to specific descriptive or sculptural forms. He reproduced natural forms for functional decorative objects, including tableware; rests for the head, arm, or wrist; hat racks; head scratchers; hairpins; earrings; cosmetic and scent boxes; incense burners; snuff bottles; palettes; ink rests; water droppers; brush and chopstick holders; chopsticks; scroll mounts; book stands; paperweights; candle snuffers; oil lamps; rice and tea spoons; fish bowls; washbasins; and garden seats. The few examples we can show only hint at the broad range of Ch'ing ceramics production, which includes high-fired, brilliant, monochrome wares of deep intensity, such as the copper reds, cobalt blues, iron-oxide celadon greens, browns, and blacks. Firing at medium temperatures yielded monochrome wares in rich yellows, greens, purples, and turquoises. In addition to these intense hues, the Ch'ing potters developed subtler ones, including the "peachbloom" pinks and *"clair-de-lune"* pale blues and greens. They were also able to re-create the earlier Sung wares so perfectly that sometimes even connoisseurs cannot distinguish between the two.

The Ch'ing kilns continued to produce prolific amounts of the blue-and-white and enameled wares so popular in the Ming. Some monochrome wares were exported to the West, but the blue-and-white and enameled wares were in the greatest demand. These ceramics, modified in terms of pattern, color, size, and shape to suit the taste of the European market, were decorated with pictures of graceful willow trees, arching bridges, moon-faced maidens, pigtailed mandarins, and pavilions. They transmitted a vision of "Cathay" to the West, and for European scholars who had read the writings of Confucius translated by the Jesuits in seventeenth-century China, the imagery on porcelain was visual documentation of the harmonious society they imagined China to be.

But as the eighteenth century drew to a close, the European vision of an ideal China faded for a number of reasons. When the foreign powers were unsuccessful in obtaining increased trade concessions from China, they became hostile and aggressive. More Europeans went to China seeking the land of their dreams, only to discover that the "land of porcelain" did not exist. Rather, China was full of injustice, poverty, and tyranny. Chinese export porcelains themselves lost some of their uniqueness, because the rapidly expanding European porcelain industry could now supply a reasonable facsimile of the new "essential" household items.

The end of Emperor Ch'ien-lung's rule in 1795 marked the beginning of the decline of the Manchu dynasty. The most creative period of Ch'ing ceramics had ended even earlier. After the mid-eighteenth century there seemed to be no artistic giants to replace the earlier great directors of the imperial kilns. Production continued, of course, but the Chinese potter of the nineteenth and twentieth centuries carried on the norms established before 1750, endlessly remaking the same garden seats, flowerpots, tea sets, vases, bureau sets, figurines, and curios for the court, the Chinese elite, and the export market.

Ch'ing and Communist art forms interestingly mirror the differences between the two regimes. Because the Manchus consciously followed Confucian orthodoxy, their art forms were an extension, a paraphrase, and an elaboration of traditional Ming forms. The Communists, by contrast, imported the foreign style of Soviet Communism and borrowed only selectively from Chinese tradition. They are still struggling to find new and truly revolutionary art forms to express the spirit of their ideology.

THE REPUBLIC OF
CHINA

234. Henry K. Murphy designed this water-pumping facility cloaked in pagoda-like exterior. Peking University (formerly Yenching University). Republican period (1912–1949).

◄235. Narrow street in the old city of Shanghai.

THE REVOLUTION of 1911 proved to be as limited as it was nonviolent. On January 1, 1912, the Republic of China was proclaimed and the monarchy toppled soon after. The revolutionaries shared a desire to rid China of foreign control and to establish some kind of parliamentary system based on political parties, and they recognized the need for a strong leader to replace the deposed emperor in maintaining the fragile unity of the country. Beyond that, however, there was little agreement among them. What kind of political ideology should be substituted for the hierarchical, authoritarian ethics of Confucianism? What kind of parliamentary system should succeed imperial rule, once governmental power derived from the Chinese people rather than from the "mandate of heaven"? What public ceremonies should symbolize and sustain the newly proclaimed values and institutions? These and many other fundamental questions had to be answered in detail if China were to create a new order and avert civil war, chaos, and further foreign intervention. All twentieth-century Chinese leaders have had to confront these questions.

Unfortunately for Sun Yat-sen and the other first-generation revolutionaries who attempted to establish a parliamentary democracy, Yüan Shih-k'ai, the experienced military leader and administrator whom they selected to bind the country together, quickly exercised his powers as president to suspend parliamentary activity and install himself as dictator. The politicians lacked the military force to resist, but Yüan lacked the vision necessary to create a new polity, and he gradually revived some of the governmental practices of the Manchus. Just before his death in 1916, he vainly sought to install himself as emperor.

From Yüan's death until the establishment of a national government by Chiang Kai-shek in 1928, China experienced the lowest point in its recent political history. While a succession of governments in Peking continued to represent China abroad and to maintain a facade of parliamentary government at home, political power in the country actually became more fragmented than ever. Disagreements in the Peking parliament led to the establishment of a rival parliament in Canton, and in both north and south the different contending groups sought to enlist the aid of locally based military leaders known as "warlords." In an effort to expand the areas under their control, these warlords, the real holders of power in their individual regions, alternately struggled against and cooperated with one another and with various politicians in endless and confusing wars and intrigues. Although they experimented with a variety of political institutions in attempting to legitimize their rule, these militarists failed to win the support of the Chinese people, who suffered greatly during this era not only from wars but also from banditry, oppressive taxation, inflation, economic disruptions, decline in public services, and a plenitude of opium.

Adding to China's humiliation, and especially felt by the increasingly nationalistic urban populace, was the expanding foreign interference in China's affairs. Warlordism had disabled the Republic and prevented it from regaining Tibet and Outer Mongolia, which had come under British and Soviet influence, respectively, after the fall of the Manchus. The successive governments in Peking followed the example of Yüan Shih-k'ai and the Manchus by borrowing huge sums abroad on terms that gave foreigners ever greater control over China's administration. Foreign banks were able to make or break governments by granting or denying cooperation. Foreign nationals were not subject to Chinese law. Moreover, in the chaotic conditions of the day, foreign enclaves in port cities and foreign spheres of influence in many parts of China assumed greater and greater importance.

Yet the decline in China's fortunes, the fragmentation of authority, and the impact of foreign ideas were combined with rapid social and economic changes in the cities, creating great political, intellectual, and artistic ferment. Individualism, democracy, egalitarianism, liberalism, populism, feminism, anarchism, nationalism, anti-imperialism, socialism, Marxism-Leninism, and a host of other ideas competed for acceptance among a new generation of politicians, administrators, businessmen, factory workers, teachers, and students, who were searching for an ideology and a political program to replace discredited Confucianism and monarchy. As the 1920s wore on, the reunification of China and the termination of foreign privileges became the dominant themes that united these diverse groups. Marxism-Leninism proved attractive to some intellectuals, because it not only offered a comprehensive "scientific" explanation of societal development and of China's backwardness in particular but also presented a specific program of action whereby a small, highly disciplined elite could seize power, as had recently happened in Russia. Yet many others were put off by the Marxist-Leninist call for socializing the means of production and mobilizing the masses of workers and peasants in a class struggle against the landlord and bourgeois classes. Thus, the new revolutionary forces that coalesced in south China—first under Sun Yat-sen and, after Sun's death in 1925, under his military aide, Chiang Kai-shek, and other leaders—reorganized their Nationalist Party (Kuomintang or KMT) under the more inclusive banners of nationalism and anti-imperialism.

Nevertheless, during the mid-1920s the Kuomintang cooperated closely with Soviet Russia; with Moscow's international instrument, the Comintern; and with members of the small Chinese Communist Party (CCP), which had been founded in 1921. After his pleas for help were rejected by the Western powers, Sun turned to Lenin for assistance in creating both a modern army and a political organization capable of seizing power and governing. He sent Chiang Kai-shek to the Soviet Union to study Soviet methods, and Soviet advisers in China helped to restructure the Nationalist Party apparatus along Leninist lines. Although the vague revolutionary ideology which Sun created—the "Three Principles of the People" (nationalism, political democracy, and people's welfare)—differed from Marxism, these advisers also aided Chiang in establishing a military academy for indoctrinating the KMT "party army" in Sun's ideology. By way of illustrating the collaboration of individual Chinese Communists with the KMT, as well as the amazing longevity of China's revolutionary leaders, we should note that half a century ago Chou En-lai served as deputy head of the political-education department of Chiang's military academy and that Mao Tse-tung had even earlier played a modest role in coordinating the efforts of the CCP and KMT party organizations.

Sun Yat-sen's program called for the implementation of his "Three Principles of the People" in three stages: first, military reunification of the country and termination of foreign control; then, political tutelage by a Kuomintang-led state; and finally, after the people were capable of self-government, constitutional democracy. In mid-1926 the Kuomintang army

236. Stairway to Sun Yat-sen's tomb,
Nanking. Built 1926–29. China's
foremost revolutionary of the
early twentieth century died in
1925, a time when the KMT
and the Communists were
cooperating in a united
revolutionary effort. Thus he is
still given full honors by the
Communists, even though he
was the founder of the KMT.

237. Looking down from Sun
Yat-sen's tomb. Its plan is
reminiscent of royal tombs: two
ceremonial gateways lead to a
blue-tiled pavilion for the
commemorative stele and then
up a great stairway to the
blue-roofed tomb itself.

under Chiang Kai-shek initiated stage one by launching from Canton the famous Northern Expedition, which was designed to end the era of warlord rule and to reunify the country. The following summer Chiang, having gained control of central China and Shanghai, and having united the left and right wings of the KMT, purged the Communist elements from its ranks. The CCP leaders who were not killed either went into hiding in the cities or fled to remote rural areas, from which they carried on what became a civil war against the KMT. Having gained the support of the business community by its harsh rejection of social revolution, the KMT established a new central government for China, with its capital at Nanking. In 1928 Chiang brought nominal unity to the country by marching north to take Peking (which he renamed Peiping) and by forging uneasy alliances with the warlords of the north, including the "Young Marshal," Chang Hsüeh-liang, who had inherited control of Manchuria from his warlord father. Chiang then announced the completion of Sun Yat-sen's first stage and the beginning of the new period of political tutelage.

Despite its continuing concerns about Communist rebellion, Japanese invasion, and warlord defection, from 1928 until Japan unleashed all-out aggression in 1937 the Nanking government, in addition to developing a professional national army, made a great effort to modernize the country and to eliminate the symbols of foreign domination. By adapting Western models to China's circumstances, it sought to implement many of the recently imported social and economic ideas without wholly abandoning Confucian values. Following the precedent set by Japan, it promulgated a European-style, comprehensive set of law codes that went a long way, for example, toward abolishing the worst abuses of the traditional family system and legitimizing the new conceptions of individualism, equality of the sexes, and emancipation of the younger generation. These codes also embodied many Western procedural and substantive protections of the individual against the arbitrary encroachments of the state. Nanking gradually extended the reach of its laws to more and more foreigners as it successfully pressed the lesser powers to surrender their extraterritorial privileges, and it regained control over its tariff schedules and the administration of its customs, salt revenues, and postal system. It coupled with this a series of fiscal and economic measures that unified China's currency and strengthened national finances, and it expanded the trans-

233

portation system and industrial base. In education, as in legal, social, and economic matters, various reforms were introduced, largely under the influence of Western-trained Chinese.

Western education, science, literature, and thought appeared to dominate China, and Christianity continued to make inroads as Chiang Kai-shek himself became a Methodist. Chiang had converted to Methodism in 1927 in order to persuade Mrs. Charles Soong, matriarch of the formidable Soong family, to permit him to marry her beautiful third daughter, Mei-ling. Mrs. Soong, whose oldest daughter Ching-ling was the widow of Sun Yat-sen and whose Harvard-educated son T.V. was a prominent financier-politician, had been reluctant to approve Mei-ling's marriage to the famous general, not only because he had fathered two sons by a peasant woman and kept many concubines, but also because she regarded him as a heathen. When Chiang agreed to dismiss the concubines and embrace Christianity, marriage to Mei-ling, a politically ambitious graduate of Wellesley College, became possible. The influence of this marriage on Chiang has been aptly summarized by his biographer, Robert Payne (*Chiang Kai-shek*, p. 137):

> He who had always been obstinate became more obstinate; and his intolerance fed on the more intolerant chapters of the Bible. The daily readings under the tutelage of his wife and Christian missionaries had the effect of confirming his belief in his mission, and it seems never to have occurred to him that he was removing himself further and further from an understanding of the real forces that moved the Chinese people. He was to enter the most fateful years of his career armed with a Bible and with a wife who had spent the greater part of her life in America and within the foreign concession in Shanghai.

Strong Western influence, combined with ineffective organization, virtually guaranteed the superficiality of this new phase of the Chinese revolution. Republican reformers were often more familiar with Western conditions than they were with those in their own countryside. They were an urban elite that concentrated on transforming the cities, where Western models had at least some relevance. Having decided to forgo social revolution and mobilization of the peasantry, the new national government allocated too few of its scarce resources to implementing programs for raising agricultural productivity and overcoming rural illiteracy. Moreover, even in the mod-

238. View of the Wu-sung (or Soochow) River in Shanghai. Buildings in a variety of foreign styles were built in the Republican period for administrative and domestic purposes in the concession areas of Shanghai.

ern sector, the effort to carry out political tutelage by gradually putting proclaimed Western democratic principles into practice left much to be desired. Instead of guiding the country toward constitutional self-government, Chiang Kai-shek, who had skillfully maneuvered himself into command of the KMT and the government as well as the army, moved steadily in the direction of establishing a dictatorship that refused to tolerate the growth of genuinely autonomous legal institutions and safeguards of individual liberty similar to those of advanced Western countries.

As an authoritative history puts it: "Despite the end of the monarchy two decades earlier, Chinese politics still required a single power-holder at the top to give final answers, which neither a presidium nor a balance of constitutional powers could supply" (John K. Fairbank, Edwin O. Reischauer, Albert M. Craig, *East Asia: Tradition and Transformation*, p. 788). Within the areas controlled by his regime, Chiang's power was limited not by the restraints of constitutionalism but by the need to balance his personal bureaucratic machine in the army, party, and government against regional or rival groups.

235

Because of the unceasing military challenges of the Communists, the Japanese, and the warlords, the influence of the military over the Nanking government became increasingly pronounced, and military expenditures, unchecked by civilian authority, did much to undermine official budgetary reforms. After the fall of Manchuria in 1931, the need to court allies for China's defense against Japan gradually blunted the Nationalists' determination to put an end to the "unequal treaty" privileges still enjoyed by Britain, France, and the United States, for this would have reduced the stake of those powers in the continuing existence of the Republic.

If progress toward reunification and modernization of the country proved to be modest during the decade of the Nanking government, it proved to be impossible after Japan's massive attack on China in 1937. Survival became the overriding concern of the Nationalist government, which was forced to move its capital to Chungking, far up the Yangtze River in the southwestern province of Szechwan, as Japanese forces occupied the vital coastal areas. Wartime pressures increased the regime's conservatism and its militaristic character, runaway inflation decimated the civil service and nourished corruption, and increasing political controls over the universities and suppression of dissent further diminished the intellectuals' support of the KMT. Although Japan's invasion and the Nationalists' retreat to the hinterland gave the regime an opportunity to mobilize the peasantry under the patriotic banner of national resistance, the government concentrated instead on a modest amount of conventional military warfare.

It was the Chinese Communist Party which took full advantage of wartime conditions. In the areas it governed it organized the peasants in the name of resistance to Japan and thereby won their allegiance. In 1937 the Communists and Nationalists had agreed to suspend their civil war in favor of a "united front" against Japan under Chiang Kai-shek; but the veneer of their cooperation soon wore thin, the Nationalists intensified their blockade of the Communists' mountain stronghold in Yenan, and each side sought to emerge from the war in a stronger position for the ultimate contest for power. While waging guerrilla warfare against the Japanese, the Communists expanded their many rural base areas to such an extent that by 1945 they could claim that they governed more than 90 million people.

After the end of World War II, in an attempt to stave off renewal of the Nationalist-Communist civil war, both the

United States and the Soviet Union sought to persuade the rivals to agree on a coalition government. These efforts proved unsuccessful. Although the Nationalists had been weakened politically and economically by the anti-Japanese struggle, their possession of vast quantities of American weapons and much larger armies made them confident of their ability to dispose of the Communists by military means. Yet, plagued by poor leadership, inflation, corruption, and jealousies, and lacking an ideology that could revitalize a weary and demoralized people, the Nationalists proved surprisingly vulnerable to the guerrilla warfare strategy that the Communists had perfected against the Japanese. Mao Tse-tung, whose genius lay in perceiving the revolutionary potential of China's million villages and in adapting Marxist-Leninist theory and practice to rural Chinese conditions, mobilized the countryside to surround the cities, gradually forcing them to surrender by cutting off their communications, and thereby acquiring more and more men and equipment for the final decisive battles. By October 1, 1949, the Communists controlled enough of the nation to justify their proclamation of the People's Republic of China, and not long afterward Chiang Kai-shek and a portion of his army, government, and followers fled from the mainland to the island refuge of Taiwan.

By the end of the Ch'ing dynasty in 1912, a limited number of Western-style structures had been built on Chinese soil. The Summer Palace, Yüan Ming Yüan, remained in ruins, but there were scores of Baroque villas with arcaded verandas and Neoclassical porticoes (plates 239, 240), designed by foreigners in "treaty ports" such as Canton. This architecture is called "colonial-style" because it was the mode generally used abroad by European nations that acquired colonies or spheres of influence from the seventeenth into the nineteenth century. There were also the railroad stations built in the International Railway Style of the late nineteenth and early twentieth centuries—a kind of Victorian stone-and-iron creation. As the foreign powers enlarged their interests in China during the Republican period, more Western-style buildings were erected (plate 238), and high-rise hotels arose along the waterfronts of Canton and Shanghai and near the Forbidden City in Peking. Administrative structures in the foreign-concession areas of the treaty ports, as well as a few Chinese official buildings, reflected the imported architectural vogue with little attempt to adapt Western styles to Chinese form or spirit.

239. Mansion on Sha-mien Island,
Canton (Kwangchow).
Nineteenth century. In 1861
the Chinese were forced to grant
Sha-mien Island to Britain and
France as concession areas. Both
countries built administrative
buildings, houses, churches, and
clubs on the island, which is
separated from the city by a
canal and accessible by only two
bridges. Handsome colonial-
style villas line the stately main
street, a wide avenue laid out
like a formal European
parkway, and huge shade trees
make the river front cool and
appealing in the hottest
weather. Although it has been
many years since European
imperialists have inhabited
Sha-mien, their former presence
lingers on through the
architecture and city plan.

240. Mansion on Sha-mien Island,
Canton (Kwangchow).
Nineteenth century. The facade
combines Baroque stone
rustication on the ground floor
with Neoclassical columns,
pediments, garlands, and
wreaths above. The Baroque
base and protruding balconies
are characteristic of colonial-style
architecture.

Considering the influence of Oriental design in Europe from the seventeenth century on, the aggressively foreign character of Western-style buildings in China seems ironic. In the twentieth century there were some modest attempts to synthesize Western and Chinese styles, and it is interesting that the two examples shown here were built by missionaries and philanthropists with a commitment to improve the lot of the Chinese. Their interest in accommodating to the Chinese spirit was far greater than that of foreign commercial firms. Like the Buddhist evangelists of an earlier era, who adapted their forms to make them more acceptable and understandable to the Chinese, some Western educators sought to give their buildings a Chinese identity. Designed by Western architects and combining Western and Chinese materials and techniques, the buildings of Peking University (formerly Yenching University; plates 234, 242), Nanking University (plate 243), and the Capital Hospital (formerly Peking Union Medical College; plate 244) possess a new spirit.

The Peking University Library is a rectangular building with a tiled roof supported by columns, as in traditional Chinese architecture. However, the columns are set into plastered walls that enclose the interior space in the Western manner. Western windows are screened with Chinese grillwork; decorative bracketing is made as if it supported the Chinese curving roof, which has gable ends and a traditional parade of guardians. Although the plan and details reflect some continuity with traditional Chinese structures, the proportions and scale, as well as the plastered walls that divide interior space from exterior environment, make the building Western, rather than Chinese. In Chinese halls of similar plan, a continuous relationship is maintained between indoors and outdoors by means of screened window-walls. Moreover, the carved-wood-and-glass walls of the Chinese hall appear light in comparison with the heaviness of solid plaster in the Western style. Even such an enormous hall as the Hall of the Preservation of Harmony, in the Imperial Palace, appears to be lighter than the smaller University Library. Another building at Peking University, the water-pumping facility, reveals no attempt to synthesize its elements. The mechanism is simply cloaked in a pagoda-like exterior—a charming masquerade.

In a relatively more successful commingling of Chinese and Western styles, the Peking Capital Hospital was built around a U-shaped courtyard. It has brick walls, sweeping green-tiled roofs with parading guardians, and a marble court with balus-

241. Church of England on Sha-mien Island, Canton (Kwangchow). Nineteenth century. Drawing on an old Christian architectural tradition, this Victorian Gothic church was doubtless as reassuring to the foreigners who worshiped there as it must have been puzzling to the Chinese who saw it.

trades carved somewhat more simply than those of the imperial monuments. Perhaps this hospital complex comes off better than the Peking University Library because the courtyard size, the levels joined by stairs, the sweeping roof lines, and the three blocks of the buildings are related in a unified composition and scale. The plan is congenial to either a Chinese palace or a Western villa with wings.

In the West, each generation in recent centuries has had, to some degree, a romance with Oriental images and ideas. Following the chinoiserie wave of the seventeenth and eighteenth centuries, Chinese and Indian forms were among the elements that made nineteenth-century Victorian "wedding-cake" architecture so picturesque. As the Impressionists and Postimpressionists of the last half of the nineteenth century were indebted to Japanese wood-block prints for new artistic resolutions of color, design, and perspective, so the creators of Art Nouveau, a few years later, were inspired by Oriental flower designs in their search for organic forms. In the twentieth century, some of the practitioners of the International Style of architecture employed Chinese and Japanese decorative arts to evoke an exotically elegant ambience. They borrowed such occasional elements from the East as the moon gates used in "1930s modern" and the sweeping roof lines of Frank Lloyd Wright's "Prairie houses" of the first decade of the twentieth century. In addition, modern architects became aware of the Oriental method of interpenetrating interior and exterior spaces. The glass curtain-walls of the modern house articulate this spatial concept. One can only mourn that the People's Republic of China has embraced the foreign formula of Socialist Realism instead of pursuing the spirit of Chinese architecture in the modern idiom.

The art of the Republican period reflects the eclectic search of Chinese intellectuals of the day, who sought the best ways to help China gain a respected place in the world community. During the last years of the nineteenth century and the first two decades of the twentieth, many Chinese went to Japan to learn a variety of disciplines from their progressive, rapidly modernizing neighbor. For Chinese art students, the Tokyo Fine Art School provided an opportunity to study Western painting, and some artists returned to China to teach and paint in the French Beaux-Arts style that they had learned in Japan. Most Chinese artists during this period, however, did not look to Western painting but continued in the tradition of their forebears with ink and paper, paraphrasing older paint-

240

242. Library, Peking University (formerly Yenching University). Republican period (1912–1949). Designed by Henry K. Murphy.

243. A professor passes a field of poppies in bloom on his way to class at Nanking University.

244. Signs: top, "Long live the unconquerable thought of Mao Tse-tung"; over door, "Serve the people"; gate, "Capital Hospital."

ings or attempting to find new expressions in the old medium. Disaffection with Japan, culminating in the May 4th Movement of 1919, directed the student flow toward Europe. Would-be artists went to Paris, where they led bohemian lives in Montmartre and were caught up in the many currents of European art, and some of them re-created a bohemian environment when they returned to Shanghai. Imperial patronage was a thing of the past, and the returned artists were alienated from the new officialdom. A small group carried on an isolated pursuit of "art for art's sake," following European models, but this movement was an intellectual and spiritual escape that hardly left a mark on Chinese art.

While painters groped for new ways to express themselves, Chinese writers succeeded in effecting a literary revolution. Hu Shih, who had been a Chinese graduate student in America, spearheaded the cause. In an article published in 1917 in a Chinese literary magazine, he called for a direct vernacular style of writing to replace the highly illusionistic, arcane writ-

242

245. A Christian church in a cityscape of Canton (Kwangchow).

ten language of the classically educated Confucian scholar. How could China modernize if even literate Chinese could not communicate in an understandable written language?

Lu Hsün (plate 246) was the literary giant of the 1920s. Writing in the new vernacular style, with sardonic wit and factual accuracy, he exposed the injustices of Chinese society and gave full expression to his disgust with the seemingly hopeless quagmire that the social system had become. He was celebrated by all literary and political reformers. However, by 1929, after Chiang Kai-shek's Nationalist Party had failed to end the oppression of the old society, Lu Hsün became confirmed in his Marxian beliefs. He had already created the short stories on which his fame rests. Thereafter, until his death in 1936, he wrote only Communist polemics and translations of Soviet literary theory. Following the Soviet example, he, like Mao Tse-tung, promoted the use of the arts as a political vehicle. He especially emphasized the political value of literature and of wood-block prints, both of which could be

243

246. *Portrait of Lu Hsün,* in the
Socialist Realism style.
People's Republic. Oil on
canvas. Shown at the Peking
Art Exhibition Center in
the People's Art Exhibition
Commemorating the Thirtieth
Anniversary of Chairman
Mao's Yenan "Talks on Art
and Literature," 1972.

cheaply produced for mass dissemination. However, even
though the Communists made Lu Hsün a revolutionary hero,
they specifically excluded his style as a model for revolutionary writing. There is no place in their mass-directed propaganda for subtle satire or sarcasm. Rather, they use large and
positive imagery that lacks the gray shadings of life's irony.
The Communist's stock-in-trade in art and literature is based
on parables of oppression and class struggle that end with
victory for the Communist cause. The legacy of Chinese art,
ancient and modern, native and foreign, was to be molded
into the image in which People's China wants to see herself.

CONTEMPORARY CHINA

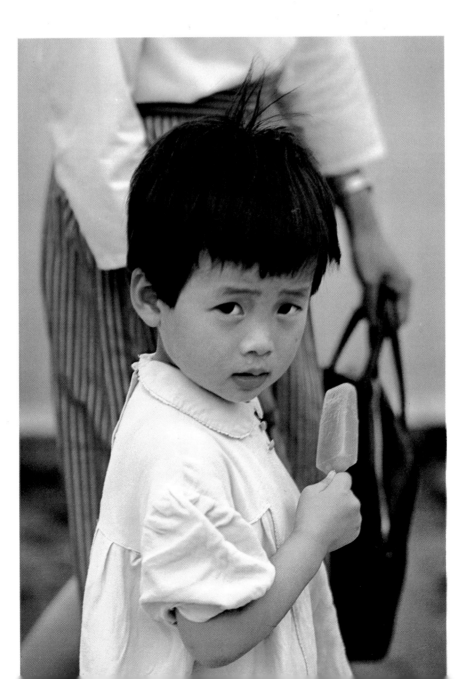

PRECEDING PAGE:

247. Peking girl cools off with a popsicle. There are approximately as many children under fourteen in China as there are people in the Soviet Union. Chinese children are as attractive and charming as those of any country, yet China's burgeoning population—well over a billion—is one of the factors in Soviet anxieties about a "Yellow Peril."

◄248. Peking boy. In youth lie the hopes of China's leaders—and their fears. Will young people become worthy revolutionary successors to Chairman Mao? Or will they become "revisionists" and succumb to what Maoists call the "sugar-coated bullets of the bourgeoisie"?

"WE ARE A DEVELOPING COUNTRY." The visitor to China often hears these words. To the uninitiated, they may seem a boast, a simple assertion of China's continuing progress. Actually, however, they reflect traditional Chinese modesty, euphemistically expressing the poverty and backwardness that confront "People's China" even after so many years of revolutionary rule. Rather than merely a slogan designed to identify China with the "Third World" countries of Asia, Africa, and Latin America instead of with the two "super powers" and the other industrialized nations, the statement represents a fact of Chinese life—perhaps the most important fact that anyone seeking to understand China should keep in mind.

Despite her ancient civilization, the China over which Mao Tse-tung and his followers seized power in 1949 shared most of the problems of the other underdeveloped countries of the world. Over 80 percent of the population was engaged in agriculture. Farming was undercapitalized, land ownership rather highly concentrated, and the bulk of the peasantry very poor. The industrial base was small; highways, railroads, and other means of communication were minimal; schools, sanitary facilities, and hospitals were limited. The government bureaucracy was swollen. Illiteracy was high, the people lacked a common spoken language, regional differences were marked, and national minorities had been imperfectly integrated into the dominant society. Although much the same could be said about many other countries, China, because of her population—the world's largest—and her vast land mass, suffered this syndrome of underdevelopment on an extraordinary scale. Moreover, nature has often been cruel to China. Floods, droughts, pests, and other disasters have regularly exacted their toll. In addition, by 1949 man-made calamities had left the country in unusually bad straits. Decades of civil war and foreign invasion had wrought unimaginable devastation and had been followed by astronomic inflation, widespread unemployment, disrupted trade, deterioration in public works, and endemic corruption. Hunger, disease, crime, prostitution, and opium had become the hallmarks of a largely demoralized population.

Even though the Chinese people had lived together in the same territory for thousands of years and shared a common culture, written language, and political tradition, many observers wondered whether any government could reunify the country, transform it into a modern nation, and make China a strong and respected member of the international community. This is the task that the Chinese Communist regime set for itself. Its ideology, organization, strategy, and tactics have all been designed to meet this challenge.

Looking at the busy yet seemingly relaxed people in both city and countryside, the visitor to China in recent years has found it difficult to escape a static view of Chinese society. Can these be the same people who witnessed the process of replacing the Kuomintang-landlord-bourgeois elite and semi-Confucian value system with a Communist Party, government, and ideology? Do they remember the Party-led mass movements of the early 1950s against counterrevolutionaries, landlords, bureaucrats, businessmen, and intellectuals? What had they thought of "Socialist transformation" of industry, commerce, and agriculture in the mid-1950s? How had they fared in the nationwide mobilization of manpower that was the Great Leap Forward and in the economic depression that followed? What role had they played in the turmoil of the Great Proletarian Cultural Revolution? It is even more difficult to keep in mind that the people one sees and meets continue to be engaged in the dynamic revolutionary process that began to gather momentum at the end of the nineteenth century and moved into high gear with the establishment of the People's Republic in 1949.

Economic Reconstruction and Political Consolidation (1949-52)

The events of the past thirty-five years in China must seem bewildering to many Chinese as well as to the "China-watcher." Viewed from the present, they can be said to have occurred in roughly eight stages. The period 1949–52 was a time of economic reconstruction and consolidation of political control. The Party, which had previously ruled widely dispersed, largely rural "liberated areas," had to make the transition to governing the entire nation, including the complex, sophisticated urban centers. A new state apparatus was created to carry out the Party's bidding, along with a network of nongovernmental local groups and mass organizations designed to enable the central Party and government authorities in Peking to extend their rule down to each household and individual. Disloyal and corrupt officials were weeded out, and large numbers of new young cadres were selected, indoctrinated, and trained for the many technical tasks required by government. Inflation was curbed, political enemies were suppressed, and land was taken away from the landlords and rich peasants and distributed to the poorer peasants. The economic and educational systems and the media were reorganized under Party domination.

In theory, the new government was a coalition in which the Communists cooperated with a group of "minor democratic parties," whose liberal leaders were given prominent posts. This was in line with the "united front" strategy that the Party had been practicing since 1936 in its efforts to enlist the broadest possible support—in the short run against Japan and in the long run against the Kuomintang. In accordance with this strategy, in 1940 Mao Tse-tung had enunciated his call for a "new democracy" that would eliminate the most glaring inequities of Chinese society and create a strong reformist coalition, while postponing the eventual socialization of agriculture, industry, and commerce, which was central to the Communist program but frightening to many non-Communists whose support the Party required. In mid-1949, on the eve of attaining nationwide power, Mao superimposed upon the "new democracy" the theory of a "people's democratic dictatorship," pledged to permit democracy for "the people"—defined as all those who supported the Communist-led government—but to root out the reactionaries who opposed it. The implications of this theory gradually became clear after a relatively tranquil first year, in which the People's Republic was genuinely welcomed by most liberal intellectuals and even some progressive businessmen, as well as by other patriotic groups who had become alienated from Chiang Kai-shek and were eager to see a strong, united China emerge from decades of chaos and humiliation.

From 1950 to 1952, as the land reform was carried out in newly liberated areas and as the Party proceeded relentlessly to crush all sources of political opposition and to rid society of criminal elements which plagued public order, the new democracy gave way to class struggle. Amid the increasing tension generated by the Korean conflict, wave after wave of government-inspired mass movements—such as the "three anti" movement instigated to eradicate official corruption, waste, and bureaucratism, and the "five anti" movement aimed against bribery, tax evasion, fraud, theft of state economic secrets, and theft of other state property—struck against China's old elite in every walk of life. Public "struggle meetings" and "mass trials" were convened by ad hoc "people's tribunals" before hordes of onlookers, who were mobilized to "speak bitterness" against and condemn their former oppressors. These thinly veiled kangaroo courts dispensed their own form of justice under Party guidance. They sentenced hundreds of thousands of "class enemies" to death. Many more were sent to long terms of "reform through labor," and millions suffered lesser sanctions combined with the "thought reform" to which virtually the entire country was subjected. During this period the regular courts also played a role, although it was not until 1953 that they were sufficiently purged of holdovers from the Nationalist government to inspire Party confidence. In addition, military control commissions continued to function and to administer punishments in large areas of the country. In many kinds of cases the civilian police also had unfettered power to investigate, detain, prosecute, and convict, and it conducted large-scale roundups of thieves, gamblers, opium addicts, pimps, prostitutes, vagrants, and other dregs of the old society, subjecting them to "noncriminal" reform measures in the course of long confinement.

In short, the army, the police, and the regular and irregular courts implemented the directive of Chairman Mao to serve as instruments for oppressing the hostile classes and for inflicting "legalized" violence or lesser sanctions on all those who were deemed "reactionaries" or "bad elements." The justification for such harsh programs had been stated by Mao in his famous 1927 "Report of an Investigation into the Peasant Movement in Hunan":

> Revolution is not the same as inviting people to dinner or writing an essay, or painting a picture, or doing fancy needlework; it cannot be anything so refined, so calm and gentle, or so mild, kind, courteous, restrained and magnanimous. A revolution is an uprising, an act of violence whereby one class overthrows another. To put it bluntly, it was necessary to bring about a brief reign of terror in every rural area; otherwise one could never suppress the activities of the counterrevolutionaries in the countryside or overthrow the authority of the gentry. To right a wrong it is necessary to exceed the proper limits, and the wrong cannot be righted without the

249, 250. Right: Boulevard in Sian. Only about 20 percent of China's population lives in urban areas. Below: Fields of wheat and vegetables against the background of a terraced hillside in western Honan province. There is an awesome quality about north China's seemingly endless plains.

251, 252. Left: Old man resting in the shade of a gateway at the Temple of Heaven complex (T'ien T'an), Peking. Above: Traffic policeman in T'ien-an-men Square, Peking. This square is the political nerve center of the country, where the principal political demonstrations take place.

proper limits being exceeded. (*Selected Works of Mao Tse-tung*, p. 27.)

Yet it would be inaccurate to depict these early years as a nightmare for the masses. For the bulk of the people "liberation," as the advent of the new regime was called, did live up to its name. For tens of millions of peasant families, land reform meant not only freedom from economic exploitation by the landlord-gentry class but also freedom from the political, social, and psychological domination of that class.

Some inkling of the process by which the landless and land-poor stood up against their oppressors can be garnered from the following account, by the chairman of a village peasants' association, of the last in a series of "struggle meetings" conducted against the village's richest landlord:

When the final struggle began, Ching-ho was faced not only with those hundred accusations but with many, many more. Old women who had never spoken in public before stood up to accuse him. Even Li Mao's wife—a woman so pitiable she hardly dared look anyone in the face—shook her fist before his nose and cried out, "Once I went to glean wheat on your land. But you cursed me and drove me away. Why did you curse and beat me? And why did you seize the wheat I had gleaned?" Altogether over 180 opinions were raised. Ching-ho had no answer to any of them. He stood there with his head bowed. We asked him whether the accusations were false or true. He said they were all true. When the committee of our Association met to figure up what he owed, it came to 400 bags of milled grain, not coarse millet.

That evening all the people went to Ching-ho's courtyard to help take over his property. It was very cold that night, so we built bonfires and the flames shot up toward the stars. It was very beautiful. We went in to register his grain and altogether found but 200 bags of unmilled millet—only a quarter of what he owed us. Right then and there we decided to call another meeting. People all said he must have a lot of silver dollars—they thought of the wine plant, and the pigs he raised on the distillers' grains, and the North Temple Society and the Confucius Association.

We called him out of the house and asked him what he intended to do, since the grain was not nearly enough. He said, "I have land and house."

"But all this is not enough," shouted the people. So then

253. Playing cards at the Ming Tombs. Public card playing was not often seen during the decade 1966–76. In the changed mood since the fall of the "Gang of Four," players may indulge openly in parks and under street lights at night, but it is illegal to play for money.

254. Far left: Drinking tea at the Western Garden Temple (Hsi-yüan-ssu), Soochow. Relaxed sociability is enjoyed all over China since the "Gang of Four" was smashed. Formerly, "indulgent" citizens might have been accused of having too low a political consciousness.

255. Left: Smoking in Peihai Park, Peking. The government has begun to warn China's youth about the health hazards of cigarettes. Peihai Park, one of Peking's most popular central playgrounds, was closed for most of the decade that began with the Cultural Revolution in 1966. Chiang Ch'ing, Mao's wife, reportedly used it as a private garden for herself and her favorites.

we began to beat him. Finally he said, "I have 40 silver dollars under the *k'ang.*" We went in and dug it up. The money stirred up everyone. We beat him again. He told us where to find another hundred after that. But no one believed that this was the end of his hoard. We beat him again and several militiamen began to heat an iron bar in one of the fires. Then Ching-ho admitted that he had hid 110 silver dollars in militiaman Man-hsi's uncle's home. . . .

Altogether we got $500 from Ching-ho that night. By that time the sun was already rising in the eastern sky. We were all tired and hungry, especially the militiamen who had called the people to the meeting, kept guard on Ching-ho's house, and taken an active part in beating Ching-ho and digging for the money. So we decided to eat all the things that Ching-ho had prepared to pass the New Year—a whole crock of dumplings stuffed with pork and peppers and other delicacies. He even had shrimp.

All said, "In the past we never lived through a happy New Year because he always asked for his rent and interest then and cleaned our houses bare. This time we'll eat what we like," and everyone ate his fill and didn't even notice the cold. (William Hinton, *Fanshen*, pp. 137–38.)

Peasants, workers, officials, educators, and others also began to enjoy more economic security than they had previously known. The Marriage Law of 1950, which provided for the equality of the sexes to an even greater degree than did the progressive Nationalist Family Law, was put into effect in a way that the Nationalist law had never been, as the Party sought to free women who felt victimized by the traditional arranged marriages and to prevent such marriages in the future. Although efforts to implement the law's divorce provisions in the early years produced a considerable amount of social upheaval and many murders and suicides, they did much to liberate women from male domination. The new regime also freed young people from the constraints of the Confucian deference to age and offered even to teenagers of proper ideological persuasion unusual opportunities for upward mobility and service to the country. The common people also benefited from the restoration of domestic order, from greater honesty and efficiency in government, and from broader access to education and health care for themselves and their children. The regime's vigorous moves to control and gradually take over Western trading and industrial interests were highly popular, although an intensely nationalistic people could not have been happy about certain economic concessions that the Soviet Union exacted in return for its "fraternal" assistance.

The Transition to Socialism (1953-57)

By the end of 1952, economic reconstruction and political consolidation had been achieved, and, with the aid of Soviet experts, equipment, and loans, China's new leaders were ready to launch their First Five-Year Plan (1953–57). It was designed along lines previously followed by the USSR and emphasized the growth of heavy industry, calling for an ordered and planned society in which economic development would take place within the context of a "Socialist transformation" that would transfer ownership of the means of production from private to public hands.

Specifically, agriculture was to be collectivized. In addition to satisfying ideological preferences and strengthening political control over the peasants, collectivization was supposed to increase total agricultural output by a more efficient use of land, labor, draft animals, and irrigation facilities. It was also desired to prevent rural surpluses from being consumed in the countryside and would place them under the control of Party cadres, who were to turn them into forced savings at the disposition of the state. This would enable the regime to obtain the capital necessary for the desired development of heavy industry and to feed the burgeoning urban population. Collectivization would also ease the Party's immediate concern about the serious inequalities that continued to exist among the peasants, for, despite land reform, the poor peasants and former landless laborers had been left with less land and capital and fewer farm tools and draft animals than the rich and middle peasants, who tended to have the additional advantages of greater literacy and management experience. The Party also hoped that in the long run the success of collectivization, together with other aspects of socialism, would provide individual peasants with greater work incentives than a system of private landowning could offer.

Collectivization was to be carried out gradually, in order to avoid the painful and disruptive consequences of Stalin's excesses in expropriating land in the Soviet Union. The initial stage was marked by the formation of many "mutual-aid teams." Perhaps four to ten neighboring households, while retaining private ownership of all their assets, pooled their labor, draft animals, and equipment to work the land belonging to each. At first these teams operated temporarily, during the busiest farming seasons, just as neighbors had often done in China before, but later they became permanent. Experiments with agricultural producers' cooperatives soon got under way. The "lower-level" or "semi-Socialist" version involved perhaps fifty families, who contributed their land as well as draft animals and tools in exchange for shares of stock in the cooperative, which generally reflected the amount of capital resources contributed. The return allocated to each household on the crops cooperatively raised was based on the amount of stock it owned as well as the labor its members had performed.

But by mid-1955 only half of China's more than 110 million peasant households had formed mutual-aid teams, and only a small percentage were in lower-level cooperatives. On July 31, 1955, Chairman Mao issued a call for a nationwide acceleration of the cooperativization movement that brought it to a sudden, frenzied climax. Within the next eighteen months, 88 percent of peasant households progressed to "higher-level" cooperatives that usually encompassed an entire village of perhaps 100 to 300 families, while almost all the remaining peasants entered lower-level cooperatives. This was a tremendous organizational achievement, and, given the nature of the higher-level cooperatives, it was extraordinary. The crucial difference between the lower and higher stages was that in the latter the peasants were compensated entirely on the basis of their labor. No longer did their income reflect their capital contribution to the cooperative. Although the cooperative generally purchased the peasants' draft animals and farm tools, albeit at prices often regarded as unsatisfactory by the former owners, it paid nothing at all for the land, which the peasants "voluntarily" contributed.

The extent to which peasants actually parted with their land voluntarily is, of course, open to serious question in a society where intense group pressures are backed by an efficient coercive apparatus. Few peasants could forget the violence and stigmatization that had been inflicted on landlords and some rich peasants and other opponents of Party policy during the land-reform campaign. Indeed, just prior to the "high tide of collectivization" in 1955, the Party launched a fierce campaign against "hidden counterrevolutionaries" in order to minimize opposition to Socialist transformation. Moreover, economic pressures manipulated by the state made it difficult for the more well-to-do peasants to continue to work their farms successfully outside the cooperatives, even if they could withstand the psychological and social pressures mobilized against them. The majority of peasants, especially the poorer

256, 257. Right: Agricultural display case with milk, eggs, and grains at the Shanghai Exhibition Hall. Below: A neighborhood grocery store in the basement of an apartment block in the East District of Peking.

258, 259. Left: Peasant tending ducks at a commune the countryside outsic Shanghai. Right: An elderly shopper holdi a basket of vegetable in the People's Market, Peking.

260. Fish at a model market in Peking. This market is shown off to foreigners, but most Chinese cannot buy here.

261. Chickens at the same market. Chinese do not eat fish or chicken except for special banquets. Grains and vegetables are their dietary staples.

ones who had more immediately to gain by joining the cooperatives, proved responsive to the Party's enormous effort through "persuasion-education" and patriotic appeals to make them take action that was promised to be in the immediate interest of the state and in their own future self-interest. In any event, once Chairman Mao issued the call for intensification of the cooperative movement, developments exceeded all expectations, and the collectivization of agriculture was achieved with far less violence and disruption than had accompanied it in the Soviet Union. The Chinese leaders' intimate familiarity with peasant conditions, their grass-roots Party organization, and their study of the Soviet experience paid rich dividends.

One Party cadre described the process of persuading the reluctant to join the cooperatives as follows:

In general, one can say that those whose land was not good were for the idea; and that those who had good land down in the valley and a lot of manpower were against it. My neighbour, Chao Teh-pa, for example, got up during the discussion and said: "I don't want to go up the hill and toil on the hill fields. I have good, fertile land down here in the valley, and this agricultural co-operative won't pay me. I can manage by myself." Well, we reckoned out properly how many days' work he would get in an agricultural co-operative and how much his fields in the valley gave him as it was. We proved to him that large-scale farming and joint effort was much more rational, and that, in actual fact, he would gain by joining the agricultural co-operative. "I'll hire people," he replied. We told him that would become rather difficult. There would be no day labourers or farmhands to be had, once we had formed our collective. They would prefer to work for themselves in an agricultural co-operative than for anyone farming on his own. In the end we proved to him that he would get much more corn and more cash for his work if he joined the agricultural co-operative.

"That isn't of any significance," he replied. "It may well be that I should earn more. But if I am to choose between earning more and having to climb up the hill and toil there, or earn less and only have to cultivate my own fields down in the valley, then I prefer to earn less and not have to clamber about up on the hill." After that, we had a serious talk with him. "You want to hire people to work for you. That's exploitation. Why do you want to become rich on other people's work? Why should only you become rich? You are not going to get anyone to exploit. Choose how you want things to be. Do you want to be rich alone, or do you want us all to be well-off together? Do you want to be a decent person or not? Think about it." He thought about it and joined. (Jan Myrdal, *Report from a Chinese Village*, pp. 160–161.)

In the cities also the period of private ownership of the means of production promised by the "new democracy" proved to be short-lived. Socialist transformation of industry, commerce, banking, and even handicrafts was basically achieved by the end of 1956. Virtually all enterprises of any significance became publicly owned. By value of output the state became sole owner of roughly two-thirds of China's industry, and most of the rest, except for 2 percent owned by cooperatives, was converted to joint state-private ownership. A joint state-private company, despite its title, was tantamount to a wholly state-owned enterprise except for the fact that the state committed itself to pay the former owners a fixed amount of interest, usually 5 percent for a certain number of years, on the value of the capital and inventory of the enterprise as assessed at the time of takeover.

As in the case of agriculture, although public ownership of industry and commerce had been gradually expanding, Socialist transformation of these aspects of the economy did not move into full swing until Chairman Mao personally called for a radical acceleration, this time on October 29, 1955. Again, a process that had originally been scheduled for completion over a period of years was concluded in a matter of months. The Party was actually more successful in mobilizing businessmen to surrender their property to the public domain than it had been with the wealthier peasants. The Party's willingness to pay was a relatively minor reason for this success. Businessmen were aware that their property was unlikely to be appraised at its true value and that the fixed interest would provide them with only partial compensation. They also knew that they would be under political pressure not to accept the interest payments or not to spend most of the interest received, and that, in any event, there would be little they could buy with the money.

As in the countryside, before the sudden final drive for Socialist transformation in the cities there was a long period of intensive ideological preparation, in which businessmen attended lectures and participated in small "study" groups that explained the desirability of Socialization and committed them to the cause. The state also used to good advantage its power to manipulate sources of supply, prices, taxes, employees, and other factors, leaving businessmen in no doubt about the harassment and anxiety they would suffer if they sought to continue private operation. Moreover, the regime had made clear that it would want the continuing services of able and loyal former capitalists in the complex task of running the economy, so that those who were cooperative could contemplate some responsible and remunerative role for themselves in the future. Finally, the Party warned that businessmen who proved uncooperative would be dealt with according to law. In these circumstances one can understand why, after the Party announced that transformation could be achieved virtually overnight, thousands of "patriotic capitalists" hastened to petition the state for the privilege of converting their companies to joint state-private enterprises. Private enterprise was eliminated in the urban sector, except for a few handicraft workers and some small family stores, street stalls, and peddlers.

The transition to Socialism was marked by structural changes not only in the economy but also in government. The new emphasis on planning and the Soviet model for industrialization was thought to require a reorganization that would create greater centralized control, predictability, regularization, and legitimacy for the regime. The year 1953–54 witnessed Soviet-style elections of local People's Congresses; they in turn elected higher-level congresses, which endorsed a single slate of Party nominees as delegates to a National People's Congress (NPC). The NPC then adopted a Constitution to replace the Common Program that had been a temporary charter of government. Under this Constitution, the NPC was to be the supreme organ of state power. In addition to its legislative and other decision-making powers, it was to choose the Chairman of the People's Republic and the heads of the Supreme People's Court and the Supreme People's Procuracy, and, upon the Chairman's recommendation, the Premier of the State Council. But, because it was composed of well over a thousand delegates and was scheduled to meet only in infrequent and brief sessions, it was obviously not expected to exercise effective power, and its Standing Committee was empowered to wield considerable authority. The principal executive body of government, however, was to be the State Council, composed of the Premier, Vice-Premiers, and heads of ministries, commissions, and specialized agencies that presided over the economy, national defense, and other spheres. Above the State Council and under the direct control of the Chairman of the Republic were two policy-planning organs: the Supreme State Conference, composed of the Chairman and Vice-Chairman of the Republic, the Premier, the Chairman of the NPC's Standing Committee and other principal officials, and the National Defense Council, composed of the country's major military leaders. Apart from outlining the functions and powers of the principal national and local institutions of government, the Constitution, which bore the marks of strong Soviet influence, also guaranteed freedom of speech, assembly, and religion, and other freedoms from arbitrary government action.

Of course, this centralized governmental structure was dominated by the Communist Party, whose top leadership also occupied the highest posts of government and was thus able to operate the levers of power as well as set the guiding policies. Responding to pressures for reorganization and regularization that were felt during this period, the Party itself enacted a new Party Constitution at the Eighth Party Congress in 1956.

Having decided to follow the Soviet political and economic model, China's leaders also decided to develop a Soviet-style legal system. The 1954 Constitution was accompanied by a series of laws that established a framework for the orderly administration of justice. With the aid of Soviet experts, criminal and civil codes were drafted; a few Chinese textbooks and law journals were published; law schools were revamped to train judges, prosecutors, and "people's lawyers" in the principles of "Socialist legality"; collectives of lawyers began to function; and, although individual judges were to serve at the pleasure of the legislative or executive agencies, in theory the courts were to be independent in administering justice. Experiments were conducted with public trials, defense counsel, and other protections of personal liberty, to the bewilderment of many Chinese Communist officials unaccustomed to legal formalities.

The campaign against "hidden counterrevolutionaries" and the pressures of Socialist transformation almost swamped the budding legal system in 1955, but shortly after Khrushchev initiated de-Stalinization in early 1956, an emphasis on legality reappeared in China as part of a general relaxation and readjustment designed to win back the support of officials, intellectuals, businessmen, and others who had been alienated by the drastic upheavals. To be sure, the Party continued to control the courts and to impose sanctions on certain anti-social elements through agencies other than the courts. But professional legal considerations began to influence judicial decision making, and the Party resorted to "non-courts" less frequently and less arbitrarily than in the past. In the spring of 1957 it appeared that China would continue to develop her legal system in a direction similar to that being followed by the USSR, which had recently launched a series of law reforms to demonstrate both to its own people and to the world its stability and its respect for human rights.

The Party's popularity had been heavily eroded by the manner in which it had tried to modernize the country, and the moderate policies of 1956–57 reflected an attempt to reduce the disaffection. In the countryside the size of the private plots that cooperatives had set aside for individual peasant households to grow their own produce was increased, and rural markets were reopened so that peasants could add to their income by selling their vegetables, hogs, homemade handicrafts, and other spare-time products. In the factories, material incentives were increased to reward ambitious workers. The measures, it was hoped, would increase production. As part of the general relaxation, teachers, writers, technicians, and other intellectuals enjoyed somewhat greater freedom.

Party leaders believed that much of the discontent was traceable to the growing separation of administrative officials from the people they governed. Therefore the Party initiated a campaign to "rectify" the "working style" of the cadres, calling on intellectuals and businessmen to criticize official arrogance, bureaucratism, and "commandism." The purpose of this campaign to "let a hundred flowers bloom, let a hundred schools of thought contend," as it was called, was not only to reform the cadres but also to provide an outlet for the frustrations and resentments pent up within the most articulate segment of the elite of the old society, thereby reducing the risk that China might suffer a violent outburst similar to those that had occurred in Hungary and Poland in the wake of de-Stalinization.

Fearful of punishment if they genuinely criticized the cadres, for a long time intellectuals and businessmen resisted the appeals to "bloom and contend." But they finally became convinced of Party sincerity, and, for six weeks from the end of April to June 8, 1957, a torrent of criticism attacked not only the cadres but also the Party policies they administered.

One major theme centered upon claims that the Party had set itself up as a new exploiting class whose members lorded it

268

over the rest of the people like "local emperors" and "plain-clothes police." At the same time, the Party was charged with committing frequent violations of "Socialist legality," and critics called for a commission to review the sanctions meted out against the innocent in past mass movements. They also asked why the much-mentioned but never-published proposal for a criminal code had not been enacted; as one comment put it, "one hears the sound of footsteps on the stairs without seeing anyone coming down." Another theme revealed the resentments that experts in many fields felt at having non-specialists from the Party dictate decisions on professional matters. "The Party committee controls everything, yet knows nothing" was a common complaint.

Journalists were bitter because newspapers could not act independently but were mere "gramophones" or "bulletin boards" for transmitting orders from upper to lower levels. Reporters bemoaned the fact that they were often regarded as spies and that their papers were dreary and dull. Teachers claimed that they were not trusted, that they were expected to attend so many political meetings that they could not do their work, and that they had to slavishly copy the Soviet Union. Professors said that the Party had adopted "Kuomin-tang methods of controlling intellectuals," that universities had become "beehives of doctrinairism," that "[t]he place is absolutely littered with feudal princes and stinking char-latans," and that "[w]hile we want to set up an institution of higher learning, they, on the other hand, want to run a depart-ment store."

Writers lamented the impossibility of being creative while churning out simplistic stereotypes for mass political appeal. Literary critics chafed under a mesh of rules and regulations. As one wrote:

> One cannot be rude, one cannot ridicule, one cannot use smart phrases; one must pay attention to authorities, to the famous writers, the new forces, the leading personnel, the old gentlemen, unity. One must consider the editor's plans, the opinions circulating in current Soviet magazines, and your own retreat in the event of future policy changes. With that many "pay attentions" and "considerations" in one's head, one's personal intentions get smaller and smaller. (Roderick MacFarquhar, ed., *The Hundred Flowers*, p. 183.)

Artists whose work failed to win Party approval told how they had lost their jobs. Businessmen questioned the adequacy

262–65. Below: Cornfields against a rugged mountain background northwest of Peking on the road to the Great Wall. Every inch of arable land is cultivated in an effort that has made the country's burgeoning population self-sufficient in food despite recurring droughts and floods. Opposite page: China is only on the verge of mechanization.

266–69. Left, above: Wheat fields against a background of terraced hillsides in western Honan province between Loyang and Sian; below: a peasant drags a cart loaded with straw at harvest time. Right and below: Sian hotel employees help with the harvest by drying wheat in the hotel parking lot.

270. Left: An old woman, whose feet were bound in childhood, toddles down a street in Loyang with the wheat she has just gleaned.

271. Right: Trees line the old Chang-he Canal, Peking. Although many examples of thoughtful tree planting may be seen in China, the government, recognizing that insufficient attention had been paid to China's forests, has recently launched a national forestation campaign.

272. Right: Pear blossoms and rape seed in the Kiangsu countryside. Spring in the rural areas is a joyous and colorful event. Pears grow in many parts of China; the yellow-flowered rape seed is used to make cooking oil.

of the "fixed-interest" compensation paid for "Socialist transformation," the need to take orders from unskilled cadres, and the Party's lack of confidence in them. The nepotism of leading cadres was also frequently mentioned. One Shanghai industrialist stated:

> There is a saying in the Shanghai China Shipbuilding Factory, "For every Lo-han [A Buddhist monk who has passed the stage of novice] there is a Kuan-yin" [Buddhist goddess of mercy], meaning that all the wives of the Party cadres in the factory have got jobs in the factory. (Roderick Mac-Farquhar, ed., *The Hundred Flowers*, p. 206.)

The scope of these attacks exceeded anything Party leaders had expected and made it clear that the old elite was not committed to the existing system but desired drastic democratic and organizational reforms that would end the Party's monopoly of power and fundamentally alter China's political and economic structure.

After a brief period of stunned inaction, the Party leaders responded with an "anti-rightist" movement that savagely struck back at their critics, including many inside the Party, and radically transformed China's political climate. The era of moderation was over, and once again discipline and mass mobilization became the order of the day.

273. Roses in the Hangchow Botanical Garden. In 1978–79, the Party revived the slogan "Let a hundred flowers bloom" to encourage new ideas and to signal a political relaxation.

The Attempted Transition to Communism and Its Aftermath (1957-62)

While the "anti-rightist" campaign got under way in the cities, the Party concentrated the main thrust of a somewhat milder "Socialist education" campaign in the countryside. This was designed to counteract the adverse effects of the period of leniency on cooperativization. Some peasant families had taken advantage of the relaxation to leave their cooperatives. Many more had spent too much time away from collective duties while farming their private plots or producing commodities for sale in the local markets. In the lexicon of the Party, the peasants were demonstrating their "spontaneous tendencies toward capitalism." The remedy, it was thought, lay in a strong dose of indoctrination regarding the necessity of Socialist transformation, combined with a renewal of pressures such as those created by restricting the size of the private plots and the peasants' access to rural markets and by reemphasizing punitive measures.

The Party's new hard line had profound implications for

the evolving system of administering justice along de-Stalinized Soviet lines. Many Party leaders had never felt comfortable about importing the formal Soviet judicial model, which to them was essentially a Western product. As a result of the "hundred flowers" debacle, they came to fear that implementation of this system would unduly limit the power of the Party and hamper "Socialist construction." Therefore, during 1957–58, while in the USSR de-Stalinization was culminating in a series of reforms that brought Soviet law closer to Western systems, in China principles of Western justice such as the independence of the judiciary from political domination and the right of the accused to a fair public trial were systematically denounced. In both theory and practice, the Party openly assumed control over individual court decisions as well as judicial policies. Moreover, the role of the courts was sharply reduced by a system of severe, police-imposed "administrative" sanctions that required no judicial approval. The most notorious of these was "rehabilitation through labor," which was used to resettle thousands of "rightists," "anti-Socialist reactionaries," and others in harsh labor camps. As Party authorities liked to put it, the reorganized coercive apparatus became "a single fist, attacking the enemy even more forcefully."

This renewed stress on indoctrination and discipline prepared the masses for another all-out effort to modernize the country, one that would challenge both nature and human nature. China's Second Five-Year Plan (1958–62), while continuing to emphasize heavy industry, called for increasing agricultural production. Party leaders had been disappointed in the economic progress of the rural sector following collectivization. The failure to generate larger agricultural surpluses was an important constraint on industrialization. Yet the leadership continued to be reluctant to allocate scarce state investment funds away from industry and into the rural sector, hoping that cooperatives would use their own funds to make improvements. Beyond that, its solution was to brighten agricultural prospects by applying massive amounts of labor in lieu of capital to the variety of tasks—such as irrigation, land reclamation, fertilizer collection, and tool manufacture—that had to be accomplished to enhance production. Moreover, in order to overcome the inefficiencies of bureaucratic overcentralization and to provide added technically qualified leadership for the mobilization of labor in the countryside, the regime shifted economic decision-making authority to lower levels and accelerated the "downward transfer" *(hsia-hsiang)* of administrative cadres to rural areas.

At the beginning of 1958 the measures taken to increase grain production appeared to be yielding results, and this encouraged Chairman Mao to believe that the time was ripe for a "Great Leap Forward" throughout the economy. Mao's optimism derived from the international as well as the domestic situation. In late 1957, after China's Soviet "big brother" successfully launched both an intercontinental ballistic missile and Sputnik, its first artificial satellite, Mao proclaimed, "The East Wind is prevailing over the West Wind." Not long afterward, the People's Republic sought to take advantage of the favorable climate to mobilize the nation for the "liberation" of Taiwan, the only significant territory controlled by the preceding government that Peking had failed to bring under its rule. The wartime atmosphere created by this campaign provided an ideal environment for enlisting the people in heroic efforts to increase production for the sake of national unification.

By the spring of 1958, however, repeated upward revisions by authorities in the capital had raised production goals beyond what was humanly possible. Cadres on the "production front" were well aware of the increasing unreality of these targets, but few dared speak out. Some Party leaders and local officials did seek to moderate Mao's utopian expectations, but their efforts were in vain.

In midsummer of 1958, as the Taiwan crisis approached its climax, the Party called for a nationwide campaign to build small-scale steel furnaces in every locality. This plan, together with the massive water-conservation projects already under way and other activities such as the construction of small factories and workshops in every township, required a vast mobilization of labor far beyond the capacities of individual cooperatives.

In early August Chairman Mao urged all of China to follow the example of Honan province by organizing "people's communes," which were formed by merging many agricultural cooperatives with the local government; the handicraft, supply-and-marketing, and credit cooperatives; and other local groups such as the Communist Youth League and the Women's Association. By the end of the year, over 99 percent of the peasants joined the communes, which the Party termed the best form for the transition to Communism. Amid intense excitement and ever-escalating production goals that made those of the spring seem modest, the *People's Daily* announced that even octogenarians would live to see Communism.

The original commune was a large unit containing perhaps twenty-five to thirty thousand people, or even seventy thousand. Its subunits were the production brigades, often corresponding to the former higher-level producers' cooperatives, and, below them, the production teams, often corresponding to the lower-level cooperatives. An aggregation of this size under unified management facilitated the mobilization of labor forces required for water conservation, steel smelting, and other large-scale projects cleared by the Party. But so many other aspects of the commune soon proved unsuitable that the institution underwent successive and significant modifications during the next few years before attaining the form we know today.

The vision of the commune presented to the peasants offered what its proponents hoped would be sufficient incentives to sustain the enormous demands that were being made on them. Women, whose labor was needed on the farms to replace that of the men who were being assigned to construction projects, were released from many domestic chores by the institution of mess halls, where the entire family was to eat food prepared by full-time cooks, and nurseries, where younger children were to be left all day. "Happiness homes" were to care for aged members of the family. Moreover, the approach of Communism was to be heralded by the free, equal, and ample distribution of basic foods—this to soften the blow dealt peasants by the abolition of private plots. Tractors were to begin to replace physical labor. The gap between city and country people was to be narrowed by commune management of new small-scale industrial enterprises and by the introduction of technology in the countryside. People were to become both "red and expert," technically skilled as well as politically enlightened. Thus, it was thought, the communes would fulfill the Great Leap Forward slogan of "more, faster, better, and cheaper" and bring about the needed increase in agricultural production.

But Mao's hopes for the commune were as romantic as his hopes for the Great Leap generally. Although communization and the Leap were not designed to shatter the fabric of the Chinese family, as some foreign critics alleged, they made more severe inroads on peasant domestic life than any previous Communist innovations had done. Because production teams had to provide their commune with a quota of male labor to be assigned to construction projects that were often carried out in distant places, family members were frequently separated for long periods. The local labor shortage created by the absence of these men increased the burdens of those left behind, especially as higher levels passed down increasingly unrealistic production targets. With virtually every waking hour devoted to work, there was no time for private life. The requirement that meals be taken in mess halls in the company of perhaps thirty to fifty other families was a further infringement on privacy and widely disliked.

If these changes had been accompanied by an improvement in the peasant's economic position, they might have been more acceptable. As it was, however, communization sharply worsened his economic situation at the same time that it infringed on his family life and made the most extreme work demands that the People's Republic had ever imposed. Peasants were pressed to donate "voluntarily" to the collective much of their remaining personal property. Farming tools and privately raised pigs and chickens had to be turned over to the team; and pots, pans, utensils, plates, tables, and chairs had to be given to the mess hall. Private plots also had to be surrendered, depriving peasants of the opportunity to eat or sell home-grown produce, and other profitable sideline occupations were prohibited to prevent the diversion of energies from the common interest. Furthermore, peasants had to strip their homes of all kinds of metal objects and contribute them to the scrap-metal drive that was to provide material for the new local steel smelters and other industrial enterprises. Even scarce cash savings were often collected in order to establish a fund for the purchase of tractors.

The new organization also virtually dismantled the individual work incentives that had been built into the cooperatives. When a commune absorbed a number of higher-level cooperatives, it tended to take their land, equipment, and animals and redistribute them throughout the commune, in effect confiscating some of the assets of the more prosperous cooperatives to the benefit of the poorer ones. Moreover, because the commune itself was made the accounting unit whose success or failure determined what segment of production would be allocated to peasant remuneration and other benefits, it became much more difficult for peasant families to see the relationship between their effort and their reward. Even if they and all their neighbors toiled heroically, their benefits would still depend on whether thousands of other families worked with equal vigor and skill. To make matters worse, the communes seemed to be deemphasizing the work-point system by which, according to one formula or another, the cooperative had implemented the Socialist principle of "to each according to his work." To the extent that the compensation of commune members was not to vary significantly with the degree of their productivity but was to reflect the Communist principle of "to each according to his need," the hardworking and competent would receive no greater economic advantage than the lazy and inept.

Peasant dissatisfactions were also increased by the many mistakes in planning, coordination, and decision making that accompanied the Leap and communization. Hasty and ill-considered efforts to expand agricultural production often proved disastrous. Just as the Party challenged human nature by mobilizing people to work beyond the limits of endurance and without material incentives, so too did it challenge nature by attempting to grow crops with seeds suited to another climate and by resorting to planting techniques that the soil could not sustain. And cadres, caught between unrealistic goals set by higher authorities on the one hand and diminishing peasant productivity and morale on the other, submitted false reports of overfulfilled quotas to their superiors, thereby reinforcing the unreality and stimulating further mismanagement. Urban areas also suffered from tremendous waste and dislocation as a result of the faulty planning, excessive decentralization, poor record keeping, absurd targets, false reporting by cadres, and squandering of energies that marked the frenzy of the Leap. The "backyard furnaces" that absorbed vast quantities of manpower and raw material but produced unusable steel came to symbolize this era.

By late 1958 the evidence of chaos throughout the nation was so great that leaders such as Liu Shao-ch'i, who had been unable to curb Mao's plans in the spring of the year, were finally able to moderate them and put him on the defensive. It is probably more than coincidental that Mao at that point decided to turn over his responsibilities as head of state to Liu and concentrate on providing policy guidance as Chairman of the Party. In any event, the Party began to address itself to the worst excesses of the commune and the Leap. Peasants were assured, for example, that they would receive adequate time for sleeping and eating, that their houses, clothes, furniture, and savings would not be taken away, that the quality of the mess halls would improve, and that their labor would continue to be compensated on the basis of Socialist rather than Communist principles. As 1959 unfolded, the Party also initiated the process of transferring responsibility for activities and financial accounting from the commune to the brigades and the teams, it again allowed peasants to grow subsidiary crops and sell them in rural markets, and it put an end to the small-scale furnaces.

The situation was destined to get much worse, however. Unusually bad weather in 1959 exacerbated China's man-made difficulties and contributed to a poor harvest. Rations fell as sharply as grain production. An attempt was made to revive the Great Leap Forward in a more moderate way, but it failed to stem what was rapidly becoming a major economic depression. The years 1959–61 proved to be extremely difficult for China. Food shortages, malnutrition, and disease were widespread. Public morale dropped disastrously. Not only did peasant enthusiasm for collective labor fall off sharply, but also many peasants and rural cadres succumbed to petty corruption. They helped themselves to harvested produce and collective funds and violated public order in other ways that included development of a flourishing black market and illegal entry into the cities. The impressive progress that new China had made during its first decade in inculcating respect for the public interest in a notoriously privately oriented people was seriously threatened.

Although the Party tried to put the best possible face on it, by 1960 the Great Leap Forward was plainly a failure, at least in terms of its immediate consequences. Even the greatest mobilization of human energy in history could not overcome the intractable facts of life. Modernization could not be attained overnight, nor could human nature be ignored, even after a decade of thought reform. The long-run consequences of the Leap, of course, may be quite beneficial to China's modernization, for it did much to shake the hold of tradition by introducing a still rural, economically backward people to technology, stirring their capacity for innovation and raising their expectations. Yet this must have been small consolation for the Party leaders, and particularly Mao, who were faced with their gravest challenge since the early days of the Party's nationwide rule. In 1949 both the cadres and the masses had been energetic and hopeful. By contrast, they were now tired and jaded. Moreover, in 1949 the People's Republic had enjoyed the support of the Soviet Union; now Sino-Soviet tensions were severe. Finally, the Chinese leadership itself, which had long been regarded as extraordinarily cohesive, was torn with dissension.

The most urgent need was to feed the people and restore production. This the Party undertook to do by going far to meet the demands of the peasants and workers and to adapt the commune to the existing situation. A new program emerged, according to which the Party at long last gave agriculture its due by allocating state investment funds to it. Most communes were reduced in size, and the Party gradually completed decentralization within the communes, transferring many operating powers to the teams and making them not only planning units but also accounting units for purposes of calculating and distributing peasant earnings.

The Party also made other concessions to the "petty capitalistic" instincts of the peasants. It fully revived what came to be known as the "three freedoms"—to farm private plots, to engage in private sideline production, and to sell the fruits of this noncollective labor in rural markets. It also ordered that the peasants be compensated for the metal items they had been forced to contribute for scrap metal. Pots, pans, chairs, small farm implements, and other private property they had surrendered to the commune at the height of the Leap were to be returned or, if that was not possible, to be paid for. Although the compensation was seldom regarded as adequate, this recognition of "bourgeois legal rights" illustrates how anxious the Communist regime was to assuage the peasants' sense of injustice.

Also, as so often happens in China after extreme Party policies have proved unpopular, the Party sought to deflect the resentment of the masses by blaming the extremism on the basic-level cadres rather than on the policies they carried out. The peasants' severe criticism of the "commandism" of these hapless scapegoats provided a convenient safety valve for social grievances, and 1961–62, like 1956–57, became a period of general political and economic relaxation following a period of mass mobilization and tension.

In the industrial sector, also, the Party restored material incentives for individual effort, while reintroducing planning, regular production modes, and reliable supply systems. By 1962 all these organizational changes and concessions to individualism began to bring about an increase in production.

The Background of the Cultural Revolution (1962-65)

Now the Party was faced with deciding how far it could safely go in making concessions to individualism and how long these concessions could last without undermining the Socialist foundations of the state and the march toward Communism. Within the Central Committee of the Party there were sharp divisions of opinion. Occasionally criticism of Mao's utopian mobilizational strategy even appeared in the press, albeit in such subtle and veiled forms that only the cognoscenti appreciated the significance of the historical or theoretical discussions or literary vehicles in which the attacks appeared. One such attack, which became famous when it was denounced at the start of the Cultural Revolution, was the play which Wu Han, a historian and deputy mayor of Peking, published concerning Hai Jui, a brave official of the Ming dynasty who had not been afraid to tell the emperor of the suffering of the peasants. The play, as insiders knew and as the Maoists later conceded, was an allegory in praise of Marshal P'eng Te-huai's unsuccessful but damaging criticism of the Chairman at a Party conference in 1959.

By the time of P'eng's attack, Mao had yielded control over day-to-day governmental decision making to Liu Shao-ch'i, who became chief of the state while Mao retained chairmanship of the Party. It was Liu and a number of other high Party and government leaders who initiated the less ideological, more pragmatic policies that restored China's economy and political stability in the wake of the Great Leap Forward. By 1962, however, Mao was convinced that the pragmatists had gone too far in catering to the private, selfish orientation of the masses and in insulating the demoralized basic-level officials from further criticism. In September he persuaded a majority of the Party's Central Committee to launch a "Socialist education movement" designed to renew the faith of the masses and the cadres in the Socialist system, put an end to the "three freedoms" to pursue private interests, reemphasize class struggle and individual self-sacrifice for the collective good, and again resort to social mobilization as the means of modernization.

The pragmatists within the leadership, concerned that a new mass campaign might undo their efforts to restore production and stability, quietly did their best to limit the scope of the Socialist education movement while publicly espousing its slogans. Because they controlled both the Party and government machinery, this strategy of "waving the red flag to fight the red flag," as the Maoists called it, proved quite effective. Mao sought to counter it in 1963 by placing the People's Liberation Army (PLA), rather than the Party or government, in charge of political indoctrination. Marshal Lin Piao, who during the darkest days of 1960–61 had renewed the PLA's faith in the regime by an intensive thought-reform campaign that focused on the works of Chairman Mao,

274. Left: Outdoor advertising for
China's Qingdao (Tsingtao)
beer in front of the trade fair
exhibition hall, Canton
(Kwangchow). Before 1979,
outdoor advertising in China
was limited to patriotic
exhortations. The Party now
permits advertising to promote
commercial products, not only
to earn foreign exchange but
also to interest domestic
consumers.

275. American lawyers explain the "joint
venture" laws of other nations at
a meeting of Chinese officials
sponsored by the China Council for
the Promotion of International
Trade, Peking, March 1979.
China promulgated its own joint
venture law a few months later.

276. The café at the Peking Hotel. When
it opened in 1979, it became
an instant center of social life for
foreigners. One can buy Coca-
Cola and foreign liquor for foreign
currency. Chinese may go there as
guests of foreign visitors, but Chinese
escorts normally do not. In the
background is one of many depictions
of famous sights (here, Kweilin)
in China that decorate the hotel.

277. *The Chinese Dragon Spouts Oil.* Card picture and gymnastic formation.
October 1, 1979, the thirtieth anniversary celebration of the PRC.
Workers Stadium, Peking. This National Day celebration was restricted
to the stadium pageant, in contrast to the massive pre-1971 and 1984
parades in the city. It featured an hour of changing images created by
thousands of people holding colored cards. Modern China was linked to
the past through the oil dragon. In Chinese mythology the first emperor
was a dragon who presided over water, the life blood of humanity. In the
twentieth century, Chinese oil is the vital fluid of modernization.

278. Shanghai District Court, 1978. A trial judge and two laymen called "people's assessors" are about to enter the courtroom to try a criminal case involving embezzlement. In 1977 the courts began to experiment with public trials, as they had in the mid-1950s.

279. Peking traffic in front of a billboard advertising traffic safety rules, 1981. Despite the fact that there are fewer cars in China than in other traffic-snarled nations, there is a high accident and traffic fatality rate. As part of a national safety campaign, the billboard admonishes drivers to stay in the proper lane and pictures a Peking boulevard with ideally ordered traffic flow, uninterrupted by jaywalkers and darting cyclists.

280. Left: A soldier instructs students in code at a Shanghai "children's palace." Many soldiers teach special skills to politically favored youngsters at these urban after-school institutions.

281. Rules for visitors are posted outside a Taoist Temple in Foshan, Kwangtung. Although the People's Republic had relatively few published laws until 1979, guidelines such as these have frequently been posted outside public buildings by local authorities. They tell people how to behave in the specific circumstances.

282. Tending tomato plants. Here "students," heirs to the traditional bureaucratic disdain for manual laborers, learn to appreciate the rigors and satisfactions of peasant life.

283. At a Shanghai "children's palace," Young Pioneers, eight to fourteen years old, learn to use rifles to shoot down enemy airplanes.

284–86. Left: Soldier carrying surveying equipment down a Peking street. Uniforms are much in evidence in China's cities. Right: Railroad police oversee platform activity at the station in T'ang-shan, an industrial city east of Peking. Below: Militia practice in Hangchow silk factory, 1978. A volunteer armed militia has long helped maintain order in the countryside. Militia units continue to serve as assistants to the police in some cities as well, although their role has diminished in many places since the fall of the "Gang of Four," which sought to use them as a counterweight against the army.

287. Soldier dragging a vegetable cart to market in Loyang, Honan province. Members of the People's Liberation Army frequently participate in civilian jobs, both rural and urban, as part of the military's effort to "serve the people" and stabilize the country in the post-Cultural Revolution period.

now attempted to refurbish the Chairman's tarnished image throughout the nation by a similar effort. Mao also initiated a "four clean-ups" campaign that was designed to mobilize lower and middle peasants to cooperate with PLA members and government cadres in attacking peasants and cadres who wanted to pursue the "capitalist path."

The year 1964 witnessed an intensification of the struggle between what, in oversimplified yet convenient terms, we may continue to call, on the one hand, the pragmatists, bureaucrats, realists or conservatives and, on the other, the ideologues, Maoists, ultra-leftists or radicals. Despite a nationwide "learn from the PLA" campaign by the ideologues, the pragmatists continued to have considerable success in resisting the unfolding of another all-out mass movement. This led Lin Piao and certain other Maoist military leaders to join with other ideologues in a new stage of the "four clean-ups" that began the following year, attacking supposed bourgeois elements within the Party who were resisting the class struggle.

Of course, the pragmatists were not really "capitalist roaders," as the ideologues were beginning to call them by the fall of 1965. Like the ideologues, they were devoted Communists. They differed from their rivals neither in goals nor in principles so much as in emphasis, timing, techniques, and approach. Yet fifteen years of experience had demonstrated the implications for modernizing China of the "struggle between the two lines." In the economic sphere the pragmatists stressed conventional planning, organization, professional management, discipline, rules and regulations, technical skills, and material incentives. The ideologues emphasized ideological indoctrination, Promethean mobilization of the spontaneous energies of the masses, charismatic leadership, and moral incentives. They believed that it would not be possible to make any significant long-run economic gains without first transforming the political consciousness of the Chinese people. The pragmatists, by contrast, thought that swifter material progress would facilitate the transformation of consciousness, which in any event could not be attained in apocalyptic leaps.

These differing approaches were reflected in other important areas. In military strategy, to the distress of many professional commanders, Mao and his "close comrade-in-arms" Lin Piao, influenced by their victories over the Japanese and the Kuomintang, continued to emphasize guerrilla rather than conventional warfare; passive rather than active defense; egalitarian rather than hierarchical relations between officers and men; ideological purity rather than technical skills; army participation in agriculture, industry, education, police, and other civilian functions rather than confinement to customary military concerns; and the training of a vast militia rather than concentration exclusively on the armed forces. They tended to play down the role of modern weapons; Mao had even called the atomic bomb a "paper tiger." By 1965 major military figures, backed by Liu Shao-ch'i and other leaders, had come to differ with Mao on military matters. They were particularly disturbed by the Sino-Soviet rift, which denied China access to Soviet aid for military modernization. They strongly urged a settlement that would enable China to regain Soviet military aid and the security of the USSR's nuclear umbrella, thereby permitting China to make a military response to American intervention in Vietnam. This would also have had the more than incidental effect of precluding Mao from continuing to use the PLA as an instrument of domestic political purification in his struggle to regain control over the pragmatists. Understandably in these circumstances, Mao opposed both reconciliation with Moscow and direct military involvement in Vietnam.

Educational policy was also a major area of dispute. Mao called it "a matter of life and death for our Party and our country." As he characterized it:

> The question of training successors for the revolutionary cause of the proletariat is one of whether or not there will be people who can carry on the Marxist-Leninist revolutionary cause started by the older generation of proletarian revolutionaries, whether or not our descendants will continue to march along the correct road laid down by Marxism-Leninism or, in other words, whether or not we can successfully prevent the emergence of Khrushchevite revisionism in China. ("On Khrushchev's Phoney Communism and Its Historical Lessons for the World," *Red Flag*, July 14, 1964.)

Who should receive higher education? For what purposes? By what means? Here, as elsewhere, the "two lines" differed. The pragmatists tended to support the view that education should go to those academically best prepared for it. They maintained that education, while not ignoring political indoctrination, should, nevertheless, feature serious academic subjects and technical training in order to produce the many kinds of specialists required by an industrializing society. As Vice-Premier Ch'en Yi had said during the relaxation of

1961: "Who wants to fly with a pilot who is ideologically pure but cannot manage the controls?" The Maoists, however, maintained that education, while not ignoring academic subjects, should strive to create new Communist men and women who would be closely integrated with the toiling classes rather than members of an elite that stood above them. In their view, devices such as entrance examinations and course examinations overemphasized the academic and gave undue advantage to the children of Party members, cadres, intellectuals, and the former landlord and bourgeois classes. The Maoists wanted to recruit most students from worker, peasant, and soldier origins; give them relatively brief, largely practical academic training; and return them to the masses to serve the people.

By 1965 the problems of education and employment had become very sensitive, because educational and job opportunities had become more limited as a result of the depression that followed the Great Leap. Disillusionment and anxiety were particularly widespread among urban youth, many of whom were not eager to respond to the Party's call to join their politically advanced comrades in moving to the countryside to develop the motherland. Chairman Mao had become increasingly preoccupied with what he perceived to be the softness and revisionism of the new generation. He clung to the notion of permanently altering human nature by replacing selfish and materialistic tendencies with selfless and altruistic ones, kindling in the population at large the collective spirit that had prevailed in the Red Army during the struggles against the Japanese and the Kuomintang.

Indeed, the Maoists sought to change the definition of happiness for China's youth. Over and over they preached that happiness does not consist of remaining with one's family in comfortable urban living quarters, eating and dressing well, obtaining higher education, working in a bureaucratic job, marrying when one wishes, having as many children as one desires, and enjoying urban entertainments. Rather, happiness is abandoning parents and education for a Spartan life of manual labor, transforming some rural wasteland in the company of like-minded patriotic youth, postponing marriage for many years, limiting the number of children one has, and devoting periods of leisure to mastery of Mao's works. What China's youth needed, Mao told visitors in 1964, was to be toughened in revolutionary struggles similar to those that the older generation had experienced. Indeed, all of China needed a revolution that would transform the existing environment and values and "touch people to their very souls." This was the background to the Great Proletarian Cultural Revolution that Mao launched in the fall of 1965 in a daring and desperate effort to mobilize the masses to overthrow the "power-holders" within the Party who had been frustrating Mao's plan for "continuous revolution."

The Cultural Revolution: The Violent Phase (1966–69)

The preliminary stage of what was to become the Cultural Revolution began innocuously enough with another of the series of attempts to eradicate "bourgeois reactionary thinking" in China's art and literature. Mao's wife, Chiang Ch'ing, played an important part in this campaign. He had met her in 1937, when, as the well-known film star Lan P'ing, she, like many patriotic artists, writers, and students, had come to the Communists' mountain stronghold in Yenan to enlist in the revolution. It had been love at first sight. Against the advice of most of his comrades, Mao had divorced his third wife, who had borne him several children—including one born during the Long March—and married the glamorous actress. This episode tarnished Mao's image as the embodiment of revolutionary austerity. His first marriage, at age fourteen, to a woman four years his senior, had been foisted upon him by his parents, and he had left her to resume his schooling. His second wife had been executed by the Nationalists in 1930, after bearing him two or three sons, one of whom was later killed in the Korean War. Comrade Chiang Ch'ing, as the Chairman's new bride came to be known, remained largely hidden from public view for over a quarter of a century, bearing him one daughter and bringing up another from Mao's previous marriage. It was subsequently revealed that she participated in the effort begun in 1964 to revolutionize traditional Peking opera; the following year she became active in transforming other aspects of art and literature.

Because the Party apparatus in Peking, under Mayor P'eng Chen, was controlled by the pragmatists, Chiang Ch'ing persuaded certain radical leaders in Shanghai to publish a criticism of Deputy Mayor Wu Han for his allegorical attacks on Mao. Actually, however, the condemnation of Wu Han had been taking place for weeks during secret meetings of the Standing Committee of the Politburo. It was understood by the pragmatists as a veiled attack on Mayor P'eng Chen, Wu's superior, and perhaps even on higher Party leaders. Interestingly, while the public manifestations of this preliminary stage of the Cultural Revolution focused on literature and art, behind the scenes the first major leader to be purged was Army Chief of Staff Lo Jui-ch'ing, whose removal from office was apparently engineered by Lin Piao.

That Mao intended no ordinary campaign but was determined to use the PLA as a principal weapon in an all-out struggle against the pragmatists became clear to insiders in late February, 1966. By April P'eng Chen and his aides, who had tried to give the impression of complying with Mao's directives while actually maneuvering to counter them, were deposed, and Mao regained command of the capital's propaganda organs. Mao then appointed a small group of confidantes headed by his private secretary, Ch'en Po-ta, and by his wife, Chiang Ch'ing, to constitute a Cultural Revolution Directorate that was to root out the remaining "counterrevolutionary revisionists." Mao sought to show that he had support for his new policy among intellectuals by persuading contemporary China's most famous literary figure, Kuo Mo-jo, to make a dramatic self-criticism before the National People's Congress, declaring that everything he had written should be "burned to ashes, for it has not the slightest value." Then Premier Chou En-lai called for expanding the struggle from art and literature to embrace education and journalism, and in late spring Mao directed Lin Piao to end the domination of "bourgeois intellectuals" over the universities and schools by having the military organize students to rebel against the Party bureaucrats in control.

Peking University became the site of the first academic conflict of the Cultural Revolution, and it was only Mao's personal endorsement that enabled the radicals to triumph over the entrenched Party authorities. His intervention unleashed a torrent of student criticism of the oppressive Party apparatus. A festive atmosphere of genuine elation prevailed. By venting their spleen on administrators and professors, students found release from the pressures of academic and political obligations, job worries, sexual repression, and tensions among the children of different classes. With Mao's blessing in the media and his new slogan "Rebellion Is Justified," the excitement spread to other universities throughout the nation.

For Liu Shao-ch'i and other pragmatic leaders, Mao's challenge represented a grave dilemma. If they opposed the Cultural Revolution, they would be attacked for suppressing the masses. If they allowed it to develop, they would be attacked by the masses for their past opposition to Mao. Their strategy, as in the past, was to appear to be implementing Mao's campaign while actually striving to control it. This they hoped to accomplish by their management of the Party work teams that were assigned to carry out the cleansing of the universities. Well aware of his opponents' dilemma, Mao waited from early June until mid-July to see how they would cope. This period witnessed a great deal of revolutionary rhetoric, considerable turbulence, and attacks on some sacrificial lambs selected by Party bureaucrats in an effort to demonstrate their ideological fervor, but the hold of the Party machine remained essentially unshaken.

At that point Mao emerged from his Hangchow retreat and captured worldwide attention by taking his now legendary swim in the Yangtze River to symbolize his vigor. The Chairman, who was then seventy-two, reportedly swam for more than an hour in the swift current and strong waves, covering a distance of over nine miles. He then returned to Peking to confront the opposition, while the *People's Daily* drove home the moral: "No one has ever learnt to swim just by standing on the shore and studying one or another aspect of the art of swimming. And the same is true of making revolution. You must take part in actual class struggle, master the laws governing revolution in the storm of class struggle and learn the art of swimming in class struggle" (July 26, 1966).

By early August Mao dissolved the work teams and criticized their operation before a long-overdue plenary session of the Party Central Committee, which he packed with his supporters in an irregular manner. He also demoted Liu Shao-ch'i and other Party Vice-Chairmen and promoted Lin Piao to be sole Vice-Chairman. While attacking the "capitalist roaders" from above, Mao also moved to undermine them from below. He mobilized the radical youth who had been forming Red Guard groups with the assistance of army units and launched an unprecedented assault on Party organizations at every level.

The "Sixteen-Point Decision" that Mao pushed through the reluctant Central Committee announced "a great revolution" that would wipe out "old ideas, old culture, old customs, and old habits of the exploiting classes." Large numbers of revolutionary youngsters were to serve as the brave vanguard of this movement, arousing the masses to eliminate the influence of "anti-Socialist rightists." Like Communist documents generally, the "Decision" contained some cautionary and ambiguous language that was undoubtedly inserted to ease the concern of high government leaders such as Premier Chou En-lai, whose support Mao needed, and who feared the consequences of chaos for China's economy and national security. Thus, the document admonished the revolutionaries not to intervene in industrial or agricultural production or to struggle against loyal scientists and technicians or to interfere with the army. The "Decision" also sought to safeguard the majority of Party members, stating that only a small number were so reactionary as to warrant dismissal.

Although the "Decision" urged the revolutionary youth to use persuasion rather than coercion, some of its language was inflammatory, and contemporaneous statements by members of the Cultural Revolution Directorate exhorted the Red Guards not to fear turmoil. Thus, shortly after Mao greeted over a million red-book-waving, slogan-chanting, hysterical Red Guard worshipers in T'ien-an-men Square on August 18 in the first of a series of enormous rallies, China's cities were subjected to the beginning of a reign of terror.

By and large, the principal victims of the first fortnight were not Party bureaucrats but a variety of helpless scapegoats—intellectuals; people who had been educated in the West before 1949; former members of the landlord, rich peasant, and bourgeois classes; people who had been branded counterrevolutionaries or "bad elements"; and even some Party members who were no longer in favor. What the pragmatists succeeded in doing during these earliest days was to divert the Red Guards from attacking the Party machinery by offering them harmless targets on which to expend their energies. Declaring war against the old world, the Red Guards sought to revolutionize all of life. They changed the names of streets, restaurants, and stores, and one group even demanded that traffic lights be revolutionized so that red would signal "go" and green "stop." More sinister were the young leftists who vandalized the homes of thousands, wantonly smashing or confiscating traditional Chinese art objects or foreign-made items, shaving the heads of people with Western hairstyles, and destroying Western clothes. Their hooliganism also extended to statues, paintings, and other objects in temples, parks, cemeteries, and other public places. Hundreds of thousands of people were publicly humiliated, intimidated, and forced to withdraw from society, and many thousands were murdered or driven to suicide. One Chinese woman who had lived in Germany during the 1930s compared the beginning of the onslaught to Hitler's infamous *Kristallnacht* pogrom against the

Jews in 1938.

Mao was not fooled by the diversionary tactics of his opponents or by their efforts to suppress or misinterpret his directives or to form their own Red Guard units to counter the Maoists by "waving the red flag to fight the red flag." At the end of August, Lin Piao and other Maoists began to urge the millions of Red Guards who flocked to Peking from all over the country to focus their attacks on the Party organization, and this word was carried from the capital as the exhilarated young rebels traveled widely through the provinces in a "great exchange of revolutionary experiences" that constituted one of the major mass migrations the world has seen. Regional and local power holders defended themselves against the Red Guards by forming worker and, in some cases, peasant units to control them. This frequently led to combat between rival groups and even between different Maoist units.

By the end of September Chou En-lai and some of the other leaders who shared Mao's enthusiasm for the Cultural Revolution but feared that it was getting out of hand strove to curb its abuses. The Red Guards were disrupting transportation, communications, the building trades, factory output, and government operations, and were even beginning to diminish agricultural production. They were also alienating important sources of Maoist support by their gangster tactics and an extreme class consciousness that excluded from their ranks the children of "feudal" families. But Chou's efforts to rein in the Red Guards yielded before the flames of revolutionary fervor fanned by Mao's wife and other members of the Cultural Revolution Directorate, and Lin Piao, invoking the precedent of the short-lived Paris Commune of 1871, called for "extensive democracy," which would allow the masses to criticize all institutions and leaders. Thus the turmoil intensified during the remainder of 1966. In mid-December the Red Guards were told to revolutionize agriculture by replacing the rural Party power elite with poor peasants under the control of new Cultural Revolution committees. Shortly afterward the Maoists were unleashed on industry. New Year's Day, 1967, found Mao urging the nation to a "general attack" on "monsters and demons anywhere in society."

This led to bloody factional strife virtually all over China as the Maoists sought to seize power from the bureaucrats. The country was exhorted to emulate Shanghai, where a coalition of radical groups had replaced the municipal Party committee. Nevertheless, although the radicals succeeded in toppling certain provincial leaders, in most areas a badly crippled Party machine retained power after violent battles that seemed to be bringing the country to the brink of civil war. The situation was made even more desperate by the fact that urban workers took advantage of the chaos to manifest their dissatisfaction with economic conditions. A series of dock and railway strikes plagued China's coastal cities, and local officials handed out extra funds to many workers in the hope of placating underpaid apprentices, insecure contract workers, and others who were demonstrating for higher wages and better terms of employment. Yet these "sugar-coated bullets of the bourgeoisie" failed to stem the tide of dissatisfaction, and hundreds of thousands of workers followed the example of the Red Guards by journeying to Peking, ostensibly to present their grievances. Urban life also became more difficult to deal with, because large numbers of former city residents who had been sent to the countryside to work with the peasants had illegally drifted back to the cities during the turbulence and had begun to support themselves through crime and black-market activities. And peasants began to help themselves to government and communal supplies and returned to private rather than collective interests.

By the latter part of January it was plain that the Maoists had to bring the situation under control or see China collapse. There was only one possible effective instrument—the People's Liberation Army. Many of the PLA leaders were seriously worried that the Cultural Revolution would weaken China's national defense by implicating the armed forces and breeding disunity. In late January Mao sought to end the chaos by directing the PLA to enter the struggle on the side of the radicals. Before doing so, however, he purged certain high-ranking officers who opposed military involvement in domestic affairs and assured those who retained command that he would take measures to contain the revolution.

Actually, the PLA had already restored order in certain areas. In doing so, it had generally failed to support the radicals, sometimes suppressing them and sometimes arranging local compromises. But in either event it had played an important political role on the local scene. After Mao ordered it into action, it behaved in a similar way on a nationwide scale, moving vigorously to promote stability, even at the cost of many very bloody clashes against Red Guard units. In February and March of 1967, while Peking propaganda organs were urging Red Guards to behave in an orderly manner and re-

288–90.
Above: A lane of workers' new apartments in the East District of Peking. A family of four or five typically has one or two rooms and may share kitchen and bathroom facilities with the family next door. Center: Traditional wooden houses with tiled roofs line a small lane in the "old city" of Loyang. Below: Traditional housing in Sian. It is of wattle-and-daub construction, with a thatched roof.

91, 292. Above: Cave dwellings in
eastern Shensi province, between
Sian and Loyang. For almost a
decade during the Sino-Japanese
War, Mao Tse-tung and his
comrades lived in cave
apartments in the hills of Yenan
in Shensi. Below: Contemporary
courtyard housing in traditional
style, near the Great Gander
Pagoda on the edge of Sian,
Shensi province. China has made
considerable progress in housing
since 1949 but still has a long
way to go to alleviate
overcrowding.

spect rather than rebel against officials, the PLA organized
military control commissions that took over police powers from
the badly divided urban public-security bureaus, formerly
the backbone of the dictatorship of the proletariat. It assumed
control over schools, universities, factories, mines, and even
rural areas. And it began the slow process of rebuilding shattered local and regional government by forging "triple alliances" of officials, radicals, and military men into disciplined
"revolutionary committees." Organization of the revolutionary
committees proved extremely difficult, since the PLA tried to
be faithful to Maoist principles, on the one hand, and to avert
anarchy, on the other. Moreover, it was often impossible to
distinguish the genuine revolutionaries among the bitterly
contending groups.

In the view of the Maoists, military efforts to restore order
went too far and threatened to end the Cultural Revolution.
Thus, at the end of March, Mao launched a new offensive designed to topple Liu Shao-ch'i and other pragmatist leaders,
to complete the purge of their followers among Party and
government officials, and to eliminate the restraints which the
PLA had imposed on the Red Guards. While again exhorting
radical youth that "Rebellion Is Justified," Mao moved to
restrict the PLA, leaving it virtually defenseless against the
mob if it followed his orders. The result was unparalleled civil
conflict throughout the spring of 1967, as youth groups battled
each other, as the PLA and workers fought radicals, and as
rival military units opposed each other. Many thousands were
killed, and the Red Guards, who had been admonished by
Mao to emulate the xenophobic "Boxer" mystics of 1900, out-
raged the world by their attacks on foreigners, diplomats as
well as ordinary nationals.

By the summer of 1967 China seemed to have reverted to
the civil war and chaos that had debilitated her during the
century prior to Communist rule. The specter of "warlordism" became very real as local military commanders ignored
Mao's restrictive edicts, particularly in July, when the Wuhan
military command rejected the order of the central authorities to side with the radicals and kidnapped the two prominent emissaries whom Mao had sent from the capital. This
Wuhan uprising, which was ended only by Peking's show of
overwhelming force, stunned the country and introduced the
bloodiest fighting of the Cultural Revolution. Mao and the
Cultural Revolution Directorate exhorted the masses to prepare for protracted war against recalcitrant military com-

305

manders and demanded a purge of the armed forces; this in turn spurred many regional military authorities to fight the Maoists more forcefully than ever. By late August the crisis had become intolerable. Although the world was ill informed about developments in the provinces, events in Peking convinced many that China had gone mad, as a torrent of Red Guard abuses against foreigners culminated in the burning of the British diplomatic mission and extreme Maoists seized power over the Foreign Ministry.

At that point Mao again had to reverse his field in an effort to end the conflict. Characteristically, he condemned the excesses as the work of "ultra-leftists," whom he purged, even though they had actually been following his orders. He commanded the Red Guards to cease attacking officials and to strive for unity, called for rehabilitation of officials who had criticized their mistakes, expressed faith in the PLA as the "chief component of state power," and authorized it to use force in self-defense against offenders. With this fresh mandate the PLA made considerable progress in restoring order and renewed the difficult task of completing the formation of revolutionary committees to replace the shattered Party and government structures. Much to the disillusionment of the Red Guards, the revolutionary committees that were organized during the following six months bore suspicious resemblances to the old structures in substance, if not in form, as the military brought veteran cadres back to power. These new military-bureaucrat coalitions tended to subordinate the "little red generals" who had been idealized during the previous years as Mao's revolutionary successors.

In March, 1968, however, the frustrated revolutionary forces burst forth again with the approval of radical leaders in Peking, who apparently feared that the pendulum had swung too far to the right. This triggered a new round of violence in the capital and savage warfare in a number of provinces, especially in south China. Once again, within a few months Mao and other radical leaders had to abandon support for their followers and solicit military assistance in reasserting central control over chaotic provinces. As Stanley Karnow has written in the leading study of the Cultural Revolution:

By the middle of summer, the trend toward moderation was firmly established and it was publicized by a lexicon of mirror-language phrases. What had formerly been justifiable "rebellion" now became "counterrevolution." Red Guards were now "anarchists" poisoned by "bourgeois factionalism" and "leftist opportunism." The restoration of law and order by the Army and its auxiliaries was no longer a "reactionary adverse current," but the imposition of "revolutionary discipline" designed to defend the "dictatorship of the proletariat" against its "class enemies." And the rationale for the new line, like the rationale for the exhortations that had launched the Cultural Revolution, would be found in Mao's immense body of doctrine. (*Mao and China,* pp. 442–43.)

Mao now prepared to bring the Cultural Revolution to a close. He not only explicitly repudiated the Red Guards but also used the PLA to control the universities and schools that had been their base. Moreover, during 1968–69 he curbed the revolutionary potential of the cities by launching the *hsia-hsiang* (down to the countryside) campaign, moving over eight million young urban students to rural areas in the next five years. This enormous migration, testimony to the continuing potency of the Chinese propaganda and coercive apparatus, temporarily reduced urban unemployment and social problems, increased rural technological capacity and public-health resources, and constituted a major step toward Chairman Mao's goal of eliminating the gap between intellectuals and peasants. Yet it was far from popular either with the peasants, who often resented the dislocations caused by the "educated youth," or with the young people, many of whom were already bitter about the course of the Cultural Revolution and the lack of educational and job opportunities in the cities and who dreaded the harsh monotony of their presumably permanent residence in the backward countryside.

In the fall of 1968 Mao moved to consolidate his hold on the battered Party apparatus. He used the vehicle of a Central Committee meeting to strip Liu Shao-ch'i of both his Party and his government offices. Although on several occasions during the previous two years Liu and his wife had admitted various errors under Red Guard pressure, unlike many of their colleagues they had refused to make the abject and exaggerated confessions demanded by the Maoists. After Liu's death and a long delay that reflected the problems Mao was encountering in reuniting the party and the country, the Ninth Party Congress was convened on April 1, 1969.

The Cultural Revolution: The Intensifying Struggle (1969–76)

The most striking fact about the Ninth Party Congress was its domination by the military, whose representatives filled a large number of the places left vacant by purged members of the previous Central Committee and Politburo. The principal radical leaders who had directed the violent phase of the Cultural Revolution remained at the very top of the Party hierarchy in the Politburo Standing Committee and the Politburo, but few of their followers held places in the Central Committee, which retained many Party bureaucrats. The Party Constitution that this Congress enacted was much less detailed and organizationally precise than its 1956 predecessor, which had sought to regularize Party procedures in the wake of Khrushchev's revelations of Stalin's abuses, and it elevated Mao and his "Thought" to heights that earlier concern about the "cult of personality" had forbidden. In addition to its emphasis on opposing Soviet revisionism and on heightening class struggle, the new document's other distinguishing feature was its designation of Lin Piao as Mao's eventual successor to the Party chairmanship.

But the new elite enshrined by the Ninth Party Congress proved to be an unstable coalition. The radical leaders must have been increasingly unhappy over the moderate policies that emanated from Peking in 1970 and 1971. Law and order became a major preoccupation. Harsh punishments were meted out to many who had acted like hooligans during the early years of the Cultural Revolution, including certain leaders of groups that had attacked foreigners and their diplomatic missions. In some cases Red Guards and other offenders were even required to make compensation for their destruction of private property. Ideological slogans began to lose some of their stridency, and the worship of Mao and the little red book of his "quotations," which had risen to extreme proportions in an effort to overcome the legitimacy of his bureaucratic opponents, began to decline. Gradually some of the cadres who had been severely attacked by the radicals returned to reconstituted Party and government units, and mass organizations such as the Communist Youth League, the labor unions, and the Women's Federation, by which the Party had formerly controlled virtually every sphere of life, began a lengthy process of reconstruction.

Economic management reflected this renewed emphasis on stability and regularization. Many of the policies the bureaucrats had used to pull China out of the depression following the Great Leap Forward were restored. Planning, expertise, technical skills, accounting, inventory and quality control, and material incentives such as private plots, sideline production, and free markets again prevailed, despite a brief effort by the ideologues to reverse the tide. China also took steps to enhance her international trading reputation, which had suffered when the chaos of the Cultural Revolution prevented her from fulfilling commitments to deliver goods.

By late 1970 it was also apparent that China, which had alienated many countries during the violent phase of the Cultural Revolution, was determined to gain acceptance by the world community. This return to a foreign policy of moderation elicited a warm response abroad, and Peking soon established diplomatic relations with many states that had previously maintained bilateral ties with the Chiang Kai-shek government. Peking also made clear its desire to replace Taipei as the representative of China in the United Nations. It even responded to America's new China policy by initiating "Ping-Pong diplomacy" in the spring of 1971 and later agreeing to the visit by President Nixon that symbolized the start of a Sino-American détente. The Soviet Union alone among the major powers maintained its hostility. Although the Sino-Soviet armed clashes of early 1969 had given way to negotiations, Peking was preparing for a possible nuclear attack by Moscow, undertaking an urban underground air-raid shelter program that demonstrated its concern.

The preeminent spokesman of China's new policy was Premier Chou En-lai, who had labored to support the Cultural Revolution and yet keep it from shattering the country. With Mao's blessing, by autumn, 1971, Chou appeared to have prevailed over those leaders who had earlier joined Mao in pushing the Cultural Revolution to extremes. Ch'en Po-ta, head of the Cultural Revolution Directorate, had dropped from sight amid rumors of disgrace. In late September the world was stunned by increasingly specific stories that Lin Piao himself, designated by the Party Constitution to be Mao's successor, had been killed in a mysterious plane crash while trying to flee to the USSR after an unsuccessful attempt to assassinate Mao. The actual cause of Lin's demise remains uncertain. Also unclear are the reasons for this spectacular and embarrassing turn of events. Among those issues commonly thought to have been involved were the Party's effort to reimpose control over the military, disputes within the armed forces concerning not only political questions but also professional matters such as strategy and weapons development, foreign-policy changes such as the turnabout toward the United States, and the struggle between Lin and Chou En-lai to determine whether Lin would become chief of state as well as Chairman of the Party.

Lin's demise accelerated the prevailing pragmatic trend. While many of Lin's followers were being removed from office, Chou En-lai reinstated increasing numbers of veteran civilian and military cadres who had been humiliated earlier in the Cultural Revolution. That bitter experience made some of them reluctant to participate in the reconstruction of Party and government, yet by the spring of 1973 many skeptical officials were persuaded that a serious attempt to re-create stability was under way. Premier Chou was obviously striving to create a new relationship with military leaders while gradually reducing their influence over both China's politics and economy. At the same time he attempted to reduce the role of the remaining "leftist" leaders without provoking further confrontation.

Renewed pragmatism became all the more essential in economic and social matters when unusually bad weather in 1972 diminished the agricultural harvest and slowed recovery from the disruptions of the previous turmoil. In these circumstances the leadership could ill afford to dispense with "reasonable rewards" based on individual worker and peasant productivity. Moreover, it emphasized improvements in the standard of living and a relaxation of domestic tensions.

In the cultural, ideological, and educational spheres, however, the influence of the radicals was far from dead. Although Western music could again be heard on occasion, and several Western orchestras were even allowed to perform in China for the first time since 1949, Madame Mao continued to promote "revolutionary model operas" in lieu of the traditional variety. Ideologically, great effort was expended to convince the Chinese people as well as foreigners that the Cultural Revolution was a necessary experience that had made important and beneficial changes in national life. The "May 7th Cadre Schools," to which officials, teachers, intellectuals, and others "voluntarily" went for labor and "thought remolding," constituted an important symbol of the continuing tangible impact of the Cultural Revolution.

During 1973 education continued to be the most visible area of struggle between pragmatists and ideologues. When university study resumed in an experimental way in 1970 after a four-year hiatus, a "Cultural Revolution in Education" had begun. Entrance examinations had been abolished, and admission standards had been adjusted to assure that the overwhelming majority of the students would be the children of workers, peasants, and soldiers. Curricular changes had been introduced to carry out Chairman Mao's directive of May 7, 1966, that students "should in addition to their studies learn other things; that is, industrial work, farming, and military affairs. They should also criticize the bourgeoisie. The period of schooling should be shortened." Course examinations had also been abolished.

Gradually, however, the pragmatists made certain inroads in an effort to improve academic quality. For example, in late 1972 reports began to circulate that university course examinations had been reinstituted to test students' knowledge. It was later learned that those who failed to meet minimum standards were being sent back to their units after a few months. As 1973 unfolded, certain radical leaders in both Peking and the provinces openly criticized this concern for quality rather than class background and political standpoint. By midyear some observers interpreted this criticism and the campaign against Confucian thought as veiled attacks not only on the bureaucrats but also on Premier Chou's "centrist" course. Observers impatiently awaited the Tenth Party Congress in order to determine the extent to which Chou could muster support for his policies and personnel changes.

Held in unusual secrecy and brevity in late August of 1973, the Tenth Party Congress of 1,249 delegates superficially appeared to consolidate the power of Chou under Mao's titular leadership. In language reminiscent of Stalin's extravagant attacks on his purged rivals, it posthumously expelled Lin Piao from the Party, denouncing him by name for the first time and labeling him a "bourgeois careerist, conspirator, counterrevolutionary double-dealer, renegade, and traitor." Although the Congress reaffirmed its faith in "Marxism-Leninism-Mao Tse-tung Thought," Chairman Mao played only a symbolic role in its activities, and the new Party Constitution deemphasized the cult of Mao that had been Lin Piao's stock-in-trade. The Congress generally endorsed existing policies, but both the personnel changes and the reports delivered reflected the delicate political balancing act that Chou had performed in order to stage the Congress.

The appointments to the new Central Committee, the Politburo, and the Politburo Standing Committee that constitutes China's most powerful decision-making body achieved a compromise on representation not only between pragmatists and ideologues but also between civilian and military leaders and between regional and central authorities. The two principal reports, by Chou and by Wang Hung-wen, a Shanghai political cadre in his late thirties who suddenly rose from obscurity to a prominent position among the leadership, suggested the continuing contest between pragmatists and ideologues for the loyalties of a Party that had swollen to 28 million members. Chou denounced Ch'en Po-ta, ousted head of the Cultural Revolution Directorate, in the same vitriolic terms he used for Lin Piao, and warned: "For a long time to come, there will still be two-line struggles within the Party . . . and such struggles will occur ten, twenty, or thirty times." Wang, by contrast, said nothing about Ch'en Po-ta and asserted that struggles like the Cultural Revolution "will have to be carried out many times in the future."

The months following the Tenth Party Congress witnessed a slow intensification of the veiled attacks on pragmatic policies, under the slogan "Go Against the Tide." More than coincidentally, the new Party Constitution stated that "all comrades throughout the Communist Party possess the revolutionary spirit of daring to go against the tide," a sentence that was probably inserted as part of the price of radical support, and Wang Hung-wen's report on that document emphasized that "a true Communist must act without selfish concerns and dare to go against the tide, not fearing removal from his post, expulsion from the party, imprisonment, divorce, or the guillotine." Although propaganda media continued to excoriate Lin Piao after the Congress, they branded him a "rightist" rather than a "leftist," linked him to the policies of Liu Shao-ch'i, whom he had helped to depose, and reaffirmed the anti-elitist values that Lin had personified only a few years earlier. Not long afterward, the intensifying attack upon Lin was linked to the campaign against the teachings of Confucius. Lin was condemned for "preaching the rubbish of Confucianism as part of his attempt to restore capitalism to China" and for opposing the "forward-looking approach to social change and the important measures" adopted by the First Chinese Emperor, Ch'in Shih Huang-ti, who in the Chinese lexicon seemed to symbolize Chairman Mao.

As the year 1974 opened, the mystery of Chinese politics deepened. Former Party General Secretary Teng Hsiao-p'ing was restored to the Politburo, despite the fact that he and Liu Shao-ch'i had been purged earlier in the Cultural Revolution as "the two leading power-holders in the Party taking the capitalist road." Mao had charged them with usurping power and treating him "like a dead parent at a funeral," and the Red Guards had pilloried Teng for his obsession with the games of mahjong and bridge. Teng had been so fond of bridge that he had sometimes ordered special planes to fly his favorite partners over a thousand miles to join his game. Nevertheless, this

293. The Chinese are especially proud of their progress in industrialization. Visitors to China are shown many factories, large and small. Here a completed Caterpillar-type tractor moves off the assembly line at China's leading tractor factory, in Loyang. The plant was built in 1955 and now produces Caterpillar and rubber-wheeled tractors as well as bulldozers. This famous factory and others like it hold the hopes for the mechanization of Chinese agriculture.

294–96. Left: Making parts in one of the
sixteen divisions of the tractor factory
at Loyang. Right: Assembly line at
the same factory. Below: Skilled
women workers at the West District
No. 1 Transistor Factory, Peking.
Many small workshops and factories
in urban residential neighborhoods
offer housewives an opportunity to
participate in production and to learn
practical skills.

297. Neighborhood housewives sewing red neckerchiefs in a basement workshop of an apartment block in Peking's East District.

enormously able organizer was rehabilitated, apparently to assist in the strengthening of the central Party and government organs in Peking.

Further evidence of the centralizing trend came with the dramatic reshuffling of most of the country's regional military commanders. This uprooted them from local power bases where they controlled not only the army but also the Party and government bureaucracies in their areas.

Yet at the same time as these efforts were being made to reinforce Peking's discipline over the country, the radicals were intensifying their campaign against so-called "reactionary tendencies." Educational institutions seemed to be on the verge of fresh upheavals. The *People's Daily* made a national heroine of a twelve-year-old girl who wrote a letter to a local newspaper denouncing the autocratic behavior of her fifth-grade teacher. She had asked rhetorically: "Are we, the youth of Mao Tse-tung's era, to be slaves to the notions of teachers' status that ruled in the old society?"

Shortly afterward, the *People's Daily* turned its guns upon Western cultural giants. Plato, Shakespeare, Beethoven, and Schubert were among those condemned. For example, the leading Party newspaper wrote that the "Unfinished" Symphony "not only has no title but it also depicts evident class sentiments, having been written in an epoch when Austria, reactionary feudal bastion in the Germanic federation, was exercising cruel oppression and exploitation of peasants and workers" (January 14, 1974). Infinitely to be preferred were the works of Maoist composers which reflected the goodness of new China. There were many signs of a disturbing anti-foreign tone that was reminiscent of the early days of the Cultural Revolution. For example, a documentary film on China by the Italian director Antonioni was castigated as a "wild provocation against the Chinese people." And Professor Owen Lattimore, a leading Western expert on inner Asia who had toured China's remote border areas as a guest of Chou En-lai in 1972, was denounced as an "international spy" for having praised Confucius in a book written almost forty years earlier. This was an obvious attack on Chou.

There were other indications of an almost self-conscious orchestration of the echoes of 1966. Particularly striking was the self-criticism of China's most famous philosopher, Feng Yu-lan. He confessed that he had mistakenly worshiped Confucius for most of his seventy-nine years and defended brainwashing by saying: "People regularly wash their faces and take baths to keep clean. Why shouldn't a person cleanse his mind of filth?"

The pendulum of Chinese politics continued to swing throughout 1974 as the forces in "the two-line struggle" jockeyed for position. The contest for power focused in part upon the new Constitution that the government of the

People's Republic needed to replace the 1954 version, which the turmoil of the preceding decades had rendered obsolete. A new draft Constitution had been prepared as early as 1970, but the principal factions had been unable to agree upon it. Finally, in early 1975, the new Constitution was promulgated. It was brief, indeed truncated, compared to its predecessor, and plainly bore the marks of a compromise between radicals and pragmatists that could satisfy neither side.

This new document was distinctive in abolishing the office of chief of state, a post that had been left vacant since the ouster of Liu Shao-ch'i and that had been coveted by Lin Piao. Another innovation was its provision for the chairman of the Party, rather than a government official, to serve as commander-in-chief of the armed forces. This enabled Mao to retain what the Cultural Revolution had confirmed to be the critical power position in China. The new Constitution reduced the number of institutional checks upon the exercise of governmental power, eliminated a few of the guaranties of personal freedom enshrined in its predecessor, confirmed the abolition of the procuracy—the prosecutor's office that was supposed to serve as a watchdog against violations of legality—and left no doubt that the courts were to follow "the mass line" rather than act independently of Party control.

At the suggestion of Chairman Mao, however, the new Constitution added a right to strike to the freedoms listed. Another novelty was its guaranty of new forms of freedom that had grown out of the previous decades, such as the right to put up wall posters and to engage in public debates. These latter freedoms and the right to strike were apparently inserted by the radicals to ensure that the reestablishment of a well-organized government would not result in curbing their resort to mass demonstrations as a weapon in the political struggle. The radicals plainly did not intend to permit those who disagreed with their views to enjoy any liberties whatever, and both before and after the 1975 Constitution they fiercely suppressed their opponents whenever possible. The best-known instance was the arrest of three young, courageous intellectuals from Canton who in late 1974 had put up, under the pseudonym Li I-che, a very long wall poster criticizing the violations of law and the hypocrisy of Party leaders and calling for democracy and a socialist legal system. Yet millions of bureaucrats of all levels and workers, teachers, students, writers, artists, and other intellectuals who never rose to prominence also suffered. Many were killed, and we learned only recently how many were driven to suicide.

Larger numbers were illegally detained for years and subjected to endless struggle meetings and harassment, while many others lost their jobs and were vilified. Moreover, not only the individuals under attack were affected, but also their families, who were frequently barred from employment or educational opportunities that would otherwise have been open.

Mass demonstrations began to plague certain Chinese cities as 1975 unfolded. Political strikes fomented by the radicals occurred in the ancient city of Hangchow, for example, forcing at least one of its major silk factories to cease production for four months. The railroads proved increasingly vulnerable to political sabotage in some key rail centers such as the cities of Chengchow and Hsuchow. Workers' morale was also suffering on economic as well as political grounds. No general pay raises had been granted to factory workers for over a decade. The willingness of pragmatic leaders like Teng Hsiao-p'ing to allow bonuses to be paid to the best workers was undercut by the radicals, who feared the property protections retained in the 1975 Constitution and used their domination of the media to wage a campaign against "bourgeois rights."

As 1976 approached, the nation was rife with tension. It was widely known that Chairman Mao, then over eighty, was in declining health and that Premier Chou En-lai was hospitalized and dying of cancer. People who thought about the fate of China, and their own welfare, worried about what would happen once these two elderly leaders left the scene.

The Smashing of the "Gang of Four" (1976–79)

1976 proved to be the fateful year. Chou died in January, leaving vacant the most important post in the government. Outside observers were betting that Chou's experienced protégé, the rehabilitated Teng Hsiao-p'ing, would be named to succeed him. The radicals, however, had other plans. They were too weak to place their own person in the premier's position but were determined to keep Teng from the post. Teng, after all, was the preeminent pragmatist. It was he who had accused the radicals of placing ideology over professional competence, quipping: "It does not matter whether a cat is black or white as long as it catches mice." Chiang Ch'ing, Mao's wife, and her ultra-leftist colleagues had been unable to prevent Teng's rehabilitation because Chou En-lai had strongly backed it. But with Chou gone, they were able to persuade the enfeebled Mao that a compromise candidate should be selected as premier, one who had no clear ties to either the radicals or the pragmatists. Thus in February it was announced that Hua Kuo-feng had been chosen to serve as acting premier. Although a vice premier and Minister of Public Security, Hua was little known even to "China watchers."

No permanent decision on the premier's position had yet been reached, and political maneuvering continued until the first week of April, when the question was resolved in dramatic fashion. Hundreds of thousands of people in a number of cities took the occasion of the annual *Ch'ing-ming* festival, when Chinese traditionally clean the gravesites of their ancestors as a mark of respect, to pay homage to the late Chou En-lai. Because of Chou's opposition to the excesses of the radicals, these demonstrations were implicit protests against their repression and Mao's sponsorship of it. In Peking, since Chou's ashes had been scattered at his request, the crowd laid wreaths containing tributes to him in the great square in front of the Forbidden City's Gate of Heavenly Peace (T'ien-an-men). The wreaths were piled at the base of the tall granite obelisk that serves as the monument to the People's Heroes. Disputes broke out and eventually, under cover of night, the "workers' militia" at the direction of certain ultra-leftist leaders sought to disperse the crowd and remove the wreaths. This triggered the most massive rioting the PRC ever allowed foreign observers to witness. Hundreds were arrested, even larger numbers of unarmed people were brutally beaten, and "the T'ien-an-men incident," as it came to be known, was declared a counterrevolutionary event.

The radicals within the leadership promptly seized upon this as the pretext they needed for attacking Teng, whom they accused of instigating the incident in an effort to mobilize popular sentiment on behalf of his candidacy for the premier's post. Teng was immediately removed from his positions of leadership in the Party and government, and it was announced that Hua Kuo-feng had been confirmed as premier. The radicals themselves, however, were not in control. They knew that, as Mao continued to decline, they had to use the little time remaining before his death to prepare for the final power struggle. Hua was an uncertain, untested leader, who had only assumed an important role in the central government in the early 1970s, after working his way up the administrative ladder in Chairman Mao's native province of

Hunan. Although it was the Cultural Revolution that enabled Hua to reach the apex of the government as a relatively young man of about 57, the extent of his loyalty to the radicals was unclear. Moreover, the ousted Teng continued to have strong support within the Party, the military, and the bureaucracy, with the people, and with other Party leaders who feared a radical coup and had been considering how to avoid it.

Plainly the demise of the charismatic Mao could be expected to plunge the nation into crisis. Nature herself seemed to anticipate the worst. In July one of the most devastating earthquakes history has recorded laid waste the city of Tangshan and caused substantial damage in nearby Tientsin and even as far away as Peking. Hundreds of thousands were killed and many more made homeless. To Chinese, who have traditionally believed that disruptions in the natural world augur disruptions in the political world, the great earthquake seemed a portent of the earthshaking events that might accompany Mao's death.

Mao died on September 9, Hua was announced as Mao's successor as Party Chairman, and within a month the power struggle came to a climax. On October 6 the group of leaders that has since been vilified as the "Gang of Four" was suddenly arrested: Mao's widow, Chiang Ch'ing, who had reportedly aspired to succeed him; Vice Premier Chiang Ch'un-ch'iao, whom many had thought a possible successor; the handsome former worker who catapulted to political stardom, Wang Hung-wen; and the famous political writer, Yao Wen-yuan, whose polemic against Wu Han's allegorical play criticizing Mao had launched the Cultural Revolution. This Shanghai group, as they were often called before their fall, were all members of the Party's ruling Politburo. They were arrested by a military unit that operated under the personal supervision of another Politburo member, Wang Tung-hsing, who had been Mao's bodyguard for many years. Other arrests soon followed, including that of Mao's nephew. Chairman Hua, backed by the aged and respected Marshal Yeh Chien-ying and the victorious pragmatists, moved to purge Party, government, and army of key supporters of the "Gang of Four."

This effort spawned a series of nationwide campaigns that denounced the Gang and held it responsible for all the troubles of Chinese life. The Gang was condemned for the terror that it had inflicted upon the Party elite as well as others for a decade, and for the economic chaos caused by its xenophobic and irrational policies and its ceaseless scheming for power.

It was also castigated for the "ten lost years" that its "fascist dictatorship" had brought to higher education; for its withering of the arts, literature, and music; and for the continuing emphasis on class struggle that had denied the nation the talents of millions of people who had unfairly been branded with labels such as "counterrevolutionaries," "rightists," and "bad elements," or who had been discriminated against because they were the children or even grandchildren of the former landlords or bourgeoisie. Indeed, as the campaigns went on and as people began to voice long-pent-up complaints, the Gang even became the scapegoat for events as far back as the late 1950s and for developments that occurred long after their arrest. Criticism of the Gang became a safe way of criticizing everything that seemed wrong with the Communist system and all the mistakes made by Chairman Mao.

The treatment of Mao, of course, was one of the most sensitive issues confronting China's new leaders. After a few days of hesitation following his death, they decided to preserve Mao's body under glass and build a mausoleum to display it, as the Soviet Union had done for Lenin. They also decided to preserve the body of Mao's Thought, but only by gradually adapting it to China's need for modernization. They began to emphasize those aspects of Maoism that seemed to promote the new leaders' pragmatic policies and categorized Mao's words not as sacred dogma but merely as basic principles that had to be flexibly applied to suit the country's evolving circumstances. Mao's successors hoped to carry out a more subtle and less disruptive form of de-Stalinization. Too sharp a break with the past might shatter the mantle of Maoism that provides the Party with its ideological underpinning. Furthermore, Chairman Hua's legitimacy derived exclusively from Mao's reported selection of him as successor. Mao supposedly passed on the torch by writing Hua a note that stated: "With you in charge, I'm at ease." Undermining Mao would thus have undermined Hua's right to rule.

By August 1977 Hua and his associates were in sufficient command of their apparatus to convene the Eleventh Party Congress and to enact yet another Party Constitution, one that resembled the 1956 Party Constitution. By early 1978 they were ready to hold the first meeting of the Fifth National People's Congress, in order to reconstitute the government. There they enacted another government Constitution that formalized a return to many, but not all, of the features of the governmental system that prevailed during the mid-1950s, just prior to the anti-rightist movement. Like its 1954 predecessor, the 1978 Constitution included certain checks upon the executive departments by the legislatures that it formally revived at the various levels of government and by the reconstituted procuracy that is supposed to serve as a guardian of legality. It also reasserted the right of an accused to defend himself in a public trial before a tribunal composed of two laymen as well as a judge.

The leadership made clear that it wished to build a formal legal system to protect the basic rights of the people and to limit the power of government to act arbitrarily. This derived from the deeply felt and widely shared need to avoid a repetition of the long nightmare of the Cultural Revolution and the "Gang of Four." But the desire for a legal system also reflected the belief that law is an indispensable tool for economic development, that the predictability and security offered by a legal system would not only encourage individuals to contribute their talents without fear of arbitrary punishment but would also facilitate the actual operation of economic institutions. For example, a contract can provide a state factory with reasonable assurance that a commune will deliver desired raw materials at the right time and place and according to prescribed standards regarding price, quantity, and quality. Moreover, government agencies, state enterprises, communes, and individuals all need rules to follow. And fair and efficient means of settling disputes and imposing sanctions have to exist if the economy is to function smoothly. Hence the new leadership's stress upon economic legislation and related institutions.

The economic goals that were announced at the fifth NPC were extraordinarily ambitious. Chairman Hua sought to make clear the new government's intention to move the country out of the economic doldrums of recent years. By 1985, he pledged, China would be producing 60 million tons of steel per year and 400 million tons of grain, and it would open ten oilfields the size of the great Taching field in the northeast and establish some 120 new industrial projects. Thus China would be well on the way to achieving what quickly became known as "the four modernizations": of industry and commerce; agriculture; science and technology; and the military.

To achieve these ambitious goals the leadership demonstrated a new flexibility toward methods of stimulating production. They endorsed bonuses, piece rates, and other means of compensating productive workers more than others, which for a long period had been ideologically unacceptable. They granted modest pay raises for certain categories of workers, the first in fifteen years, in a general effort to raise the morale of a labor force that seemed to have lost the proverbial Chinese will to work. The regime also moved more vigorously to restore the jobs and reputations of officials, workers, and intellectuals who had been unfairly treated during the previous decades, and often compensated them for losses suffered. It also began to open up employment to people formerly barred on arbitrary grounds. Those who still wore "rightist caps" from the late 1950s finally had them removed, thanks largely to the efforts of Teng Hsiao-p'ing, who was himself rehabilitated a second time in 1977 and gradually restored to both his membership in the Party Politburo and his government office as a Vice Premier.

The government made clear that the long-standing Maoist precept of China's "self-reliance," which had often been interpreted to prevent close economic cooperation with other countries, would no longer stand as a barrier to trade. Indeed, without foreign equipment and technology, Peking acknowledged, China would be hard pressed to achieve its goals. Thus the arrest of the "Gang of Four" set in motion forces that led to a considerable expansion of China's foreign commercial activity. During 1978 the PRC contracted for the importation of billions of dollars of capital equipment and technology from Japan and the industrialized West, and foreign businessmen and bankers rushed to China to discuss the PRC's even more ambitious plans.

The new leaders also moved to restore the nation's educational system in order to overcome the severe damage inflicted since the Cultural Revolution. Modernization requires scientists, technicians, doctors, economists, lawyers, and a host of other experts and skilled workers. China had lost over a decade of training time and had to offer opportunities not only to the current high school graduates but also to the "lost generation" of talented youth who had never had an opportunity for meaningful higher education. Thus the government reestablished nationwide examinations, which many millions took even though the newly restored institutions of higher learning had facilities to enroll a maximum of 300,000 new students each year.

The leadership recognized that greater freedom of expression is a necessary concomitant of this effort to renew China's modernization drive. People were still afraid to innovate, make suggestions, teach, or criticize, for experience had taught them that the Party line could soon change. The

People's Daily conceded that many mid-level government officials were afraid to carry out the new policies. Government efforts to encourage people to use some of the freedoms enshrined in the 1978 Constitution culminated by the end of that year in an extraordinary democratic movement that flourished in Peking and some other major cities. In the capital, for example, at what came to be known as "Democracy Wall" on the city's main street and at several other locations, hundreds of people began to speak out freely and to put up posters that voiced searching criticism of the regime. Some unapproved pamphlets and magazines were also openly circulated, a mind-boggling event in the PRC, where the printed word has always been under government control. Chinese who never previously dared to speak with foreigners proved willing and eager to do so, and some began to wear more colorful, Western-style clothing. Even disco dancing with foreigners was permissible in certain places. Visitors to China in the winter of 1978–79 witnessed and occasionally participated in an exciting intellectual ferment. When Teng Hsiao-p'ing was reportedly asked by angry comrades why the leaders tolerated this bewildering and potentially subversive spectacle of open criticism of the Party and its leaders and policies, he replied: "Let them criticize us. The heavens will not fall. It may do us good."

During this period Teng plainly seemed to be China's most powerful leader. The PRC's new democratic movement, its ambitious economic plans, and the normalization of diplomatic relations with the United States all appeared to bear his stamp. The third plenary session of the Party Central Committee in December was dominated by Teng, his supporters were being named to fill key Party and government posts, his remaining opponents within the Politburo were becoming increasingly isolated, and the difference in emphasis between his speeches and those of Chairman Hua seemed to be diminishing as Hua drew closer to the pragmatic line. Moreover, the Party reversed itself and announced that the 1976 "T'ien-an-men incident" had been a revolutionary event. Teng's historic visit to the United States in early 1979 saturated the media in the PRC as well as abroad and placed him more than ever in the spotlight.

Yet his dominance did not go unchallenged, and neither China's sudden surge of trade with the industrialized world nor its sudden surge of freedom were destined to last in pristine form. During the spring of 1979 each policy was modulated. Foreign trade policies had to undergo a "readjustment." The goals for 1985 that had been enunciated just the previous year were, it was now admitted, too ambitious. A series of fiascos had demonstrated that more careful planning and coordination would be necessary to rebuild the economy, and this would require time. It would do no good to rush to build a fertilizer plant if there were no trucks to carry the fertilizer to the farms. A steel plant could offer little satisfaction if, in order to run it, the government had to deprive the area in which it was to be located of virtually all electricity. Moreover, China's buying spree abroad had brought home the fact that it was dreadfully short of foreign exchange and would have to tailor its purchasing to its pocketbook. Thus, in order to enhance short-run foreign exchange earnings, the government began to give agriculture and light industrial projects preference over its ambitious heavy industrial plans.

The "readjustment" of trade plans was not designed to reduce China's long-range economic cooperation with other nations but to facilitate it through better-balanced development. This became clearer as 1979 unfolded. The PRC for the first time arranged to borrow many billions of dollars from a variety of foreign banks in order to have the funds required for necessary purchases abroad. It demonstrated increasing receptivity to a range of devices for attracting foreign investment, which had always been anathema to China's nationalistic leaders. Compensation trade, joint ventures with Chinese enterprises, and even wholly owned foreign enterprises became possible, and Peking revived several pre-Cultural Revolution institutions for attracting funds from overseas Chinese. All of this dynamism brought forth a number of new PRC institutions for planning and regulating economic activities, and one of the first of the laws promulgated by the recently revived National People's Congress set forth the principles for joint ventures.

A similar readjustment took place regarding freedoms of expression in the spring and summer of 1979. The tolerance that had endeared Teng to outspoken intellectuals in the winter diminished by late March. A number of wall poster writers were arrested, while many others were plainly intimidated by a crackdown that stimulated city governments to post notices of disputed legality that sharply limited dissident activities. In addition, unauthorized contacts with foreigners were prohibited. The new freedom had led to some socially undesirable consequences, including a lack of public discipline, and high-level opponents of the liberal policy had seized upon these developments to put Teng on the defensive. In Shanghai, for example, crowds of "educated youth" who had been sent down to the countryside, but who had come home for the traditional New Year's celebrations, had rioted in protest against having to return to the rural areas; they disrupted city traffic and for a day even suspended railroad operations. In several Chinese cities the relaxed atmosphere at dances and in universities had led to social contacts between foreign men and Chinese women that involved sexual relations and even prostitution; given the background of Chinese nationalist resentment against pre-Liberation exploitation of women by foreigners, this was more than the new leaders could stomach. And amid the tense atmosphere generated by China's springtime border war with Vietnam, some Chinese were accused of selling state secrets to foreign reporters.

Teng Hsiao-p'ing, also under attack because of his associations with the overly optimistic economic policy and the Vietnam war, sought to steal his opponents' thunder by himself declaring limits to the liberalization. He announced what came to be known as "the four basic principles." Criticisms were to be permitted so long as they did not challenge socialism, the proletarian dictatorship, Party leadership, and "Marxism-Leninism-Mao Tse-tung Thought." Thus the posters on "Democracy Wall," now closely monitored by the plainclothes police, became less interesting, and people were forbidden to put up their own posters in most other locations. Chinese stopped going to dances attended by foreigners, and casual conversations with foreigners occurred less often and were more strained than during winter.

Nevertheless, this springtime narrowing of freedom of expression did not constitute a return to the repression of the past. It was unevenly enforced, especially outside the capital, and by May controls had relaxed considerably as the liberal forces within the Party rallied in a counterattack. The convening of the second session of the fifth NPC in late June gave them a welcome boost that culminated in the promulgation of six laws in addition to the joint venture law: revised statutes regulating elections, local government, the courts and the procuracy, and newly minted codes of criminal law and procedure, the first ever enacted by the PRC. These laws, on the whole, provided important support for those who wanted to move China toward a more open society. Furthermore, the press, which during the winter had featured discussions of major legal topics of great sensitivity, such as the need for broad areas of free speech, for independence from Party control in judicial decision-making, and for equal justice under law, by summer renewed its discussion of such former taboos.

Other developments in the legal system also suggested the possibility of gradually evolving legal checks on government action. The restoration of the "people's lawyers" of the 1950s and of the Ministry of Justice, the actual recruitment of manpower to staff the procuracy, the increasing resort to model public trials, the renewed publication of law journals to inform and guide officials, the development of the Law Institute within the Academy of Social Sciences and of university law departments and other law colleges all indicated that the Party was in the process of creating a new interest group composed of legal professionals who might increasingly be expected to oppose a return to arbitrary rule.

By midyear the new leadership had been strengthened through the return to power of experienced senior officials such as Chen Yun, the economic planner, and P'eng Chen, one of the earliest high-ranking victims of the Cultural Revolution, who became a vice chairman of the National People's Congress and head of its Law Committee. Teng Hsiao-p'ing, again on the move, continued to install a younger generation of able administrators. Differences between Teng and Chairman Hua appeared to be muted, although Teng plainly wanted to abandon the doctrine of class struggle while Hua preferred merely to deemphasize it. Relations among the expanded leadership had become increasingly complex, even leaving aside the minority in the Politburo who were outside the mainstream, unenthusiastic about the new policies, and under persisting pressure. In his mid-seventies, Teng appeared to be wistfully contemplating retirement once his version of China's revolutionary line seemed secure.

Toward Reform and Modernization (1979–84)

But there could be no security for the new line so long as Teng's supporters did not occupy the leading positions in the Party, the government, and the military. The top post in each of these systems was held by Hua, who in a determined effort to remain in power was increasingly giving lip service to Teng's policies. During the next two years, in what amounted to a gradual and peaceful coup d'état, Teng successfully maneuvered to oust Hua from all three positions and, together with his protégés Zhao Ziyang and Hu Yaobang, constituted a new triumvirate to lead China toward reform and modernization.

Zhao, a talented, dynamic administrator who had used Teng's pragmatic policies to invigorate the economy of Szechuan province in the late 1970s, was appointed to the Politburo in the fall of 1979 and became a member of its Standing Committee, the power center of China, early the next year. Hu, a veteran of the Long March who, like Zhao, had been purged in the late 1960s, was not only elected to the Politburo's Standing Committee but was also chosen to fill the newly revived position of General Secretary of the Party, a post evidently designed to curb the power of Mao's anointed successor, Chairman Hua.

By the fall of 1980 the stage was set for Hua's withdrawal from managing the government. The press had prepared the public to expect this dramatic change. As the official New China News Agency had put it: "The patriarchal system of lifetime tenure and the system of designating successors by the 'patriarch' cannot make the patriarch and his designated successor 'wiser.' " In September Hua had no choice but to tell the National People's Congress that he had decided to resign as premier in favor of Zhao. Hua was still Party Chairman and Chairman of the Military Affairs Commission, however, and enjoyed considerable prestige and support.

Teng subtly manipulated the trial of the "Gang of Four" to further undermine Hua. The Gang had proved a problem even in captivity. What was to be done with them? They could have been secretly executed or left to die in hideous prison conditions, as they had dealt with so many of their rivals. At the other end of the spectrum, they could have been given a genuine public trial under the newly enacted Criminal Procedure Law that enables accused to defend themselves and to appeal a conviction. Or they could have been "brainwashed" or drugged to confess their crimes at a "show trial" like those staged by Stalin for some purged Soviet Party leaders in the 1930s.

Teng chose a fourth option: a truncated televised show trial in which the defendants were neither programmed to confess nor allowed a full opportunity to defend themselves. Two special tribunals were actually formed to handle cases that were regarded as distinct yet related. One involved the "Gang of Four" and another civilian leader, Ch'en Po-ta, formerly Mao's private secretary. The second involved the so-called "Lin Piao Clique," five senior military figures who had not been heard of since Lin's death in 1971. In long indictments the ten alleged counterrevolutionaries were charged with having, through collusion, "framed and persecuted Communist Party and state leaders in a premeditated way in an attempt to usurp Party leadership and state power." Mao's widow, Chiang Ch'ing, and her three comrades were accused of persecuting and slandering over 700,000 innocent people and causing the deaths of some 30,000, including the President of China, Liu Shao-ch'i, either directly or indirectly.

The tribunals were not staffed exclusively by professional judges but included a cross section of the elite who had been restored to their positions after the Cultural Revolution. The behavior of the defendants ranged from the silence of Chiang Ch'un-ch'iao to the contrition and cooperation of Yao Wen-yuan to the escalating defiance of the star performer, Chiang Ch'ing, who more than once shouted her rebuttals to the hand-picked audience and official television cameras and had to be dragged from the courtroom for "disrupting order." The defendants did not present their own witnesses, cross-examination was minimal, and only one of the "Gang" chose the assistance of counsel. Although almost every night during the two-month trial the public was treated to long, carefully screened television excerpts and there was a general media blitz, the Chinese were never allowed to learn the full trial record.

The evident lack of fundamental fairness in the trial may have aroused some sympathy for the spunky Chiang Ch'ing, who was plainly made to bear the burden of many offenses that everyone knew had been committed in collaboration with her late husband. Perhaps this, as well as a reluctance to create martyrs and further divide an already fractured society, was the reason why she and Chiang Ch'un-ch'iao, the other principal culprit, were given suspended death sentences instead of being executed. In any event the public seemed to be not only entertained but also basically satisfied with the proceedings, which, despite shortcomings that were perceived by many Chinese, represented a more legitimate way of handling genuinely hated offenders than could have been expected had the tables been turned.

The trial, of course, explicitly condemned the Cultural Revolution and implicitly condemned Chairman Mao, who, everyone recognized, was in effect an unindicted co-conspirator. Indeed, his widow claimed that Mao had approved of everything she did during the Cultural Revolution. "If you beat the dog, you should also beat the master," she said. This further weakened the position of Hua Kuo-feng, who, although spared accusation at the trial, was undergoing intensive criticism within the Politburo for the Maoist background and outlook that led him to embrace "the two whatevers," that is, "we firmly uphold whatever policy decisions Chairman Mao made, and we unswervingly adhere to whatever instructions Chairman Mao gave."

Informed Communist sources reported that a deal had been struck with Hua prior to the trial, according to which he would not be prosecuted for presiding over the suppression of the T'ien-an-men protesters in 1976 as Minister of Public Security if he would agree to step down as both Party Chairman and Chairman of the Military Affairs Commission at the next meeting of the Party Central Committee. Whatever the truth of the report, Hua did resign both posts when that long-delayed meeting was finally held in late June 1981. Hu Yaobang replaced him as Party Chairman and Teng Hsiao-p'ing became Chairman of the Military Affairs Commission, thereby testifying to the crucial importance of controlling the PLA. Teng, who had retired as a Vice Premier the previous year and still talked of withdrawing from day-to-day responsibilities, apparently did not think that circumstances yet allowed him that luxury.

In addition to toppling Hua, the June 1981 meeting of the Central Committee issued a long-awaited assessment of the role of Chairman Mao in the history of the PRC. This resolution took over fifteen months to prepare and was discussed and revised by literally thousands of senior Party officials. It condemned Mao for a succession of "left" errors beginning with the Great Leap Forward of 1958 and culminating with numerous mistakes during the Cultural Revolution, which it said was "responsible for the most severe setbacks and the heaviest losses suffered . . . since the founding of the People's Republic." Nevertheless, although Mao had initiated this "catastrophe," the resolution pleaded mitigating circumstances on his behalf. His, after all, "was the error of a great proletarian revolutionary" who had acted out of the noblest of motives in a misguided attempt to preserve the revolution he had done so much to create before 1949 and to establish in the early 1950s. He was, the resolution suggested, a leader who had excelled in war and fierce class struggle but had not been able to make the transition to a new era of socialist construction.

The resolution echoed a theme from some of Teng's recent speeches: That what was under way was not merely a struggle over power between hostile personalities but was, more significantly, a clash over policies and, even more fundamentally, over governmental philosophy. Under Mao, power had become excessively concentrated in the hands of too few people in the capital. Laws were needed to allow power to be exercised by various agencies, including local governments, state enterprises, and social units. The Party should stop usurping the day-to-day functions of government, and, in accordance with Leninist concepts, should revert to its earlier role as the formulator, not the executor, of policy. The resolution maintained that the existence in China of "the evil ideological and political influence of centuries of feudal autocracy" had contributed to a situation in which arbitrary individual rule and a personality cult had flourished within the Party, and this had to be overcome by creating a "highly democratic socialist political system."

The humiliation of Hua Kuo-feng was not yet complete, for in losing the post of Party Chairman he became a Vice Chairman and remained one of seven members of the Standing Committee of the Politburo. It was not until the Twelfth Congress of the Chinese Communist Party, held in September 1982, that Hua was removed from the Politburo. Moreover, he lost his position as Party Vice Chairman because the Twelfth Party Congress streamlined the leadership organization by abolishing the offices of Chairman and Vice Chairman. This relegated Mao's supposed heir to relative anonymity and powerlessness as an ordinary member of the Party Central Committee. This also left Hu Yaobang, who remained General Secretary, in command of the Party apparatus, even though his Chairman's office had been eliminated.

The Twelfth Party Congress also made other institutional changes. In order to encourage the Party's elderly leaders to give up their active government and Party responsibilities, it created a Central Advisory Commission through which the elderly could enter semiretirement with dignity, comfort, and continuing opportunities to be heard on policy matters. Teng Hsiao-p'ing sought to make membership on this Commission more attractive by assuming the post of Chairman while retaining his chairmanship of the Party's Military Affairs Commission. In order to enhance the Party's effectiveness in combatting corruption, favoritism, and other acknowledged evils of the bureaucracy, the Twelfth Party Congress strengthened the Discipline Inspection Commission.

As the Party eased its hold upon the day-to-day administration of government, the need to strengthen government as well as Party institutions became apparent, and at the end of 1982 a new PRC Constitution was promulgated that contained numerous improvements over its March 1978 predecessor, which had reflected the ambivalence and tensions of a post-Mao leadership that Teng Hsiao-p'ing had not yet come to dominate. The new Constitution gave legal form to many of the institutional reforms that Teng had been advocating. For example, the role of the National People's Congress and its Standing Committee, China's highest lawmaking body, was bolstered in an effort to breathe life into what the Western press had called a "rubber stamp" following its revival in the late 1970s. Moreover, the new Constitution required "all political parties" as well as other organizations to abide by the Constitution and the laws, thereby making it clear that even the Communist Party does not enjoy the privilege of being above the law. It also restored several features that the 1975 and 1978 Constitutions had removed from the original 1954 version, including the statement that "The people's courts shall, in accordance with the law, exercise judicial power independently and are not subject to interference by administrative organs, public organizations or individuals." This left to debate, interpretation, and practice the question whether the Party too was barred from interfering with court decisions.

The new Constitution also boosted the foreign business community's confidence in China's recent desire to welcome foreign investment. Despite the PRC's post-1978 "open door" policy and the spate of joint venture, tax, foreign exchange, trademark, and patent legislation promulgated to effectuate this policy, many foreigners feared that their investments might someday be seized as inconsistent with earlier constitutional provisions generally limiting ownership of China's "means of production" to state and collective enterprises. To assuage this fear, Article 18 of the 1982 Constitution specifically authorized foreign investment and promised to protect it "in accordance with law."

By 1983 Teng Hsiao-p'ing was more firmly in control than ever, despite the fact that he no longer was Vice Premier and was outranked by Hu Yaobang in Party protocol. Indeed, the publication of his *Selected Works* and the accompanying campaign exhorting people to study them, made some observers wonder whether a new cult of personality was developing. Nevertheless, the very necessity Teng felt to continue his leading responsibilities as he approached the age of eighty indicated doubts on his part that General Secretary Hu, Premier Zhao, and their comrades could in his absence meet the challenge of keeping China on a pragmatic, modernizing course. This was not only because of the intrinsic difficulties of reforming the economic, social, and political systems but also because of still deep-seated opposition to many of the new policies by both "leftists" and "conservatives" among the central and provincial cadres of the Party, the government, and the military.

One of the attacks that domestic critics have leveled against Teng's economic innovations and his "open door" policy is that they have led to a relaxation of social discipline that has produced a crime wave. Murder, rape, robbery, and serious economic crimes against the state have increasingly troubled a country that previously tried to convince the world that it had both an unusually low crime rate and an unusually effective system for reforming offenders. In an effort to reduce the crime rate, during 1983–84 the Party presided over a massive campaign that resulted in the execution of thousands of offenders and the confinement in labor camps and prisons of many more. The criminal procedure law and substantive criminal law were amended to facilitate the task of promptly convicting suspects and to expand the number of offenses for which the harshest penalties may be imposed. Although many Chinese intellectuals were troubled by this apparent setback to the cherished criminal justice reforms of 1979, some were frank to admit that the vigorous anticrime drive had made life safer for them and their children.

Less welcome to people who enjoyed contacts with foreigners was the spy scare created as part of the effort to suppress crime. The convictions for spying of numerous visitors from Hong Kong and Taiwan as well as local people were designed to create an atmosphere that would curb the growing contacts between Chinese and outsiders. The news that China would emphasize the detection of espionage even more than in the past by establishing a new Ministry of State Security had a similarly chilling impact upon many, but not all, friendships between Chinese and foreigners. Although toasts continued to be drunk to "mutual understanding" at every banquet for visitors, it seemed clear that, despite its "open door" policy, the Party did not want foreigners to understand too much about China, or Chinese to understand too much about other countries.

To protect China against other undesirable effects of the "open door" policy, at the same time as it carried on the anticrime drive the Party also launched a campaign against

334

"spiritual pollution," said to emanate from the outside world. It sought not only to eliminate pornography, rock music, and youthful preoccupation with sex, style, and money, but also to reimpose orthodoxy and conformity upon the many writers, artists, musicians, and other intellectuals who had hoped that the new leadership would revive the unprecedented freedoms of 1978–79. Significantly, this campaign met with broad opposition both inside and outside the Party and, by mid-1984, had run its course.

By this time the Party leaders had begun to focus on plans for a long-awaited nationwide campaign to rectify the Party itself, which had swelled to more than forty million members. The goal was to purge "leftists" and corrupt and incompetent elements and to make the organization more manageable as a result of the projected three-year "consolidation."

After Thirty-five Years

This summary of the first thirty-five years of the People's Republic necessarily focuses on dramatic mass movements, policy clashes, power struggles, personal rivalries, and purges. All this is essential background for understanding contemporary China—its problems, its accomplishments, and the fragility of its leadership as it strives to make the transition from Chairman Mao's charismatic rule to a more stable second-generation system. As should be clear by now, PRC policies are, above all, dynamic and swiftly changing, and we can expect this situation to continue as the elite strive to articulate the correct "line" for the nation's development.

Yet we should not become mesmerized by the fascinating task of tracing the pendulum nature of China's post-1949 development, which apparently embodies the Marxist dialectic of a recurring process by which thesis evokes antithesis to create synthesis. Before concluding, we should also step back from reviewing the succession of trees to ask about the forest. How successful does this Promethean effort to break the hold of tradition seem to be?

When we were preparing the second edition of this volume, in the summer of 1979, we presented what was then, on balance, a muted assessment of the PRC's record. Today, any overview must be more positive in tone. There are two basic reasons for this. The first is that China's economic performance during the first years of the 1980s has been very impressive, owing to a variety of recent changes and experiments. The second is that the new leaders have initiated a corresponding range of social and educational reforms that

335

have improved the quality of life despite the fact that individual freedoms continue to be significantly restrained.

In 1979 we noted that economic achievements in the 1970s had failed to match the substantial progress of the PRC's earlier years and that the post-Mao leadership had begun a massive effort to restore productivity. We also reported that, as part of this effort, for the first time in two decades, the PRC was considering a major revision of its agricultural system, one that would go beyond the existing changes, which had already decentralized planning and management of farm labor and crops from the commune to production teams of a few dozen families. Until then, it had been hoped that by making each team rather than the vast commune the accounting unit for calculating profits and losses, by encouraging teams to become self-reliant, by using a "work point" system that afforded greater compensation to more productive people, and by allowing families to farm private plots in their spare time and to sell their produce in rural markets, the regime had found an optimum socialist "mix" between collectivism and individual incentives. Agricultural reformers, however, realized that the production team was itself too large an accounting unit and that even smaller units had to be formed in order to foster individual work incentives by enabling people to see a clearer relationship between their labor and their gain.

As a result, beginning in 1979, some variation of the so-called household responsibility system was adopted throughout most of the Chinese countryside. Under this system, in addition to the "private plot" already allocated to family farming, an individual family is given the responsibility for farming a section of the fields that were formerly farmed collectively. Each household makes a contract with local commune or state officials to sell a fixed amount of the output from its field at a prescribed price. The household can keep its excess production, sell it to the official units at a premium above the prescribed price or, in the case of vegetables and other produce, sell it at the free markets that have expanded in both cities and rural areas. In order to give the peasants confidence that this very popular reform will not be abolished, and thereby encourage them to invest in improving the land assigned to their families, in 1984 the Party recognized the need to allow long-term contracts, and it authorized contracts of fifteen to twenty years' duration instead of the one to three-year periods originally adopted. This gives farmers many of the advantages of the land ownership that in

298. The head of a production brigade at the Hangchow Dragon Well Tea Commune stands in front of a "billboard of honor" that praises the production achievements of certain brigade members.

principle is denied them by the socialist system.

Related rural reforms have also had a dramatic impact upon productivity. Particularly striking is the emergence of the so-called specialized households, families or individuals who, for example, buy their own tractor or truck and contract with local people or organizations to plow fields or transport produce for them. Many engage in other specialized occupations such as large-scale poultry raising, fish farming, and processing; even the private raising of pigs, cattle, and sheep is becoming possible. Moreover, the size of the "private plots" allotted to families has been doubled in many places. Even more significantly, farmers can now, within limits, hire others to help them. Thus, private enterprise has developed, and the Chinese press currently features stories of rural entrepreneurs who have become rich and who should be emulated rather than interfered with by zealous cadres and neighbors who have not yet adapted to the new era.

337

The results of these changes have been startling. Grain output in 1982 and 1983 reached record heights. Since 1979 agricultural labor productivity has increased by an average of 2.7 percent each year, while the *total* increase between 1953 and 1978 was only 2.7 percent! Agricultural output per capita has gone up by approximately 36 percent in the past five years, and the PRC claims that net income per peasant has more than doubled. Both economists and visitors to the Chinese countryside testify to a recent enormous improvement in standards of living.

Yet the task of overcoming the widespread and desperate poverty of the Chinese countryside is far from complete, and there are many obstacles to further progress. Perhaps the greatest is the very small amount of arable land for so vast a population. Countries such as India and Japan have a much more favorable ratio of cultivable land to population, and even Bangladesh and Indonesia are better off. As Premier Zhao has noted, China must feed almost one quarter of the world's population on 7 percent of its cultivated land. And every year at least 13 million people are added to the population.

Future gains in productivity will have to come not from increasing the amount of available land but from increasing crop yields. Although China has already done much to do so, more can still be accomplished through extensive and appropriate application of chemical fertilizers and improved insecticides. But funds will be in short supply as the government, which has subsidized and invested heavily in the rural areas in recent years, will be pressed to emphasize other sectors of the economy, such as energy, transportation, and telecommunications, and will not be able to continue its recent favoring of agriculture. Thus, in assessing the future of the rural economy, the respected *Far Eastern Economic Review* has written:

> The real key to further gains will be inducing Chinese peasants to invest their increased income in their own fields and to undertake small- and medium-scale cooperative projects in areas such as irrigation, drainage and road-building using their own funds. (*Asia 1984 Yearbook,* p. 151.)

We can therefore expect the "household responsibility" and "specialized household" systems to endure and be strengthened, despite their repudiation of the Party's egalitarian tradition and the consequent opposition that they arouse among "leftist" local officials, who often seek to frustrate implementation of these reforms. In fact, in order to make farming more efficient by expanding the size of the land tilled by a given family and by developing an increasingly sophisticated division of labor, China may even allow families to assign their rights to till contracted lands to other families. This would free the assigning family to engage in specialized pursuits while receiving income from the assigned land. The goal is to leave farming to those who can do it best while others pursue what they are good at and enjoy.

Reforms in industry have not yet been as comprehensive, dramatic, or successful as those in agriculture, although the PRC reported a 10.2 percent rise in industrial output in 1983. Nevertheless, these reforms are significant, as the Party cautiously but steadily continues its program to transform bureaucrats into businessmen. State enterprises that formerly received all their financing from their government superiors and handed over any profits to those superiors have increasingly come to take on some of the characteristics of independent corporations responsible for their own profits and losses. When they need funds, they now are generally required to borrow them from state banks. The banks will assess the soundness of their projects and their ability to repay the loans, with interest, and will subject their business performance to continuing scrutiny. If the enterprises earn a profit, they no longer hand all of it back to the state, but pay an income tax and keep a share of the after-tax profit. This can be used, within limits, for renovation, purchase of new technology and equipment, bonuses for management and workers, and other purposes. Although state enterprises remain subject to the controls of a socialist planned economy, some enterprises are increasingly experimenting with sales to and purchases from a gradually evolving, supplementary market economy. Unsuccessful enterprises are now experiencing strong pressures to become more efficient or go out of business, a previously unthinkable option, and some have been closed. Moreover, the State Economic Commission has warned enterprises that continue to lose money that they will also lose their substantial state subsidies if they cannot earn a profit.

Corresponding changes in industrial labor policies are also under way. The Party has denounced the "iron rice bowl" tradition, according to which workers in state enterprises could not lose their jobs (their "rice bowl") no matter how poor their performance. Some factory managers have fired indolent and incompetent workers. The PRC has also denounced the long-standing practice of "eating from the same pot," that is, paying workers without rewarding those who are especially productive. In order to demonstrate a connection between performance and income, Chinese factories have been experimenting with a variety of bonus systems. Some have also introduced innovations such as administering tests to job applicants, requiring probationary periods before confirming employment, and entering into employment contracts that permit the firing of incompetent or insubordinate employees.

Some of the stimulus for industrial reform has come from the PRC's felt need to cooperate with foreigners in large numbers of joint ventures and coproduction, compensation trade, processing, and assembly projects that provide technology and capital. Some of the most interesting industrial changes are taking place in the "special economic zones" of southern China that were established in 1979 and in the "economic development zones" of fourteen coastal cities that were established in 1984. Moreover, the joint exploitation of China's offshore petroleum resources that over twenty foreign oil companies recently began with the China National Offshore Oil Corporation has been helping to modernize the oil sector of industry. In addition, Sino-foreign enterprises are even setting up in the interior of the country, as far from the urbanized east coast as Sinkiang province in the northwest and Yunnan province in the southwest.

In the hope of both reducing the serious unemployment problems and improving the quality of services available in the cities, the Party has encouraged private entrepreneurs to undertake many activities, including the operation of small restaurants, informal markets, motor vehicle transportation for people and goods, and tailor shops. By 1984, spurred by various state incentives such as tax benefits, the right to hire up to eight employees, and inexpensive bank loans, there were more than 7.5 million self-employed shopkeepers, vendors, and other small businessmen in China, compared to 140,000 in 1978. The new Constitution pledged protection for "the lawful rights and interests of the individual economy," and many localities have created "individual workers' federations" to look after the self-employed much as the trade unions protect industrial workers. To demonstrate the importance the state now attaches to private entrepreneurs, who used to be condemned as "the tail of capitalism," in 1983 two representatives of this group were among the deputies elected to the National People's Congress for the first time. One runs a wine shop with his sisters, and the other is a commercial photographer. In 1984 Premier Zhao announced that small state-owned shops and restaurants will be leased to individuals or small groups of workers to run. The Party has even authorized peasants to move to nearby towns to enter nonfarming businesses, as part of a plan to reduce the farming population to between 20 and 30 percent of the total rural population. This has aroused considerable opposition among local "leftist" officials, who have tried to sabotage the policy by measures such as denying business licenses, refusing to permit the peasants to change their household registration, and rejecting rental applications. They have also invented various obstacles to frustrate peasants who do manage to set up shop.

The underlying premise of this new program is the need to release China's productive forces from the stifling effects of a monolithic, tightly controlled system by giving localities, enterprises, and individuals the freedom to take initiatives and enhance their earnings. "We must encourage competition and prevent monopoly," Premier Zhao recently told the National People's Congress. To do so, he introduced reforms to promote competition among state-owned, cooperative, and private enterprises. The basic features of socialism—public ownership of the major means of production and planning of the principal aspects of the economy—will remain, but within this context the state will rely less on direct administrative orders telling production entities what to do and more on their independent operation under the indirect influence of the state's price, tax, and credit policies.

This, of course, presupposes the readiness of the state to articulate policies appropriate to the new program. Although the PRC has moved boldly on tax and credit matters, it has proved extremely cautious in changing a pricing system that is widely acknowledged to be irrational and that rests upon enormous state subsidies to consumers and other interests. Many of the prices fixed by the State Price Bureau bear little relation to the value of the commodity in question in terms of supply and demand. A bag of sand can cost more than a bag of coal. Yet if prices were suddenly decontrolled and market forces allowed to assert themselves, the social and political reverberations would be profound even if the

299–302. The transportation system that the Chinese Communists inherited was extremely inadequate. They have made slow but steady progress in improving the situation, yet human power is still a basic means of moving materials from one place to another.

303, 304.

Top: Barges on the Wu-sung (Soochow) River in Shanghai. Shanghai is not only China's
largest city but also its greatest industrial and commercial center. China's inland waterways are vital
parts of the national transportation network and are crowded with all kinds of boats. Bottom: An
ocean-going freighter on the Huang-p'u River in Shanghai. Although now self-sufficient in food
production, China continues to import foreign grain into its coastal cities rather than impose too
great a strain on its internal transportation system within China.

305. The bridge that spans the Yangtze River at Nanking. With evident satisfaction, Chinese guides report that foreign engineers had said it was impossible to build a bridge across the Yangtze, but that in the late 1950s Chinese engineers succeeded.

subsidies that now impose a great burden upon the state budget were maintained. The Party leaders, mindful of the tragic, absurd inflation of the 1940s that helped bring the Communists to power, have always sought to minimize price increases in order to foster stability. They realize, however, that steps must gradually be taken to adjust prices if the new modernization program is to succeed, and they have begun to do so by balancing increases in the prices of certain commodities with decreases in the prices of others, in the hope of softening the impact on the public.

Even if we assume that China's renewed emphasis upon achieving greater industrial and agricultural productivity will continue to prove successful, this effort alone cannot assure that the growth in production will keep ahead of the country's growth in population. The latter, in part reflecting a declining death rate as a result of improved health conditions and the absence of war and famine, drastically declined during the 1970s from well over 2 percent per year to 1.2 percent by the decade's end. Even this impressive achievement, however, was not enough to meet China's need to limit its population in the year 2000 to 1.2 billion. Moreover, in the early 1980s the natural growth rate crept up to 1.4 percent, and a baby boom was expected because of the large number of people reaching marriageable age. Thus the Party imposed a strict new policy that called for each couple to have only one child, with limited exceptions in hardship cases, as when a couple has a retarded or disabled child or when one of the partners to a second marriage has not had a child. The hope is to reduce the annual population growth to less than 1 percent in each of the remaining years before 2000. Otherwise the PRC's economic gains will be eaten up by the large number of additional mouths to feed, and per capita production may even diminish, as has happened in some Chinese provinces during the past generation. The greatest progress in reducing the birthrate has been made in the cities. The challenge persists in the countryside, however, where traditional preference for male children continues to stimulate large families. Rural women are under enormous pressure to produce sons, not only because of "feudal" traditions but also because farm families need male labor and daughters leave the family after marriage, which involves an expensive dowry despite its prohibition under the marriage law. In 1983, for example, fifteen women from Anhwei province wrote to the *People's Daily* saying that, although they already had three to nine daughters each, they would rather die than give up the chance to have a son, for failure to produce a son was worse than death. They wrote:

> We all know that limitless childbearing gives us nothing but troubles and fading health. None of us would have become what we are now if not for the deadly longing for a son. For mothers like us here nothing is more painful than what we have to suffer from discrimination and ill-treatment.

Another woman—obviously not a dedicated Communist—even said she would give up her Party membership, if necessary, to have a son. In the countryside, women who give birth to girls are frequently beaten by their husbands, abused by their mothers-in-law, and even criticized by their own parents. As anticipated by those who know rural China, the strict one-child policy has also led to many cases of female infanticide, so that the parents can try again for a boy, and this has begun to threaten a long-term serious disparity between the sexes. The *People's Daily* warned not long ago: "In 20 years a great number of young men will be unable to find spouses if parents cling to feudal thinking and kill or abandon their unwanted female babies." Yet the courts have been lenient in punishing those responsible for infanticide. For example, a man who snatched his newborn daughter from the delivery table and killed her by stuffing cotton in her mouth and throwing her in a bucket of nightsoil received a three-year prison sentence, less than the sentence given to people convicted of illegally removing intrauterine contraceptive devices from women!

Gradually, even rural areas should feel the impact of intense educational and social pressure. Especially effective in the cities have been the efforts of women cadres who convene group meetings of the women in their neighborhood or work unit so that the group can discuss the importance of birth control and agree on a specific plan for allocating births among the group. The most popular birth control technique in the cities is the oral pill, while intrauterine devices predominate in the countryside. China is engaged in intensive research on new contraceptive devices. All contraceptives are issued free of charge, and normally women can be sterilized and men vasectomized at no cost. Unwanted pregnancies are commonly terminated by inexpensive legal abortion, and many women have been "persuaded" or even physically compelled to undergo abortion or sterilization by overzealous local cadres determined to prevent a second child.

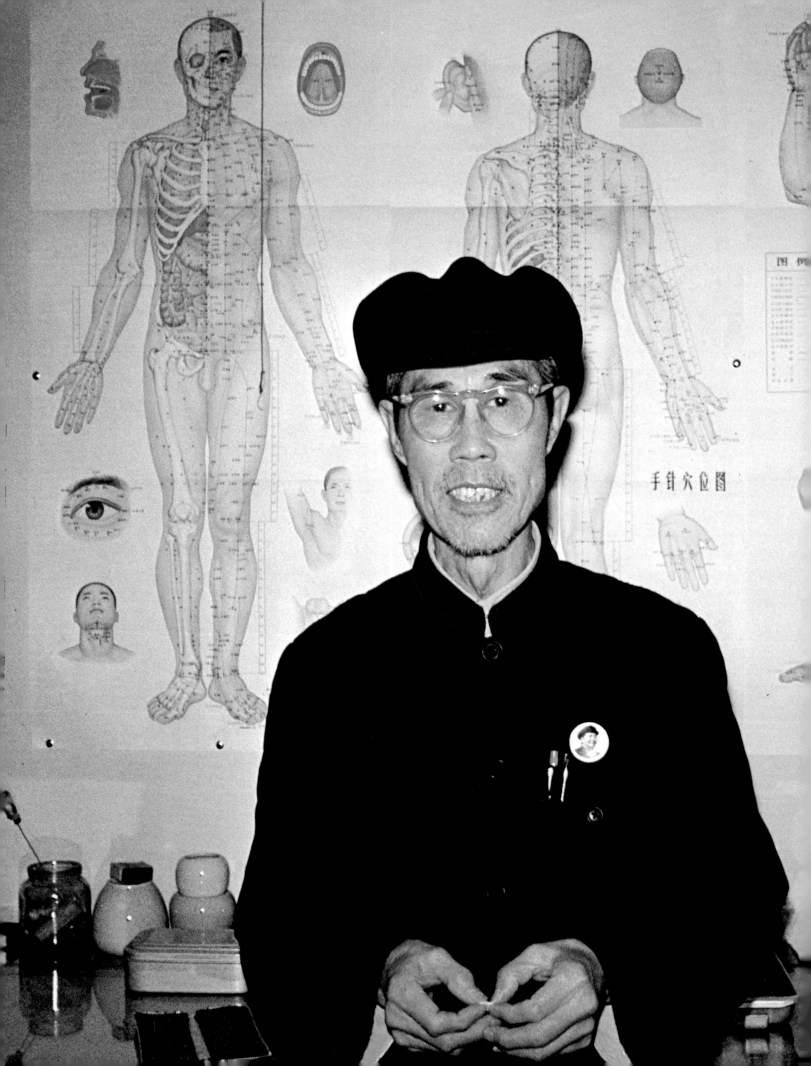

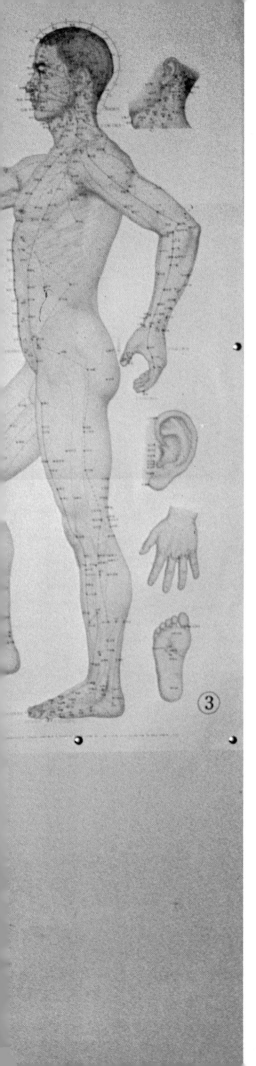

③

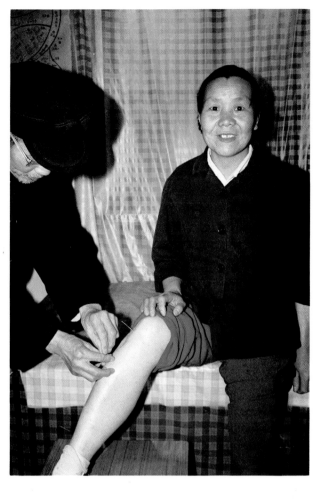

306–8.
Opposite page: Medical
worker at a neighborhood
clinic in the basement of
an apartment block in the
Eastern District of Peking.
Behind him are the charts
that guide his application
of acupuncture for the
treatment of various
ailments. One of new
China's outstanding
achievements has been the
extension of low-cost,
competent medical care to
the masses. A combination
of traditional Chinese and
Western medicine is used.
Above: Medical worker
at a neighborhood clinic
applies acupuncture to the
leg of a smiling resident.
Below: A Young Pioneer
learns to find the "pressure
points" for acupuncture
treatment by practicing on
herself. She is attending
an acupuncture class at a
Shanghai "children's palace."

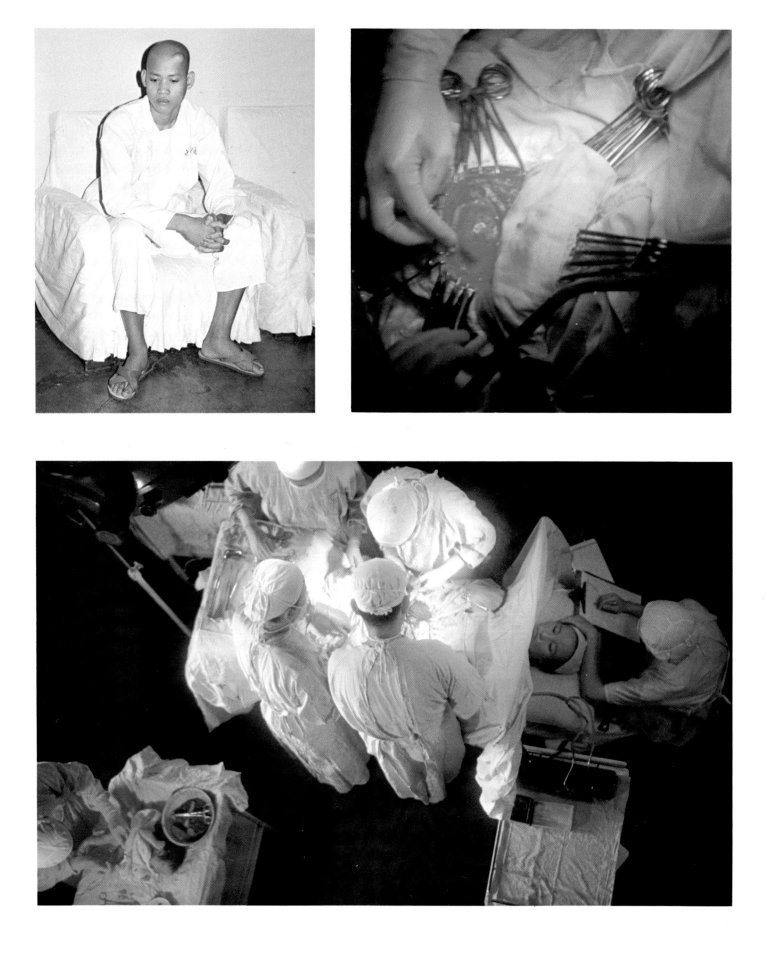

309, 310. Far left: Patient about to undergo surgery to remove a cranial tumor. The operation was successfully performed, with the aid of acupuncture anesthesia, by the staff of Teaching Hospital No. 2, Chung-shan Medical College, Canton (Kwangchow). Left: A doctor points out the cranial tumor being removed by surgery. Drills were used to cut out the diseased section of the cranium. A fiberglass plate was inserted to replace the section removed.

311. Using acupuncture anesthesia, doctors deliver a baby by cesarean section. The baby is on the table at the left. The mother is being sewn up on the right. This is a frequent occurrence at Teaching Hospital No. 2.

The most effective birth control technique, of course, is abstinence, and the People's Republic has sought to pressure young people, not always successfully, to postpone marriage until their mid- or late twenties and to refrain from pre-marital intercourse.

Implementation of family planning is the responsibility of provincial governments rather than of the central authorities in Peking, and the measures adopted vary somewhat from province to province. Some are purely psychological, such as holding mass rallies at which huge red flowers are pinned on the chests of women who promise to meet the new goal of the one-child family. Yet, only 10 percent of China's 180 million women of childbearing age have signed the one-child contract, and fully a third of all these women still use no form of contraception. To induce them to conform, most measures are practical, such as free schooling and medical treatment for an only child, periodic cash bonuses to his parents, and added housing space allotments. To remove the need for large families as insurance against old age, Peking is contemplating improved pensions for elderly childless couples and parents of merely one child. Moreover, Kwang-tung province offers an additional incentive by providing that when a worker's only child is a girl, she can take over her father's job if she has the right qualifications. People who violate the one-child policy are subject to various sanctions, including fines. Yet many violations occur.

This is a far cry from the PRC's earlier lack of concern for population control, epitomized by Chairman Mao's statement that the more people China had, the better things would be. In order to demonstrate this 180-degree change in policy, the Party Central Committee recently admitted that the Party had been wrong many years earlier in criticizing one of China's most famous economists, Ma Yin-chu, who had been dismissed from the presidency of Peking University in 1960 for having opposed Mao's stand. Had Ma's advice been heeded, China today would have almost 250 million fewer people, as the ninety-eight-year-old scholar pointed out at the time of his public rehabilitation. Although it is frequently pointed out that over one million people were killed during the Cultural Revolution, it has only recently come to light that 120 million people were added to China's population during the years 1966–71 because of a complete lack of concern with birth control. This nearly equaled the entire population growth during the period 1840–1949!

Because of the desperate race between production and

349

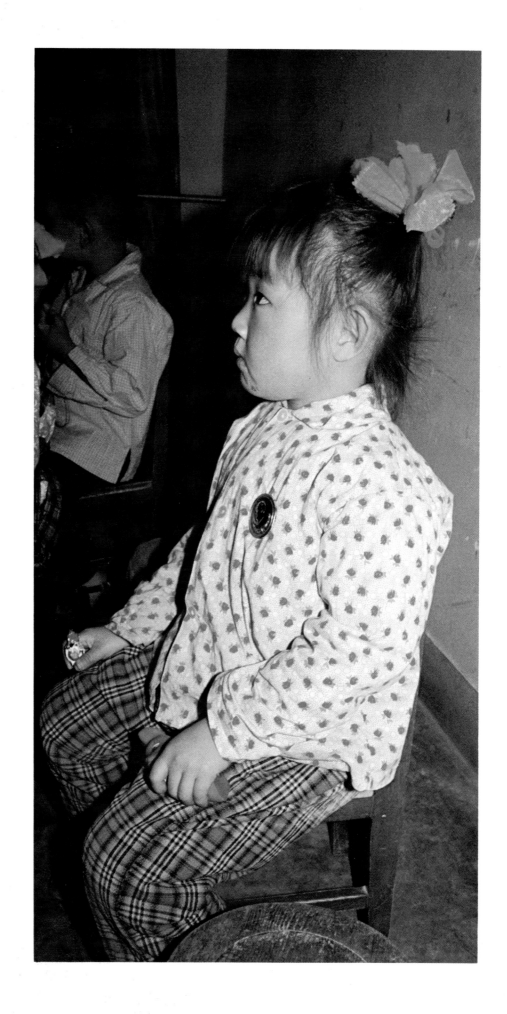

312-15. Left: Toddler in a day-care nursery run by a neighborhood residents' committee in the basement of an apartment block in the Eastern District of Peking. If mothers work and no grandparent is available, infants may be enrolled in nurseries two months after birth. Above: Young Pioneer learning woodworking at a "children's palace" in Shanghai. Center: Young Pioneers learning how to braid plastic thread into flowers and animals at a Shanghai "children's palace." Paper cutouts are displayed under glass on the table. Standard approved designs for plastic objects and paper cutouts are given to schools and clubs all over China. Below: Experiment under way in the physics laboratory of Peking University.

316. According to a Chinese proverb: "In heaven there is paradise, on earth there are Soochow and Hangchow." Soochow retains its earlier scale and charm. Here, laundry dries on lines attached to the spreading plane trees.

317. Looking at a collection of photographs of
theatrical stars in a shop window, Soochow.
Since the fall of the "Gang of Four,"
collecting pictures of popular entertainers has
again become permissible.

318. Soochow mother and child. According to
Chinese tradition, the most beautiful women
of China come from Soochow.

population, rationing is a continuing fact of Chinese life. Cotton cloth, cooking oils, and grain are among the major items rationed throughout the nation, and other items that are temporarily in short supply in certain areas, such as meat, are rationed locally. Ordinary people use public telephones, which are located in every neighborhood. They have to shop daily because they lack refrigerators. Yet, since 1979 China has increasingly become a consumer society as the Party has moved to improve living standards. People are no longer content to buy sewing machines, bicycles, and watches. Now they are acquiring color television sets, electric fans, tape recorders, and even washing machines and living-room furniture. Moreover, the advent of installment buying has made it easier to obtain these products. And, since the spring of 1979, commercial advertisements in print and on television and billboards—a truly revolutionary innovation in China's political culture—have spurred consumer spending.

Expense, of course, is a relative matter in what remains a very poor society. By American standards an ordinary industrial worker's salary of perhaps seventy yuan per month (roughly $35) is infinitesimal. Yet, he receives a large number of subsidies for items that range from rent, medical care, and transportation to haircuts, meals, and cold drinks. These subsidies account for 40 percent of the state budget. Such workers and ordinary government officials, whose salaries are comparable, used to be the envy of their countryside cousins, whose cash income is irregular and only a fraction of an industrial worker's. In recent years, however, although the income of urban dwellers has risen, that of rural people has improved much more dramatically, creating certain social tensions. In both city and countryside, frugality is absolutely necessary to make ends meet, unless there is more than one breadwinner in the family, especially because prices have been rising as the state has recently begun to set them higher in order to stimulate agricultural production and improve peasant income. Nevertheless, many urban families manage to save money and deposit it in savings accounts that earn interest. These savings finance the occasional purchase of a major consumer item.

There is little danger that China will seek to emulate the automobile-dominated culture of the United States. Although privately owned bicycles seem to be everywhere and individuals are gradually buying motorbikes, trucks, and even small tractors for transportation, there are still virtually no private automobiles. The cars one sees, some made in

China and others abroad, are for government or collective use. In the cities a modest number of taxis are available, but they are expensive for Chinese, if not for foreigners. Buses, minibuses, and other motor vehicles are also in short supply, as are railroad cars and airplanes. The People's Republic has increasingly established small factories in rural areas not only to alleviate unemployment but also to minimize the transportation burden of distributing manufactured goods to consumers. Because the Chinese make do as best they can, walking is very much in vogue, people as well as beasts still pull carts in city and countryside, and "carrying water on both shoulders" is not a figure of speech but a familiar sight. China continues to rely on internal transport via rivers and canals and even imports large quantities of foreign grain by ship to relieve the burden of transporting domestic grain from the western part of the nation to the populous coastal areas.

Housing is one of the regime's sore points. Most people now have a roof over their heads, and this achievement must not be underestimated. Some tall new buildings have attractive, if spare, quarters. Yet, despite serious construction efforts, especially during recent years in the major cities, many families continue to live in appallingly crowded conditions. The alleys a few paces from the main thoroughfares of Canton evoke the Middle Ages. Many charming courtyard residences in Peking and other cities have been subdivided among several families. New housing in the cities has often been constructed as part of new factory complexes, the long multiple-entry, four-to-five story, red-brick buildings resembling public-housing projects in the West. A typical post-1949 building will have four walk-up apartments on each floor of an entry, with a bathroom and kitchen shared by two apartments. A family of four or five may have one or two rooms. Space is at less of a premium in rural areas. Peasant families, like some city families, often live in individual one-story wattle-and-daub, brick, or cement houses with tiled or thatched roofs. These houses have several rooms and frequently open onto a small courtyard that may be shared with another family. Some of the new housing in communes consists of two-story buildings divided into four to eight individual duplex units. In some places in arid north-central China people still live in caves that have been converted into simple homes. In the cities most houses as well as apartments are owned by the state, which leases them at rents calculated according to floor space, but people are now being urged and helped to build and buy their own homes. In the countryside private ownership of houses is widespread, although the land on which the houses stand is, of course, collectively owned.

Perhaps new China's most widely acknowledged and least controversial achievement is in medical care. The world is now familiar with, and even beginning to benefit from, China's development of the ancient art of acupuncture in place of chemical anesthesia for certain types of surgery. Although since 1979 some of the exaggerated claims for acupuncture have been punctured, visitors never fail to be impressed when, thanks to acupuncture, babies are delivered by cesarean section or tumors are removed while the patient remains awake but free of pain. Chinese media have also given great publicity to the accomplishments of surgeons who have successfully restored severed limbs and of medical researchers who have succeeded in synthesizing insulin.

Yet China's gains in organizing the delivery of medical services and the spread of preventive public-health measures, though less spectacular than the well-known medical feats, are undoubtedly more important in the long run. Although poorly equipped by Western standards, a variety of large and small urban hospitals offer competent treatment for the range of serious human ailments. City neighborhoods have easily accessible health stations staffed by paramedical personnel who treat emergencies and minor problems, give vaccinations, and dispense advice and contraceptives. Larger factories also offer medical care. More remarkably, this system has been extended to the countryside. Production brigades and some production teams have paramedical personnel called "barefoot doctors." They operate modest health stations or often clinics that provide outpatient care and sometimes hospitalization, and a commune headquarters generally has a small hospital. Serious cases are often sent to larger, more specialized medical facilities in the county seat or provincial capital.

Both Western and traditional Chinese medical practices are used, depending on the nature of the problem and, at least in the first instance, on the preference of the patient. Perhaps the most notable aspect of the system is that the cost of medical services is reasonable, even in Chinese terms. Thus, medical care is now more readily available to the ordinary people of China than ever before. This and endless health-education campaigns and organized attacks on unsanitary conditions, such as the legendary fly-swatting movement of the late 1950s, have made China a relatively healthy place, despite the existence of primitive economic conditions. One notable accomplishment, for example, is the almost complete obliteration of venereal disease, which was made possible by the regime's stern measures, shortly after it assumed nationwide power, to suppress prostitution. The conquest of schistosomiasis, or snail fever, has proved more elusive, but China's doctors and scientists hope to meet this challenge before long. The country still has a long way to go in improving the quality of rural medical practice and the basic sanitary habits of the masses. It also urgently needs to increase the number of its medical schools and acquire better facilities and equipment. Yet progress to date has been impressive.

The educational accomplishments of the People's Republic present more of a mixed bag. It has made enormous progress in reducing illiteracy in a population where few could read and write prior to 1949. By reducing both the number of Chinese characters used in publishing and the number of strokes in writing the characters, it has facilitated the success of massive adult-education programs. Today, approximately three-quarters of the people are able to meet at least minimal reading and writing standards. In what may well be the most impressive quantitative expansion of education the world has known, the PRC is approaching its goal of universal primary and lower-middle-school education. A generation ago only 20 percent of school-age children attended primary school, while now over 80 percent do, despite a massive increase in population. Whereas formerly even an elementary education set a person apart, now many children advance to lower middle school, and their parents need pay only a few yuan per year for tuition and books. In this respect, as in others, change has been slower in remote rural areas, particularly those inhabited by minority nationalities.

Because mothers have been recruited into the labor force, many urban children and some rural ones as well, before they reach kindergarten, spend much of their time first in nurseries and then in nursery schools. Some return home every evening, while others board throughout the week. This prepares them for what is to come, socializing them in a collective atmosphere suffused with patriotism, political indoctrination, concern for the welfare of the group, and conformity. This orientation persists through their formal schooling, which emphasizes reading, writing, arithmetic, science, and arts and crafts, as well as political study and group activities that make useful contributions to society.

For example, even nine-year-olds march to the fields to help with the harvest, often with festive songs and chatter that give their excursion a holiday air.

Many Chinese children do not go beyond lower middle school. By age sixteen they take up full-time work at farms or factories. Those who have an opportunity to attend upper middle school—a growing number—continue with math, science, politics, and a foreign language, increasingly English, and take up world history. Schools also feature a variety of sports and musical drama and dance programs with explicit political themes.

Given the fact that education has traditionally constituted the most prestigious ladder of success in China, a major point of tension is the extremely limited educational opportunity for senior-high-school graduates. Because of the lack of teachers and facilities in institutes of higher learning, 96 percent of them will not be able to study in colleges and universities. Yet many high schools, in order to boost their own prestige, have concentrated on preparing their best students for enrollment in higher education. Many college professors nevertheless report that their current students are not as well prepared as students were before the Cultural Revolution, a situation that is only gradually being rectified. The task of training the nation's 220 million primary and secondary school students is prodigious.

No facet of Chinese life more vividly demonstrates the damage done by the Cultural Revolution than higher education. The "ten lost years" that Chinese now attribute to the discredited Lin Piao and the "Gang of Four" were actually the result of the application of Chairman Mao's policies. The Cultural Revolution temporarily put an end to China's efforts to emulate the Soviet model of universities as elite centers where the most academically qualified students learn to become the technical specialists required by industrial society. Liu Shao-ch'i and his followers were willing to risk the emergence of a "new class" in China as the price of modernization, but Chairman Mao was not. Virtually no higher education took place in China from 1966 to 1970, during the successful struggle to overthrow Liu, and when universities did begin to reopen, they were very different from their predecessors. Mao's vision of proletarian education required them sharply to reduce their curricula by excising "irrelevant" academic subjects and concentrating on practical and applied courses, thereby cutting back the time spent in residence to half or even less than that formerly prescribed. Students were also supposed to spend half of their reduced programs in manual labor. Moreover, high school graduates were required to engage in full-time labor for at least two years before being considered for college admission, even though they often forgot so much during the intervening period that it became necessary for them to begin again in certain basic subjects. Admission standards and procedures were markedly changed to accommodate Mao's insistence on a student body largely composed of workers, peasants, and soldiers. Entrance examinations were abandoned and candidates were recommended by their units on the basis not of their academic quality but of their political orthodoxy and hard work, thus filling institutions of higher learning with people unprepared for advanced study. Similarly, examinations concerning the subject matter of various college courses were either replaced by practical exercises that deemphasized booklearning or were simply done away with. Many fewer students were enrolled in higher education than before the Cultural Revolution, and the atmosphere of terror created by "the struggle between two lines" hardly made the period 1970 to 1976 a fruitful time to teach or study.

Since Mao's death and the arrest of the "Gang of Four," China's new leadership has reversed these policies. Of course, even before 1976 the pragmatists had made some progress in modifying implementation of the most extreme Maoist vision of higher education, but only in recent years has the PRC again begun to train large numbers of scientists, engineers, doctors, economists, linguists, teachers, and the other specialists required by an industrializing society. High school graduates are no longer required to spend years in manual labor before applying for college, nationwide entrance examinations now evaluate their scholastic qualifications, curricula again feature academic subjects and have returned to normal duration, course examinations have been reinstituted, students spend less time in labor, and the political atmosphere for teaching and study has considerably improved in accordance with the current Party slogans of "seeking truth from facts" and "liberated thinking." This does not mean that the current leadership is insensitive to the desirability of creating a higher educational system that is open to the masses and in close contact with them, and that sends many graduates back to "serve the people." The leadership realizes that such egalitarian measures solidify the nation's internal cohesion; it will undoubtedly seek to implement them, but only to the extent consistent with training the highly educated personnel demanded by the "four modernizations." The leaders are also aware that it will make no sense to "over-educate" large numbers of students to fill positions that do not or should not exist at China's present stage of modernization.

Nor do the new educational policies imply the advent of full academic freedom. University life has been relieved of the nightmare symbolized by the "Gang of Four," but it continues to be dominated by the Party apparatus and an ideological orthodoxy that maintains restraints upon individuality, creativity, and free inquiry. Fewer limitations exist in scientific and technological education than in the social sciences, the liberal arts, and the fine arts. Yet even the former are not unrestricted, and all educators are constantly mindful not only of current restrictions, but also of the possibility that the pendulum might again swing in a "leftist" direction.

A similar situation prevails in the many research institutions that have been restored to prominence. Scholars at the Academy of Sciences, the Academy of Social Sciences, and other research units are busily rebuilding their libraries, convening discussion groups, publishing essays, beginning to publish books, and establishing contact with counterparts all over the world in an effort to make up for lost time. They may read virtually whatever they need, are relatively free to exchange ideas informally, and can publish unorthodox views on certain subjects and analyze other subjects that were formerly taboo. Yet there are many things that they cannot state in print or even utter at public meetings, and they must continue to be cautious in their contacts with foreigners.

Education and research are specific aspects of the leadership's broader problem of attempting to cope with freedom of expression by steering between the Scylla of "leftist" reaction and the Charybdis of a "rightist" tendency that advocates going beyond the "four basic principles" by allowing even criticism of socialism, the Party leadership, the dictatorship of the proletariat, and Marxism-Leninism-Mao Tsetung Thought. As the *People's Daily* itself conceded, the leaders' reaffirmation of the four principles was interpreted by many people as "the signal for another movement to oppose the rightists," as occurred after the "hundred flowers bloom" era of 1956–57. To counter this interpretation the *People's Daily* in a series of articles exhorted people, in the interest of modernization, to "express their opinions freely so that they dare to speak, dare to criticize, dare to debate."

As one essay put it:

> In order to build up the country, everyone may and should air his views as regards the state's politics, the economy, culture, education, and arts as well as other fields of work, so that the Party and government can hear all kinds of opinions, improve their work, and avoid making mistakes.

People who speak out need not fear the possibility of being prosecuted for counterrevolutionary crimes as under the "fascist" dictatorship of the "Gang of Four," the newspaper stated. Under the Criminal Code enacted in mid-1979, it noted, nobody can be convicted for his thinking, theory, or viewpoint, since counterrevolutionary offenses are limited to acts committed "with the aim of overthrowing the political power of the dictatorship of the proletariat and the socialist system."

Of course, what worries the millions who are being urged to speak out is the breadth and vagueness of even the newly revised definitions of counterrevolutionary offenses and the ease with which a Party-dominated judicial system can infer counterrevolutionary intent from freely expressed, well-intended criticisms. Thus, film-makers who complain, as some have done, that China's feature films are below standard because of "too much bureaucracy and censorship" and that "without democracy, no art can exist," are taking a chance that their remarks may be misinterpreted. For this reason China's writers will take a long time to cast off what they call their "mental burden" and freely indulge their creative instincts. As the well-known poet Ai Ch'ing, who was imprisoned as a "rightist" in 1957 and prevented from engaging in normal literary activity for twenty years, has stated: "Once beaten, twice shy." Another writer, Li Tuo, has described the problem as "perennial" and advised other writers to expect little improvement from a Party that believes that writers, like journalists, need only "pass down to the masses the policy guidelines of the Party." Li wrote: "There is one way; use your pen as an ax to trim down your thoughts, for if you do not do so, others will do it for you anyway." It is therefore no surprise that China's writers today envy the relative freedom that their predecessors enjoyed during the T'ang dynasty over twelve hundred years ago, and are fascinated by the flourishing culture of ancient Greece and the Renaissance.

Will the current relative liberalization prove more enduring than previous similar periods in PRC history? Plainly, another severe clampdown would have adverse effects upon the "four modernizations" and reinforce the cynicism, discontent, and inertia of many of the most articulate and talented. Yet too sudden a movement toward an open society would prove hard for the present leaders to tolerate, for the ability truly to speak out would inevitably lead to public recognition that the errors of the past thirty-five years are not solely the product of the "Gang of Four," Lin Piao, and the other former leaders who are currently excoriated. This could threaten the already shaky credibility of the Party and its monolithic ideology and organization, and even raise the specter of another era of disintegration and chaos. If the PRC leaders manage to maintain a steady course, however, slowly but steadily moving toward a more open society, they may not only facilitate economic modernization but also bring China to a more pluralistic, sophisticated stage of political development.

Although the theory and practice of Maoism approached religious proportions during the Cultural Revolution, conventional religion has been an obvious target of Chinese Communism. In 1949 there were only about three million Catholics and one million Protestants in China—less than 1 percent of the population. This situation contrasted sharply with that in Communist Eastern Europe, where the Church's hold was great. Moreover, China's churches were dominated by foreign missionaries, whom many Chinese patriots, non-Communist and Communist alike, had for decades believed to be political instruments of imperialism. Ideological principles reinforced the Communists' nationalistic hostility to Christianity, which they deemed incompatible with "scientific Marxism." After seizing nationwide power and severing foreign ties with China's Christian institutions, the Communists recognized that the new national churches thus created represented little threat to the government, except perhaps through subversion. Official policy until the Cultural Revolution purported to permit freedom to worship, as well as freedom not to worship, in accordance with the Constitution's guarantee of freedom of religion. Actually, however, explicit ideological opposition to religion, tremendous political and psychological pressures against those engaging in religious activity or revealing religious attitudes, a ban on religious instruction, imprisonment of priests who remained loyal to the Vatican, and close control over the churches' hierarchies contributed to a withering of Christian influence.

The Cultural Revolution put an end to all formal Christian worship as the remaining churches came under severe attack by the Red Guards, and even Party-sponsored "patriotic" religious organizations such as the "Three-Self Movement," which stands for self-government, self-support, and self-propagation and which was composed of dozens of Protestant denominations under a single umbrella, were suppressed. Yet Christians continued to worship in their homes throughout the decade of intense persecution. Following the downfall of the "Gang of Four," Mao's successors resumed the Party's earlier toleration of carefully controlled religious activities and revived the national mass religious organizations, such as the Three-Self Movement and the China Catholic Patriotic Association, through which the Party exercises its leadership. At least 1,200 churches have been reopened to serve the three million Protestants the regime concedes now exist in China, and a similar number of Catholic churches have been reconverted from warehouses and factories to their original use for the estimated three million Catholics in the country. A few seminaries have been restored to train pastors and priests and to publish treatises and magazines, although no religious schools or universities for ordinary people are allowed. Contacts with foreign religious groups are again permitted, but only through official arrangements.

Christians may not instruct or seek converts among persons under eighteen years of age, nor may they participate in unregistered worship groups. This last prohibition is designed to suppress the so-called house churches that kept the faith alive during the Cultural Revolution and that expanded rapidly—in the case of Protestants to far beyond their pre-1949 numbers—during the liberal years 1979–81. Since then, enforcement of these rules has led to serious clashes between the authorities and house-church Christians in several parts of the country, and hundreds of Christian activists have been jailed for printing and distributing "unofficial" church literature and tape recordings of sermons. Some Catholic priests who served long sentences in the 1950s have been sentenced to prison again for counterrevolutionary acts that consisted of trying to split Catholics away from the Party-approved Church. Even students at China's main academic centers, Peking University and Ch'ing Hua University, were ordered to turn in philosophical material printed outside China, to admit any religious belief, and to report the names of fellow students who believed in religion. Those concealing information reportedly faced interrogation and expulsion. During the years 1983–84 the simultaneous waging of the campaigns against "spiritual pollution" and crime and the purge of Party ranks provided a convenient cover for the regime's suppression of "abnormal religious activity," that is, conduct that is outside approved channels. China's new Constitution, while protecting the right of citizens to "enjoy freedom of religious belief," forbids the use of religion for "counterrevolutionary activities" and declares that "no religious affairs may be dominated by any foreign country."

Although Buddhism claimed more adherents in China than in any other country and in earlier centuries exerted enormous influence on Chinese life, precisely because of its traditional hold on the populace, the Party has been careful not to allow it an unfettered restoration in recent years. Largely in order to win favor with the Buddhists of other Asian countries, the People's Republic spent large sums on the restoration of temples in the 1950s. During periods of relaxation such as 1956–57 and 1961–62, the temples were filled with worshipers, some of them youthful, who ran the risk of being accused of "feudal thinking." In 1963, however, the regime initiated a policy of eliminating Buddhist activity that reached its climax in the sacking of temples during the Cultural Revolution. Since 1972, as part of Peking's resurgent "people's diplomacy," foreign visitors have again been permitted to visit some repaired monasteries and to meet Chinese Buddhist leaders. The monasteries and temples were at first only displayed as historic monuments that demonstrate the building skill and artistic creativity of China's laboring people in centuries past. By the late 1970s, however, ordinary Chinese were being allowed to worship there and aging monks were training their successors. Since then, in virtually all the cities likely to be frequented by foreigners, Buddhist houses of worship have been crowded with people burning incense, making offerings, and bowing before the images. In the remote countryside, however, there have been many incidents in which Buddhists have been forced by local officials to tear down recently resurrected temples or to call off religious processions. Believers were invariably subjected to heavy doses of "education" that reportedly persuaded them that "prosperity depended not on begging to Buddha but on the Communist Party."

The fate of Taoism, an indigenous religion with deep and broad roots in traditional China that has maintained its popularity in rural areas, has run a similar course. In the countryside, Taoism, like Buddhism and other Chinese folk

364

religions—including spirit worship—often becomes intermingled with sorcery, witchcraft, and other "superstitious activities" that are regularly repressed.

It seems clear that the regime allows somewhat greater religious latitude to national minorities than to the Han people. Chinese Moslems have been less restricted, for example, not only because of their minority status but also because a number of Moslem nations take an interest in them. Similarly, Tibetans have been allowed to flock to their temples since the downfall of the "Gang of Four" relaxed the cultural suppression of twenty years.

The Party's current philosophy is that religion cannot be stamped out but that it can be contained. Eventually, Party theorists declare, "religion will come to its natural end only when all the objective conditions have been prepared through long years of socialist and communist development." For now, the Party appears to accept with equanimity the growth in the number of religious believers, so long as they are controlled. Not only does the existence of worship provide an outlet to disaffected citizens but it also makes for good propaganda in the many other countries that share Buddhism, Islam, Catholicism, and Protestantism, as a recent Central Committee document acknowledged. In the current view, it is not surprising that some young Chinese become religious: "Some of them grew up in religious families. Others seek consolation in religion either because they failed to correctly approach their setbacks in study, work or daily life or because they were disillusioned when their personal problems were not promptly solved." But members of the Communist Youth League and of the Communist Party must remain atheists even though it is permissible for them to marry believers.

Some of the costs of contemporary China's achievements are not apparent to the casual observer. If one works where he is told, if he says only what is permitted, if he volunteers to undertake actions that seem against his interest, it is not only "thought reform" and group social pressure that make it possible to give many individual acts a veneer of "voluntarism." The basis of the entire well-regulated society is a public-security system that unobtrusively extends to every household and work site and that has subjected many millions of people to a spectrum of efficient sanctions. This system has cut China off from the world and even from its own past, except on terms approved by the Party. It is the unspoken premise of social action.

Yet the coercive apparatus is not very much in evidence. In the cities one frequently sees soldiers on holiday or taking part in the labor force. But, except for guards at major buildings, airports, and railroad stations, the only visible sign of police control is the traffic cop on duty. Although one of the few smartly attired figures in China, he hardly symbolizes a police state. Trucks, buses, bicyclists, and pedestrians rarely seem to heed his flailing arms or shrill whistle. How, then, do the Chinese do it?

In the cities what is usually called the "street office" is the primary level of government and is responsible for an area embracing as many as 65,000 people. In addition to cooperating with the public-security station for the area in settling interpersonal disputes and imposing sanctions against persons whose misbehavior is not serious enough to warrant treatment as "criminals," the salaried officials of the street office lead or coordinate myriad local activities, including schools, medical care, sanitation, welfare, production, service facilities, and propaganda.

Each street office is assisted by a number of "residents' committees," which are semiofficial organizations of perhaps seven to eighteen locally elected volunteers, who are mostly housewives and retired workers. A single residents' committee may be responsible for an area including several thousand people. These people are in turn subdivided into small groups of about fifty persons, each group having an elected volunteer leader who is linked to the residents' committee.

Each of the dozen or so patrolmen assigned to a public-security station cooperates with one or more residents' committees in maintaining public order in a given area. Certain members of each committee are assigned the duty of protecting public order, mediating disputes, and generally acting as the eyes and ears of the police in every lane and apartment complex. The Communist Youth League, the women's organization, and other groups of volunteer "activists" also operate in the area, and civilian militia groups, which have long been active in the countryside, assist the police in certain cities. This entire apparatus is usually directed by the Party.

This thorough grass-roots network, which also reaches into factories and workshops, has in recent years been unable to stem a rising crime and delinquency rate. The present wave of executions has made clear to all what close observers have long known—the People's Republic continues to be troubled not only by espionage, subversion, and other political offenses that range from actual sabotage to public dissent, but also by murder, rape, theft, and other conventional criminal activity. People are careful to lock their bikes, and bicycle stores even chain together the outermost bikes in each rack. Among the most difficult public-order problems of late are the many "educated youth" who, unreconciled to their enforced resettlement in the countryside, illegally return to the cities and become drifters, black marketeers, and occasionally rioters and even prostitutes. More sinister are the gangs of hoodlums that fight each other, rape, rob, and generally intimidate citizens, who have consequently become afraid to go out at night, even to work. Embezzlers, smugglers, and other economic offenders have proved to be an enormous problem. Increasing attention has also been focused on the rapes, seductions, black market dealings, and assaults of "gilded youth," miscreants protected by parents who are high officials.

Not only is the public-security network engaged in detecting interpersonal disputes and antisocial infractions, but it also plays an important role in disposing of them in a variety of ways. Even though certain members of street offices and residents' committees are designated to look after mediation and public order, virtually everyone in the official and semi-official network tends to participate at one time or another. For example, a dispute between tenants over sharing a bathroom or kitchen might be mediated by any residents' committee member, the small-group leader, or the group itself. Chronic quarreling would be dealt with in a series of discussion and "study" sessions that involve not only street office officials, residents' committee members, family, friends, and the parties themselves but also representatives of the factories or other units where the parties are employed.

A petty thief might in the first instance simply receive some private "persuasion-education" or criticism from his small group. But if he failed to reform, he might be censured by a meeting of the entire neighborhood convened by the residents' committee. An especially recalcitrant offender might be made the target of intense verbal abuse at a "struggle meeting," stigmatized as a "bad element," and given one of several possible forms of compulsory labor by the public-security apparatus. The situation is similar in the rural communes. Every production team has people who participate in security and mediation work under the direction of production-brigade and commune personnel, who in turn work with the county public-security bureau and its agents.

An effort is made to reduce the risk of arbitrariness in imposing sanctions, which, although nominally "noncriminal," are recognized as being severe. Before subjecting someone to the humiliation of being censured at a public meeting, for example, it is said that the leaders of a production team or brigade must obtain the approval of commune officials.

The role of the judiciary in the sanctioning process is rather small. Most civil disputes never reach the courts. Occasionally, however, if mediation of a divorce case proves ineffective, and if one of the parties is dissatisfied with the decision of the street office or commune to grant or deny divorce, the dispute may be taken to court. Except for a brief period in the mid-1950s, until recently, following the implementation of the new criminal procedure code, the work of the court had largely been confined to a closed-door review of cases serious enough to be denominated "criminal." Now courts frequently hold public trials of nonpolitical criminal cases, although foreigners generally cannot attend these trials without permission. Operating under the control of the local Party apparatus, the court has the final say in determining whether the accused is guilty and whether he should be sentenced to prison, to "reform through labor" in a remote labor camp, or to death. Yet it is the public-security force, guided by the Party, that assumes the major responsibility for criminal cases. Even though it now must receive the approval of the newly revived procuracy each time it wishes to bring a criminal prosecution, it decides in the first instance whether to charge as a criminal someone suspected of a serious offense or whether to subject him to "noncriminal" sanctions that can include "rehabilitation through labor" in a labor camp. It also has a major voice in recommending the appropriate sentence in criminal cases and in determining whether to announce the sentence at a "mass trial" before a throng of onlookers.

Until the spring of 1979, to Westerners, especially to Americans, and even to citizens of the USSR and East European Communist states, perhaps the most striking aspect of the legal system in China was the absence of practicing lawyers. When questioned in the mid-1960s about whether there were lawyers in the PRC, as there had been in the mid-1950s, a Chinese diplomat who had just defected to the West uncomprehendingly replied: "What do you think China is—the Soviet Union?" An independent legal profession has little support in Chinese tradition, and the official view for two decades stressed the meddlesome, obstructive, divisive aspects of lawyers, much as China's emperors inveighed against "litigation tricksters." Since the end of 1978 that official view has yielded to one that emphasizes the valuable role of lawyers in promoting socialist legality and economic development, and lawyers have begun to appear in court, to give advice to state enterprises as well as individuals, and to participate in negotiations that Chinese companies conduct with foreigners. At this writing, there are already over ten thousand lawyers operating in law firms and legal advisory bureaus, and more than thirty law schools are training thousands more.

Similarly, for two decades prior to 1979 China was unusual from our perspective and that of the Soviet bloc in its extremely limited body of published legislation. A frequently ignored Constitution and a handful of vaguely worded laws that were promulgated during the regime's earliest years provided less guidance to the populace than did received notions of right and wrong supplemented by the "Thought" of Chairman Mao and the current Party line enshrined in the *People's Daily*. That situation began to change with publication in 1979 of codes of criminal law and procedure and revised laws relating to the courts, the procuracy, local government, arrest and detention, and elections. Joint venture laws, environmental protection legislation, and tax, foreign exchange, banking, contract, trademark, patent, business registration, and civil procedure laws are the first examples of the many economic laws that are expected in the near future. Many other laws have also been enacted, including a much-needed revision of the 1950 Marriage Law and the PRC's first nationality law.

One legal innovation of which Chinese judicial authorities claim to be proud is the suspended death penalty. In many, but far from all, capital cases execution is postponed for two years to allow the convicted criminal an opportunity to demonstrate his capacity for rehabilitation. If he makes satisfactory progress during this period, his sentence will be commuted to life or a period of years in prison. The Chinese call this a humanitarian measure that is highly successful in stimulating reform and saving lives. The availability of this punishment gave the Party a face-saving way of sentencing Mao's widow, Chiang Ch'ing, to death without having to risk the consequences of executing her. Her sentence was subsequently commuted to life imprisonment.

How should one evaluate the contemporary legal system? Plainly, its emphasis on extrajudicial institutions builds on the traditional Chinese preference for local groups to deal

369

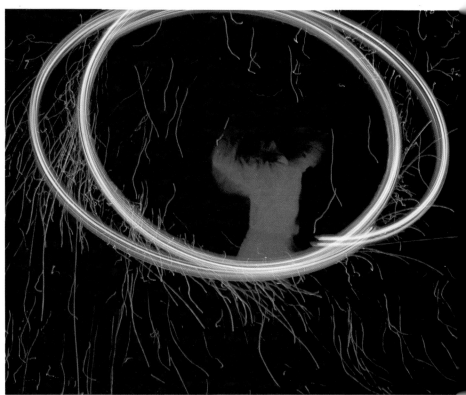

319, 320. Far left: Summer Palace visitors enjoy a picnic lunch on the terrace of an old imperial hall. Left: A People's Liberation Army soldier views golden Buddhist sculptures in the Temple of the Azure Clouds, Fragrant Hills, Peking. Many Buddhist temples were vandalized and shut down during the Cultural Revolution. Recently some have been renovated and reopened as historical monuments. Few priests or worshipers are in evidence.

321, 322. Far left: The Kaifeng Acrobatic Troupe offers a dazzling display of coordination. Left: A juggler twirls a fiery baton. This is one of the troupe's most spectacular acts.

with their own affairs and to conserve the resources of the state. But the contemporary system has adapted past practices to revolutionary needs. The grass-roots neighborhood organizations not only provide the parties to a dispute with inexpensive and relatively speedy means of resolving it but also indoctrinate them and the community in Communist moral and legal norms. Similarly, familiar methods of group pressure and social ostracism have become powerful instruments for inculcating the new values.

The system surely has much to commend it in the resolution of civil disputes, although fairness to politically disfavored persons is not always assured. But even taking into account the extent to which individual rights have traditionally been subordinated to those of the group and the state in China, the criminal process has proved unsatisfactory in direct proportion to the severity of the sanction imposed. This is a major reason why the demand for socialist legality, especially the protection of basic rights of the person, is so widespread in China today and why the government has sought to appear responsive to this demand in nonpolitical cases, even while ignoring it in sensitive political cases, including the trial of the "Gang of Four." People want to be protected against crime, but they also want to curb the ability of both private groups and government officials to impose severe sanctions upon them outside the courts—they want to do away with arbitrary arrests, incommunicado confinement, endless "struggle meetings," midnight interrogations, and other intimidations that have coerced false confessions and often led to suicide and murder. They also want to prevent any further possibility of unfair defamation and dismissal from employment of millions of persons on the basis of hearsay, speculation, and inadequate evidence, and without any opportunity for a hearing or review. This helps to explain why new laws have been promulgated, the procuracy, lawyers, law professors, and legal scholars have been resurrected, and the courts strengthened.

There is broad agreement that in the past the judiciary was totally unable to protect individual rights. Indeed, it was itself too often the instrument of illegality, being used by the dominant political forces to suppress those who opposed them. It is too early to predict the extent to which the courts will vindicate the hopes that are being placed in them. They have few personnel with legal training adequate to the challenge. Moreover, judicial officials, like others, remain afraid to carry out the policies of the new leaders, for fear that

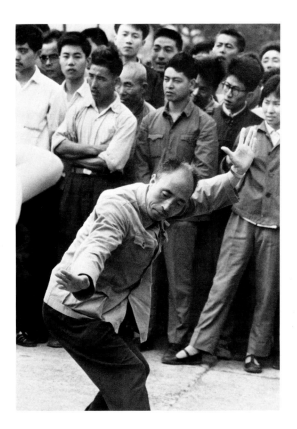

323–25. Left: Early morning crowd watching traditional Chinese sword-dancing exercises. This is a daily occurrence near the Peace Hotel on the Bund in Shanghai. Above: Practicing the traditional Chinese exercise *t'ai-chi ch'üan* on the Bund before an admiring throng.

the line will change yet again. The most important question that bears upon the future role of the courts, however, is whether the Party will allow them the freedom to decide concrete cases on their own, remaining content to set the policies, prescribe the laws, select and train the judges, and criticize or even remove them after an "incorrect" decision. Thus far, the record in political cases seems to be discouraging. The courts may enjoy more autonomy in ordinary criminal cases, but the outside observer cannot determine this. One prediction seems safe—that the PRC is likely to be preoccupied with questions of justice for many years, for, as a recent visitor noted, "the country seems to be teeming with people smarting under injustice."

The sense of injustice goes far beyond legal matters and the rehabilitation of the millions who unfairly suffered in the past. It will not end even if the Party follows through on its current policy of reducing the discrimination it has practiced against people from the old society's bourgeois, landlord, official, and other families that enjoyed the benefits of pre-1949 China. Nor will it end even if the Party should release scholars, intellectuals, writers, and artists from the still significant political and cultural restraints and the consequent uniformity and mediocrity that are imposed upon them. For the sense of injustice also appears to be widespread among the masses.

In part it is fueled by the resentment that many hardworking people feel against many others who do not work hard but who nevertheless suffer no sanctions. Chinese often say that one of the costs of socialism is that "rice bowls are made of iron," that "whether they work or not, people will still get two and one-half meals a day." This was brought home to some visitors when they discovered their escort, a professor of English, loading their large suitcases into an undersized taxi in the scorching heat while five hotel "service personnel" looked on. One of the foreigners tried to put the best face on this embarrassing situation by saying: "This certainly shows the difference between the old China and the new. In the old society, a professor would never do physical labor while the bellboys watched." Instead of smiling in satisfaction at social progress, the professor looked exasperated and said: "That's the trouble with the Cultural Revolution." When asked what he meant, he replied: "Before the Cultural Revolution we were never allowed to think for ourselves, but now we are. Thinking for yourself is good, isn't it? The only trouble is

374

that those guys," he said, pointing to the service personnel, "are thinking for themselves, and you know what they're thinking—they're going to get their rice bowl filled whether they work or not."

By adopting a policy of more pay for more work the Party runs certain risks, of course. Morale in the People's Republic has been strengthened by the fact that no new wealthy classes have been allowed to develop until now. Indeed, China has sought to achieve rapid economic growth while minimizing inequalities in income distribution. Substantial progress was made in reducing disparities during the 1950s. But the pace was slowed in the 1960s out of deference to economic growth. The Party's recent emphasis on bonuses, the "household-responsibility system" and "specialized households," and its exhortations to "overcome egalitarianism" are already leading to greater income differentiation that may sap public morale even while seeking to enhance it.

Perhaps the most substantial source of popular resentment has been the privileges and corruption of the official class. Traditionally the social distance between ordinary people and officials was enormous. The Party has sought to reduce that distance and generally to bridge the vast gap between urban and rural life and between intellectual and manual labor. Many of the innovations of the Cultural Revolution were designed toward those ends. For example, the "May 7th Cadre Schools" were established so that officials and educators could "learn from the peasants" by combining agricultural labor with ideological study for periods that ranged from one to three or four years. These schools have now been phased out, as have many of the other innovations, yet the need to subject officials to continuing indoctrination and discipline is as great as ever. Indeed, by recently encouraging the media to begin honestly revealing instances of corruption—even by developing the role of letters to the editor and investigative reporting—the Party has heightened popular resentment against corruption in the hope of subjecting the bureaucracy to greater control and demonstrating the Party's concern with the problem.

Thus the *People's Daily* has attacked officials "who misappropriated public funds to live the good life" and "who used power to get their children and family in by the back door." Many high officials who educate the masses to abide by the law, to engage in self-sacrifice, and to work hard have themselves used public resources to build their own homes. In mid-1979, for example, a factory worker in Shansi province claimed that in his county "more than thirty motor-cars and tractors are mobilized every day for private home building" and that 150 homes were being built for high-ranking county officials, factory chiefs, and hospital heads. While a member of the PRC's Politburo, former Party Vice Chairman Wang Tung-hsing, under attack by the dominant Teng Hsiao-p'ing group ostensibly for clinging to Maoist fundamentalism, was criticized by wall posters alleging that he had diverted over $4 million in public funds to build a personal pleasure dome within the leadership's residential compound in the heart of Peking. As the *People's Daily* stated, without mentioning Wang's case: "If Party members are asked to reform their lifestyle, the Party managers should do the same first. But if they are asked to reform their lifestyle, then the senior executives should do the same, and if senior management reforms its style, then the highest leaders should do so first." Party disciplinary commissions, government procurator's offices, the new criminal code, and economic branches of the people's courts all reflect the Party's determination to suppress official corruption.

Stamping out "walking through the back door"—that is, using connections to gain entrance to a desired university or job—will be much harder to accomplish. Influential Chinese, today as in the past, want the best for their children and, like most of their counterparts in other countries, are often willing to pull strings even if doing so violates their personal principles. This breeds a great deal of resentment among ordinary people, as does use of official cars for private purposes, dining out at public expense, and other perquisites enjoyed by the elite. Although it is difficult for foreigners to discern, a social wall persists between Party members and others, and it will be a long time, if ever, before status and class distinctions are removed from Chinese life. Moreover, bureaucratism plagues the country that invented bureaucracy some two thousand years ago. Red tape, buck-passing, arbitrariness, and arrogance too often characterize an administration that is frequently slow to act, whether out of laziness, fear, or indifference.

Nevertheless, the masses of people are in many ways better off than they were prior to 1949, even if they tend to take for granted the many improvements in their lives and instead focus on what they lack. One very important aspect of social progress is the emancipation of women. By fostering a new ethic and by creating facilities such as nurseries and collective dining halls to lighten domestic burdens, the Party has made it possible for women to take part in production and thereby to increase their independence. Today women play important roles in virtually every field, often providing the bulk of the work force in factories, farms, hospitals, schools, offices, and stores. Although they are frequently assigned less remunerative work than men or are paid less for the same work, these differentials are gradually disappearing, and more and more women are assuming managerial responsibilities. Less than perfect equality still seems to prevail between the sexes in the allocation of housework and in family decision-making. Chinese cadres, both male and female, seem surprised at the respect with which American men treat the opinions of their wives. Again, however, Party ideological education is slowly making inroads on traditional male chauvinism. Ironically, women continue to be grossly underrepresented in the highest levels of the Party and government. Many of the best-known female leaders appear to have reached prominence because of their marriages to principal figures. Progress at the basic levels should eventually be reflected at the top, but even the former will take time.

The Chinese family has managed to survive the vast changes of the past quarter century. It remains the basic social unit. With a twinkle in his eye, Premier Chou En-lai occasionally gave visiting Americans the impression that Chinese parents, unlike Americans, no longer have to look after children. Actually, however, Chinese parents still are responsible for the upbringing of their children, and children continue to be responsible for the welfare of aged parents. Indeed, one can argue that on balance the Communist revolution may have strengthened the family as an institution rather than weakened it. Surely some of the traditional sources of family tension have been reduced by curbing the tyranny of husband over wife, of mother-in-law over daughter-in-law, and of parents over children. Although campaigns against arranged marriages and related customs, including expensive dowries, betrothal gifts, and wedding banquets, have been only partially successful, they have to that extent relieved families of a substantial financial burden and the worries associated with it. Also, improvements in the political and economic environment have eliminated many of the anxieties that formerly plagued home life. Natural calamities can still spell hard times for peasant families, but collectivization has given them much greater assurance against complete economic disaster than they have ever had before. Similarly, the Cultural Revolution to the contrary notwithstanding, the regime has enhanced the family's sense of protection against violent intrusions such as the banditry, civil war, and foreign invasion that formerly laid waste many parts of China. In these circumstances, and with a gradual increase in the standard of living, more relaxed, warmer family relations are now possible, at least during periods when no mass movements are taking place.

This is not to say that the vast changes wrought since 1949 have not exposed families to new tensions. Simply adjusting to the often bewildering succession of policies, values, and institutions created by the People's Government has produced considerable strain among family members. Husbands have had particular difficulty in coping with the liberation of women and children. Having both parents employed outside the home has challenged the family in China as well as elsewhere, but grandparents continue to play an important role in child care, often living with their children and grandchildren; and one of the most frequent and touching sights in China is that of an elderly person walking hand in hand with a grandchild. It is, of course, difficult to maintain close ties in families where, because of the absence of resident grandparents, children board away from home the bulk of the time. Families also reflect current political worries, such as the widespread fear of Soviet aggression and the continuing concern over renewed "struggle between two lines." Recently, the advent of the "one family, one child" policy has confronted many families with difficulties, not the least of which is how to avoid rearing a "spoiled brat" in a household without siblings.

During the 1960s and 1970s, divorces were few and far between in China. The policy of easy divorce that marked the regime's early years and produced a good deal of social disruption soon gave way to a highly conservative policy of maintaining family stability. Visitors to urban street offices, for example, were frequently told that there had been only one or two divorces granted in the past year for a population of some fifty or sixty thousand people. Under the newly revised Marriage Law, however, divorce has been more available, although neighborhood mediators, cadres from the street offices or rural production brigades, and judges patiently admonish husbands and wives who seek divorce to return home and try harder to alleviate marital misunderstanding.

From our distant vantage point it is not easy for Americans, the world's most voracious consumers, to keep in mind the satisfactions that China's much simpler life can hold for the common people today. Although Spartan, it is far from un-relieved drabness. The one day off per week that urban workers receive might be spent visiting relatives or going to a park or zoo, a cultural or historic monument, or a concert, movie, opera, or variety show. Rural people have less frequent access to such diversions, especially during the seasons when little time can be spared from agriculture. But mobile film units, entertainment by local groups, and other events break the tedium, and trips to the city can occasionally be made during slack periods. Moreover, roughly 90 percent of the population can now watch television, if not on their own set, at least on that of their work or residential unit. Younger people everywhere are avid sports enthusiasts, and basketball, Ping-Pong, volleyball, and gymnastics are particularly popular. Chinese of all ages like to be spectators at frequently held athletic events.

Work days are busier, of course, but despite political, neighborhood, and family obligations, there is still time for Chinese chess, card games (mahjong and gambling are prohibited), and gossip. The visitor to China in recent years has found the pace of life more relaxed than in Hong Kong, Japan, or the West. Some people begin the day by practicing a traditional series of slow, rhythmic movements called *t'ai-chi-ch'uan* or by performing a variety of more martial exercises. Jogging and calisthenics are common. Young couples go for walks in the evening and, despite the Party's puritanical strictures, lovers can be seen embracing in the shadows in parks or along riverbanks. In China privacy is a scarce commodity, especially during the searingly hot summers. One popular pursuit for Chinese men at any hour is sitting with a few friends at their favorite wine shop, sipping beer, sweet wine, brandy, or a fiery sorghum distillate, while nibbling assorted cold snacks. For ordinary Chinese there is no "night life" to speak of in the Western sense, and to conserve electricity most people go to bed by ten o'clock and rise by six.

The success of the People's Republic in restoring China's unity and independence has been a major source of satisfaction to all the Chinese people. The theme that "China has stood up" against imperialism and modern revisionism after a "century of humiliation" has continued to elicit the support of the masses. Despite their recent admiration for Western achievements, national pride marks all Chinese contacts with foreigners, as a British shipping executive discovered. A Chinese ship en route from Shanghai to Japan was destined to call at Hong Kong. Eager to load freight on the ship, the executive repeatedly cabled Shanghai from Hong Kong asking about space but received no reply. Finally, in desperation, he cabled: "Imperative. Must know today." This drew an immediate response from his Chinese counterpart: "Imperative an imperialist term. Please rephrase." The sense of nationhood is enhanced by instilling pride in China's past as well as her present. To this end many historic monuments have been repaired, and excellent exhibitions of archaeology and traditional art rival displays of contemporary "people's art."

Another major factor contributing to national unification is the progress that has been made in spreading a single spoken language over the entire country. Of course, local dialects continue to be very much in use, and many older people have failed to learn *p'u-t'ung-hua*, "the common language," or Mandarin, as Westerners call it, because it was the official language of imperial China. It is also not unusual to find even recent high school graduates in central and southern China who do not understand Mandarin well and who speak it with difficulty. Yet there is no doubt that oral communication has been greatly facilitated. Newspapers, theater, radio, television, films, and other media have combined with the expansion of literacy and education to create a new political culture. Indeed, the Party's skill in communicating the satisfactions of collective effort to "serve the people" and to "defend the motherland" will be important for many years to come because of China's continuing need for national unity and for massive applications of manpower to compensate for what is lacking in mechanization.

THE ARTS
IN CHINA TODAY

PRECEDING PAGE:

326. *Make Grain the Key,
Boost Agriculture!* Poster.
Printed 1979 in both Chinese
characters and romanization,
such posters help the masses
pronounce the message in the
standard national spoken
language. The jolly tone reflects
post-1976 campaigns and is a
welcome relief from the harshly
militant posters of the Soviet
style.

◄ 327. Giant sculpture of Chairman
Mao in front of the tractor
factory in Loyang, Honan
province. The sculpture stands in
a square in front of the great
gateway adorned with a Maoist
slogan.

THE ROLE OF ART was carefully defined in planning for the revolution. Lenin had pronounced art to be a cog in the wheel of revolution. In the 1920s and early 1930s the Chinese Communist leadership began to use the arts to spread their message. The period from 1935 to 1948, after the Long March and before the final battles against Chiang Kai-shek, when the Communists enjoyed thirteen years of relative stability in Yenan in the northwest, proved to be a good time to experiment. Drama groups began to use psychodrama techniques to play out the injustices of the oppressed, trying to raise the consciousness of people who passively accepted their lot. The Lu Hsün Academy of Arts was organized to provide training for the nation's cultural leaders in the decades ahead.

In 1942, Mao Tse-tung delivered the central document, his "Talks on Art and Literature," to the Yenan Forum. Its theme was deceptively simple: "There is in fact no such thing as art for art's sake, art that stands above classes or art that is detached from or independent of politics." Mao said that art and politics interact in a dialectical way. "Literature and Art are subordinate to politics but in turn exert a great influence on politics." The role of art is to inspire the masses with the revolutionary spirit and unify them in the cause. To serve the masses art must be made understandable to workers, peasants, and soldiers.

How to do that has been the major educational challenge confronting artists under Communist rule. Mao drew on his own experience when he vividly prescribed how the Communist artist must approach this problem of communication with the masses. "I began life as a student and at school acquired the ways of a student; I then used to feel it undignified to do even a little manual labour, such as carrying my own luggage in the presence of my fellow students, who were incapable of carrying anything, either on their shoulders or in their hands. At that time I felt that intellectuals were the only clean people in the world, while in comparison workers and peasants were dirty. I did not mind wearing the clothes of other intellectuals, believing them clean, but I would not put on clothes belonging to a worker or peasant, believing them dirty. But after I became a revolutionary and lived with workers and peasants and with soldiers of the revolutionary army, I gradually came to know them well, and they gradually came to know me well too. It was then, and only then, that I fundamentally changed the bourgeois and petty-bourgeois feelings implanted in me in the bourgeois schools. I came to feel that compared with the workers and peasants the unremolded intellectuals were not clean and that, in the last analysis, the workers and peasants were the cleanest people and, even though their hands were soiled and their feet smeared with cow-dung, they were really cleaner than the bourgeois and petty-bourgeois intellectuals. That is what is meant by a change in feelings, a change from one class to another. If our writers and artists who come from the intelligentsia want their works to be well received by the masses, they must change and remold their thinking and their feelings. Without such a change, without such remolding, they can do nothing well and will be misfits."

Most artists would not voluntarily follow this prescription, but in periods of high political tension such as the Cultural Revolution they have been forced to work in the countryside to acquire this remolding.

If this artistic training of hard labor sounds harsh, one must consider the privileged place the artist holds in Communist society. He receives a state salary that is high on the scale. In periods of political relaxation he is invited to stay in good hotels and resorts and is offered the use of a car and theater tickets. He can receive cash bonuses for paintings plus royalties on published works.

Yet, in periods of political tension, he is attacked for his bourgeois interests and accused of wanting to restore capitalism. The style and content of art are carefully controlled. The Soviet revolutionary example was an object lesson because it included some of the most radical artists of the first three decades of the twentieth century. Their vocabularies of abstraction and the unconscious were understandable only to a tiny avant-garde. This was no more acceptable to the Soviet leaders than it would later be to the Chinese ones, for both believe that artists should paint things that are recognizable and understandable to the masses. Realism is an important aspect of this new revolutionary style. It is crucial to be able to identify heroes and historical scenes.

Finding a form of revolutionary art that will unite and educate the masses is not easy. It was natural for the Chinese to accept Soviet art forms along with Soviet revolutionary ideology and technology until the Sino-Soviet romance withered in 1959. And Soviet influence was great even after that, in painting, sculpture, and architecture, in the theater, and especially in classical ballet.

Socialist Realism, the principal style, was the major vehicle for portraits of revolutionary heroes and for heroic landscapes. The general pattern of Socialist Realist paintings includes pink-cheeked, vigorous giants engaged in some admirable pursuit, carefully outlined and modeled in a convincingly three-dimensional landscape. It preaches virtue through demonstration by model people.

The roots of such paintings go back to eighteenth-century England and Sir Joshua Reynolds, who in his *Discourses on Art* pronounced history painting about noble deeds to be the most truly worthy endeavor. He called for "grand-manner" paintings, large, important, and with messages, and throughout the nineteenth century many academic artists continued to paint moral and historical lessons to teach and elevate the spirits of their viewers.

The mythological and religious subjects of the West were rejected by the Socialist Realist painters, who had a different "class" orientation. Communist subjects must be from the working class. Socialist Realism is particularly suited to class struggle—to show bravura battles involving nationalist causes and the emancipation of the oppressed. The paintings feature romantically depicted heroes, differentiated by their costume from the revolutionary heroes of America and Europe. The classical drapery of the Statue of Liberty and of France's Victory and Justice is dropped in favor of proletarian garb.

Oil painting was the technique that came with the style. The technique had been taught in Chinese art schools since the second decade of the twentieth century, and of course many students studied abroad. However, it had limited prestige and exposure until Socialist Realism in oil technique became the official state style.

Images of Chairman Mao Tse-tung in painting and sculpture are archetypal examples of the Chinese version of Socialist Realism. The giant cast-plastic sculpture in Loyang (plate 327) is built on the Lenin prototype; the elongated figure even has a long windblown coat to add flourish. His raised

328. *An Army of Peasants Welcomes Mao Tse-tung.* Artist unknown. Oil on canvas. Shown at the Kwangtung Province State Guest House in 1972. Removed in 1978. This type of large painting in the Socialist Realism style was often executed by a provincial artistic collective.

hand is oversize—especially big to let the leader bless, protect, and reassure his flock—as one often secs in Buddhist sculpture.

These large sculptures of Mao are to be found in important public places such as airports, government buildings, and memorial squares. During the Cultural Revolution there was such a profusion of Mao posters and buttons that China seemed to have created a religious cult of Mao. The vast majority of these images disappeared after the Cultural Revolution.

A second Socialist Realist prototype is the large oil painting of the Chairman accompanied by many workers, peasants, and/or soldiers. The figures are arranged to focus attention on the Chairman. A painting which hung in the Kwangtung Guest House until 1978 (plate 328) focuses on the Chairman at its apex. The dark patch on the left leads the eye back, and the tilted oval composition gives the picture gusto. The flourish is reemphasized in the flags and raised arms of the soldiers.

The prototypes in the Soviet landscape style featured didactic tales of ample fields and proudly productive peasants. However, the Soviet girl and her tractor are usually outlined against darkly somber grain fields. The Chinese, disliking the dreariness of these Russian scenes, created their versions with a brighter palette (plate 326). After 1959 Mao specified a Chinese version of Socialist Realism which he called "revolutionary romanticism and revolutionary realism."

Portraiture was a third model imported from the Soviet Union. The hero is shown life-size or bigger and in the flush of good health. Features are rendered with photographic precision, yet the subject always manages to look like a hero. The four patriarchs of Communism—Marx, Engels, Lenin, and Stalin—were always depicted in such a manner. Before 1979, giant portraits of the four were to be seen in T'ien-an-men Square. Smaller versions used to abound as posters and printed on fabric (plate 329), and were hung in official meeting rooms with framed pictures of Chairman Mao on the principal wall; Marx, Engels, Lenin, and Stalin were on the opposite wall. An occasional variant on this formula would be Mao's portrait hung next to that of a Communist hero of another country, such as Kim Il Sung, whose visage adorns the Chinese-Korean Friendship Commune.

Since the easing of political tensions after 1976, Communist patriarchs have been removed from many official meeting places. In some rooms the space remains unfilled, in others it is filled with calligraphy of Mao's poetry or with landscape paintings.

A temporarily important post-Mao image during 1978–79 was a large double portrait of the two chairmen, Mao and Hua Kuo-feng (plate 330). The title and visual message convey the official version of Mao's words: "With you in charge, I am at ease." Mao's hand over Hua's indicates his confidence in the younger leader. Hua leans forward eagerly, showing both his deference to the great Mao and his energetic determination and competence to take over. The relatively informal scene seems to be set in Mao's office, with his own books prominently displayed, reassuring the viewer that Hua will follow Mao's revolutionary line. It is an intimate moment blown up to "grand-manner" scale because it is a matter of national importance. Everyone must be informed exactly how the mantle of revolutionary leadership passed to Hua.

329. Members of a street-revolutionary committee in the Eastern District, Peking, explain their activities to foreign visitors in a typical pre-1976 meeting room. Colored posters of Marx, Engels, Lenin, and Stalin hang on one wall; a portrait of Mao hangs on the opposite wall (not shown).

330. Double portrait of chairmen Mao and Hua. c. 1978. Tapestry based on an oil painting. This picture was an important document in the legitimizing of Hua's rule. The giant tapestry pictured here was at the Shanghai airport, 1978–79, until Hua's fall from power, when it was replaced by flower paintings.

331. Shanghai Exhibition Hall (formerly the Palace of Sino-Soviet Friendship). The facade has a mixture of borrowed elements, including Baroque columns, gingerbread turrets, and a churchlike steeple.

The picture becomes a principal legitimizing image. In some important places, the double portrait of the chairmen had replaced individual portraits of Mao until 1979, when Hua's pictures disappeared, signaling his political eclipse. By 1980 Hua's image was nowhere to be found.

Mao, still recognized as a great leader, has been demoted from his solitary godlike position in the revolutionary pantheon and has been reunited with his revolutionary confrères, the late Premier Chou En-lai and military hero Marshal Chü Te, and former President Liu Shao-ch'i. Each has been given a commemorative room in the mausoleum built for Mao.

Soviet influence may be seen in two enduring examples of 1950s architecture. One is the Shanghai Exhibition Hall (plate 331), formerly called the Palace of Sino-Soviet Friendship, from which only the Russian onion dome is absent. Its facade has intertwined and patterned columns, gingerbread turrets, Neoclassic colonnades, and a soaring steeple. Yet the borrowed finery of the exterior does not extend to the interior. The vast, bare semicircular space, reminiscent of an airplane hangar, is devoid of warmth.

The other is the ultimate state colossus, the Great Hall of the People in T'ien-an-men Square (plate 332). This showpiece of new proletarian architecture covers over half a million square feet and is said to be larger than the palaces of the Forbidden City. It is a massive monolithic block that gives no hint of its functions; it contains a banquet hall for 5,000 people, a theater that seats 10,000, and countless smaller rooms (plate 333). It is here that the Communist Party holds its national Party and government congresses and here that China's leaders wine and dine their guests. The exterior is decorated with Neoclassic columns and cornices. There is none of the flamboyance that marks the Shanghai Exhibition Hall—the grandeur of this edifice lies in its scale. The vast interior spaces climax in mountainous staircases. Perhaps the Chinese designers had in mind the Forbidden City, where vast courtyard approaches make human scale almost meaningless. The awesome ceremonial approaches to the Great Hall of the People are through cavernous entranceways and up great stairways. Visitors pose for photos in front of a huge Chinese landscape painting.

Classical ballet is another significant Russian import. It was the White Russians who introduced ballet to China in the 1920s, but like oil painting its importance grew enormously with state sponsorship. Moreover, Soviet troupes and schools

389

332. The Museum of History and of the Revolution in the foreground; the Great Hall of the People in the background; looking southeast toward T'ien-an-men Square, Peking.

333. A reception and dining room in the Great Hall of the People, Peking. Hosts and guests sit in armchairs, with adjoining tea tables, in a large circle. Interpreters and cadres sit in the rear.

334. Nationalities' Cultural Palace (Min-tsu wen-hua-kung), Peking. This building includes a theater, cultural center, library, and museum.

offered renewed opportunities and contacts for the ballet. A number of classical ballets, including *Swan Lake*, were performed in China from Liberation until 1966, as were newly styled ones about the revolution, such as *The East Is Red*.

During the Cultural Revolution, when Chairman Mao's wife Chiang Ch'ing became cultural czar, she banned *Swan Lake*, denouncing it as decadent and bourgeois. Nor were any other Russian classical ballets performed for a decade. When *Swan Lake* was revived in 1979 (plate 335), there was great excitement and appreciation—along with a tremendous amount of curiosity by people who might otherwise not have been so interested.

Nationalism and Tradition in Art Forms

The Chinese Communist movement has always had strong elements of nationalism. When Sino-Soviet friendship ended in 1959, Chinese tradition became the cultural keynote. This is not to say that the PRC had ignored traditional paintings, operas, and other arts in the decade since 1949, because indeed, they had been simultaneously patronized along with Soviet-inspired arts. But from 1959 to 1966 traditional Chinese forms were supported by the government as the leading force in the arts.

In the search for Chinese forms to fill modern needs, the Nationalities' Cultural Palace (plate 334) attempts to combine traditional curving tiled roofs with a typical Socialist U-shaped block-and-tower model. The central block and towers are partially covered with a tiled roof. The pagoda-style central tower is crowned by blue-green-tiled "dragon-back" roofs replete with decorations suggesting the roof-line parade of guardian figures seen on old buildings.

Chairman Mao said: "Let the past serve the present," and this principle was applied to Chinese opera. The old stories were overhauled to eliminate anything that might be construed as antirevolutionary; the singing was somewhat simplified, doing away with the most artificial falsetto styles; and subtitles were projected beside the stage to help the audience understand the action. During the Cultural Revolution, Chinese opera met the same fate as classical ballet—it was denounced as backward and bourgeois. No traditional operas were performed, costumes and props were sold as curios, and performers were sent to the countryside to be reeducated.

The current version of *The Monkey King Wreaks Havoc in Heaven* (plate 336) is one of the many traditional works re-

335. *Swan Lake* performed by the Shanghai Ballet Troupe in the Sun Yat-sen Memorial Hall, Canton, in 1979. The principals performed with great skill, freshness, and feeling.

336. Chinese actors of the Soochow Opera Company pose as gods in a 1979 performance of *The Monkey King Wreaks Havoc in Heaven*.

vived after 1976. Monkey was not invited to the banquet of the gods, so he stole their feast of peaches and the elixir of immortality. The gods gathered in fury, but they were no match for the nimble and cunning monkey. The story is based on a perennially popular sixteenth-century novel. Perhaps its greatest appeal is the humorous way in which the rebellious monkey makes fun of the pompous establishment.

There had been a great debate as to what art style served Mao's call for a revolutionary art. Would it be built on traditional Chinese painting, or would it be based on folk art such as New Year's painting? In 1957, when the Chinese painting academies were established in Peking, Shanghai, and Nanking, the future of Chinese traditional painting was assured. From 1959 to 1966, when old Chinese art forms were featured by the government as the leading cultural force, Chinese traditional painting regained its prestige and vitality.

During the early 1960s, as a result of heightened nationalism, Fu Baoshi's painting received great recognition. His mastery of the traditional Chinese brushstrokes and his understanding of classical Chinese painting allowed him to paint with skill, freedom, and subtlety. He had gone to Japan in the 1930s, where he was exposed to many modern trends, but he returned to a traditional frame. His little fan painting

337. Fu Baoshi. *Not Quite Huang Shan.* 1965. Chinese ink on paper fan. Private collection. This intimate painting is traditional in subject, fan format, and brushwork, yet it is unmistakably modern because of the gamboling couple who are holding hands. In a Chinese work painted before 1900 they would be part of the passing scene, or sages and poets who seek to harmonize with nature's rhythm.

338. Gate of Heavenly Peace
(T'ien-an-men), Peking. Ming
dynasty (1368–1644), with
renovations of the Ch'ing
dynasty and the People's
Republic. Signs: left, "Long
live the People's Republic of
China"; right, "Long live the
solidarity of the people of the
world."

(plate 337) seems intimate. Yet the brilliantly brushed mountains and tree are vast, stark, and uninhabited except for two tiny figures, a young couple frolicking in the mountains. It is a charming idyll, but the artist is working with universal ideas and scale. Nature is vast and enduring. Man is small and frail.

Architectural monuments are easy places to let the past serve the present. The great T'ien-an-men (plate 338) is one of the gates to the Imperial Palace. It is the center of the capital, the heart of the nation, where the leaders appear on national days to review parades and make speeches. Before 1911, imperial messengers put imperial edicts into the mouth of a golden phoenix here and lowered the bird to the civil servants who spread the word to the nation. Only the emperor himself could be carried through the central gateway. Now, adorned with Mao's portrait and revolutionary mottoes, it has become the national symbol of the People's Republic.

395

339· Peasant Movement
Institute, Canton (Kwangchow).
In 1926, Mao trained peasants
to be cadres in an old Ming
dynasty temple of Confucius
(foreground roof). In the early
1970s a new building was erected
to train cadres (background
tower with torch).

The Peasant Movement Institute (plate 339) is a fine example of the militant spirit of a Cultural Revolution production. It has virtually the same massive U-shaped block-and-tower plan as the Nationalities' Cultural Palace (plate 334), except that in lieu of a Chinese tiled roof there is a symbol of international Communism—a great red plastic windblown torch. Surrounded by four little torches that rise triumphantly from the tower, this five-pointed roof crown, with four elements arranged around a central one, is like five dots on a die. It is ironic that this purports to create a revolutionary style, because few of its forms are new, and one may note that this arrangement is like the cluster of onion domes on medieval Russian cathedrals, the Buddha figures in esoteric Buddhist sculpture, and the towers of Angkor Wat—none of which could be called standard revolutionary prototypes.

During the Cultural Revolution, Chiang Ch'ing became the architect of a new order in the arts. She had only been a minor movie star in Shanghai in the 1930s, and after her marriage to Chairman Mao, politics required her to remain backstage. She also suffered bad health and spent a long period in the Soviet Union. It was not until 1964 that she began to play a leading role in reshaping the arts, and the Cultural Revolution gave her the power to impose her model revolutionary formula upon all of them.

Red Guards took over the schools and creative art groups, and almost constantly, for three years, accused artists of trying to restore capitalism. Virtually all the official artists were denounced and humiliated. Many were forced to move out of their homes, and their possessions were vandalized and confiscated. Like many other intellectuals, they were forced to do the lowest sorts of menial labor—cleaning latrines, pulling handcarts, sweeping streets. The events were so traumatic that some artists broke down mentally or physically. Some took their own lives.

Chiang Ch'ing denounced all the art produced before the Cultural Revolution—she said the arts had not lived up to the goals Mao set in his Yenan talks and that they were reactionary.

The ballet received the lion's share of Chiang Ch'ing's attention. *Red Detachment of Women* (plate 340) was one of eight model revolutionary opera-ballets she created. Its story is typical of the others—that of a peasant girl who is oppressed and exploited by a landlord. She escapes into the jungles of

340. Ballet performance of *Red Detachment of Women*, Peking. *Red Detachment* is performed in ballet and opera forms developed during the Cultural Revolution under the guidance of Chiang Ch'ing, wife of Chairman Mao.

341. Pan Chaichun, an artist in the People's Liberation Army. *I Am a Seagull*. Oil on canvas. Shown at the 1972 People's Art Exhibition. In this typical Socialist Realism painting, with its large figure, dramatic lighting effects, and romantically brushed-on pigments, the poetic seagull metaphor is applied to the hard work of industrialization.

Hainan Island and joins the Red Detachment. They return to kill the landlord in another Communist victory. The simple plot shows only very good or very bad characters. All intermediate shades of gray have been removed so that the heroine stands out clearly as a model for the masses. Her story is a revolutionary parable. The dance and music fuse Chinese and Western elements. Classical ballet underlies the movements yet it has been purged of its feminine grace. The army in Bermuda shorts is militant, with emphatic Chinese repertory gestures. The music has romantic climaxes modeled on Beethoven, but passages sound like the marine band playing Rimsky-Korsakov with an occasional Chinese melody. Red handkerchiefs on the guns are the only soft touch on the no-frills guerrilla army. Although the revolutionary heroine starts out as a victimized peasant girl, her revolutionary transformation is tough, effective, and unisex.

After the fall of the "Gang of Four" in 1976, these model operas were condemned as "stereotyped hackwork."

Essentially the same heroine Chiang Ch'ing created also starred in Socialist Realism paintings. Brushed in oil, larger than life and pink-cheeked, the electrical worker is shown with a romantic flourish. She is a paragon of revolutionary consciousness, ignoring the wind and rain; her own personal comfort is nothing in the face of the task she must perform for the people. The title, *I Am a Seagull* (plate 341), suggests that she is like the bird, not letting the elements bother her. Once again the heroine stands out boldly; her story is a revolutionary parable. This formularized propaganda painting communicates—without subtlety, originality, or good technique—qualities generally associated with high art. It has been suggested that such a work could be a parody.

The veteran teaching the youth about pre-Liberation evils and oppression was another Cultural Revolution model subject, both in painting and performing arts. *A Splendid Red Sun Will Shine for 10,000 Generations* (plate 342) features the stock character, a gray, baggy-suited old woman who has seen it all and teaches the healthy and eager heroes of the future. Pink sets the sweet tone for the painting, and the cherry blossoms reinforce the metaphor of continuing the revolutionary tradition.

The painting style is a variation of Socialist Realism, having absorbed some elements of traditional New Year's paintings such as watercolors in warm, bright colors and rigidly balanced, bold, precisely outlined compositions. Although the Chinese refer to these paintings as New Year's types, the point of view is that of Socialist Realism.

399

342. Kang Zuotian. *A Splendid Red Sun Will Shine for 10,000 Generations*. Ink and colors on paper. Shown in the 1972 People's Art Exhibition. Painted in Socialist Realism style, this picture of the classroom in springtime conveys the ideal spirit of learning in the new utopia of Chinese Communist society.

343. Opposite page: Li Keran. *Marching Through Loushan Pass at Sunset* (an episode in the Long March). 1971. Ink and colors on paper. Chinese style. The multiple perspective points, mountains, trees, and mist all recall traditional Chinese landscape painting. However, the columns of Red Army soldiers and the strong red-orange tone that bathes the scene are politically motivated innovations that inject revolutionary content.

Traditional Chinese painting did not totally cease during the Cultural Revolution, but the government favored the Socialist Realism style. What was done in the traditional medium had to be loaded with revolutionary content. Li Keran (born 1907) has been recognized as a leading artist since the 1950s. But that did not save him from being criticized along with other artists, nor did his age save him from being sent to a manual labor camp for several years, together with his colleagues from the Peking Central Academy of Fine Arts. He and a few other artists were rescued from this exile on the eve of President Nixon's 1972 visit. They were recalled to Peking to paint pictures for public buildings. *Marching Through Loushan Pass at Sunset* (plate 343) dates from this period, and to assure the political correctness of his painting he used two lines from one of Mao's poems as inspiration: "Green mountain looking like the ocean/the setting sun the color of blood." Bathed in the red sun, a revolutionary color, the army columns with red flags thread their way

400

344. Yang T. H. *The Masses Criticize Lin Piao and Confucius.* Hu Hsien peasant painting from Shensi Province. 1974. Bright colors, strong design, and lively crowds in animated scenes from the countryside characterize this kind of painting. Although the masses gather to denounce Confucius, in fact the campaign against the sage was a metaphorical attack on Premier Chou En-lai by the "Gang of Four."

345. Above: *Peasants, Soldiers, and Children March to the Fields Together as the Red Sun Rises* (detail). Paper cutout. Shown at the 1972 Exhibition of People's Art. The masses working together in the fields are Chinese heroes. The red sun rising is a symbol of the revolution.

through the pass. It is a successful blend of old mountain mist and revolutionary consciousness.

A third important trend cultivated by the officials of Chinese art has been called "peasant painting." In theory, untrained and untrammeled peasants should be able to paint in a national style genuinely expressive of the masses. The Hu Hsien peasant paintings (plate 344) are the best known because the Chinese government not only sent exhibitions to Europe and America from 1973 to 1976, but because it also published catalogues. These painters from Hu Hsien banded together during the Great Leap Forward of 1958 to form a school. Some of the painters were peasants, a few were cadres. Their subjects were mostly life on the farm, rendered in bright gouache colors—happy people enjoying their work. The paintings are joyous and cartoon-like. Their stylistic roots come from New Year's paintings, drawn annually to decorate one's house, and traditional paper cutouts. A group of professional artists was sent to Hu Hsien to help the artists prepare for the international exhibitions. The paintings that resulted were reproduced and circulated at home and abroad.

Paper cutting continued to be a zesty, popular art form even when high political content was emphasized during the Cultural Revolution. Perhaps it is the crisp freshness of the cutout form that saves it from being too cute (plate 345). Mao buttons, the jewelry of the masses, were another politically popular Cultural Revolution item. The design, of course, was based on Socialist Realist art (plate 312).

The Post-Mao Era (1976–1984)

Even before the "Gang of Four" was "smashed" in October of 1976 there were signals of a shifting artistic atmosphere. After Chiang Ch'ing's forced exit there was a dramatic change in the art scene. Literature began to re-emerge, and an outpouring of novels, short stories, plays, and films that came to be known as the "literature of the wounded" sought to describe and understand what China had just experienced. Visual and performing arts forbidden during the dominance of the "Gang of Four" were revived, and art exhibitions were filled with works that had almost no political content. The Chinese government officially rehabilitated the slogan "Let a hundred flowers bloom, let a hundred schools contend," inviting a profusion of styles.

Freedom and artistic excitement peaked during and after Teng Hsiao-p'ing's visit to the United States early in 1979. Underground artists appeared at "Democracy Wall" with

346. "Lotus Dance" in the Sun Yat-sen Memorial Hall, Canton, 1978. Angel-like Chinese flower beauties in flowing costumes—including portable leafpads—perform a dance that has elements of a 1940s Hollywood pageant. Choreographed by Chinese dance pioneer Dai Ailian, the work revived a graceful ideal, a dramatic change from the exclusively militant Cultural Revolution style.

347. Wang Keping (b. 1949).
Blind and Silent. 1979.
Wood. Exhibited in Star
Star exhibition in Pei-hai
Park, Peking, November
1979. After the group
successfully picketed for
space, this was one of the
pieces shown in the first
Star Star exhibition.
Wang's sculpture makes
the point that most
Chinese stood mute and
blind to uncivilized
behavior during the
Cultural Revolution.

their paintings and made speeches protesting government
oppression and demanding guarantees of continued freedom.
New and sometimes unauthorized publications appeared.
Intellectuals organized groups that discussed many previously forbidden subjects. Once again one could hear
Western music. Female performers dressed in form-fitting
gowns and used makeup reminiscent of Hollywood glamour
styles of the 1940s (plate 346).

Yet many recalled what happened in 1957, when those who
spoke out against officialdom in response to the same "hundred flowers" slogan were denounced as "rightists" a few
months later and punished. In an effort to reassure the understandably skeptical, the Party claimed that this would not
happen again, but many intellectuals remained unconvinced.
Events soon demonstrated that, although there was no
return to the nightmare of the Cultural Revolution or the
earlier antirightist movement, the Party would not tolerate
the heady, total freedom of early 1979. Limits had to be
imposed if the Party was to retain its power, and since that
time Party leaders have struggled to draw the line that de-
lineates permissible artistic expression. Typical of the sort
of compromise that has been attempted was the official statement at the Fourth Congress of Writers and Artists, held in
November 1979 (the first such Congress in nineteen years),

that "The Art Association will legally defend the artist's right to individual expression . . . as long as the artist does not subvert the goals of the Communist Party."

Amid this tense and shifting atmosphere many amateur artists as well as professionals all over China formed groups and held exhibitions using previously taboo subjects, such as nudes and abstraction, and formerly forbidden Impressionist and other Modernist styles. The group movement was extremely meaningful, because for the first time since 1949 Chinese artists organized themselves privately, based on aesthetic concerns. They took their art outside of government-run art organizations and into their own hands, if only for a brief interval.

The Star Star group of amateur artists picketed the National China Art Gallery and marched in protest to demand Peking gallery space in the fall of 1979. The pioneering thirty-member Star Stars succeeded in exhibiting work that was politically critical as well as abstract, and did so again in August 1980. They stretched the limits of style and content of the art establishment.

348. Feng Guodeng (b. 1948). *Self-portrait.* 1979. Oil on canvas. Oil Painting Research Association Exhibition, Pei-hai Park, Peking, October 1979. This tortured scene, haunted by swirling brooms, describes the artist's frustration with his own work. Assigned the job of sweeper in a factory, he therefore has little time to paint.

349. Zhao Yixiong (b. 1934). *Desert Jeep*. 1981. Oil on canvas. The theme of "developing China" illustrated by this desert survey team continues to be a stock subject in the post-Mao era, but the heroes of progress have been scaled down to life-size. A realism based on observation is characteristic of the new generation of artists. Zhao shows old and new China: desert camels near today's Jeeps.

350. Chen Danqing (b. 1953). *Tibetans*. 1980. Oil on canvas. Exhibited at the Central Academy of Fine Arts, Peking, 1980. The government officially encourages artists to paint the minority peoples of China, and Tibetans are one of the fifty groups. Chen's painting has been trend-setting, with fine technique, more authentically naturalistic figures, and in a smaller scale format than the earlier melodramatic Socialist Realism norm. The figures have psychological depth as well as immediacy.

407

351. Chen Yifei (b. 1946). *Looking at History from My Space*. 1979. Oil on canvas. Exhibited at the Shanghai Painting Academy, 1980. This historical painting uses video-like, flashback images in the sepia-toned background to tell the story of China since 1912. In a self-portrait in the foreground, the artist views this patchwork of events. Such a composition is surprising in the Chinese context, since the Party line supports individual recognition only for designated martyrs and heroes.

Wang Keping, one of the Star Star leaders, who had been a Red Guard ten years earlier, showed *Blind and Silent* (plate 347), a face with one eye patched over and a cork in the mouth. "This is an image of myself and of all the Chinese people who have been oppressed," Wang Keping told *Los Angeles Times* reporter Linda Mathews. "See one eye is shut so we can't see much of what's going on around us, and the mouth is corked, like a Thermos bottle, so we cannot speak. I've taken the cork out of my own mouth for a while at least, but eventually, of course, somebody may stuff it back in."

Wang Keping's sculpture is strong and direct. He produces powerful and amusing political indictments as well as a satisfying object. His forms have a naturalness deriving from the wood he selects.

The political satire, abstract styles, and sexually suggestive works in the Star Star exhibitions offended much of the Chinese art establishment. The Star Star Group had refused to edit out pieces that presented ideological and stylistic problems, even after suggestions were made to them by the head of the Artists Association. They chose to exhibit all their work.

By the end of 1980 the Party line had shifted from the "hundred flowers" tolerance of many styles, including modern, foreign-influenced ones, to a harder line purging outside influences, abstractions, and nudes as well as cracking down on exhibition policies for private groups. The Star Stars were repeatedly criticized for "slavish imitation," which meant uncritical copying of the West. Although they promised to follow the Party line, they were not allowed to exhibit again as a group.

Another pioneering group, the Oil Painting Research Association, has proved more enduring. It grew out of a New Spring Art Exhibit shown in Chung-shan Park, adjacent to the Peking Palace Museum, in March 1979. The newly rehabilitated head of the Artists Association wrote an introduction to that show calling for creativity, free choice of subjects, the forming of private groups, and the selling of paintings. All of these points represented a reversal of official policy of the past decade and lifted the hopes of the artists who had endured much humiliation and suffering during the Cultural Revolution. This new group was formed by thirty-six of China's leading oil painters, ranging in age from thirty to sixty, who used a variety of styles, including Post-Impressionist. Their stated goal was to improve the level of oil painting as well as provide opportunities to exhibit their work and exchange ideas.

The most adventurous and controversial piece in the Oil Painting Research Association exhibit of October 1979 was *Self-portrait* (plate 348) by Feng Guodeng, born in 1948. Feng was one of the three amateurs in the group. When he finished high school, he was assigned to work in a factory as a cleaner. This painting, which has both expressionist and surrealist qualities, shows him, tortured and red-headed, among flying brooms. The traditional Asian demon has red hair. Employment in China is generally for a lifetime, and in this painting, he seems to be in purgatory. In the November 1980 exhibition of the Oil Painting Research Association, Feng Guodeng entered works even more abstract and surrealist, reminiscent of Dali and Miró. They quickly became a target when the Party moved from the tolerant "hundred flowers" policy of 1978–80 to hard-line "socialist morality" in 1981. The new line allowed limited experimentation by the Oil Painting

352. Luo Zhongli (b. 1950). *My Father.*
1980. Oil on canvas. National
Youth Art Exhibition, China Art
Gallery, Peking, 1980. This giant
photo-realist portrait became an
instant sensation. The old man's
sweating, lined face is a monument
to the Chinese peasant, who
endures a very hard life. Luo
painted a ball-point pen tucked
into the turban so the viewer would
be aware of the time warp.

353, Above: Yuan Yunsheng (b. 1937).
354. *Water Festival, Song of Life.* 1979.
Acrylic on canvas in plaster. Peking
International Airport. Two details.
This vast narrative mural shows
groups of Dai people, a Chinese
minority living in southwestern
China, celebrating their springtime
water festival at the beginning of
the hot season. The two nudes
(plate 354) were the center of
controversy until March 1981,
when that section of the painting was
walled over.

Research Association, as well as other artists, and, unlike the
Star Stars, they were permitted to exhibit again, although
under closely censored conditions.

Zhao Yixiong, born in 1934, is more typical of the Oil
Painting Research Association artists than is Feng Guodeng.
A graduate of the Central Academy of Fine Arts, he is older
and more conservative in his approach to a new Chinese art
style. He went to paint the great and terrible Takla Makan
Desert in the northwestern province of Sinkiang, which is
rich in resources. Admirably painted and realistic in style,
Desert Jeep (plate 349) shows old and new China. A candid
view of the Jeep's front seat is in the foreground, and camels
and a survey team are seen through the window. Camels
have been the primary "silk road" transport for thousands
of years, and the surveyors symbolize the modern development of the desert. The carefully composed objective figura-
tion needs no bravura gestures to make its point.

Another important group that formed during the "hundred
flowers" period called themselves the Contemporaries. They

411

355. Yuan Yunsheng (b. 1937). *Black Figure*. 1981. Ink on paper. Exhibited in *Painting the Chinese Dream*, Smith College Museum of Art, 1982. This figure symbolizes the agony and humiliation Chinese artists, intellectuals, and officials have suffered in China, especially during the Cultural Revolution.

356. Opposite page: Kong Boji (b. 1932). *Buddha*. 1980. Oil stick on paper. Inspired by a fourteen-hundred-year-old Buddha image from the cave paintings at Tun-huang, the haunting figure has been repainted in a contemporary expressionist mode. The Tun-huang murals offer new Chinese sources of style and substance to writers and dancers as well as artists.

are thirteen young male oil painters in Peking who share similar ideas about how to liberate themselves from Sino-Soviet orthodoxy. A number of works from their show in July 1980 were bought by the National China Art Gallery for its permanent collection, giving the artists an official seal of approval. Some use Post-Impressionist and Modernist styles that stop short of abstraction; others, like Chen Danqing, draw inspiration from nineteenth-century European academic painters such as Millet.

A young teacher at Peking's Central Academy of Fine Arts, Chen is one of a new generation of realists and is especially appreciated for his gifts of objectivity and forthrightness. In contrast to the highly dramatic compositions of the over-scaled Socialist Realist hero paintings, *Tibetans* (plate 350) has a credibility that is both freshly observant and classically composed. Chen's figures, painted in rich earth tones, have a haunting beauty. Chen records his Tibetan subjects; he does not glamorize them. He seeks to convey their nature through deft inner portraits that penetrate unusually handsome features and the marvelously exotic combination of furs and jewelry that is their daily wear.

357. Liu Haisu (b. 1896). *Clouds at Huang Shan*. 1978. Ink and colors on paper. Hong Kong Museum of Art. Liu pioneered oil painting in China, but his finest work is in traditional materials.

Chen Yifei, from the Shanghai Painting Academy, is another leading younger-generation realist painter. In honor of the thirtieth anniversary of the PRC in 1979, Chen Yifei painted a large historical work, *Looking at History from My Space* (plate 351). It was inspired by Soviet models but goes well beyond Socialist Realism into the new generation's more objective vision. In the foreground the artist paints both a strikingly lifelike self-portrait and his studio chair, in a trompe-l'oeil technique. His fresh approach to the narrative content of Chinese history since 1912 is a succession of sepia-toned, video-like images. The artist used old photographs and film in his research, and by adapting their style he depersonalized his statement. Chen's use of both documentary images and flashback style broke new ground. Moreover, because revolutionary consciousness dictates the submersion of the individual, it was shocking to see the artist place himself in a central position in the painting.

Another important leader of the wave of new realism is Luo Zhongli, from Szechuan. His giant photo-realist portrait of a peasant, called *My Father* (plate 352), received first prize in the National Youth Art Exhibition in December 1980. The father, sweating beneath his towel turban, has a lined, weather-beaten face. He holds his soup bowl, waiting patiently. Luo had seen a portrait by the American photo-realist Chuck Close in a Chinese art magazine. This inspired him to transform his academic peasant subjects, similar to those of Millet, into a monumental Chinese "everyman"

358. Wu Zuoren (b. 1908). *Goldfish.*
1980. Ink and colors on paper.
Peking's Central Academy of Fine
Arts Exhibition in Hong Kong,
1980. Wu Zuoren's images have a
remarkably lifelike quality although
the artist effects a transformation
of ink to fish without illusionistic
shading. Still within the frame of
traditional painting, Wu's work is
lively and fresh.

on whose labor the nation depends. Luo Zhongli said that the man was a half-frozen peasant guarding the latrine which contained the manure that was to fertilize his own meager plot. Luo described the peasant's immobile figure, silent, staring, and anesthetized. Luo was moved by his sincerity and unquestioning acceptance. The peasant wouldn't speak for himself, so the artist said he would shout for him and others.

Along with the new realism, the most significant art trend of the post-Mao era is the wall-painting movement. Conceptually, it includes many more artists than those who literally paint on walls. It includes all those who have been influenced by several sources: the Buddhist wall paintings at Tun-huang that use "heavy color" (opaque, rich colors) to depict both narrative and decorative subjects; the richly colored Ming dynasty decorative bird and flower paintings; and the expressionistic Socialist Realism of the Mexican muralists of the 1930s and 1940s—Rivera, Orozco, and Siqueiros.

The wall-painting movement emerged as a major force at the October 1, 1979, opening of the Peking International Airport. Veteran painter Zhang Ding, then Dean of the Peking Central Academy of Arts and Crafts, was commissioned to decorate restaurants and lounges in the airport. He gathered painters from all over China to create murals in a variety of media, subjects, and styles.

Among the many well-conceived, mature works at the airport, one that stands out is *Water Festival, Song of Life* (plates 353–354) by Yuan Yunsheng. Yuan had criticized Stalinist

415

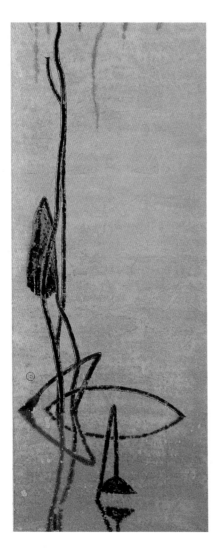

359. Wu Guanzhong (b. 1919). *Two Swallows*. 1980. Ink on paper. Exhibited in a one-man show, 1981, Pei-hai Park, Peking. Wu Guanzhong works interchangeably in ink and oil with highest skill and feels that the traditional ink medium does not give a painting its "Chinese-ness." The house is a vision of where he spent his youth, and it has a kind of magical realism.

360. Yang Yanping (b. 1934). *Brown Lotus*. 1982. Ink on paper. Exhibited in *Painting the Chinese Dream*, Brooklyn Museum, 1983. Private collection. Like many of the new wave of Chinese painters, Yang paints in both oil and ink. Her ink paintings have a particular delicacy and disciplined selectivity. She uses an old subject in a personal and innovative way.

art in 1957, but after the Party line condemned Soviet influence, he had been permitted to return to Peking from a seventeen-year exile in the northeast, during which he corrected amateur paintings in a Workers' Palace. *Water Festival* is a vast narrative painted from life studies the artist made when he lived among the Dai people in Yunnan, in southwestern China. Most of the figures are celebrating by throwing water, bathing, and dancing in a verdant jungle. The artist rejoices at the people's annual celebration commemorating the death of the tyrant who oppressed them, an important theme in China since the "Gang of Four" was smashed.

The great strength of Yuan Yunsheng's work is his dynamic composition, in which figures flow into and through vast spaces and around doors. It has unity and action and is richly colored and decorative. Yuan developed a personal style that has grown from Socialist Realist roots more Mexican than Soviet but also features expressionism. Yet he elongates his figures like Botticelli, whom he deeply admires, and they also resemble the angel-like Apsarases at Tun-huang. Some people in the art establishment condemned *Water Festival* because of its "distortion," but it was controversial principally because of the two nudes among its hundred-odd figures. In April 1980 a curtain was installed to veil the section with the nudes; in March 1981 they were walled over. Officials claimed that the Dai people had objected to the nudes.

Yuan Yunsheng works in both oil and ink. Like many Chinese artists, he had to depict the oppression through which they had lived during the past years. In Yuan's inky *Black Figure* (plate 355) a man is kneeling, bowed head on the ground, hands raised high to the rear, tied to a rope. This pose of humiliation, referred to as the "jet airplane," was the posture artists, intellectuals, and leaders were forced to assume when they were being publicly criticized during the Cultural Revolution. The expressionist composition is executed with power and economy against a vaguely inhospitable gray, mottled ground. The artist says that he does not begin to paint with a specific image in his head but finds the form stroke by stroke.

Kong Boji is another good artist among the important new wave inspired by wall paintings. Shanghai artist Kong says that he seeks "to combine ancient tradition with contemporary feeling."

In 1979 and again in 1983 Kong Boji went to northwestern China to see the Buddhist cave paintings at Tun-huang. What he saw profoundly affected his work. He copied intently—then later reinterpreted the Buddhas, Bodhisattvas, beauties, and demons on the cave walls. With oil-stick medium, he uses bright spots of Impressionist color, as well as the dark outlines of expressionism. The paintings have a numinous quality, as if transmitted by dream. A painting such as *Buddha* (plate 356) is profoundly touching, and the Buddhist content has a genuine spiritual tone.

Kong Boji's painting has been somewhat controversial. When he had an exhibition in 1980 in Wuhan, a bastion of conservatism, some art school teachers forbade their students to see such innovative work.

Most artists, including traditionalists, were rehabilitated by 1979. They enjoyed renewed prestige and were given exhibitions. The aged pioneer of painting and art education, Liu Haisu (born 1896), had his post as President of the Nanking Art College restored and had his first exhibition in twenty-two years. Termed a "rightist" in 1957, he had lived in disgrace all those years because he was outspoken and had called the Soviet painting teacher sent from Moscow "third-rate." But that had not been his only serious difference with the official line of the 1950s. Liu Haisu had found the Post-Impressionists, who were then taboo, interesting and relevant to new Chinese art. During the Cultural Revolution his personal collection of his own and others' paintings, as well as his books and other possessions, were confiscated or destroyed.

Liu Haisu is a self-taught artist who founded the first modern painting academy in 1912, when he was sixteen years old. At that time, he introduced oil painting into the curriculum as a regular subject.

Throughout Liu Haisu's long career he has painted both in oil and in ink. However, his most successful integration of the old and the new is seen in his works in ink and color. Liu uses brilliant blues and reds on the mountains in a kind of symbolic expressionism reminiscent of Les Fauves of 1908 (plate 357). Yet he continues to use the deeply brushed images of tradition.

Wu Zuoren (born 1908) was president of Peking's Central Academy of Fine Arts from 1953 to 1979. He had taken over at the death of his teacher and mentor, China's most celebrated pioneer in modern art, Xu Beihong. Wu Zuoren is one of many modern Chinese artists of his generation who was trained in Western painting but reverted to traditional techniques. Wu's most famous paintings, of yaks, camels, and pandas, are in ink; his pandas have appeared on postage stamps.

But his luminous goldfish (plate 358) are his most graceful achievement, a traditional subject that has a freedom of design and image-form that marks its modernity.

Wu Guanzhong, born in 1919, is China's most distinguished oil painter of his generation. Yet he has also chosen to work interchangeably with traditional ink on paper. He believes that when a Chinese artist uses oil, his work, by definition, becomes a Chinese painting. Wu Guanzhong has been an outspoken advocate of broadening Chinese artistic possibilities. He points out that abstract elements, such as decorative marble patterns, weirdly shaped garden stones, calligraphy, and "splashed ink" styles, have existed in Chinese tradition. Wu Guanzhong argues for liberated thinking about the essence of beauty. In "Exploration of Beauty," published in *Chinese Literature* in July 1981, he wrote:

> I was brought up in the country and my family were all country people. My schoolmates and I went around barefoot. When we caught sight of a local girl who'd been married off to somebody in Shanghai and had come back fashionably dressed, hair permed and lips rouged, we'd all run giggling behind her. Later on, at the Institute of Fine Arts in Hangzhou, I not only became used to permed hair and rouged lips, but began to appreciate different types of human beauty, even the distorted beauty prevalent in Western modern art.

In one of his ink masterpieces, *Two Swallows* (plate 359), he imagines the house of his youth, handsomely geometric and whitewashed, south of the Yangtze River. Tiny birds, specks in the distance, fly by this classically composed scene. Focusing his artistic intensity on this ideal, he creates an image of deep serenity.

Yang Yanping works at the Peking Painting Academy. She and Wu Guanzhong are both members of the Oil Painting Research Association and, like Wu, she often does her best work in ink on paper. In *Brown Lotus* (plate 360) she shows herself to be an observer of the natural world, focusing on a segment of reality and isolating it. Yang could be described as one of the new realists. By selection, she reveals a universal form. The brown lotus is observed from life but then artistically transformed in an evocative way.

Huang Yongyu, born in 1924, is one of China's most dynamic and successful artists. He has pioneered new visions and

361. Qiu Deshu (b. 1948). *Natural Order, Series IV.* 1981. Collage and ink on paper. Exhibited in *Painting the Chinese Dream*, Smith College Museum of Art, Boston City Hall Gallery, and the Brooklyn Museum, 1982–83. Searching for new ways to use old Chinese materials, young Qiu let the ink flow, wavelike, on wet paper. A white path through the ink was allowed to remain; the image evokes a waterfall. The black band on top is decoratively strewn with seal marks. These were made with uncut stones, and then they were torn up and pasted on.

techniques. Although he has absorbed a great deal from Chinese traditional painting, including materials and subject matter, his work shows abstract techniques artfully blended with traditional Chinese "flung ink" technique.

During the Cultural Revolution, like many of his colleagues, he was criticized, his house was vandalized, and he was sent to the countryside for labor reeducation. In 1974 he was singled out for particularly harsh treatment during the "black paintings" campaign. An owl painting that Huang had made for an artist friend was seized and shown in an exhibition of "black paintings." It was criticized because one eye of the owl was open and one closed. Chiang Ch'ing's deputy said this implied criticism of the government. Huang Yongyu was hounded by inquisitors, isolated from his family and friends, and exiled to a miserable room without any amenities for more than two years.

When Huang Yongyu was rehabilitated after 1976, he was commissioned to do a tapestry for the mausoleum commemorating Chairman Mao. He was also given a one-man show that exhibited mostly large bird and flower paintings, traditional Chinese fare. His compositions have a richly decorative and vital quality which is not confined to his lotus flowers (plate 361) but embodies the entire complex life cycle of a swamp. His works are international in spirit and combine the traditions of East and West.

Qiu Deshu is one of the most brilliant painters of the younger generation, doing innovative and substantial work in traditional materials. Like the scholar-painters of the past, he is a master calligrapher and seal-carver. He has studied the work of the ancients and, like the wall painters, focuses on Chinese art before the Sung dynasty (960–1279). He is much influenced by the dynamic hunting scenes of the late Chou dynasty of twenty-five hundred years ago and the Han tomb tiles of two thousand years ago. Qiu strives to paint the nature of existence, the structure of matter, and the forces of creation and change. To paint these themes, he has broken through conventional brush handling by pouring ink onto wet paper and piercing the paper itself. To control patterning and to express universal rifts, he uses torn paper to create giant collages. He makes prints—from his own fancifully carved seals as well as from uncarved beach stones—which he tears up and scatters within his compositions. Like the Ch'an (Zen) Buddhist sages, he values the untrammeled spirit and was able to recognize the liberation achieved by Jackson Pollock. Qiu Deshu saw one Pollock painting in

362. Huang Yongyu (b. 1924). *Red Lotus*. 1978. Ink and colors on paper. Collection of Chuan Ruxiang. Exhibited in *Painting the Chinese Dream*, Smith College Museum of Art and Boston City Hall Gallery, 1982–83. This intense painting radiates energy that combines traditional "flung ink" brushstrokes and flower subjects with a contemporary viewpoint and color scale. Blossoms stretch effortlessly, on stems far too wispy, over restlessly brushed blue-black water patterns.

1981, when the Boston Museum sent the first exhibition of American painting to China.

It is clear that the creative juices of China have begun to flow again, albeit in restricted channels. Moreover, since 1978 more international influences have been allowed to stimulate the scene. Foreign ideas are no longer limited to those of the Communist bloc countries as they had been in the years 1949–59. Nevertheless, the Party line has been drawn and redrawn in a continuing effort to define the extent of creative freedom. "So long as the work does not subvert the goals of the Communist Party" is a vague guideline that is given varying meanings in different periods. For example, the "spiritual pollution" campaign of 1983–84 cast a pall upon the art world through the intimidation and abuse of experimental artists and writers; by April 1984, however, the Party line had swung back to a more tolerant position.

The dream of a new art, modern yet identifiably Chinese, persists. It will continue to be a challenge for artists, in creating works of art, to be true to themselves and yet to abide by Party proscriptions.

BIBLIOGRAPHY

Akiyama, Terukazu, Kosei Ando, Saburo Matsubara, Takashi Okazaki, and Takeshi Sekino. *Arts of China: Neolithic Cultures to T'ang Dynasty* (coordinated by Mary Tregear). Tokyo and Palo Alto, Calif.: Kodansha International, 1968.

————— and Saburo Matsubara. *Arts of China: Buddhist Cave Temples.* Trans. Alexander C. Soper. Tokyo and Palo Alto, Calif.: Kodansha International, 1969.

Andersson, J. Gunnar. *Children of the Yellow Earth.* London: Kegan Paul, Trench, Trubner & Co., 1934.

Art Treasures of Dunhuang. Dunhuang, People's Republic of China: Dunhuang Institute for Cultural Relics; Hong Kong: Joint Publishing Co., 1981.

Ayers, John. *The Baur Collection: Chinese Ceramics,* 4 vols. Geneva: Collections Baur, 1972.

Barnett, A. Doak. *Communist China: The Early Years, 1949–55.* New York, Washington, and London: Praeger, 1964.

—————. "There Are Warts There Too." *New York Times Magazine,* April 8, 1973, pp. 36, 37, 100–106.

de Bary, William Theodore, Wing-tsit Chan, and Burton Watson (compilers). *Sources of Chinese Tradition.* New York: Columbia University Press, 1960.

Bennett, Gordon A., and Ronald N. Montaperto. *Red Guard.* Garden City, N.Y.: Doubleday, 1971.

Birch, Cyril (compiler and ed.). *Anthology of Chinese Literature.* New York: Grove Press, 1965.

Bonnichon, André. *Law in Communist China.* The Hague: International Commission of Jurists, 1956.

Bulling, A. "Historical Plays in the Art of the Han Period." *Archives of Asian Art,* XXI. New York: The Asia Society, 1967–68.

—————. "Hollow Tomb Tiles." *Oriental Art,* XI, no. 1. Spring, 1965.

Bunker, Emma C., C. Bruce Chatwin, and Ann R. Farkas. *"Animal Style" Art from East to West.* New York: The Asia Society, 1970.

Bush, Susan. *The Chinese Literati on Painting.* Cambridge, Mass.: Harvard University Press, 1971.

Cahill, James. *The Art of Southern Sung China.* New York: The Asia Society, 1962.

—————. *Chinese Painting.* Geneva: Albert Skira, 1960.

—————. *Hills Beyond a River: Chinese Painting of the Yuan Dynasty, 1279–1368.* New York and Tokyo: John Weatherhill, 1976.

—————. *Parting at the Shore: Chinese Painting of the Early and Middle Ming Dynasty, 1368–1580.* New York and Tokyo: John Weatherhill, 1978.

Carter, Thomas F. (rev. by L. Carrington Goodrich). *The Invention of Printing in China.* New York: Ronald Press, 1955.

Chang, Kwang-chih. *The Archaeology of Ancient China.* 3rd edition. New Haven: Yale University Press, 1977.

—————. *Early Chinese Civilization: Anthropological Perspectives.* Cambridge, Mass.: Harvard University Press, 1976.

Ch'en, Jerome. *Mao and the Chinese Revolution.* New York: Oxford University Press, 1965.

Chen, Jo-shi. *The Execution of Mayor Yin and Other Stories from the Great Proletarian Cultural Revolution.* Trans. Nancy Ing and Howard Goldblatt. Indianapolis: Indiana University Press, 1978.

Ch'en, Kenneth K. S. *Buddhism in China.* Princeton, N.J.: Princeton University Press, 1964.

—————. *The Chinese Transformation of Buddhism.* Princeton, N.J.: Princeton University Press, 1973.

Chinese Art Treasures. Geneva: Albert Skira, 1961.

Chinese Cultural Art Treasures. Taipei, Republic of China: The National Palace Museum, 1967.

Chinese Jade Throughout the Ages (Exhibition organized by the Arts Council of Great Britain and the Oriental Ceramic Society, Victoria and Albert Museum, May and June, 1975). London: Oriental Ceramic Society, 1975.

Chuka jinmin kyowakoku shutsudo bumbutsu ten (Exhibition of Archaeological Treasures Excavated in the People's Republic of China). Kunio Fujita and Sumio Kuwabara, eds. Tokyo: Asahi Newspapers Ltd., 1973.

Clapp, Anne de Coursey. *Wen Cheng-ming: The Ming Artist and Antiquity.* Ascona, Switzerland: Artibus Asiae, 1974.

Cohen, Jerome Alan. "China's Changing Constitution." *China Quarterly,* December, 1978, pp. 794–841.

—————. *The Criminal Process in the People's Republic of China, 1949–1963: An Introduction.* Cambridge,

Mass.: Harvard University Press, 1968.

———— and Hungdah Chiu. *People's China and International Law*. Princeton, N.J.: Princeton University Press, 1974.

Cohen, Joan Lebold. "Aesthetics in China—Since the Gang of Four Was Smashed." *Smith Alumnae Quarterly*, February, 1979.

————. "From Mao to Michelangelo in Chinese Art Education." *Asian Wall Street Journal*, May 31, 1979.

————. "From Red Flags to Red Flowing Plums." *Asian Wall Street Journal*, October 11, 1979.

————. "Painting the Chinese Dream: Thirty Years after the Revolution." Exhibition of painting and sculpture, 1978–81. Northampton, Mass.: Smith College Museum of Art, 1982. Subsequent exhibition enlarged, Boston: City Hall Gallery, 1982; New York: The Brooklyn Museum, 1983.

Creel, Herrlee Glessner. *The Birth of China*. New York: Frederick Ungar, 1967.

Croizier, Ralph C. (ed.). *China's Cultural Legacy and Communism*. New York: Praeger, 1970.

Cultural Relics Unearthed in Sinkiang Museum of the Sinkiang Uighur Autonomous Region. Peking: Wen-wu Press, 1975.

Dawson, Raymond. *The Chinese Chameleon*. New York: Oxford University Press, 1967.

———— (ed.). *The Legacy of China*. Oxford: Clarendon Press, 1964.

Domes, Jurgen. *China After the Cultural Revolution: Politics Between Two Congresses*. Trans. Annette Berg and David Goodman. London: C. Hurst, 1977.

Donnithorne, Audrey. *China's Economic System*. New York and Washington, D.C.: Praeger, 1967.

Dubs, Homer H. (trans.). *The History of the Former Han Dynasty* by Pan Ku, 2 vols. Baltimore: Waverly Press, 1938.

Eliséeff, Vadime, and M. T. Bobot. *Trésors d'Art Chinois*. Paris: Petit Palais, 1973.

Fairbank, John K., and Edwin O. Reischauer. *China: Tradition and Transformation*. Boston: Houghton Mifflin, 1977.

Fairbank, John K., Edwin O. Reischauer, and Albert M. Craig. *East Asia: Tradition and Transformation*. Boston: Houghton Mifflin, 1973.

Fairbank, Wilma. *Adventures in Retrieval*. Cambridge, Mass.: Harvard University Press, 1972.

Feuerwerker, Albert (ed.). *History in Communist China*. Cambridge, Mass.: MIT Press, 1968.

Fitzgerald, C. P. *China: A Short Cultural History*. New York: Praeger, 1961.

Fourcade, François. *Art Treasures of the Peking Museum*. New York: Harry N. Abrams, 1965.

Gardner, John. *Chinese Politics and the Succession to Mao*. London: Macmillan, 1982.

Gernet, Jacques. *Daily Life in China on the Eve of the Mongol Invasion, 1250–1276*. Trans. H. M. Wright. Stanford, Calif.: Stanford University Press, 1970.

Goldman, Merle. *Literary Dissent in Communist China*. Cambridge, Mass.: Harvard University Press, 1967.

————. *Modern Chinese Literature in the May 4th Era*. Harvard East Asian Series 89. Cambridge, Mass.: Harvard University Press, 1977.

Granet, Marcel. *Chinese Civilization*. Trans. Kathleen E. Innes and Mabel R. Brailsford. New York: Meridian Books, 1958.

Grousset, René. *Chinese Art & Culture*. Trans. Haakon Chevalier. New York: Grove Press, 1961.

————. *The Rise and Splendour of the Chinese Empire*. Trans. Anthony Watson-Gandy and Terence Gordon. Berkeley and Los Angeles: University of California Press, 1964.

Hinton, William. *Fanshen, A Documentary of Revolution in a Chinese Village*. New York and London: Monthly Review Press, 1966.

————. *Hundred-Day War, The Cultural Revolution at Tsinghua University*. New York and London: Monthly Review Press, 1972.

Historical Relics Unearthed in New China. Peking: Foreign Languages Press, 1972.

Ho, Ping-ti. *The Ladder of Success in Imperial China*. New York: Columbia University Press, 1962.

————. "The Loess and the Origin of Chinese Agriculture." *American Historical Review*, LXXV, no. 1, 1969.

————. "The Significance of the Ch'ing Period in Chinese History." *The Journal of Asian Studies*, XXVI, no. 2. Association for Asian Studies, Inc., 1967.

Hobson, R. L. *The Later Ceramic Wares of China*. London: Ernest Benn, 1925.

Honey, William B. *The Ceramic Art of China and Other Countries of the Far East*. London: Faber & Faber, 1945.

Hsia, C. T. *A History of Modern Chinese Fiction 1917–1957*. New Haven: Yale University Press, 1961.

Hsia Nai. "Opening an Imperial Tomb." *China Reconstructs* (Peking), VII, no. 3, March, 1959.

Hsi-an Pan-p'o [*The Neolithic Village at Pan P'o, Sian*]. Archaeological Monograph, XIV, ser. D. Peking: Wen-wu Press, 1963.

Hsiao, Kung-chuan. *A History of Modern Political Thought*. Princeton, N.J.: Princeton University

Press, 1979.

Isaacs, Harold R. *Images of Asia*. New York: Capricorn Books, 1962.

Jenyns, R. Soame. *Later Chinese Porcelain*. London: Faber & Faber, 1951.

——. *Ming Pottery and Porcelain*. London: Faber & Faber, 1953.

Kaltenmark, Max. *Lao Tzu and Taoism*. Trans. Roger Greaves. Stanford, Calif.: Stanford University Press, 1969.

Kao, Mayching Margaret. *China's Response to the West in Art, 1898–1937* (Ph.D. thesis). Stanford, Calif.: Stanford University Press, 1972.

Kaplan, Frederic M., Julian M. Sobin, and Stephen Andors. *Encyclopedia of China Today*. New York: Harper & Row, 1979.

Karnow, Stanley. *Mao and China*. New York: Viking, 1972.

Keightley, David N. *Sources of Shang History: The Oracle Bone Inscriptions of Bronze Age China*. Berkeley and Los Angeles: University of California Press, 1978.

Keswick, Maggie. *The Chinese Garden*. London: Rizzoli International, 1978.

Kuo Hsi. *An Essay on Landscape Painting*. Trans. Shio Sakanashi. London: John Murray, 1959.

Lattimore, Owen. *Inner Asian Frontiers of China*. New York: American Geographical Society, 1940.

Lee, Sherman E. *Chinese Landscape Painting*. New York: Harper & Row, n.d.

——. *A History of Far Eastern Art*. New York: Harry N. Abrams, 1964.

—— and Wai-Kam Ho. *Chinese Art Under the Mongols: The Yüan Dynasty (1279–1368)*. Cleveland: The Cleveland Museum of Art, 1968.

Legge, James. *The Chinese Classics*, 7 vols. Taipei, Taiwan, 1966.

Levenson, Joseph R. *Confucian China and Its Modern Fate*, vol. 3. Berkeley and Los Angeles: University of California Press, 1958, 1964, 1965.

Leys, Simon. *Chinese Shadows*. New York: Viking, 1977.

Liang Heng and Judith Shapiro. *Son of the Revolution*. New York: Alfred A. Knopf, 1983.

Li Chi. *Anyang*. Seattle: University of Washington Press, 1977.

——. *The Beginnings of Chinese Civilization*. Seattle: University of Washington Press, 1957.

Lin Yutang. *Imperial Peking*. New York: Crown, 1961.

Loehr, Max. *Chinese Painting After Sung*. New Haven: Yale Art Gallery Ryerson Lecture, March 2, 1967.

——. "The Fate of the Ornament in Chinese Art." *Archives of Asian Art*, XXI. New York: The Asia Society, 1967–68.

——. *Relics of Ancient China from the Collection of Dr. Paul Singer*. New York: The Asia Society and Arno Press, 1976.

Loewe, Michael. *Everyday Life in Early Imperial China*. New York: G. P. Putnam's Sons, 1968.

Loh, Robert, and Humphrey Evans. *Escape from Red China*. London: Michael Joseph, 1963.

MacFarquhar, Roderick (ed.). *The Hundred Flowers*. London: Stevens & Sons, 1960.

Mahler, Jane Gaston. *The Westerners Among the Figurines of the T'ang Dynasty of China*. Rome: Istituto Italiano per il Medio ed Estremo Oriente, 1959.

Malone, Carroll Brown. *History of the Peking Summer Palaces Under the Ch'ing Dynasty*. Urbana, Ill.: University of Illinois, 1934.

Mao Tse-tung: On Literature and Art. Peking: Foreign Languages Press, 1977.

Mao Tse-tung. *Selected Works of Mao Tse-tung*, vol. 1. London: Lawrence & Wishart, 1954.

Meisner, Maurice. *Mao's China: A History of the People's Republic*. New York: The Free Press, 1977.

Miduno, Seiiti (Mizuno, Seiichi), and Toshio (Tosio) Nagahiro. *A Study of the Buddhist Cave Temples at Lungmen, Honan*. Tokyo: Zauho Press, 1941.

Mino, Yutaka. *Ceramics in the Liao Dynasty*. New York: China Institute in America, 1973.

Munro, Eleanor C. *Through the Vermilion Gates*. New York: Pantheon Books, 1971.

Myrdal, Jan. *Report from a Chinese Village*. Trans. Maurice Michael. London: Heinemann, 1965.

Needham, Joseph (with research assistance of Wang Ling). *Science and Civilization in China*, 5 vols. Cambridge, England: Cambridge University Press, 1954–1971.

New Archaeological Finds in China. Peking: Foreign Languages Press, 1972.

New Archaeological Finds in China (II). Peking: Foreign Languages Press, 1978.

Pasqualini, Jean, and Rudolph Chelminski. *Prisoner of Mao*. New York: Penguin Books, 1976.

Payne, Robert. *Chiang Kai-shek*. New York: Weybright and Talley, 1969.

Perkins, Dwight H. "Looking Inside China: An Economic Reappraisal." *Problems of Communism*, May-June, 1973, pp. 1–13.

——. *Market Control and Planning in Communist China*. Cambridge, Mass.: Harvard University Press, 1966.

Pope, John Alexander, Rutherford John Gettens, James Cahill, and Noel Barnard. *The Freer Chinese Bronzes, I*. Washington, D.C.: Smithsonian Publication 4706, 1967.

Pye, Lucian. *Mao Tse-tung: The Man in the Leader.* New York: Basic Books, 1976.

Reischauer, Edwin O. *Ennin's Travels in T'ang China.* New York: Ronald Press, 1955.

Rice, Edward E. *Mao's Way.* Berkeley, Los Angeles, and London: University of California Press, 1972.

Schafer, Edward H. *The Golden Peaches of Samarkand.* Berkeley and Los Angeles: University of California Press, 1963.

Schneeberger, Pierre F. *The Baur Collection, Geneva: Chinese Jades and Other Hardstones.* Geneva: Collection Baur, 1976.

Schram, Stuart. *Mao Tse-tung.* New York: Simon and Schuster, 1966.

Schurmann, Franz. *Ideology and Organization in Communist China.* Berkeley and Los Angeles: University of California Press, 1966.

Seckel, Dietrich. *The Art of Buddhism.* Trans. Anne E. Keep. New York: Crown, 1964.

A Selection of Archaeological Finds of the People's Republic of China. Peking: Wen-wu Press, 1976.

Shangraw, Clarence F. *Origins of Chinese Ceramics.* New York: China Institute in America, 1978.

Sheridan, James E. *China in Disintegration: The Republican Era in Chinese History 1912–1949.* New York: The Free Press, 1975.

Sickman, Laurence, and Alexander Soper. *The Art and Architecture of China.* Baltimore: Penguin Books, 1960.

Sirén, Osvald. *The Chinese on the Art of Painting.* New York: Schocken Books, 1963.

——. *Gardens of China.* New York: Ronald Press, 1949.

——. *A History of Early Chinese Art*, 4 vols. London: Ernest Benn, 1928.

——. *The Imperial Palaces of Peking*, 3 vols. Paris and Brussels: G. Van Oest, 1926.

——. *The Walls and Gates of Peking.* New York: Orientalia, n.d.

Sivin, Nathan. *Chinese Alchemy: Preliminary Studies.* Cambridge, Mass.: Harvard University Press, 1968.

——. "The Theoretical Background of Chinese Alchemy," in Joseph Needham, *Science and Civilization in China*, vol. 5, sec. 33. Cambridge, England: Cambridge University Press, 1954–71.

Snow, Edgar. *The Other Side of the River.* London: Gollancz, 1963.

Solomon, Richard. *Mao's Revolution and the Chinese Political Culture.* Berkeley, Los Angeles, and London: University of California Press, 1971.

Spence, Jonathan D. *Emperor of China: Self-Portrait of K'ang-hsi.* New York: Vintage, 1974.

——. *The Gate of Heavenly Peace.* New York: Viking, 1981.

Ssu-ch'iu chih-lu (The Silk Route). *Han T'ang chih-wu* (Objects from the Han and T'ang). Edited by the Work Group for the Exhibition of Unearthed Archaeological Treasures of the Wei-wu-er Autonomous Regional Museum of Tibet. Peking: Archaeological Treasures Publishing Co., 1972.

Sullivan, Michael. *The Arts of China* (rev. ed.). Berkeley and Los Angeles: University of California Press, 1977.

——. *Chinese Art in the Twentieth Century.* Berkeley and Los Angeles: University of California Press, 1959.

Swann, Peter C. *Chinese Monumental Art.* London: Thames and Hudson, 1963.

Terrill, Ross (ed.), *The China Difference.* New York: Harper & Row, 1979.

——. *The White-boned Demon.* New York: William Morrow, 1984.

Treistman, Judith M. *The Prehistory of China.* New York: Doubleday, 1972.

Tseng Yu-ho Ecke. *Chinese Calligraphy.* Philadelphia: Philadelphia Museum of Art, 1971.

Tuchman, Barbara W. *Stilwell and the American Experience in China, 1911–45.* New York: Macmillan, 1971.

Tung, Robert (ed.). *Revelations that Move the Earth to Tears: A Collection of Post-Cultural Revolution Poems and Essays by Chinese Youths.* Lund: Scandinavian Institute of Asian Study Monographs, 1978.

Twitchett, Denis, and John K. Fairbank (eds.). *The Cambridge History of China*, vol. 10, part 1: *Late Ching 1800–1911.* London: Cambridge University Press, 1971.

Vanderstappen, Harrie A. *The T. L. Yuan Bibliography of Western Writings on Chinese Art and Archeology.* London: Mansell, 1975.

Vogel, Ezra. *Canton Under Communism.* Cambridge, Mass.: Harvard University Press, 1969.

Waley, Arthur. *An Introduction to the Study of Chinese Painting.* London: Ernest Benn, 1958.

Watson, Burton. *Early Chinese Literature.* New York: Columbia University Press, 1962.

——. *Records of the Grand Historian of China* (trans. from the *Shih-chi* of Ssu-ma Ch'ien), 2 vols. New York: Columbia University Press, 1961.

——. *Su Tung-P'o, Selections from a Sung Dynasty Poet.* New York: Columbia University Press, 1965.

Watson, William. *Early Civilization in China.* New York: McGraw-Hill, 1966.

Watt, J. C. Y. *A Han Tomb in Lei Cheng Uk.* Hong Kong:

City Museum and Art Gallery, 1970.

Welch, Holmes. "Buddhism Since the Cultural Revolution." *The China Quarterly* (London). October-December, 1969.

———. "The Buddhists' Return." *Far Eastern Economic Review* (Hong Kong), vol. 81, no. 28, July 16, 1973.

Wan-hua to-ko-ming ch'-chien ch'u-t'u wen-wu (Archaeological Treasures Unearthed During the Period of the Great Proletarian Cultural Revolution). Edited by the Work Group for the Exhibition of Unearthed Archaeological Treasures. Peking: Archaeological Treasures Publishing Co., 1972.

Whitfield, R. *Chang Tse-tuan's Ch'ing-ming Shang-ho t'n* (thesis). Princeton, N.J.: Princeton University Microfilms, 1965.

Willetts, William. *Chinese Art*, 2 vols. Baltimore: Pelican Books, 1958.

———. "The Treasures of Wan-li: Gold, Jade and Porcelain from the Newly-Discovered Tomb of a Ming Emperor." Supplement to the *Illustrated London News*, Feb. 27, 1960, p. 353.

Witke, Roxane. *Comrade Chiang Ch'ing*. Boston: Little, Brown, 1977.

Wittfogel, Karl A. *Mao Tse-tung: Liberator or Destroyer of the Chinese Peasants?* New York: Free Trade Union Committee, American Federation of Labor, 1955.

Wright, Arthur F. *Buddhism in Chinese History*. New York: Atheneum, 1965.

——— and Denis Twitchett (ed.). *Confucian Personalities*. Stanford, Calif.: Stanford University Press, 1962.

Wu, Nelson I. *Chinese and Indian Architecture*. New York: George Braziller, 1963.

———. "The Toleration of Eccentrics." *Art News*, vol. 56, no. 3, May, 1957.

———. "Tung Ch'i-ch'ang: Apathy in Government, Fervor in Art." Fifth Conference on Chinese Thought, Sept. 12–17, 1960.

The Yunkang Caves. Compiled by the Committee in Charge of Cultural Relics and the Institute for the Preservation of the Yunkang Caves of Shansi Province. Peking: The Cultural Relics Publishing House, 1977.

INDEX

Italic type indicates references to plate numbers.

Academy of Social Sciences, 55, 328, 360
Acrobats, 87–88; *74, 149–50, 321–22*
Acupuncture, 338, 356; *306–11*
Agriculture, 55, 247, 257–66, 277–84, 313, 330–31, 336–37, 344, 354; *27–28, 39, 88, 250, 256, 258, 262–69, 272, 282*
Ai Ch'ing, 361
Akiyama Terukazu, 94
Alchemy, 142–44
Altars, Ming, 177–80; *178, 181, 184*
Amphora, 160; *157*
Amusements. *See* Recreation
An Lu-shan, 140–41
Anderson, J. G., 44
Animal forms in art: Ch'ing, 222, 224–25; *229, 232*; Han, 90–91, 94, 99, 101, 103, 171; *75–78, 81, 84–87, 93–95, 174*; Ming, 171; *13, 170, 174, 202*; People's Republic, *180*; Shang, 59; *47*; T'ang, 138–40, 142; *127, 133, 138*; Yang-shao, 50–51; *45*. *See also* Art; Dragons; Nature in art
Anti-: Americanism, 18; Buddhists, 115, 130; corruption, 32; crime, 334–35; foreigners, 317; elitism, 312; imperialism, 230–31; Japanese, 237; rightists, 277–78, 299, 322–23, 405
Antonioni, Michelangelo, 317
Anyang excavations, 44–45
Apartments, imperial, 193–95; *201, 203*
Apsarases, 120, 417; *108*
Archaeology, 35, 43–46, 55, 89, 97–99, 173, 380
Architecture: Ch'ing, 219–22; *210, 222–23, 225–28*; colonial, 237–39; *239–41*; influence of, 72, 154, 219, 237–40; Ming, 176–95, 204, 206; *26, 181–203, 211–19, 224*; People's Republic, 175–76, 240, 380, 383–84; *180, 331–32, 334*; proletarian, 389; Sung, 133–35; *124–25*; T'ang, 130, 132–33; *120–21*; Yüan, 157–58; *154–56*
Art: Buddhist, 116–17, 130; Communist, 384; Cultural Revolution, 396–404; education, 418; exhibitions, 39; forms of, 392–96; pictorial, 160; post-Mao, 404–21; role of, *139*, 225, 381–92; traditional, 38
Art and Architecture of China, The (Sickman and Soper), 127
Artists Association, 406–9
Arts of China: Neolithic Cultures to T'ang Dynasty (Akiyama *et al.*), 94
Atheism, 365
Authoritarianism, 148, 229

Ballet, 36, 377, 380, 384–85, 389, 392, 396, 399; *335, 340, 348*
Balustrades, 191; *194, 225*

Bells, bronze, 62; *52*
Billboards, 33, 182, 212; *30, 220*
Birth control, 332–33, 345, 349
Black Figure (Yüan Yunsheng), 412, 417; *355*
Blind and Silent (Wang Keping), 405, 408; *347*
Blue-and-white ware: Ch'ing, 165, 226; Ming, 164–66; *165, 168*; Yüan, 165–66; *167*
Boats, 107–8, 219–20; *97–98, 102*
Bodhi trees (pipal), 135; *125*
Bodhisattvas, 113, 117, 119–20, 127; *105, 117*
Bonus system, 323, 340, 349, 375
Book burnings, 78, 111
Botanical Gardens, Canton, *18*
Boxer Rebellion, 223, 305
Bridges, 187–88, 211; *18, 219, 222, 305*
Bronze: castings, 44–45, 59, 62, 65, 91, 94, 99; Chou, 48, 59–60, 62, 99; *48–50, 52, 56*; Han, 90–91, 94, 99, 103; *75–81, 85, 94–95*; Ming, *11*; Shang, 99; *47*
Brown Lotus (Yang Yanping), 419; *360*
Buddha (Gautama), 113, 412, 418; *356*; art, 116–17, 158; cave paintings of, 112, 417; images of, 121–22; temples for, 136
Buddha Vairocana, 127; *100, 115, 117*
Buddhas: sinicization of, 117, 121–22; Sui, *110*; T'ang, 122, 129, 158; *100, 108, 110–11, 113–15, 117–18*; Wei, 117, 119, 158; *36, 104–5, 107, 109*; Yüan, 158; *155–56*
Buddhism, 65, 112–14, 117–19, 122, 127, 158, 365; Chinese, 122, 130; classical language of, 158; and Cultural Revolution, 114; Indian, 112; Mahayana, 113; Northern Wei, 113, 116–17, 158; in People's Republic, 114, 351–53; persecution of, 122–27, 129; as religion, 112, 147; and sculpture, 40, 113–16, 136; symbols, 119–20; T'ang, 121, 129–30, 158; and temples, 136
Buddhism in China (Ch'en), 117
Bulling, Dr. A., 83–84
Bureaucracy, 147, 157, 215, 235, 250, 300, 308, 316, 332, 375–76
Burial figurines, 140
Businessmen, 10, 32, 230, 248, 265–66, 269, 277

Cadres, 264, 268, 282–83, 306, 308, 377
Calligraphy, 103, 148–49, 201; of Mao, 182, 375
Camels, 407, 419; *133, 349*; Bactrian, 138–39; *133*
Canton, 121; *18, 237–41, 274*
Canton Commune Rising of 1927, 175; memorial tumulus for, *180*
Canton Fair, 78
Capital Hospital, 239–40; *244–45*
Cash, string of, 67; *143*
Castiglione, Giuseppe, 219

Catholicism and Catholics, 362–63, 365
Cave dwellings, *291*
Cave of Ten Thousand Buddhas, 122; *112–14*
Cave sculpture and paintings, 112–17, 119, 122, 127, 129–30, 417; *100, 102–18*
CCP. *See* Communist Party, Chinese
Ceilings, 171, 193; *176, 201*
Celadon ware, 161–63; *93, 122, 157–61*
Central Advisory Commission, 332
Central Committee, 308, 311, 331
Centralized government, 147, 157, 267, 311, 316
Ceramics, 45–52, 133, 160, 165–66, 223–25; Ch'in, *67–68*; Ch'ing, 223–26, 375; Five Dynasties, *158, 160*; Han, 87–89, 101–3; *74, 87, 89–93, 98*; Lung–shan, 46; *41*; People's Republic, 375; *341*; Six Dynasties, 105, 160; *96*; Sung, 160–65; T'ang, 133, 139–41, 160; *35, 99, 122, 131–36, 157, 159*; Yang-shao, 46, 49–52; *40, 45–46*; Yüan, *145, 164, 166*. *See also* Blue-and-white ware; Celadon ware; Chün ware; Porcelain; Three-color ware; Ting ware; Tz'u-chou ware; Yüeh ware
Ch'ang-an, 83–84, 112, 121, 133, 135–36, 140–41. *See also* Sian
Chang Ding, 400
Chang Hsüeh-liang, 70, 233
Chang Tse-tuan, 149–50
Chao Teh-pa, 264
Chariots, 91; *77–78*
Ch'en, Kenneth, 117
Chen Danqing, 407, 412; *350*
Chen Jo-hsi, 11
Chen Mu-hua, 333
Ch'en Po-ta, 298, 309, 312, 329
Ch'en Yi, 295
Chen Yifei, 408, 414–15; *351*
Chiang Ch'ing, 13, 57, 78, 297–98, 319–20, 321, 330, 369, 396
Chiang Ch'un-ch'iao, 321, 330
Chiang Kai-shek, 45, 70–71, 116, 175, 216, 243, 309; and the Republic, 229–37, 383
Chiang Kai-shek (Payne), 234
Chiang Nan-hsiang, 343
Ch'ien-lung, Emperor, 204, 216–17, 219, 226
Children, 247, 332, 343–48, 362; *1–3, 10–11, 13, 25, 247–48, 312–15*
Children's Hospital (Peking), 40
Children's palaces, 345; *1, 280, 283, 315*
Chimes, stone, 62; *51*
Chin dynasty, 157
Ch'in dynasty, 77–78, 83–84, 136, 157, 165, 215; *67–68*
Ch'in Shih Huang-ti, Emperor, 77–78, 80, 83, 111, 312
China National Offshore Oil Corporation, 340
China Travel Service, *6*
"China watchers," 10
Chinese Art (Willetts), 161

Chinese Art Under the Mongols (Lee), 158
Chinese Dragon Spouts Oil, 288; *277*
Chinese and Indian Architecture (Wu), 180
Chinese-Korean Friendship Commune, 387
Chinese Shadows (Leys), 11
Ch'ing dynasty, 43, 136, 149, 165, 215–16, 222–26
Ching-ho, 255–56
Ch'ing Hua University, 363
Ch'ing-ming festival, 149–51, 320; *149–50*
Chou dynasty, 43, 55–71, 77, 99, 111
Chou En-lai, 13, 39, 57, 71, 78, 298, 300–1, 309–12; "centrist" course of, 311; and the Republic, 71, 231, 319–20
Chou-k'ou-tien caves, 44
Christians and Christianity, 226, 234, 351–52, 362–63
Chü Te, Marshal, 389
Chu Yüan-chang, 169
Chü-yung-kuan Pass, 157–58; gateway, *154–56*
Chün-ware, 163; *162*
Churches, 352; *241*. *See also* Temples
Civilization, development of, 38, 43, 45, 48, 52, 57
"Class" orientation, 376, 385
Class struggles, 39, 322, 328, 331
Classics, Confucian, 43–45, 67, 130, 148, 169, 182
Clothing: Han, 140; Ming, 203; *179*; People's Republic, 25; *15*; T'ang, 140; *134–35*; Wei, 140
Cloud Terrace, *154–55*
Clouds at Huang Shan (Liu Haisu), 414; *357*
Coins, 65–67, 144; *56, 143–44*
Cold war responses, 9
Collectivization, 257–65, 268, 277, 336
Columns. *See* Pillars
Communes, 279–84, 318, 387; *298*
Communications: internal, 77–78; oral, 20, 380. *See also* Transportation
Communism, primitive, 52, 55
Communist Party, Chinese (CCP); and art, 9–10, 154–55, 211, 371, 383–84; Central Committee, 308, 311, 331; and Confucianism, 56; Congresses, 267, 307, 311–12, 322; historians, 56; ideologues vs. pragmatists, 248–50, 258–65, 267–78, 284–317; in Republican period, 231, 233, 236–37
Communist Youth League, 279, 308, 354, 365–66
Competition encouraged, 341
Confucianism: attacks on, 56, 78; bureaucracy in, 215; and education, 130; and filial piety ideals, 113; preservation of, 215; role of, 148, 158. *See also* Classics, Confucian
Confucius, 56, 78, 312; temples honoring, *36*
Confucius Association, 255
Constitution, new, 114, 266–67, 311, 317–19, 322–23, 333, 340–41

Constitutional restraints, 235
Cooperatives, 257–64, 268, 281–82
Corruption, 32, 237, 248, 250, 332, 375–76
Counterrevolutionaries, 32–33, 248, 258, 267, 329, 361, 364
Court system, 367–69, 371, 374
Courtiers, 141; *136*
Courtyards, 188–93; *192, 199, 223, 227*
Cowrie shells, 65; *55*
"Cradle of China," 44, 48
Craig, Albert M., 149, 235
Crime, 334–35, 353–57, 363–64, 366–68
Criminal law codes, 327, 361
Cuisine, 29–33, 35, 140; *22–23*
Cultural Revolution, 9, 13–14, 29, 39, 78, 87, 114, 154–55, 181–82, 211, 297–309, 372, 380, 384, 396
Cultural Revolution Directorate, 298, 300–301, 305, 384
Culture presentations, 24, 50, 215
Cutouts, paper, 65, 391–92, 404; *345*

Dai Ailian, 404; *346*
Dai people, 411, 417; *353–54*
Dancers, 62, 87, 325, 404; *346*; sword, 85, 89; *70*
Dancing, 358; *22, 70*
Decentralization, 336
Democracy, 230, 249, 318, 325, 361–62
"Democracy Wall," 327, 404
Demonstrations, mass, 318–19
Desert Jeep (Zhao Yixiong), 407, 411; *349*
Diplomatic relationships, 10, 14, 28
Discipline Inspection Commission, 332
Divorce, 256, 363, 368, 378. *See also* Family life
Dragon bones, 58–59
Dragon-cloud motif, 180, 186, 189–91; *171, 191, 194*
Dragon King, 142
Dragons, 72, 91, 99, 142, 166, 220; *59, 77, 83, 127, 138, 176–78, 211, 215*
Drama groups, 383

Earthenware. *See* Ceramics
Earthquakes, 321
East Asia: Tradition and Transformation (Fairbank, Reischauer, Craig), 149, 235
Eastern Chou, 56, 64, 111
Eastern Han dynasty, 101
Eastern Wei, 121
Economic development, 40, 308, 323–24, 329, 334–36, 362; Socialist planned, 339
Education, 114, 234, 269, 339–50; *280, 312–15*; adult, 357; art, 418; Confucian, 130; and Cultural Revolution, 295–96, 298, 310–11; health, 356; opportunities for, 307, 319; in People's Republic, 357–58; "persuasion," 264; pragmatic, 359; proletarian, 358; quality of, 33, 311, 324; and Red Guards, 396; reforms, 336; in rural areas, 357; Socialist, 277–78, 285; technological, 360
Eleventh Party Congress, 322
Elgin, Lord James, 217, 219
Elitism, 312
Engels, Friedrich, 375; *329*
Essay on Landscape Painting, An (Kuo Hsi), 153
Eunuchs, 193–97, 215

Execution of Mayor Yin and Other Stories (Chen Jo-hsi), 11
Expression, freedom of, 326, 360
Expressionism, 409, 415, 417

Fairbank, John K., 149, 235
Family Law, Nationalist, 256
Family life, 113, 256, 280–81, 355, 377–78
Family planning, 344–46, 349–50
Fang-Hu, *48*
Fanshen (Hinton), 256
Far Eastern Economic Review, cited, 338
Feng Guodeng, 406, 409–11; *348*
Feng-hsien Temple, 127; *100, 115–17*
Feng Yu-lan, 317
Ferghana blood-sweating horses, 90–91, 139
Feudal society, 55–56, 78, 173, 332; tradition of, 344–45
Fifth National People's Congress, 322
Five Year Plan: First, 257–78; Second, 278–84
"Flung ink" painting technique, 420; *362*
Forbidden City. *See* Imperial Palace
Foreign relations: with Great Britain, 216–17; influence of, 18–20, 29, 32, 39–40, 233, 317, 333, 421; with Japan, 70–71, 220, 222–23, 236–37; with Soviet Union, 15, 231, 279, 283, 309; trade policies and, 121, 138, 141–42, 324–26; with United States, 9–11, 14–15, 18, 309; with visitors, 24–25, 29–30, 39, 317
Foreigners in T'ang China, 135–38; *131–32*
"Forest of Steles, The," *146*
Fourth Congress of Writers and Artists, 392–93, 405
Freer Chinese Bronzes, The (Pope), 60
Fu Baoshi, 394; *337*
Funerary customs, 52, 57, 60–62, 64–65, 87–91, 94–102
Funerary objects: ceramic, 105, 133, 136–40; Ch'in, 78–80; Chou, 59–62; *48–50*; Han, 87, 89–98, 136, 139; *74–94, 98*; Shang, 57, 64; *47, 53–54*; Six Dynasties, 105; *96*; T'ang, 133, 136–40; *35, 99, 122–23, 131–36*
Funerary suits, 60–65, 94–99; *69, 82–83*
Furnaces, backyard, 279, 282–83
Furnishings: Ch'ing, 193–95, 219; *203, 224*; Ming, 203, 211; *217*; People's Republic, 377; *333*; Republican, 240

Games. *See* Sports
Gang of Four, 13–14, 24–25, 57, 155, 319–24, 358, 371, 387, 392–93, 399, 404, 417
Garden of the Master of Nets (Soochow), 154
Gardens: beauty of, 154–55, 203–4, 206, 212; *18, 228*; Ming, 204–11; *211–19*; People's Republic, 154–55, 211–12; *34, 220–21, 273*. *See also* Rocks
Gardens of China (Sirén), 204
Gate of Heavenly Peace, 184–87, 320
Gate of Heavenly Purity, *193*
Gate of the Midday Sun, 187
Gate of Military Prowess, *29*
Gates: Ming, 177–80, 187, 193; *182,*

190, 200, 212; Yüan, 157–58; *154–56*
Gazebo, 72; *60*
Genghis Khan, 155, 157
George III, King, 216
Glass, imported, 142; *141*
Glazing, 140, 166
Gold, 142, 222; *138, 229*
Golden Horde, 155–57
Golden Peaches of Samarkand, The (Schafer), 136, 139
Goldfish (Wu Zuoren), 415, 419; *358*
Government: Ch'in, 77–78; Han, 89; Ming, 169, 195–97, 215; People's Republic, 248–57, 266–78, 284–97, 307–17; Republic, 229–37; Shang, 56; Sui, 121; Yüan, 157
Great Gander Pagoda, 130–33, 385; *120–21*
Great Hall of the People, 35, 184, 377; *332–33*
Great Leap Forward of 1958, 279–85, 296, 308–9, 331, 403
Great Proletarian Cultural Revolution of 1966–76, 9, 297
"Great Spirit Who Resides in Heaven," 60, 177; *50*
Great Wall, 36, 75–78, 80; *63–65, 67–68*
Group pressures, 345, 365, 371
Guardians, 158, 193; *60, 116–17, 156, 196, 198*

Hai Jui, 285
Hall of Eminent Favors, 171–73; *176–77*
Hall of Military Prowess, *192, 202*
Hall of Perfect Harmony, 188–89, 191
Hall of Prayer for Good Harvests, 176, 180–81, 184; *187–88*
Hall of the Preservation of Harmony, 189, 191; *67–68*
Hall of Repose, *210, 223*
Hall of Supreme Harmony, 188–89, 191; *26, 191*
Han dynasty, 64, 83–108, 111, 121; *66*
Handicrafts, 393; *346*
Handles, 99–101; *85–86*
Hangchow, 151, 157, 419
Health resources, 307, 356–57, 366
Hinton, William, 256
Historians: Communist, 52, 55–56, 173; Han dynasty, 84
Historical Museum (Sian), 171; *99, 126, 146, 174*
Horses, 90–91, 139; *35, 75–76, 78*
House-church Christians, 363
Household responsibility system, 336–38, 375
Housing: Neolithic, 48; *42*; People's Republic, 338, 355; *288–92*; prehistoric, 48–49, 51; Republican, 237; *239–40*
Hsia dynasty, 43–45, 55
Hsia Nai, 141, 144, 173
Hsia-hsiang (down to the countryside) movement, 279, 307
Hsiang Yü, 83–85; *72*
Hsien-feng, Emperor, 222
Hsü Wei, 201; *208*
Hsüan-tsang, 130–33
Hu Hsien peasant painting, 391–92, 403; *344*
Hu Shih, 242–43
Hu Yaobang, 328–29, 331–33
Hua Kuo-feng, 15, 18, 320–25, 328–32, 387, 389; *330*
Hua-ch'ing-kung, 67–72; *57–62*
Huang Yongyu, 420; *361*
Huang-p'u River, 304
Human sacrifices, 57, 87

Humanism, 80, 148
Hundred Days of 1898, 223
Hundred flowers period, 268–77, 360, 404–5, 409, 411
Hundred Flowers, The (MacFarquhar), 268–69, 277
Hung-wu, Emperor, 169
Huns, 89–90

I Am a Seagull (P'an Chia-chün), 387, 399; *341*
I Ho Yüan Summer Palace, 219–22; *222, 225, 228, 255*
Ideologues, 311–12, 394–96
Ideology, 308, 319
Images, 415; *358*; of Buddha, 121–22, *117*; of Mao, 36
Immortality, elixir of, 142–44
Imperial Academy, 149, 151, 153
Imperial Heavenly Vault, 180; *184–86*
Imperial Palace, 36, 38, 163, 169, 176, 182–84, 187–95, 395; *4, 13, 17, 189–203, 223–24, 239*; displays at, 165–66, 204, 215, 224
Imperialism, 230–31
Impressionism, 406
Incense burners, 91–94, 142, 166, 191; *79, 137, 168*
Incentives, work, 336, 341
Income distribution, 340, 354, 375
India, 122, 132, 338; religion of, 112; treasures of, 45
Industrialization, 265–66, 313, 339–40, 344, 359
Industry, 277–84, 301–2, 308–9, 318–20; *293–97*
Ink, 103–5; painting technique, 420; *360, 362*
Inkstone case, 103; *94*
Institute of Fine Arts (Hangzhou), 419
Instruments, musical, 61–62, 87; *51–52*
Intellectual repression, 19
Investments, 326, 333
Islam, 365
Ivory, 66

Jade, 94–99; *69, 82–83*; disks, 63–64; *53–54*
Japan, 70–71, 220, 222–23, 236–37, 338
Jewelry, 64, 222, 392; *54, 179, 229*
Journalism, 10, 13, 29, 269, 298
Judiciary, role of, 368–69, 371, 374
Jurchens, 151, 157

Kaifeng, 149–51
Kaifeng Acrobatic Troupe, 321–22
K'ang-hsi, Emperor, 219
Kang Zuotian, 399; *342*
Kansu, bronze horses from, 103
Kao Tsu, Emperor, 83–85, 89
Karnow, Stanley, 306–7
"Killing Three Knights with Two Peaches," 87; *73*
Kong Boji, 412, 417–18; *356*
Korea, 10, 249, 297, 387
Ku Yen-wen, 97
Kuang-hsü, Emperor, 222–23
Kublai Khan, 155–58, 169
K'un-ming Lake, 219, 222; *226*
Kung, Prince, 222
Kuo Hsi, 153–55
Kuo Mo-jo, 55–56, 87, 238, 298
Kuo-chieh-t'a Gateway, 157–58; *154–56*
Kuomintang (KMT) Party, 231–36, 243, 249, 256, 294
Kwangtung Province State Guest House, *14, 328*

428

Labor force and productivity, 308, 338, 357, 366
Lakes and ponds, 72, 211, 219, 222; *19, 58, 62, 216, 218, 226, 228*
Lamaism, 158
Lamps, 94, 136; *80, 127*
Lan P'ing, 297
Land: ownership, 247, 265; reform, 249–65, 268, 277, 336–37
Landscapes: Ming, 198, 201; *153, 205–6*; painting styles, 150–53, 155, 160, 386; People's Republic, 388; *343*; Sung, 151–54; *151–52*
Language, 57–59, 158, 242–43, 365–68
Lattimore, Owen, 317
Law Institute, 328
Lawyers, role of, 367–69, 371, 374
Lee, Sherman, 157–58
Leftist leaders, 307, 310, 319–20, 335, 339, 341
Legal system, 267–69, 277–78, 323, 356–58, 367–69; *275, 278*
Lenin, V.I., 231, 332
Leopards, 103; *174*
Leys, Simon, 11
Li Keran, 400; *343*
Li Po, 136–38
Li Shou-li, cache of. *See* Pin, Prince, cache of
Liberalization policies, 18–19, 255
Lin Piao, 285, 294, 298–99, 301, 308–12, 318, 329–30, 358, 362
Literature, 46, 63, 198, 242–44, 269, 298, 404. *See also* Classics, Confucian
Liu Haisu, 394, 396, 414, 418; *357*
Liu Pang, 83–85, 89, 169
Liu Shao-ch'i, 282, 285, 295, 312, 318, 330, 358, 389; Cultural Revolution and, 298–99, 305–7
Liu Sheng, 91, 94, 96–97, 99, 101
Living standards, 354. *See also* Family life
Lo Jui-ch'ing, 295, 298
Long March, 329, 383
Looking at History from My Space (Chen Yifei), 408, 414; *351*
Lotus Dance, 404; *346*
Lotus Flower Cave, 120; *109*
Lotus flower designs, 420; *112, 361*
Loyang, 40, 69, 83, 87, 101, 111–12, 114, 121; *289, 327*
Lu Hsün, 243–44; *246*
Lu Hsün Academy of Arts, 371, 383
Lung-shan culture, 46–52, 112, 116, 158; *41*
Luo Zhongli, 411, 414; *352*

Ma Yin-chu, 349
Macartney, Lord George, 216
MacFarquhar, Roderick, 268–69, 277
Mahayana Buddhism, 113
Mahler, Jane Gaston, 140
Manchu dynasty. *See* Ch'ing dynasty
Mandate of heaven, 43, 67, 84, 169
Mao and China (Karnow), 307
Mao Tse-tung: in art, 371–72; *243, 330*; charismatic rule of, 335; death of, 321; images of, 36; influence of, 13, 57, 78, 231, 237, 248–55, 258, 265, 279–80, 282–307, 310–11; military leadership of, 294, 305; poetry of, 182, 400; posters and buttons, 386; statues of, 211; *327*; "Thoughts," 182, 308, 322, 369
Marching Through Loushan Pass at Sunset (Li Keran), 400; *343*
Markets, 308–9, 336–37; *24–25, 256–61*
Marriage, 256, 333, 369, 378; *32*

Marx, Karl, 375; *329*
Marxism-Leninism, 55–57, 230–32, 237, 243–44, 360
Masses Criticize Lin Piao and Confucius, The (Yang T.H.), *344*
May 7th Cadre Schools, 310, 359–60, 375
Medical care and medicine, 59, 142–44, 307, 338–39, 356–57, 366; *306–11. See also* Acupuncture
Military Affairs Commission, 329, 331
Ming dynasty, 136, 149–50, 165–66, 169–81, 191–98
Ming Huang, Emperor, 140–41
Ming Imperial Academy, 153
Ministry of Justice, 328
Ministry of State Security, 334
Missionaries, effects of, 112, 121, 234, 239, 362
Moderation, policy of, 309
Modernization programs, 10, 322, 324, 328–29, 334, 344, 360–62
Monarchical form of government, 55–57
Monasteries and monks, 129–30
Money. *See* Cash, string of; Coins; Cowrie shells
Mongols. *See* Yüan dynasty
Monkey King Wreaks Havoc in Heaven, The, 392; *336*
Monsters. *See* Animal forms in art
Moon gates, 57, 121
Morale in People's Republic, 375
Morality, socialist, 408–9
Moslems, 365
Mountain landscapes, 153; *153*
Murphy, Henry K., 229
Museum of History, 184; *332*
Museums, 20, 36, 38, 136
Music and musicians, 61–63, 88, 136, 310, 358, 393, 405; *108, 347–48*
Mutual-aid teams, 257–58
My Father (Luo Zhongli), 411, 414; *352*
Myrdal, Jan, 265
"Mysterious Orient," 9
Mythology, 9, 43, 45, 288, 385; *277*

Nanking Art College, 418
National China Art Gallery, 406
National People's Congress, 266–67, 298, 326, 333, 341
National Youth Art Exhibition, 411; *352*
Nationalism, rise of, 9, 38, 223, 392
Nationalist Party. *See* Kuomintang (KMT) Party
Nationalities' Cultural Palace, 380, 392, 396; *334*
Natural Order, Series IV (Qiu Deshu), *361*
Nature in art, 50–51, 59, 154–55, 225. *See also* Animal forms in art; Gardens; Lakes and ponds
Needham, Joseph, 107
Neo-Confucianism, 148
Neolithic cultures, 44–52
New Archaeological Finds in China (Hsia Nai), 141, 144, 173
Ni Tsan, 198, 201
Ninth Party Congress, 307–8
Nixon, Richard M., 309, 400
Normalization policies, 14, 18, 325
North Temple Society, 255
Northern Celadon glaze, 159, 163; *161*
Northern Sung dynasty, 149–50
Northern Wei Buddhist art, 116–17, 158
Northern Wei dynasty, 112–13, 117, 119, 121, 127

Not Quite Huang Shan (Fu Baoshi), *337*
Nurhachi, 215
Nurseries, horticultural, 212; *37, 219*
Nursery schools. *See* Children; Education

Offerings. *See* Funerary customs; Funerary objects
Oil Painting Research Association, 406, 409, 419; *348*
Oil painting, technique of, 385, 389, 409, 418
Open door policy, 334–35
Open society, 19, 327–28, 362
Opera, 36, 297, 380, 392, 399; *279, 336*
Opium War of 1839–42, 56, 147, 216
Opportunism, educational, 307, 319–20
Oracle bones, 58
Orchid Garden, *34*
Ownership, private, 247, 265, 336–37, 355–56

Pagodas, 130–33, 135, 239; *119–22, 124, 234*
Painting: abstract, 198; calligraphy as extension of, 148; cave, 112–17, 119, 122, 127, 129–30, 417; *100, 102–18*; Che school of, 153; classical, 392; and expressionism, 409, 415, 417–18; flung ink, 420; *360, 362*; Han, 83–87; *70–71, 73*; and impressionism, 406, 409, 418; landscape, 150–53, 155, 160; *153*; Ming, 150, 153–54, 197–203; *147–49, 153, 204–9*; modernistic, 412; oil, 385, 389, 409, 418; peasant, 403; Peking Academy style of, 396–97, 400, 411–12, 415, 418; in People's Republic, 380, 382–83, 385–92, 394–420; *337, 341, 343–45, 351, 353–55, 358, 360–62*; pictorial, 160; post-Mao, 404–21; in Republican era, 240–42; Socialist Realist, 385–87, 399–400, 403–4, 412; *350–51*; Southern Sung, 153; Sung, 150–55; traditionalism in, 392, 394, 400, 417–19; *358*; Western influence in, 219, 408, 414, 419–21; Wu school of, 201; Yüan dynasty, 198
Painting the Chinese Dream, 412; *355, 360–62*
Palace of Orderly Clouds, *226*
Palace of Permanent Peace, *200*
Palace of Sino-Soviet Friendship, 389
Palace of Virtue and Harmony, *227*
Pan Chaichun, 399; *341*
Pan Ku, 84
Pan-p'o village, 45–52; *38, 42–48*
Paper cutting (art form), 65, 391–92, 404; *345*
Park of the Martyrs of the Canton Commune Uprising, 175–76; *180*
Parliamentary government, 229–30
Pasqualini, Jean, 10
Patriarchal system, 329
Pavilions, 72, 206–11, 220; *57, 213–14*
Payne, Robert, 234
Pearl River, *33, 97*
Peasant life, 147, 202, 247, 256–58, 264, 355, 403
Peasant Movement Institute, 384, 396; *339*
Peking, 13, 157, 169, 176, 215, 233; *2, 19, 21, 24, 255, 258, 271*

Peking Central Academy of Arts and Crafts, 415
Peking Central Academy of Fine Arts, 388, 396–97, 400, 407, 411–12, 418; *350, 358*
Peking Children's Hospital, 40
Peking man, 44, 176
Peking Painting Academy, 419
Peking University, 239–40, 298, 349, 363; *3, 234, 242*
P'eng Chen, 294, 297–98, 328
P'eng Te-huai, 285
People's Art Exhibition, *342*
People's Daily (cited), 317, 325, 344–45, 360, 369, 375–76
People's Liberation Army (PLA), 285, 294, 302–7; *5, 67, 287*
People's Market, *2, 19, 24, 259–61. See also* Markets
People's Republic of China (PRC), activities of, 9–40, 216, 237, 247–84, 297–317, 325, 357–58, 375
Persecution, 115, 122–27, 129–30
Personality, cult of, 308, 332
"Persuasion" education, 264
Phoenix hat, 175; *179*
Photography, 35–36; *16, 20, 317*
Pigs, 101, 255; *87–88, 337*
Pillaging of national treasures, 45
Pillars, 180–81, 186
Pillows, 99, 163–64; *82–83, 163–64*
Pin, Prince of, cache of, 141–44; *137–44*
Ping-Pong: diplomacy, 10, 309; matches of April 1971, 9
Pin-yang cave, 117–20; *104–5*
PLA. *See* People's Liberation Army
Police, 353, 366; *252, 284–85*
Politburo Standing Committee, 308, 329, 332–33
Political developments, 13, 18–19, 198, 229–30, 317, 384, 387, 408. *See also* political parties by specific name
Pollution: noise, 29; spiritual, 19, 335, 364, 421
Polo, Marco, 9–10, 157
Pope, John A., 60
Population growth, 147, 344–45
Porcelain, 160–61, 163, 203; Ch'ing, 165, 223–26; *230–33*; exportation of, 226; Ming, 164, 166; *145, 169*; Sung, 163–64; *161, 163*; Yüan, 165–66. *See also* Ceramics
Portraits: Ming, 197–98, 201–3; *204, 207–9*; People's Republic, 375; *327. See also* Painting
Post-Cultural Revolution, 114
Post-Impressionism, 406, 409, 418
Posters, 18, 327, 376, 386; *30, 326*
Pottery. *See* Ceramics
Pragmatism, policy of, 294–95, 297, 310, 312, 318–22, 329, 334, 359
PRC. *See* People's Republic of China
Prehistory, 43, 48–52
Prehistory of China, The (Treistman), 49
Printing, invention of, 122
Prisoner of Mao (Pasqualini), 10
Private plot system, 336–37
Production brigades, 280, 283
Proletarianism, results of, 358, 389
Propaganda, 19, 38, 57, 302, 307, 366
Protestantism, 362–63, 365
Psychodrama techniques, 383
Public security, 353–56, 366–68

Qiu Deshu, 420–21; *361*

Radiant King, *126*
Radicalism, 318, 320

429

Reactionary tendencies, 316–17
Reading standards, 357
"Rebellion is justified" philosophy, 298, 305
Record of the Western Regions (Hsüan-tsang), 130
Recreation, 136, 138, 296, 363–65; *319–25*
Red Detachment of Women, 384, 396; *340*
Red Guards, 18, 299–307, 312, 363, 396
Red Lotus (Huang Yongyu), *362*
Reforms, 328–29; agricultural, 336–37; educational, 336; industrial, 339–40; land, 249–50, 258; rural, 337; social, 223, 230, 233–35, 336; "thought," 365
Reischauer, Edwin O., 149, 235
Relic box, 133; *123*
Religion, 112, 114, 121–24, 129–30, 147, 234, 239, 351–53, 362, 364. *See also* Buddhism; Catholicism; Protestantism
Report from a Chinese Village (Myrdal), 265
Repressive measures, 19
Republic of China, 43, 70, 223, 229
Residents' committees, 354–55, 366
Revolution of 1911, 43, 223, 229
Revolutionary activities, 9, 305–6, 392
Rhyton (onyx), 142; *142*
Rightist movement, 277–78, 299, 312, 322–23, 361, 405
Rocks, 203–4, 206, 211–12; *210*
Roofs, *101*; Ch'ing, 222; Ming, 177–80; *183*, *188*; People's Republic, 380, 384; Republican, 71–72; *60–61*
Rural areas, 356–57, 375

Sabotage, political, 319
Sacred Way, 171; *170*, *173*, *175*
Sakanashi, Shio, 153–54
Sanskrit classical language, 158
Satire, use of, 408
Schafer, Edward, 136, 139
Scholar on a Donkey (Hsu Wei), 201; *208*
Schools. *See* Children's palaces; Education; May 7th Cadre Schools
Schubert, Franz, 317
Science and Civilization in China (Needham), 107
Screen-gates, 193; *199*, *200*
Sculpture, 405; *347*; Buddhist, 40, 113–16, 136; Han, 171; *174*; high and low relief, 117; Ming, 171, 186; *170*, *175*; People's Republic, 211, 373, 384; *32*, *327*, *362*; Socialist Realist, 211; T'ang, 136; *126*; Yüan, 158; *155–56*. *See also* Animal forms in art; Cave sculpture
Self-portrait (Feng Guodeng), 406, 409; *348*
Sha-mien Island, *10*, *239–41*
Shang dynasty, 43–46, 55–59, 65, 67, 99
Shanghai Exhibition Hall, 377; *331*
Shanghai Painting Academy, 408, 414; *351*
Shen Chou, 201, 204–6; *206–7*
Shomu (Japanese Emperor), 141
Shōsōin treasure house, 141–42
Sian, 67, 69; *128–30*, *249*; Historical Museum at, 171; *99*, *146*, *174*. *See also* Ch'ang-an
Sickman, Laurence, 127
Silk and Silk Road, 90–91, 105, 138–39, 142, 161, 319, 411
Silver, 142, 144; *137*, *139–40*, *143–44*

Sino-American détente, 9–10, 30–31, 309
Sino-foreign enterprises, 340
Sino-Japanese War, 220
Sino-Soviet relations, 283, 295, 385, 389. *See also* Soviet Union
Sirén, Osvald, 204
Six Dynasties, 105, 116–17, 160
Sixteen Point Decision, 299–300
Slave Society, 55–57, 78
Sleeve weights, 94; *81*
"Snow" (Mao Tse-tung), 182
Social life, *22–23*, *253–54*, *276*; pressure, 345, 365, 371; progress, 376; reforms, 336; tensions, 307, 354
Socialist movement: economy, 339; education, 277–78, 285; industry, 265–66, 313; morality, 408–9; rightists, 299
Socialist Realism, 211, 240, 373–75, 385–87, 399–400, 403–4, 407, 412, 414, 417; *246*, *327–28*
Socialist transformation, 257–58, 264–66, 277, 339
Socialization, 265–66, 277
Society: adjusting to, 35, 50, 52, 56, 99, 243, 247–50; Ch'ing, 148–49, 215; Communist, 384; industrialized, 359; open, 19, 327–28, 362; slave, 55–57, 78
Sociopolitical institutions, 58
Soochow, 154; *316*, *318*
Soong family, 234
Soper, Alexander, 127
Southern Sung, 150, 153, 157
Soviet Union, 15, 18, 283, 295, 385–86, 392
Specialized household systems, 337–38, 375
Speech, freedom of, 328
"Spiritual pollution," 19, 335, 364, 421
Splendid Red Sun Will Shine for 10,000 Generations, A (Kang Zuotian), 399; *342*
Sports and games, 9, 36, 363–65, 379
Ssu-ma Ch'ien, 84
Stalin, Joseph, 375; *329*
Standard of living, improvement in, 18, 310, 338
Star Star Group, 405, 408; *347*
Statuary, 29, 116, 158
Steles, 147, 171; *36*, *146*, *172*
Stone Age, 44
Stoneware. *See* Ceramics
Street revolutionary committees, 353–55
Strike, right to, 318–19
Struggle meetings, 250–57
Subsidies, granting of, 344
Sui dynasty, 69–70, 121
Summer Palace, 36, 38, 72, 191, 217–22, 237; *221*, *225–28*
Sun Yat-sen, 229, 231–34; *236–37*
Sun Yat-sen Memorial Hall, 404; *346*
Sung dynasty, 87, 129, 147–55, 157, 160
Superstitions, 58–59, 63, 365
Swan Lake, 389; *335*
Symbols, use of, 9; *119–20*

Tai Chin, 153; *153*
T'ai Tsung, Emperor, 121
Taiping Rebellion, 217
Taiwan, 10, 14, 116, 237, 279, 334
Tall Tree, Bamboo, and Stone (Wang Fu), *205*
T'ang dynasty, 69–70, 108, 112, 115–17, 121–44, 147, 158
T'ao Ch'ien, 197

T'ao Yüan-ming, 197–98; *204*
Taoism, 94, 142–44, 148, 364
Tartars, T'o-pa, 113–14. *See also* Wei dynasties
Technology, 21, 136, 147, 225, 307, 339, 360
Temple of Agriculture, 176
Temple of Great Good Will, 130, 132–33; *121*
Temple of Heaven, 176, 180–81, 184, 186, 191; *182*
Temple of Heaven complex, 176–82; *181–88*, *215*, *251*
Temple of the Six Banyan Trees, 133–35; *124–25*
Temples: Confucian, 36; Buddhist, 136
Temur, 169
Teng Hsiao-p'ing, 14–15, 18, 312–16, 319–29, 331–36, 376, 404
Tensions, political and social, 283, 295, 307, 354, 384, 387
Tenth Party Congress, 311
Theatre, 84
Thought: classical, 148; Mao's, 182, 308, 322, 369; reform, 365
Three-color ware, 139–40; *123*, *133–35*, *164*
Three freedoms, 284–85
Three Principles of the People, 231–33
Three-Self Movement, 362–63
Tibet, 20, 365; *6*
Tibetans (Chen Danqing), 407, 412; *350*
T'ien-an-men Gate, 184–87, 320, 325; *171*, *338*
T'ien-an-men Square, 184–87, 331; *252*
Tiles, painted, 83–87; *70–71*, *73*
Ting ware, 163; *163*
Tomb figures. *See* Funerary objects
Tombs, 80, 83, 87, 91, 94, 97, 101–3, 169–76, 191; *86–87*, *180*, *236–37*
Tools, Neolithic, 49; *43–44*
Tou Wan, 91, 94, 96–97, 99, 103
Tourist industry, 21, 31, 38
Trade policies, 10, 121, 138, 141–42, 216–17, 226, 236, 309, 324–26
Tradition, 38, 44–45, 55, 57, 72, 99, 344–45, 392, 394, 400, 417–19
Transportation: Ch'in, 77; Han, 105–8; *78*; internal, 21, 24, 237, 289, 340, 354–55; *279*; People's Republic, 28, 335; *12*, *16*, *21*, *97*, *299–304*; T'ang, 138–39
Treasures of Chinese Art, 39, 103
Treaties, 217, 237
Treistman, Judith, 49
Truman, Harry, 10
Twelfth Congress, 332
Two Swallows (Wu Guanzhong), 419; *359*
Tz'u-chou ware, 164; *145*, *164*
Tz'u-hsi, Empress Dowager, 195, 220–23

Underground artists, 404–5
Unemployment, 307, 340–41, 355
Unions, growth of, 308, 340–41
United Nations, 309
United States, 9–11, 14–15, 18, 30–31, 309, 325

Valley of the Thirteen Tombs, 170–75; *170*, *172–73*, *175*
Vietnam War, 15, 327
Visitors, influence of, 24–25, 29–30, 39, 258, 310, 317
Voluntarism, 258, 310

Wall painting, 400–3, 415, 417; posters, 18, 376
Walls, 177–80, 187–88, 206; *128*, *182–83*, *190*, *195*, *211*. *See also* Great Wall
Wan-li, Emperor, 46, 166, 173–75
Wang-ch'eng Park, 111–12
Wang Chung-yü, 197–98; *204*
Wang-Fu, 198; *205*
Wang Hung-wen, 311–12, 321
Wang Keping, 405, 408; *347*
Wang Tung-hsing, 321, 376
Warlordism, 229–31, 233, 236, 305
Warring States period, 65
Water Festival, Song of Life (Yüan), 411, 415, 417; *353–54*
Water pumping facility, 239; *234*
Weapons, 49, 57; *47*
Wei dynasties, 112–14, 116–17, 120–21
Western Chou, 56, 60
Western painting, 419
Westerners Among the Figurines of the T'ang Dynasty of China, The (Mahler), 140
Willetts, William, 161
Women: People's Republic, 256, 280, 332, 361; *5–7*, *12*, *15–16*, *31*, *270*, *295–96*; role of, 52, 195, 327, 345, 357, 366, 376–78; T'ang, 140; *134–35*
Women's Association, 279, 308
Workers' Palace, 417
Wright, Frank Lloyd, 240
Writing and writers, 18, 57–59, 103–5, 357, 361. *See also* Calligraphy
Wu, Nelson, 180
Wu Guanzhong, 419; *359*
Wu Han, 285, 297
Wu-sung River, *238*
Wu-Ti, Emperor, 89–90, 94, 180–82
Wu Zuoren, 415, 418; *358*
Wuhan uprising, 305, 418

Xu Beihong, 418–19

Yang, 203–4
Yang, Minister, 141
Yang Kuei-fei, 70, 140–41
Yang-shao culture, 44, 46–52; *38*, *40*, *43–46*
Yang Su, 203; *209*
Yang Yanping, 419; *360*
Yeh Chien-ying, 321
Yellow River, 44, 48
Yi River, 116; *102*
Yin, 203–4
Young Pioneers, 15, 283, 308, 313–15
Yu Ch'in, 203; *209*
Yü Yüan, 40, 204–12; *211–17*
Yüan dynasty, 149, 153, 155–58, 164–66, 169, 195; *145*
Yüan Ming Yüan, 217, 219, 237
Yüan Shih-k'ak, 229–30
Yüan Yunsheng, 402–3, 415, 417; *353–54*, *356*, *360*
Yüeh-chih (nomads), 89–90
Yüeh ware, 105, 160–63; *158*, *160*
Yung-lo, Emperor, 169–71, 173, 176; *172*, *178*

Zhang Ding, 405
Zhao Yixiong, 407, 411; *349*
Zhao Ziyang, 328–29, 333, 338, 341
Zodiac, 101
Zoomorphic tradition, 99

CHRONOLOGY

Neolithic period		
Yang-shao culture	?4000–?2000 B.C.	
* Hsia dynasty	?2000–?1200 B.C.	
Lung-shan culture	?2000–?1200 B.C. (with scattered later survivals)	
* Shang dynasty	?1523–?1027 B.C. (traditional ?1766–1122 B.C.)	
* Chou dynasty	?1027–256 B.C. (traditional ?1122–256 B.C.)	
Western Chou	?1027–770 B.C. (traditional ?1122–770 B.C.)	
Eastern Chou	770–256 B.C.	
Spring and Autumn era	770–481 B.C.	
Warring States era	403–221 B.C.	
Ch'in dynasty	221–206 B.C.	
Han dynasty	206 B.C.–A.D. 220	
Western Han	206 B.C.–A.D. 8	
Wang Mang Interregnum	A.D. 9–23	
Eastern Han	A.D. 25–220	
Six Dynasties	220–587	
		Three Kingdoms 222–264/280
Western Chin	265–304	
		Sixteen Kingdoms 304–386
Eastern Chin	317–420	
		Northern Wei (T'o-pa) 386–534
Liu Sung	420–447	
Southern Ch'i	479–502	
Liang	502–577	
		Western Wei 535–557 Eastern Wei 534–550
		Northern Chou 557–581 Northern Ch'i 550–557
Ch'en	557–589	
Sui dynasty	581–618	
T'ang dynasty	618–907	
Ten Kingdoms	907–979	Five Dynasties 907–960
		Liao dynasty (Khitan Tartars) 947–1125
Sung dynasty	960–1279	
Northern Sung	960–1127	
		Chin dynasty (Jurchen Tartars) 1115–1234
Southern Sung	1127–1279	
Yüan dynasty (Mongols)	1279–1368	
Ming dynasty	1368–1644	
Ch'ing dynasty (Manchus)	1644–1912	
Republic	1912–1949	
Kuomintang	1928–1949	
	(in Taiwan, 1949–)	
People's Republic	1949–	

* *The dating of the Hsia and Shang dynasties and the Chou invasion have not been indisputably established. Most modern scholars use the dates given first in the chronology and used in the text, rather than the traditional dates shown in parentheses.*

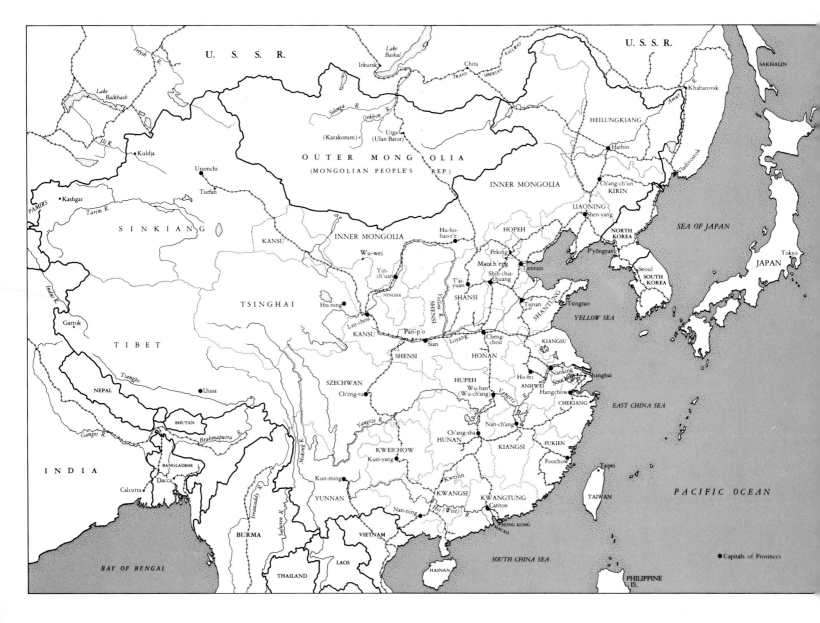